W9-AVN-447

The
ICING
ON THE CAKE

The ICING
ON THE CAKE

GREG ROBINSON & MAX SCHOFIELD

E. P. DUTTON   NEW YORK

First published in the United States in 1989 by E. P. Dutton,
a division of Penguin Books USA Inc.,
2 Park Avenue, New York, N.Y. 10016.

Originally published in Great Britain by
Bloomsbury Publishing Limited.

Library of Congress Catalog Card Number: tk

ISBN: 0-525-24747-5

1 3 5 7 9 10 8 6 4 2

First American Edition

The Icing On The Cake
was produced by Nigel Osborne
115J Cleveland Street, London W1, England.

Art Director Nigel Osborne
Editor Linda Sonntag
Photography Mark French
Artwork Fraser Newman

CONTENTS

UTENSILS

When buying cake making equipment, particularly cake tins, knives, tips and cutters, it really is worth spending just that little bit extra on high quality items that will last you a good many years. Other items such as food colour pens, cake boards and pillars are widely available and of excellent quality and variety. It is worth buying a small work box in which to put all your food colours, piping bags, modelling wire, florists' tape and paint brushes, so as to keep them in good condition.

1 Cake tins
2 Pastry brush
3 Rolling pin and spoon
4 Mixing bowl
5 Sieve and cooling rack
6 Whisks, knives and spatula
7 Icing cutters
8 Icing smoother
9 Pillars, board and candles
10 Tissue paper, foil and scalpel
11 Food colour in jars and pens
12 Skewers
13 Florists' tape
14 Pastry bag and tips

SCALES *

Accurate measures have been used throughout the book for weighing ingredients. A set of scales should last a lifetime and it is worth investing in a good pair which will serve all your ordinary requirements.

NOTE TO THE US EDITION

Though measuring by weight yields the most accurate results, those who do not have a kitchen scale or prefer to measure by volume rather than by weight may use the following equivalents:

1oz all purpose flour
 = $3/16$ cup = 3tbsp

1oz sugar, granulated or brown
 = $1/8$ cup = 2tbsp

1oz powdered sugar
 = $1/4$ cup = 4tbsp

1oz powdered sugar, sifted
 = scant $1/3$ cup = 5tbsp

1oz butter (and other moist ingredients, including ricotta cheese)
 = $1/8$ cup = 2tbsp

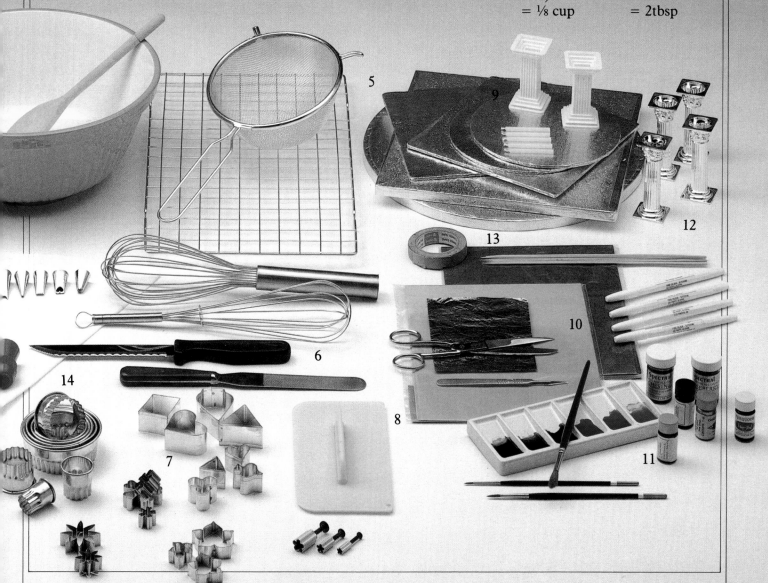

BASIC TECHNIQUES

The cakes in this book have been invented with one aim in mind — to give pleasure, to the decorator as well as to everyone who looks at and eventually eats the cake. Thirty projects are presented. Step-by-step photographs and clear instructions show you exactly how to create everything from a jaded Statue of Liberty to a teddy bears' picnic, all in cake, marzipan and icing.

Some of the cakes demand a degree of dexterity. There is a panda, for instance, sculpted out of three cakes placed one on top of the other. The effect is stunning. Other cakes, such as the crab and the rosette, can be made to look really professional by absolute beginners.

Various skills are taught in this book, among them modelling, moulding and marquetry in marzipan and icing and handpainting with food colours. Learning these techniques and their application will inspire you to invent cakes of your own. Tips and timesavers are included for busy cooks.

There is a cake to fit every conceivable occasion, from Christmas to Valentine's Day. For a wedding, there is a traditional three-tiered cake exquisitely decorated with flowers, or as an alternative wedding cake we offer a breathtaking hot air balloon. The decorations on many of the cakes form gifts in themselves. They may be edible, but they are too good to eat, and they can be taken off the cake before it is cut and kept as a permanent reminder of the occasion.

THE CAKE

A wide variety of cakes can be decorated, not just the rich fruit cake traditionally baked for Christmas and weddings. The criterion is that the cake should retain its shape during and after decorating. You should bear this in mind when inventing new designs or decorating bought cakes.

If the cake is to provide a platform for surface decoration, as with the Opening Night Cake or the Partridge in the Pear Tree, then any firm cake, including fruit cake, will be suitable. If the cake is to be sculpted, as in the Panda or the gondola for the alternative wedding cake, then a fine and close-textured madeira cake will be ideal, as it will not break and crumble under the carver's knife. Parkin is another cake that responds well to delicate knifework. Soft cakes too can be decorated — a Genoese sponge forms the basis of our strawberry and cream tea cake and a chocolate truffle cake which requires no cooking provides the basis of a pair of Piscean fishes.

In most cases a cake will rise during cooking, and usually we cut off the resulting dome to make a regular block of cake. An exception is rich fruit cake. This we turn upside down, filling the gap between cake and board with marzipan. The surface of the cake is then perfectly flat and level.

Offcuts of cake need never be wasted. Eat them straight away, crumb them for use in truffle

cake, or use them in trifle. Remember to plan for extra baking time in projects that consist of more than one cake – each cake should be baked separately in the centre of the oven for the correct temperature. We have used size 2 eggs throughout unless otherwise stated.

A final point: many of the cakes featured here have been made big enough to decorate on a generous scale: they will serve quite a number of people. You can of course make your own cakes as large or as small as you wish.

MARZIPAN

The purpose of marzipanning a cake – apart from adding something delicious – is to seal the moisture in. This makes the cake keep longer and provides a firm dry basis for the icing, which should on no account be allowed to get damp.

Marzipan – almond paste – comes in two colours, yellow and white. In the US only white (natural, actually) is generally available. For recipes in this book where yellow marzipan is required for visual reasons, colour your own by kneading in a touch of yellow colouring to achieve the desired tint. Keep marzipan at room temperature and roll out according to the recipe instructions. It handles like pastry. The cake is spread thinly and evenly with apricot jam and the marzipan, usually about ¼″ (5mm) thick, is stuck to it. Be as accurate as you can in marzipanning, as irregularities and bumpy seams are likely to show up on the icing.

ICING

Four kinds of icing are used in this book; each has different characteristics and is used for a different purpose. With the exception of tragacanth, the cost of each is minimal, so much so that you can make up a batch of icing and experiment with the different decorations in the book, and ideas of your own, before deciding which project to tackle.

ROLLED FONDANT

Fondant is used to cover most of the cakes featured in this book. It handles rather like pastry and produces a soft moulded finish that is easy to cut and does not splinter – unlike traditional royal icing. Fondant remains soft for several hours after application – even fingertip pressure will mark it. It also shows up any irregularities in the marzipan, especially likely round the seams. However, fondant gives a very professional finish and is quick to use after a little practice. Wrap any leftovers in cling film for later use. If it begins to feel rather dry as you roll it out, add a few drops of water and knead until soft and pliable. Sometimes air bubbles may appear in the icing. Prick them with a pin to release the air.

To make fondant icing
1lb + ¼ cup powdered sugar
1 egg white
2 tablespoons (30ml) liquid
glucose
cornstarch

Put the powdered sugar, egg white and glucose into a food processor if you have one, or work by hand. Blend until the mixture resembles lumps of breadcrumbs. Tip into a mixing bowl and knead until it takes on the consistency of bread dough. Add a little cornstarch as necessary to prevent the mixture from becoming too sticky. The icing is ready when it

no longer feels sticky and can be rolled out on a work surface lightly dusted with cornstarch without sticking. You can use it straight away, though some people prefer to leave it overnight wrapped in cling film and sealed in an airtight container.

GELATIN AND TRAGACANTH ICING

Gelatin and tragacanth (gum paste) are used for moulding decorations, particularly small delicate shapes such as flowers. Both dry very hard. Gelatin is cheaper and easier to make and can be used on all occasions instead of tragacanth. Tragacanth is more elastic and hardens less quickly, but there are problems with making it. It can be difficult getting hold of tragacanth and unless there is a good supplier of caking making and decorating equipment near you, you may have to order it. Tragacanth can only really be made in a food processor. Before you begin you should make sure the motor is strong as the icing mixture is very dense and may well ruin a small machine. Gum paste mixes are easier to handle. Tragacanth is delightful to use if you have the resources to make it, but if not, use gelatin, which is excellent for the purposes we recommend.

To make gelatin icing
1lb + ¼ cup powdered sugar
½oz (12.5g) gelatin powder
4 tablespoons (60ml) water
2 teaspoons (10ml) liquid
glucose
cornstarch

Put the water in a heatproof bowl and add the gelatin. Leave to soak for two minutes. Place the bowl in a pan with ½" (1cm) water and set on the stove. Heat gently until the gelatin dissolves. Remove from the heat and stir in the liquid glucose. Allow to cool for two minutes. Turn the mixture into a bowl containing the powdered sugar and mix in. If the mixture seems wet add a little more powdered sugar. Add sufficient cornstarch to allow the icing to be worked like bread dough. The finished icing should not be sticky. Wrap in cling film and place in an airtight container until ready to use.

To make tragacanth icing
1lb + ¼ cup powdered sugar
5 teaspoons (25ml) cold water
2 teaspoons (10ml) powdered gelatin
3 teaspoons (15ml) gum tragacanth
2 teaspoons (10ml) liquid glucose
4 teaspoons (20ml) white vegetable shortening
white of 1 egg

Put the water in a heatproof bowl and sprinkle on the powdered gelatin. Place the bowl in a pan with ½" (1cm) water and heat until the gelatin dissolves. Remove from the heat and add the liquid glucose and shortening. Stir until dissolved and well mixed. Tip into a food processor or blender with the powdered sugar, egg white and gum tragacanth and work until well combined. To begin with the icing will appear almost beige in colour. Turn the speed of the mixer up to maximum for a minute or two until the icing is very white and a little stringy. Put the icing in a plastic bag and refrigerate overnight.

ROYAL ICING

Royal icing used to be used exclusively to cover cakes, but it is immensely hard and brittle and fondant is now much preferred. However, its soft paste-like consistency and quick setting quality make it ideal for creating peaks of 'snow', as in the Christmas Tree, and for piping, as in the Get Well Basket of Fruit. The larger the opening of the piping tip, the stiffer the icing needs to be. In this book royal icing is used mainly for fastening decorations in place – it is an excellent edible glue that sets rock hard.

To make royal icing
1 egg white
12oz (350g) sifted powdered sugar

Beat the egg white to break it up and add the powdered sugar in batches, mixing after each addition. Add sufficient powdered sugar to make the required consistency. Cover the icing with cling film, pressing it down gently on the surface to remove any air bubbles. Keep until required, but do not store in the fridge as it will absorb moisture and this will alter the consistency.

CUTTING THE CAKE

First remove the decoration. This can be reassembled and kept as a souvenir. If the cake is square or irregular, cut it in half, then cut the half in slices. Cut the slices into portions. Cut wedge shaped slices from a round cake. In the case of the Champagne Bucket, remove the bottle and napkin and slice the bucket down the seams. In the case of the Valentine cake, lift off the box before cutting.

CORRECTING MISTAKES

● In sculpting, if you carve off too much cake by mistake, either stick the piece back on with jam or replace it with a piece of marzipan.
● If, when the marzipan has dried, you find one of the seams is irregular, fill the crack and round off the edge with royal icing – it will set like cement and make a smooth base on which to apply the fondant.
● If, once the icing has dried, you find a fault in it, disguise this by painting with food colours.
● If you make a mistake in painting, wait for the paint to dry, then paint over it.

ADAPTING ARTWORK TO SIZE FOR YOUR OWN CAKES

The designs for all the cakes can be found on pp.182-190. Naturally they have had to be reduced in size to fit the pages. You will thus have to increase the size to fit the cake you wish to decorate. You can either go to a photocopying or print shop, where this will be done for you very cheaply to your specifications, or you can do it yourself. Trace out the design and draw a square round it to fit as tightly as possible. Divide each side of the box into ten equal parts, then join the lines from top to bottom and side to side to make 100 squares. Now draw a square that just fits the size of cake you want to decorate. Divide this into 100 squares as well. Copy the design, square by square, from the smaller onto the larger grid. Though you are drawing freehand, you will have reproduced the design exactly.

USEFUL EQUIPMENT

● Graphite paper – like carbon paper – is useful for transferring a traced design on to icing, where it will be painted over. Note, however, that the trace left contains lead, so this method should not be used on anything that is to be eaten.
● As the photographs show, we always use a scalpel for cutting out icing shapes. The fine sharp blade of a scalpel, a modelling knife or an X-acto knife will give more accurate results than most kitchen knives.

FOOD COLOURS

Specialist cake making and decorating shops offer a wide range of food colours, from the light pastel shades best used only with traditional piped royal icing to rich thick paste colours that look almost black in their pots. Gold and silver paints and coloured lustre powders are also available. Though edible, they do have a slightly metallic taste and should not be consumed in great quantities.

You can increase the range of colours in your palette by blending and mixing. Picture 1 shows the paler shades that result from adding water. Picture 2 shows how two colours are brushed together while still wet to create a third shade. Picture 3 shows how pale blue and dark blue are worked together by dabbing and stippling to create the illusion of watery depths – this is the technique used in the Teddy Bears' Picnic. In picture 4 grass is produced by splaying out the bristles coated in green food colour, then lightly stippling over the lines while the paint is still wet. Picture 5 shows the effect that can be achieved by applying colour with an open-textured sponge. A closer-textured sponge gives a softer and subtler effect, provided it is not too wet, as in picture 6. In picture 7 a potato print is demonstrated. In picture 8 we reproduce a wood grain effect. First brush the surface with pale brown and allow to dry. Then drag a medium sized paintbrush, bristles coated in dark brown, along the 'grain', swerving to allow for knot holes – concentric circles of dark brown.

On one or two occasions in this book we have used an airbrush, which allows for a subtle and even application of colour. However, as this is not a piece of equipment likely to be found in most homes, we have always given alternative directions for producing the same effect.

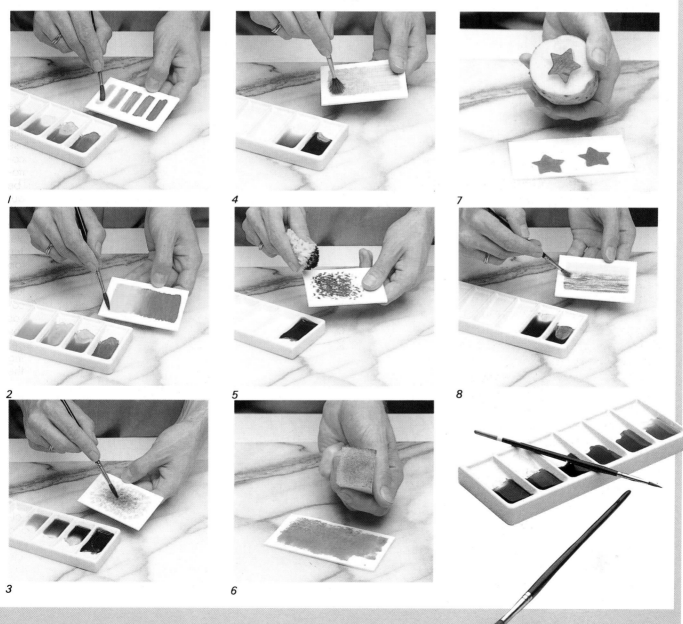

1

2

3

4

5

6

7

8

AFTERNOON TEA CAKE

A stencil is a simple and inexpensive way of decorating the delicious moist walnut cake pictured on p. 17. Take the design for the stencil from the back of the book, use a paper doily or devise a geometric or flower pattern of your own. You can make the design more intricate by using a number of colours. Take care to leave one colour to dry before applying the next or you may smudge the outline. This is a versatile decoration that can be used to great effect on any number of cakes.

To make the cake. Mix together the butter or margarine, sugar and syrup, and beat until light and fluffy. Add the eggs one at a time and incorporate into the mixture. Follow each egg with a spoonful of flour. Fold in the remaining flour and the chopped walnuts. Grease a 9″ (23cm) round cake tin and line with waxed paper. Spoon in the mixture and level off the top. Cook in a preheated oven at 160°C/325°F/Gas mark 3 for about 1 hour to 1 hour 10 minutes, or until firm to the touch. Check the cake after 40 minutes and if browning too quickly, cover the tin with a double thickness of paper or kitchen foil. Turn out the cake and allow to cool.

For the filling, mix together the butter or margarine and sugar and beat until smooth. Add vanilla and spread on the split cake.

TIMESAVERS

TIMESAVER If time is very short use only one colour and complete the stencil in one move.

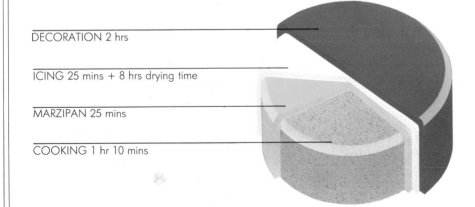

DECORATION 2 hrs

ICING 25 mins + 8 hrs drying time

MARZIPAN 25 mins

COOKING 1 hr 10 mins

2 Using the design on *p. 182* trace out the stencil pattern on to a piece of waxed or parchment paper. If necessary increase the size of the pattern to fit your particular cake. With graphite paper transfer the design on to thin card. In this photograph the stencil has been divided into four sections to allow for the use of an airbrush with four different colours. However, if a paintbrush is being used, do not divide the stencil. With a sharp knife or scalpel, cut out the stencil pattern.

1 On a work surface lightly dusted with powdered sugar roll out 8oz (225g) marzipan. Using the tin in which the cake was baked as a guide, cut out a circle the size of the cake. Spread the top of the cake with apricot jam and fix the marzipan to the cake. Wrap a piece of string around the cake to determine its circumference and measure its depth. Roll out the remaining marzipan and cut out a strip to the measurements just taken. Cut the strip into two equal lengths for ease of handling. Spread the side of the cake with apricot jam and fix the marzipan in place. Let it dry for about two hours. On a work surface lightly dusted with powdered sugar roll out the fondant icing into a sheet large enough to cover the cake. Place the icing over the cake and smooth to fit the sides. Using a large flat-bladed knife held against the side of the cake, trim off any excess icing. With a plastic sheet, smooth the icing on the sides of the cake to produce a neat finish. Allow the icing to dry for eight hours or overnight.

3 Choose your colours and decide which sections will be painted with which. Lay the stencil on the surface of the cake. Put some colour on your paintbrush without making it too wet. Gently brush over those sections of the stencil you wish to colour first. Of course the whole stencil may be painted in one colour, but if using more than one, there are two ways of proceeding. If you are neat in your painting it is possible to paint the whole stencil with several col-ours in one process, but keep it as free of smudges as you can to avoid colours 'straying' to other sections and mixing with other shades. If you are not confident of doing this, remove the stencil after you have applied the first colour and allow to dry for at least an hour. Wipe the stencil clean with a tissue. Reposition the stencil when dry and proceed with your second colour. Continue in this way until you have completed the design.

4 When the stencil is complete and has dried, you can add further detail should you wish to, such as small highlights in silver or shadows in a deeper shade of one of your chosen colours. Do not attempt this if you feel you may spoil the effect.

5 Stencils are available in many large stores in response to a renewed interest in craft and individualized interior design. You could select a bought stencil of the right size instead of using the design on *p.182*, or you could use a doily. Carefully pin the doily of your choice to the surface of the cake, being sure to count all the pins and take them out afterwards.

6 Apply the paint in the same way, being careful not to break the delicate doily. Do not overload the brush with colour. You can paint the whole design without removing the doily. If you do need to remove it between colours, use a fresh doily of the same design rather than trying to wipe the first one clean.

7 When the design is complete, you can tidy up smudges with a paintbrush, or indeed add further detail.

ALLEY CAT

The dustbin is made from three 6″ (15cm) round chocolate chip madeira sponges with a chocolate fudge filling. The 'rubbish' is sweets, which makes the cake ideal for any children's party – if time allows, you could make icing 'rubbish' to go inside the dustbin, such as tin cans, bottles, an old TV set and a few fishbones. The cat is modelled from marzipan. This cake offers plenty of scope to anyone handy with a paintbrush. The finished cake can be seen on p. 23.

To make the cake. Grease a 6″ (15cm) round cake tin and line with waxed paper. Cream together the butter or margarine and sugar until light and fluffy. Beat in the eggs one at a time, followed by a tablespoon of flour. Sift the remaining flours together and fold into the mixture, followed by the lemon juice and chocolate chips. Spoon the mixture into the tin and level off the top. Bake in a preheated oven at 160°C/325°F/Gas mark 3 for about an hour or until firm to the touch. Cool in the tin for 5–10 minutes. Turn out of the tin and allow to cool on a wire rack. Cut each cake in half to sandwich with the chocolate filling.

To make the filling, put the chocolate and butter in the top of a double saucepan or in a heatproof bowl over a pan of gently simmering water. Heat until the chocolate melts. Remove from the heat and beat well until smooth. Beat in the egg yolks and sufficient sugar to give a thick smooth spreading consistency. Allow to cool slightly and use to sandwich the cakes together.

TIMESAVERS

TIMESAVER If you would like a less pristine looking dustbin, miss out the vertical marzipan strips and concentrate on giving the bin a more battered appearance suitable for a back alley.

TIMESAVER To simplify the colouring of the bin just add a little black food colour to the icing and knead to produce an even grey. A few highlights can then be added in black or silver.

TIMESAVER The marmalade cat is quite easy to make, but you could use a bought marzipan cat or a favourite toy instead.

INGREDIENTS

Cake (for one cake)
4oz (125g) butter or margarine
4oz (125g) sugar
2 eggs
4oz (125g) self-rising flour
2oz (50g) all purpose flour
2 teaspoons lemon juice
6oz (175g) chocolate chips

Filling
8oz (225g) semi-sweet chocolate, broken into pieces
4oz (125g) butter
4 egg yolks
8oz (225g) sifted powdered sugar

Decoration
10″ (25cm) round cake board
1lb (450g) white marzipan for the cat
1lb 8oz (675g) yellow or white marzipan for the dustbin
1lb (450g) fondant icing for the dustbin
8oz (225g) gelatin icing for the dustbin lid handles
sweets
apricot jam
a little royal icing

Equipment
food colour
modelling wire

DECORATION 2 hrs
By simplifying the decoration as above, up to 1 hr 45 mins can be saved.

ICING 45 mins + 5 hrs drying time

MARZIPAN 1 hr 30 mins

COOKING 1 hr per cake

1 Spread the chocolate filling on the cakes and sandwich them together. Measure the height of the cake and, using a piece of string or thread, measure the circumference also. Spread the top and sides of the cake with apricot jam.

2 Roll out the marzipan and using the base of the tin in which the cakes were cooked as a guide, cut out a circle of marzipan and fix on top of the cake. Roll out the marzipan again and cut out a rectangle according to the height and circumference measurements already taken. Fix to the sides of the cake.

3 Once again, measure the circumference of the cake. It will be slightly bigger now, because of the layer of marzipan. Roll out the marzipan and cut out two strips ¾" (2cm) wide and long enough to go around the cake. Spread the strips with apricot jam and fix round the top and bottom edges of the cake.

4 Measure the distance between the two strips of marzipan just applied. Roll out the remaining marzipan and cut into strips about ¼" (5mm) wide and long enough to fit between the two strips at the top and bottom of the cake. Spread them with apricot jam and fix in place as shown.

5 Measure the circumference of the cake along the top edge. Measure the height of the cake and add on ¾″ (2cm) so that the icing when applied will extend above the top edge of the cake. Brush the middle section of the cake between the upright strips with water to help the icing stick to the sides. Roll out 1lb (450g) fondant icing on a surface dusted with cornstarch. Cut out a piece of icing according to the measurements taken. Fix to the sides of the cake, smoothing the icing into the joins between the upright strips. Allow to dry for at least 4 or 5 hours.

7 Roll out the icing and cut out two shapes for the handles (being cut out in the photograph) and one handle for the lid (on the marble surface; also see p. 21).

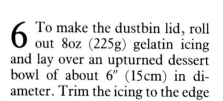

6 To make the dustbin lid, roll out 8oz (225g) gelatin icing and lay over an upturned dessert bowl of about 6″ (15cm) in diameter. Trim the icing to the edge of the bowl and allow to dry overnight. Gather up the remaining icing and knead together (add a little water if it has dried out).

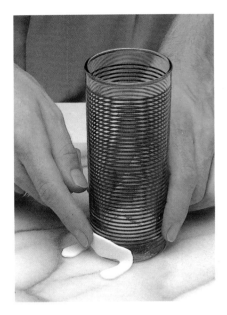

8 Allow the dustbin handles to dry against a glass as illustrated. Fix to the sides of the dustbin with royal icing.

10 Using food colours, mix up several shades of blue and decorate the cake as illustrated. Paint all over in a light blue and leave to dry. A second coat of colour can be applied as in the photograph with the bristles of the brush splayed out, dabbing the food colour on to the icing to produce a mottled effect for character.

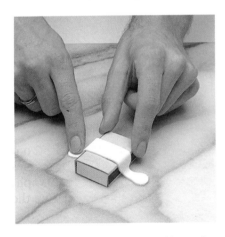

9 Allow the handle for the dustbin lid to dry over a matchbox with the ends of the handle flat against the work surface. Fix to the dustbin lid with a little royal icing.

11 Using a darker blue paint one side of each groove of the dustbin to create shadow. Leave to dry.

12 Using silver food colour, add highlights to create the illusion of light striking the dustbin.

14 Fix the pieces of the cat together with royal icing and allow to dry for an hour or so before decorating.

13 To make the cat, take the white marzipan and model as illustrated in the photograph. Make the ears by pinching the marzipan and shaping it into triangles. Score the details of the eyes into the marzipan with a toothpick, and likewise the details on the paws. The whiskers are made from 1″ (2.5cm) long pieces of modelling wire. If this is not available, toothpicks or wooden skewers are just as good. Make sure young visitors do not put them in their mouths.

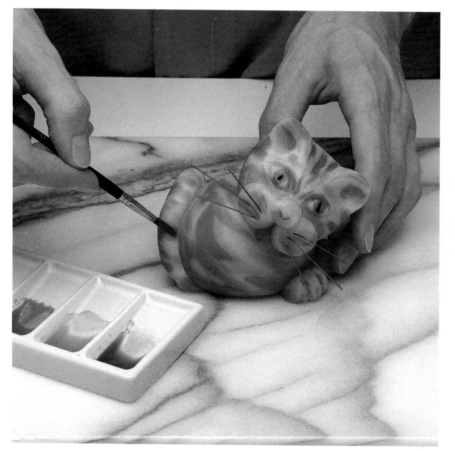

15 Make up a series of yellows and oranges with food colours and paint strips on the cat. Paint the eyes green and the tongue red. Insert the whiskers into the cheeks.

ASSEMBLY

Place a handful of brightly coloured sweets inside the dustbin and place the lid on top at an angle. Put the cat at the base of the dustbin and scatter a few sweets around it. Put an empty wrapper between its paws.

EASTER CAKE

The traditional simnel cake relies heavily on the use of marzipan and the finished cake is usually browned lightly under the grill for a golden toasted look. These alternative Easter cakes (pictured on p. 29) retain the use of eggs to represent the twelve apostles. The main technique employed here is working in marzipan – one cake features a basketwork design and the other a plait. Neatness is the secret of a professional finish.

Simnel cake is very similar to the rich fruit cake used in the Three-tier Wedding Cake (p. 120), though some recipes leave out the glacé cherries and vary the proportions of dried fruit and candied peel. For these designs we have used the recipe for the top tier (8"/20cm) of the wedding cake. The first illustration shows how a layer of marzipan is baked in the centre of a traditional simnel cake. If you would like to include it, use 8oz (225g) marzipan for the sandwich filling and take extra care when testing to see if the cake has cooked, as a toothpick stuck into the marzipan will always come out moist and sticky. The marzipan filling can quite easily be left out, as there is a large amount of marzipan in the decoration of both cakes.

TIMESAVERS

TIMESAVER To simplify the decoration of the eggs, dip them into a solution of food colour and water. Allow the eggs to dry and dip again. Repeated dippings will produce deeper colours. A subtle effect can be achieved by wrapping an egg in the outer skin of an onion. Tie the egg and onion skin in a handkerchief to secure and boil gently for 15 minutes. The egg will be marbled brown and purple, and sometimes green. Allow to cool and rub the eggshell with a little lard for a beautiful sheen.

TIMESAVER Replace the sugared marzipan eggs with chocolate eggs wrapped in coloured foil if you have no time to make them.

INGREDIENTS

Basket of eggs
Decoration
10" (25cm) round cake board
1lb (450g) yellow marzipan
12oz (350g) white marzipan
apricot jam

Equipment
wire coathanger
ribbon
poster paints
flowers
feathers

Plaited marzipan cake
Decoration
10" (25cm) thin round cake board
1½lb (675g) yellow marzipan
12oz (350g) white marzipan
4oz (125g) sifted powdered sugar
1 tablespoon warm water
1 teaspoon orange flower water
apricot jam
2oz (50g) superfine sugar

Equipment
food colour

DECORATION 4 hrs
By simplifying the decoration of the eggs an hour can be saved, by using existing eggs 1 hr 30 mins can be saved

MARZIPAN 1 hr 30 mins

COOKING 2 hrs 45 mins

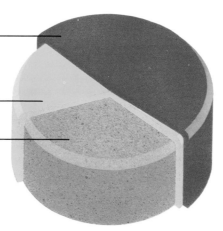

BASKET OF EGGS

1 Blow the eggs that you are going to use in the cake mixture rather than breaking them, so that you can use the shells in the decoration. Insert a needle into the egg at both ends, being sure to puncture the membrane and pierce right through to the yolk. Do not be afraid to break the shell with the needle – you will find that it chips away in small pieces. The hole should be only the size of a pinhead. Place a bowl beneath the egg and blow steadily into one of the holes. It can take a lot of blowing to begin with, but then the egg should trickle out quite easily. Shake the egg to check that it is empty. If you are not happy at the prospect of blowing the eggs, simply hard-boil them before decorating.

2 Using a sharp knife cut the cake into an oval shape with slightly sloping sides. Spread the sides of the cake with apricot jam.

TIPS

In the traditional simnel cake a layer of marzipan is placed on half the un-cooked mixture, then the remaining mixture is spooned on top.

3 Roll out 12oz (350g) yellow marzipan and 8oz (225g) white marzipan on a work surface dusted with icing sugar. Cut the yellow marzipan into about 5 strips ½" (1cm) wide and long enough to reach half way round the cake. Cut the white marzipan into strips the same width and long enough to stretch from top to bottom of the cake. Lay the yellow marzipan strips next to one another on the work surface and secure the ends by laying a ruler or a light weight over them. Fold back alternate strips of the yellow marzipan and insert a strip of the white marzipan up to the edges of the folded back pieces. Once in place, fold back the yellow strips. Now fold back the second lot of yellow strips and repeat the process. Continue like this until you have 'woven' a piece of marzipan long enough to cover half the side of the cake.

6 As an additional feature (see photograph p. 29), the top of the cake and the handle can be decorated with twisted strips of marzipan. Take the remaining yellow and white marzipan, roll out and cut from each three strips ¾″ (2cm) wide. Place a yellow strip on top of a white one and stick them together using egg white or apricot jam. Gently twist each yellow and white strip and decorate the handle as shown. Fix the first end in place by pinching it, wind the strip round then pinch the second end to join the first.

4 Before attaching the marzipan to the cake gently press the top and bottom edges and each end of the woven piece with the ruler so that the individual strips are squeezed together. Do not press so hard as to cut through the pieces, just aim to 'weld' them together. Stick the marzipan to the cake with apricot jam – another pair of hands could come in useful here if you are worried about breaking the weave. Repeat the entire process and marzipan the second half of the cake. Make sure that the seams are at the ends of the cake so that they can be covered with ribbon bows.

7 As the eggs are not to be eaten they can be decorated in any number of ways. In this instance poster paints are used to create bold and colourful designs.

TIPS

Tie two bows of yellow or gold ribbon and attach at the base of the handle so that the bows cover the seam of·the woven marzipan. When the paint on the eggs has dried, pile them on top of the cake and fill in any gaps with flower heads, ribbon bows or feathers.

5 To make the basket handle, take a piece of wire – a wire coathanger is ideal. Fold it into a gentle curve and wrap in yellow or gold ribbon. Cover each end of the handle with a small piece of cling film and insert into the cake.

PLAITED MARZIPAN CAKE

1 Turn the cake upside down and prepare it for decoration as for the Three-tiered Wedding Cake on p. 120. Using a piece of string or thread, measure the circumference of the cake and note down the measurement. Take 1lb (450g) of the yellow marzipan, roll it out on a work surface lightly dusted with powdered sugar and cut three strips ¾″ (2cm) wide. To determine the length of the strips, add 3″ (7.5cm) to the measurement of the circumference. This additional length will be taken up in the plaiting. Lay the three strips on the work surface and pinch the ends together to secure. To plait the marzipan, take the piece on the right and lay it over the piece in the centre. Take the piece on the left and lay it over the piece now in the centre. Continue right over centre, left over centre, until all the marzipan is plaited. Spread a little apricot jam around the sides of the cake. Fix the plait to the cake.

TIPS

If you want to cut down on the marzipan weaving, cut fewer strips of marzipan and make them wider. Bigger strips are easier to handle, but the result will of course look less intricate.

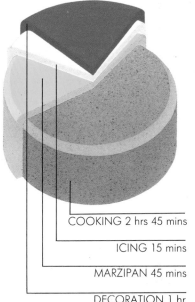

COOKING 2 hrs 45 mins

ICING 15 mins

MARZIPAN 45 mins

DECORATION 1 hr

2 Take the remaining 8oz (225g) yellow marzipan and repeat step 1 to make a plait long enough to go round the top inside edge of the cake. Attach to the cake with a little apricot jam.

3 To fill the top of the cake with glacé icing, take the sifted sugar and add the warm water. Mix together gently and avoid getting air bubbles in the mixture if possible. Mix in the orange flower water, or an extra teaspoon ordinary water if orange flower water is not available. Carefully pour the icing into the centre of the cake.

4 Allow the icing to spread to the edges of the plaited circle. If any air bubbles should appear in the icing, pop them with a needle and withdraw the needle carefully.

5 To make the eggs, take the white marzipan and divide into 12 equal pieces. Roll each piece into the shape of an egg, each egg to represent an apostle, as is the tradition.

TIPS

As an alternative to rolling the marzipan eggs in coloured sugar, you could knead food colours into the marzipan to produce several pastel shades.

6 Take the superfine sugar and put in a screw-topped jar with one or two drops of food colour. Screw on the top and shake vigorously to colour the sugar. Paint the eggs with a little egg white, then roll in the coloured sugar. Place on waxed paper and allow to dry. Speckled eggs can be made with two or more different colours of sugar.

An alternative way of decorating the eggs (as in the photograph on p. 26) is to paint them red and allow to dry. Dip a paintbrush or old toothbrush in silver food colour and flick spots of colour on to the eggs to produce speckles.

ASSEMBLY

Place the eggs at regular intervals around the plaited top.

PARCEL PATISSERIE

*This cake (shown on p. 33) is made with two 12″
(30cm) square sponge cakes. It is relatively easy to model
as it requires very little cutting. A variety of techniques is
employed in the decoration, from which you can choose
according to the time available and your degree of
confidence. The neat little parcels are individually
wrapped in marzipan and icing – some feature a
marbled finish achieved by incompletely kneading food
colour into the icing. The finishing touches are added
with an icing gift tag and ribbons.*

To make the cake. Cream together the butter or margarine and
sugar until light and fluffy. Add the eggs two at a time and mix
well, followed by a tablespoon of flour. Sift the remaining flours
together and fold into the mixture, followed by the lemon juice.
Grease a 12″ (30cm) square cake tin and line with waxed paper.
Spoon the mixture into the prepared tin and level off the surface.
Cook in a preheated oven at 160°C/325°F/Gas mark 3 for 1 hour 15
minutes. The cake is ready when risen and firm to the touch. Cool
in the tin for 5 minutes. Turn out of the tin and allow to cool
completely. Remove the lining paper.

For the filling, use unsalted ricotta cheese and sweeten with
powdered sugar to taste.

TIMESAVER It takes time to plan and
paint the sophisticated peach and silver
stripes on the carrier bag – a simpler
and bolder effect can be achieved by
sponge-printing colours on to the icing.
A cut potato shape can also produce
interesting results.

TIMESAVER In place of the cake
parcels you could put real gifts in the
mouth of the carrier bag.

TIMESAVER Instead of painting the
label on to the bag, make one from
gelatin icing and allow to dry for four
hours. The name can be marked out in
sweets or fake jewels instead of hand-
painted.

DECORATION 2 hrs
1 hour can be saved by
simplifying the decoration

ICING 1 hr 20 mins + drying time

MARZIPAN 1 hr + 6 hrs drying time

COOKING 1 hr 15 mins per cake

INGREDIENTS

(for one cake)
15oz (425g) butter or margarine
15oz (425g) sugar
8 eggs
15oz (425g) self-rising flour
8oz (225g) all purpose flour
3 tablespoons lemon juice

Filling
12oz (350g) ricotta
powdered sugar
15oz (425g) mandarin orange
segments

Decoration
16″ (40cm) square cake board
1½lb (675g) marzipan
1lb (450g) fondant icing
apricot jam

Equipment
food colour
ribbon of various colours
silk flowers if required

1 Cut the two square cakes into oblongs measuring 12″ × 9″ (30 × 23cm). Keep the cut-off pieces. Spread the sweetened ricotta on one of the cakes. Drain the mandarin oranges in a sieve and press the fruit gently to extract all excess juice. Too much juice can soften the marzipan and seep through to the icing. Place the second cake on top and press gently so that the filling is consolidated.

2 Using a sharp kitchen knife, Cut diagonally through the length of the cake from the back edge to a point just above the filling at the front edge so that you end up with a long wedge shape as shown. Now cut a wedge shape into each of the longer sides of the cake as illustrated to give the effect of a carrier bag lying flat.

3 Measure the height and width of the cake at the back and along the sloping edge. Spread the surfaces of the cake with apricot jam. Roll out the marzipan and cut pieces to the dimensions noted. Fix them to the back, sides and top of the cake. Allow to dry for 5 or 6 hours.

4 Lightly dust a work surface with cornstarch and roll out the fondant icing. Cover the cake in one piece and smooth the icing on to all the surfaces, pinching it at the corners to make neat seams. With a sharp knife, trim the icing to the edges of the cake. To trim the corners, use scissors. You should then be able to seal the corners neatly. Moisten the edges with water if necessary and press gently together. Keep any icing trimmings. Allow the icing to dry for several hours.

skewer, gently draw over the letters and score the name into the icing. Do not press too hard – even gentle pressure will leave a clear impression. Paint or draw over the indentations using food colour or a food pen.

5 Cut the remaining pieces of cake into shapes to represent parcels spilling out of the mouth of the bag. Spread the parcels with apricot jam and cover with marzipan.

7 After the icing on the bag has had a chance to dry, mark out the design for the label on the bag (*see p. 185*), making sure you leave enough space for all the letters in the name. Using waxed or tracing paper trace the design. Cut the design out of the paper and place on the cake. Mark it out on the cake with a food colour pen or paintbrush and food colour. Paint stripes on the bag in the colour of your choice. Food colour pens are easier to use than a paintbrush, if you are not particularly handy with one. The stripes and label look good painted in silver. The sides of the cake can be painted a solid colour with silver to emphasize certain details.

9 An additional gift tag can be made from a small amount of gelatin icing. A simple heart shape is pretty, but a square or oblong is just as effective. With an icing cutter or a sharp knife cut a hole and tie a piece of ribbon through it. Choosing whichever greeting is appropriate (*see p. 185*), either mark out the greeting on the surface of the icing while it is still soft as in step 8, or if the gift tag is not to be eaten, you could use graphite paper. Gently lay the graphite paper over the tag and place the tracing paper with the greeting on top of it. Write over the words of the greeting. A graphite trace of them will be left on the gift tag. Paint over the trace.

6 To ice the parcels, divide the remaining icing between them and mix in various food colours. It is possible to produce a slightly marbled effect by adding food colour to the icing and kneading only briefly so that the colour is not spread evenly throughout it. Cover the marzipanned parcels and trim the icing neatly at the edges.

ASSEMBLY

Place the parcels at the mouth of the carrier bag. They can be prettily decorated with ribbons and silk flowers from the haberdashery department of any large store. The ribbons could be made of coloured icing if you want them to be edible, as could the flowers. Finally make handles for the carrier bag from a thin strip of fondant icing. Attach to the top of the cake as shown with a dab of royal icing.

8 The name of the recipient can be painted or drawn on the bag using any of the alphabets on *p.185*. Use tracing or waxed paper to trace the chosen letters. Place the name in position on the cake. Using a needle, toothpick or

CHAMPAGNE CELEBRATION

Two 8″ (20cm) round madeira sponges layered with fruit preserves and sweetened ricotta cheese form the basis for this special celebration cake, pictured on p. 41. To make the bottle and the champagne bucket, gelatin icing is moulded on to an empty champagne bottle and a flowerpot – a simple technique that produces spectacular results. Carefully dismantled, each piece of the decoration can be safely removed and reassembled as a permanent souvenir of the party.

To make the cake. Cream the butter or margarine and sugar together until light and fluffy. Add the eggs one at a time and beat into the mixture. After each egg is incorporated add a spoonful of flour and mix again. Sift the remaining flours together and fold into the creamed mixture followed by the lemon juice. Turn the mixture into a greased tin lined with waxed paper and level off the top. Place in a preheated oven at 160°C/325°F/Gas mark 3 for about 1 hour 25 minutes or until risen and firm to the touch. Turn out on to a wire cooling rack.

For the filling, use unsalted ricotta cheese and sweeten with powdered sugar to taste. Split the cakes in half and sandwich together with the sweetened cheese mixture and a layer of fruit preserve.

INGREDIENTS

(for one cake)
8oz (225g) butter or margarine
8oz (225g) powdered sugar
4 eggs
8oz (225g) self-rising flour
4oz (125g) all purpose flour
4 teaspoons lemon juice

Filling
1½lb (675g) ricotta
powdered sugar to taste
1½lb (675g) fruit preserve

Decoration
10″ (25cm) thin round cake board
1½lb (675g) marzipan
2½lb (1.1kg) gelatin or tragacanth icing
a little royal icing

Equipment
8″ (20cm) plastic plant pot
empty champagne bottle and cork
ribbon

TIMESAVERS

TIMESAVER Instead of moulding a champagne bottle from icing, you could put a half-bottle of real champagne in the iced bucket. Either cut into the cake to support the bottle or serve it standing upright leaning against the napkin. A chocolate champagne bottle of the right size wrapped in green foil would also fit the bill.

TIMESAVER Soft pink tissue or a cotton napkin could replace the icing napkin, saving time and providing a contrasting texture to the icing.

DECORATION 2 hrs + 12 hrs drying time
An hour can be saved on the decoration by using the two timesavers

ICING 1 hr + drying time

MARZIPAN 30 mins

COOKING 1 hr 25 mins per cake

1 Assemble the cake as illustrated.

2 Wrap the plant pot in a sheet of bakers' parchment and secure with tape. Trim the paper to the top and bottom edges of the plant pot.

4 Using a sharp knife, cut the cake to the same shape as the pot but slightly smaller than it. The champagne bucket will be exactly the same size as the plant pot – the cake should fit inside it and still leave a ½″ (1cm) gap all round. Now roll out 8oz (225g) of marzipan on a work surface lightly dusted with powdered sugar and cut out a circle to fit the top of the cake. Spread the top of the cake with the fruit preserve. (It is a good idea to blend it in a processor first.) Place the marzipan on top of the cake. Roll out 1lb (450g) marzipan plus any leftover trimmings. Place the paper pattern on top of the marzipan and cut around it. Spread the sides of the cake with fruit preserve and fix on the marzipan. Leave to dry for a few hours.

3 Using a sharp pair of scissors or a knife cut a straight line through the paper from the top to the bottom edge. Open out the paper. The pattern you have made will act as a guide for marzipanning and icing the cake.

5 Trim off any excess marzipan.

6 Roll out 1lb (450g) of gelatin or tragacanth icing. Lay the paper pattern on top of it and cut around the edge. Save any trimmings and wrap tightly in cling film.

8 Using sticky tape, secure the paper pattern to help keep the icing in place while it dries. Gently smooth the icing into any detail that there is on the pot. Turn the pot upside down and leave the icing to dry for 12 hours or overnight.

7 Lay the icing piece on top of the paper pattern so that the edges match exactly. Place the plant pot on the icing sheet and wrap round.

9 When the icing is dry, remove the paper pattern. Carefully cut the bucket in half with a sharp knife as shown. After 12 hours the icing may still feel rather soft and pliable. If so, it is safest to wrap it back inside the pattern once cut and allow it to dry out completely.

Icing dries as air circulates around it. Wrapping the icing in paper against the plant pot means that very little air can get to it. Once the bucket has been cut, however, you can place both halves inside the plant pot and allow the air to get to the inside of the pieces.

TIPS

Silver food colouring is safe to eat, but if you don't like the taste, you could add a small amount of black food colour to the icing to make it pale grey. To add a shine to the finished bucket, dust with edible lustre powder. For a golden wedding you could paint the bucket gold or yellow instead.

10 Place the two halves of the bucket around the cake and fix together with a little royal icing gently smoothed along the edges. Leave to dry for an hour or so.

11 Paint the bucket with silver food colour.

12 Take any icing trimmings left from making the bucket and roll out again to a sheet about ¼″ (5mm) thick. Using a sharp knife cut out four circles, two of which are 1½″ (4cm) in diameter and two of which are ¾″ (2cm) in diameter. Cut two circles of icing ¼″ (5mm) thick for the handles. Cut out a piece from each handle leaving a ¾″ (2cm) gap. Leave the icing pieces to dry completely.

13 Paint the bucket details silver and fix on to the bucket as shown with a little royal icing.

TIPS

Instead of painting the bottle green, which could leave brushstrokes, you could knead green food colour into the icing before laying it over the bottle. You might not end up with the same intensity of green, but you won't have to wait for the paint to dry to continue.

14 To make the champagne bottle, take a real (empty) champagne bottle and dust lightly with a little cornstarch. Roll out 8oz (225g) gelatin or tragacanth icing and lay over the bottle so that it covers half of it. Gently smooth the icing to the shape of the bottle.

15 Using a sharp knife, trim the icing while soft so that exactly half the bottle is covered. You will find that most bottles are made in two halves and that the glass has a seam running down it. Try to cut the icing to the seam so that you have two exact halves. Because the bottle will be seen sticking out of the bucket, you will not need an entire bottle, and will need to trim off about a third. Allow the icing to dry over the bottle overnight or for 12 hours. As with the icing bucket, it may be that when you remove the icing from the bottle it will still be pliable. If time permits, allow the icing to sit on the bottle until it is completely hard, or if not, tie several pieces of ribbon around the icing to keep it in shape and let it dry out completely in the air while you make the other half of the bottle.

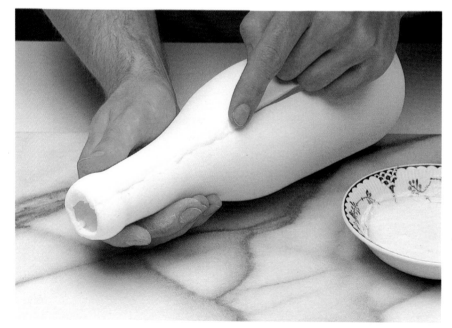

16 Fix the two halves of the bottle together, spreading the seams with a little royal icing. Allow to dry for a couple of hours.

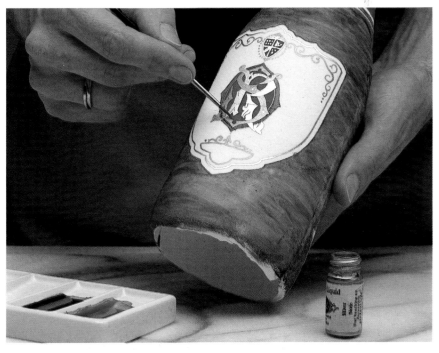

17 Using the label designs and monograms on *p.183* mark out the bottle with the help of a sheet of graphite paper. Paint the bottle green.

18 Using gold, red and silver food colours, paint on the detail as illustrated.

TIPS

If you decide to colour the icing green you will need to use gold foil for the label and round the neck of the bottle, as gold paint won't take on top of coloured icing. Or you could make a label from gelatin icing and fix it to the bottle with royal icing.

19 Place the bottle inside the bucket, fixing it to the surface of the cake with royal icing.

20 Take the remaining 8oz (225g) gelatin or tragacanth icing and colour it pink. Roll out the icing and cut into oblong shapes for the napkin.

Drape around the bottle and arrange decoratively with at least one or two pieces hanging over the edge of the bucket.

ASSEMBLY

Cut two lengths of ribbon and thread through the bucket handles and all around the cake. Place the cork at the base of the bucket.

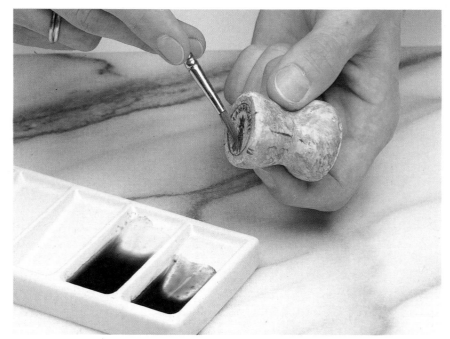

21 Take any remaining icing and shape into a cork. When the icing has dried, stipple it with brown food colour and leave the paint to dry.

CHRISTMAS WREATH

The Christmas Wreath pictured on p.47 is a quick and simple 10" (25cm) round Christmas fruit cake in a time-honoured tradition. The wreath itself can form part of your Christmas decorations both before you serve the cake and after you have eaten it.

INGREDIENTS

Decoration
12" (30cm) round cake board
2½lb (1.1kg) marzipan
2lb (900g) white fondant icing
12oz (350g) fondant icing
coloured Christmas red
1¾lb (825g) gelatin icing
apricot jam
royal icing

Equipment
wire for modelling
artificial leaves for the wreath
stiff cardboard
fir cones
food colours
various Christmas decorations
5 tall thin candles

TIMESAVERS

TIMESAVER The wreath on top of the cake can become part of your Christmas decorations once the cake has been cut. If you are not intending to eat any of it, then you can save time by omitting the poinsettias and Christmas roses, which are moulded from icing, and using in their place any suitable tree ornaments. Or you could use shop-bought edibles such as chocolate figures wrapped in foil, nuts and dried fruit.

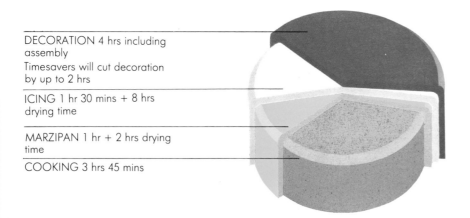

DECORATION 4 hrs including assembly
Timesavers will cut decoration by up to 2 hrs

ICING 1 hr 30 mins + 8 hrs drying time

MARZIPAN 1 hr + 2 hrs drying time

COOKING 3 hrs 45 mins

1 Turn the cake upside down. Place a saucer in the middle of the cake and cut round it and right through the cake with a sharp knife to remove the centre. Hold the knife perfectly vertically to make a neat and regular hole. Wrap the cut-out centre for decoration later.

3 On a work surface lightly dusted with cornstarch roll out the white fondant icing into a circle about 18″ (46cm) in diameter. Moisten the surface of the cake with a little water on a pastry brush. Lay the icing sheet over the cake and smooth to the outside edge. Using a large flat-bladed knife held against the side of the cake cut off and keep any excess icing. Cut neatly around the top inside edge with a sharp knife and remove the small circle of icing. Roll out the icing remains and cut into a strip according to the measurements previously taken for the inside of the cake. Brush the inside of the cake with a little water and fix on the icing.

2 Take 8oz (225g) marizpan and roll into a long sausage. Press the marzipan into the gap between the cake and the board, as in the wedding cake (see *p.121*). Trim the marzipan to the edge of the cake with a flat-bladed knife and keep any leftovers. Wrap a piece of string round the cake to measure its circumference and measure its height. Roll out 1lb (450g) marzipan into a strip. Cut a piece to the measurements just taken. Cut in half for ease of handling. Spread the outside of the cake with jam and fix the marzipan to it. Gather together all the leftover pieces of marzipan. Measure the circumference of the cutout centre and cut out a piece to fit (the height of the cake has already been noted). Spread the marzipan with apricot jam (it would be too tricky and messy to spread jam on the inside of the cake) and fix the marzipan in position. Roll out 1lb (450g) marzipan. Use the tin in which the cake was baked as a guide and cut out a circle. Place the saucer in the centre of the circle and cut round it. Keep the cut-out circle. Spread the top of the cake with apricot jam and fix the marzipan to it. Allow to dry for two hours.

4 Trace the pattern for the decoration on *p.190* on to bakers' parchment, ensuring that it is long enough to stretch over the cake from the bottom outside to the bottom inside edge. Cut out the pattern.

6 Take a piece of stiff cardboard. Place the cake tin on the cardboard and draw around it with a pen or pencil. Place the saucer in the centre of the marked-out circle and draw around it. Take a sharp knife or pair of scissors and cut out the circle for the base of the wreath.

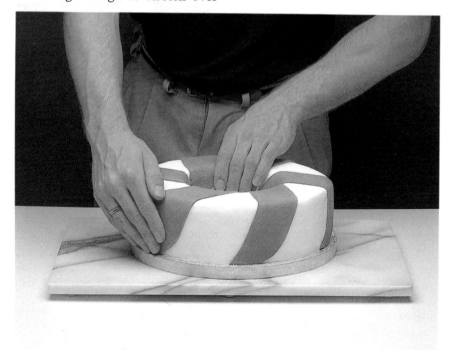

7 Assemble the various Christmas decorations that are being used.

5 On a work surface lightly dusted with cornstarch roll out the Christmas red fondant icing. Lay the pattern on the icing and cut around. Place the icing strip over the cake. Dab a little water on the inside of each end of the strip, then smooth down against the sides of the cake. Six of these strips are sufficient to decorate the cake.

8 Take the leaves that form the basis of the wreath and fix to the card circle with tape, staples or glue. Place the first lot decoratively round the outside of the circle, then fill in the inside.

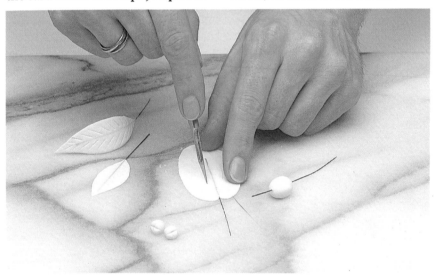

9 To make the poinsettia take 4oz (125g) gelatin icing and divide into 10 balls the size of hazelnuts. Cut the modelling wire into 4″ (10cm) lengths. Insert a piece of wire into each ball of icing and roll out so the wire extends well into the icing. With a sharp knife cut five of the icing discs into petals 3″ (7.5cm) long and the other five into petals 2½″ (6.5cm) long. Score veins into the petals with a toothpick and allow them to dry over a tin, so that they take on a curved shape, for four hours or until completely dry. Repeat to make enough petals for three poinsettias. Take 4oz (125g) gelatin icing and roll into 18 small balls the size of peas. Cut a small cross into the top of each ball and allow to dry for two hours.

10 Paint each petal Christmas red and allow to dry for an hour or so.

11 When dry, collect the petals together so that you have five larger petals at the base of the flower and five smaller ones on top. Twist the petal wires together to hold the flowers in shape. Make three flowers. Paint the bottom half of the 18 balls green and the top half yellow. Leave to dry for an hour, then paint the crosses red. Fix six balls into the centre of each poinsettia with dabs of royal icing.

SPECIAL FINISHES

To make the centres for the roses cut out 12 2″ (5cm) lengths of yellow thread. Hold the pieces together and fold in half so that the ends meet in a bunch. Tie together at the bottom with another piece of thread. Fan out the thread strands to form a circle. Put a dab of royal icing in the centre of each flower and fix the thread centres in place. Cut out three ½″ (1cm) circles of icing a little thicker than a nickel from the trimmings left over. Prick the surface all over with a toothpick. Allow to dry for an hour then paint pale yellow. Fix in the middle of the thread centre with a dab of royal icing. When dry, dust the roses with gold lustre powder. Place a layer of fir cones on the wreath, fixing them in position with royal icing or glue. Fix on the poinsettias and Christmas roses. Fix the remaining decorations on the wreath and allow to rest until the glue or icing has hardened.

Paint the red strips of icing with a thin edging of silver food colour. Paint small dots of silver on the white icing. Allow to dry for about an hour. Place the wreath on top of the cake. Take the five candles and cut to different lengths. Fix the candles in the centre of the cake, securing them to the board with Stick-um™ or other candle adhesive or royal icing.

12 To make the Christmas roses cut out a heart-shaped piece of cardboard about 1½″ (4cm) across. For each rose take 4oz (125g) gelatin icing and roll out as thinly as possible. Cut round the cardboard to make five heart-shaped petals. Gently press the edges of the petals between thumb and forefinger to make them as thin as possible, and allow to dry in small bowls, so that they take on a curve, for four hours or until completely dry. Make 15 petals, which will make three roses. Keep any leftover icing.

13 When the petals are dry fix together with small dabs of royal icing to hold the flowers in shape. Allow to rest for at least two hours to give the icing a chance to harden.

ASSEMBLY

Be sure not to leave icing the cake until the last moment. It should have plenty of time to dry out completely before you put the wreath on top, or the decoration will stick to the cake and make a mess when you take it off.

GET WELL FRUIT BASKET

A rich farmhouse cake is transformed by the addition of simply modelled marzipan fruit into an imaginative get-well gift. The basket of fruit (see p.53) and the cake board on which it stands could even be wrapped in cellophane secured at the top with a bow. This is a straightforward cake to decorate and its appearance will boost the morale of anyone feeling under the weather.

To make the cake. Sift the flour and spice together and set aside. Cream the butter or margarine with the sugar and molasses until light and fluffy. Beat in the eggs one at a time followed by a tablespoon of flour. Fold in the remaining flour with the fruit and milk and mix thoroughly.

As the cake needs to cook for 2–2¼ hours, the tin should be prepared as for a wedding cake. Grease and line the tin with two layers of waxed paper. Tie a double layer of waxed brown or newspaper round the tin. Spoon the mixture into the tin and level off the top. Cook in a preheated oven at 160°C/325°F/Gas mark 3. To see if the cake is done insert a skewer into the centre. If no mixture sticks to the skewer, remove the cake from the oven and allow to cool for 5 minutes in the tin. Turn out on to a wire rack and allow to cool.

TIMESAVERS

TIMESAVER Using royal icing to produce a basketweave effect is quite simple after a little practice. However, if you do not want to use a pastry bag, you could marzipan the cake in the usual way and then cover it in fondant icing. You could then paint the icing brown to make it look like a basket, or print or stencil the sides of the cake to turn it into a bowl of fruit rather than a basket.

TIMESAVER For a true lover of marzipan this cake is an added inducement to getting well, filled as it is with marzipan fruit. If time does not allow, or the recipient of the cake is not a lover of marzipan, you could fill the basket with real fruit instead.

INGREDIENTS

8oz (225g) self-rising flour
1 teaspoon ground mixed spice
5oz (150g) butter or margarine
5oz (150g) light brown sugar
1 tablespoon molasses
2 eggs
4oz (125g) chopped dates
5oz (150g) golden raisins
4oz (125g) currants
3 tablespoons milk

Decoration
9″ (23cm) thin round cake board
1lb (450g) yellow marzipan
1¾lb (825g) white marzipan
royal icing made with 1 egg white
4oz (125g) gelatin icing
apricot jam

Equipment
2 × 12″ (30cm) lengths coathanger wire
2 yards (2m) baby ribbon
12″ (30cm) of 1″ (2.5cm) wide ribbon
food colours
lustre powder
edible baker's glaze

DECORATION 2 hrs + 4 hrs drying time

ICING 45 mins + 1 hr drying time

MARZIPAN 30 mins

COOKING 2 hrs

1 Turn the cake upside down. Using a sharp knife, cut the square on the diagonal into an oval shape. Trim the sides to produce a gently sloping edge.

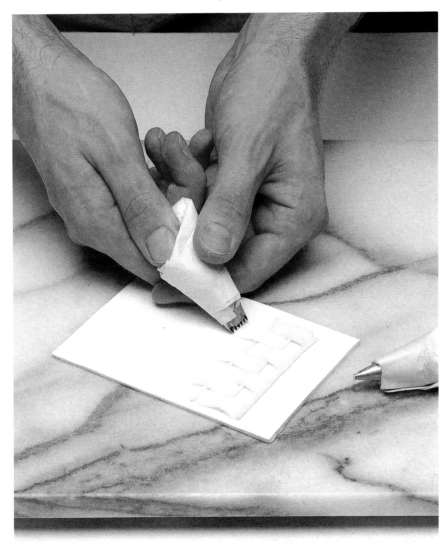

2 On a work surface lightly dusted with powdered sugar roll out 8oz (225g) yellow marzipan. Spread the top of the cake with apricot jam and place it jam-side down on the marzipan. With a sharp knife trim round the edge of the cake and then smooth the marzipan surface, making sure that the edges are neat. Measure the depth of the cake. Wrap a piece of string round the cake to determine its circumference. Roll out 8oz (225g) marzipan and cut out a strip to the measurements just noted. It can be a good idea to cut the piece into two halves to make handling easier. Spread the sides of the cake with apricot jam and fix the marzipan to the sides.

3 This photograph shows the basket weave on a separate piece of icing to make the steps easier to see. The weave is created using icing tips Nos 2 and 9. Fix each tip to a separate pastry bag and fill with 2 tablespoons royal icing. Begin by piping two vertical lines ½″ (1cm) apart with nozzle No 2, working from top to bottom of the cake. Take the bag fitted with nozzle No 9 and hold against the top edge of the cake right up to the first vertical line. Pipe a 1″ (2.5cm) length of icing stretching over the second vertical line. Pipe a second similar piece of icing leaving a gap the thickness of the icing tip between the first and sec-

ond lengths. Continue in this way to the bottom of the cake leaving gaps between each 1″ (2.5cm) piece. Take the bag fitted with tip No 2 and pipe a third vertical line joining up the ends of the 1″ (2.5cm) pieces just piped. Take the bag fitted with tip No 9 and hold against the second vertical line. Begin piping 1″ (2.5cm) lengths in the gaps left, stretching over the third vertical line. Take the bag fitted with tip No 2 and pipe a fourth vertical line joining up the ends of the 1″ (2.5cm) pieces just iced. Continue piping in this way until the whole cake is iced, then leave to dry for one hour.

4 Make up a number of brown food colours and paint the sides of the cake in several shades. Allow to dry for an hour.

5 Dust the side of the cake with edible gold lustre powder.

TIPS

Instead of using a piping bag, you could plait basketwork for the side of this cake in marzipan, following the technique for the Easter cake.

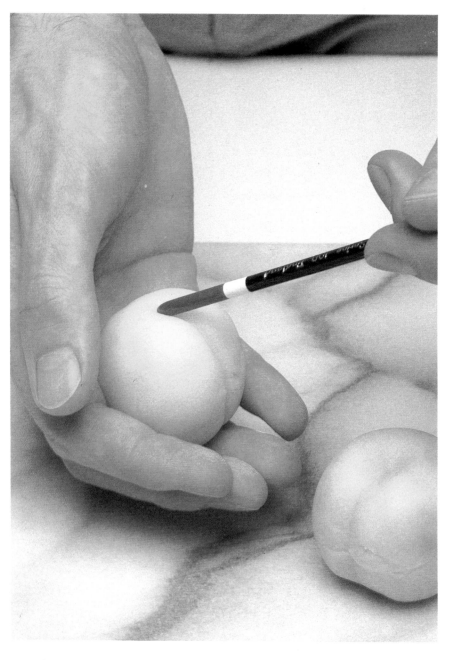

6 A dozen pieces of fruit and grapes are enough for this cake. Each fruit is moulded from about 2oz (50g) white marzipan. For the peaches, oranges and apples, begin by rolling a ball of marzipan. For the oranges and apples, add dimples by pressing the end of a paintbrush into the top and bottom of the ball before allowing it to dry. In the case of the orange, the effect of the skin is created by gently stippling with the end of a fine paintbrush all over the fruit. For the peach gently press the handle of a paintbrush into the side of the fruit to create the characteristic indentation. Make the grapes from smaller slightly elongated marzipan balls. For a banana roll a sausage shape and mould the ends into rounded points. Bend into shape. Flatten the sides slightly as in a real banana. To make a pear, pinch and mould one half of the ball to create the required shape. Add other fruits of your choice. Allow to dry for four hours before proceeding.

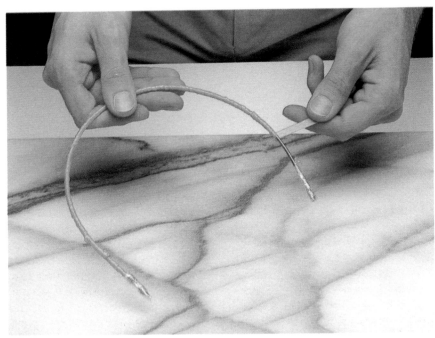

7 To paint the fruit make up a series of shades of food colour relevant to your choice of fruits. In most cases a simple wash of one colour can be brushed on to the fruit and left to dry. However, if you feel adventurous, several shades can be painted on the same fruit. Merge the colours where they meet to produce a delicate bloom. This is done with a moistened brush while the colours are still wet.

8 Take two 12″ (30cm) lengths of coathanger wire and bend into a horseshoe shape. Wrap both wire pieces in lengths of baby ribbon. Wrap the ends of the wire in cling film, as they will be pushed into the cake to the depth of 1″ (2.5cm).

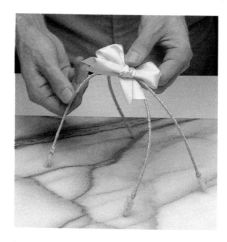

9 Tie the handles in position with a ribbon bow at the top.

10 Gently press the handles into the cake.

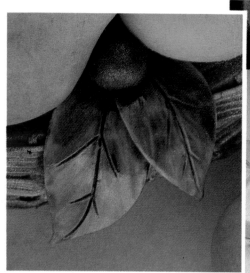

11 Take the 4oz (125g) gelatin icing and roll into a sheet on a work surface lightly dusted with cornstarch. With a sharp knife cut out 12 spear-shaped leaves about 1½″ (4cm) long. Score veins into the leaves with a toothpick. Allow some leaves to dry over a rolling pin and bend others up at the edges to produce a 'v' in cross-section. Leave for four hours to dry. When dry paint green and allow to dry for a further hour. Add a shine to the surface of the leaf with edible baker's glaze.

ASSEMBLY

Pile the fruit on top of the cake. If necessary fix in place with a dab of royal icing. Fill any gaps between the fruit with leaves. Place one or two pieces of fruit on the board for a pleasing effect.

HAND OF CARDS

This striking design (see p.57) is based on blocks of cake bought in a supermarket. We have used four blocks measuring about 6 × 4″ (15 × 10cm). The cakes are arranged quite simply and the cards are made from gelatin icing and fanned out on top. You can use the symbols on the cards to convey a message. The King and Queen of Hearts joined by the Ace of Diamonds would be suitable for an engagement party, and a hand of blackjack adding up to 21 would make an unusual 21st birthday cake.

INGREDIENTS

Decoration
12″ (30cm) square thin cake board
1lb (450g) marzipan
1lb (450g) fondant icing
12oz (350g) gelatin icing
apricot jam
royal icing

Equipment
food colours
ribbon

TIMESAVERS

TIMESAVER A quicker cake to make on the same theme would be a card table. Cover the cake with green icing to represent baize. When it has dried you could lay out a real hand of cards, say a dummy hand of bridge. Other items such as scoring pads and pencils could be arranged on the cake as part of the gift.

TIMESAVER The cards could be placed in a run instead of fanned out in a hand to avoid the need to cut and shape. Display them slightly overlapping in a straight line. Bear in mind that number cards take less time to paint than royal cards, especially if you are using cutters to make the symbols.

DECORATION 2 hrs 30 mins + 5 hrs drying time
Decoration could be cut to 30 mins, see Timesavers

ICING 30 mins + 8 hrs drying time

MARZIPAN 45 mins + 2 hrs drying time

1 Assemble the cakes by placing three side by side lengthways and the fourth cake below the other three as shown. The size of the individual cards is dictated by the size of the cake block. In this instance the assembled cakes allow for cards that are 7″ (18cm) long and 4½″ (11.5cm) wide. Take your measurements and draw three cards on a piece of parchment or tracing paper with each card at an angle to the others, in such a way that the resulting template fits within the block of the cake. Cut out the template.

2 Place the template on the block of cake and cut the cake to its shape.

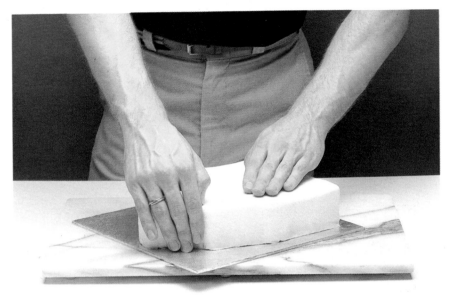

3 Spread the top of the cake with apricot jam. On a work surface lightly dusted with icing sugar roll out 8oz (225g) marzipan. Place the template on the marzipan and cut around the edge. Fix the marzipan to the surface of the cake. Measure the depth of the cake. Take a piece of string and wrap round the edge of the cake to determine its circumference. Roll out the remaining marzipan and cut a strip to the depth of the cake and the length of the sides. It will be easier and perhaps produce a neater edge if this strip of marzipan is cut in half and applied in two sections. Spread the sides of the cake with jam and fix on the marzipan. Allow to dry for two hours.

4 On a work surface lightly dusted with cornstarch roll out 1lb (450g) fondant icing. Place the icing over the cake and gently smooth along the edges. Using a flat-bladed knife held against the side of the cake, trim off the excess icing. Allow the icing to dry overnight or for about 8 hours. Now when the cards are placed on the cake they will be easily removable. If the icing is even remotely tacky or sticky to the touch, the cards may stick, which would make cutting difficult.

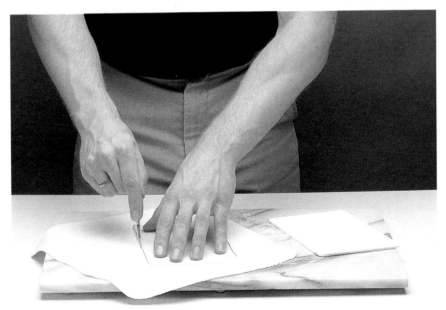

5 On a piece of parchment or tracing paper mark out the shape of one card. Roll out 12oz (350g) gelatin icing and using the template for the single card, cut out three shapes. Allow to dry for at least 4 hours until completely dry.

6 Take a pack of cards and select the three to be used in the cake. Trace the designs on to parchment or tracing paper, increasing the size of each motif if necessary to match the size of your cards. Put a piece of graphite paper over the icing card and lay the tracing on top. Draw over the design to transfer each motif into position on the icing card. Make the three cards in this way and paint with the appropriate food colours. Allow to dry for an hour or so.

8 If you are a little hesitant about painting with food colours, the various symbols for the suits can be cut out of gelatin icing with pastry cutters and fixed on the card with dabs of royal icing. You can buy school rulers from certain shops which feature stencils of letters and numbers. One such could be used, in conjunction with food colour pens, to mark out the letters and numbers on the cards.

7 To assemble the cake place the three cards overlapping on the surface of the cake. Ribbon of various colours, possibly chosen to match those in the cards, can be added to the sides of the cake and fixed in place with royal icing.

HALLOWEEN PUMPKIN

A warm, spicy parkin will keep out the cold on Halloween. This pumpkin (pictured on p. 61) is made of three 9″ (23cm) round cakes piled one on top of the other and features simple carving. Parkin lends itself admirably to this technique as it is moist and dense and therefore easy to cut. The orange fondant icing 'skin' and the candle flame flickering behind the cut-out features complete the illusion.

To make the cake. Grease a 9″ (23cm) round cake tin and line with waxed paper. Place the flour and oats in a mixing bowl and sift in the soda, salt and ginger. Place the butter or margarine, molasses, syrup and sugar in a saucepan and heat gently until the fat has melted. Cool slightly and add to the dry ingredients together with the milk. Mix thoroughly. Pour the mixture into the tin and bake in a preheated oven at 180°C/350°F/Gas mark 4 for about 50 minutes, or until firm to the touch. Leave the cake in the tin for 15 minutes, then turn out to cool on a wire rack. Store for several days before eating. Do not be anxious if your parkin appears to sink slightly on cooling. Parkin tends to do this, but as you will see in the step-by-step instructions, the centre of each cake is cut out and not used in the finished pumpkin.

TIMESAVERS

TIMESAVER If you lack either the time or the confidence to hollow out the centre of the pumpkin to take the candle, a whole pumpkin with a candle sitting on the top would be a quicker alternative. You can paint the features in black on the surface of the cake.

TIMESAVER You can ice the cake in one go. Roll out the coloured fondant into a circle large enough to cover the entire cake, and lay it on the cake board, which you have lightly dusted with cornstarch. Put the marzipanned cake in the centre of the icing and moisten the marzipan all over to make it sticky. Fold the icing up the sides of the cake without bothering to smooth out the creases. Twist the surplus at the top into a stalk and leave to dry. The stalk can be painted afterwards.

INGREDIENTS

Made with 3 × 9″ (23cm) round parkin cakes.

(for one cake)
8oz (225g) wholewheat flour
8oz (225g) rolled oats
½ teaspoon bicarbonate of soda
½ teaspoon salt
1 teaspoon ground ginger
4oz (125g) butter or margarine
4oz (125g) molasses
4oz (125g) golden syrup
4oz (125g) light brown sugar
6 fl oz (175ml) milk

Decoration
12″ (30cm) round cake board
2lb (900g) yellow marzipan for the pumpkin
8oz (225g) white marzipan for the spider
1½lb (675g) fondant icing coloured orange
apricot jam
a little royal icing

Equipment
one or two candles or a nightlight
food colour

DECORATION 1 hr + drying time
Not hollowing out cake will save 30 mins
Icing the cake in one go will save 20 mins

COOKING 50 mins per cake

ICING 45 mins

MARZIPAN 1 hr 30 mins + drying time

1 Cut the centre out of each cake using a teapot lid as a guide. Keep the centres and enjoy them later with friends and a cup of tea!

3 Pile the cakes one on top of the other.

2 Roll out a small amount of the marzipan and cut out a strip to the depth of the cake. Measure the circumference of the teapot lid to determine the length of the strip.

Brush the marzipan with a little apricot jam and fix on to the cut inside edge of the cake. Repeat with the other two cakes.

This will tell you how wide each of the marzipan segments should be at the top, in the middle and at the bottom, and allow you to take into account the curve of the cake. Roll out the marzipan and, using a sharp knife, cut out 6 segments according to the measurements just calculated. Gently press the edges of the segments to round them off – this will emphasize the segments once applied to the pumpkin. Brush each segment with apricot jam and fix to the side of the cake. Allow to dry for several hours or overnight before proceeding.

4 Using a sharp knife, carve the pile of cakes as illustrated into the beginnings of a pumpkin shape.

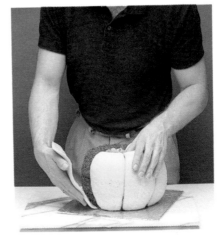

TIPS

There is no filling between the layers of this particular cake and none is required as parkin is so moist that the layers will stick to each other with no danger of moving while they are being carved.

5 The pumpkin will be made with 6 individual marzipan segments, so to find out how big each will be, use a piece of thread or string to measure the height of the cake and its circumference at the widest point. Measure the circumference of the cake again around the opening on the top and around the bottom where the cake meets the board. Note down each of the circumference measurements, then divide each figure by 6.

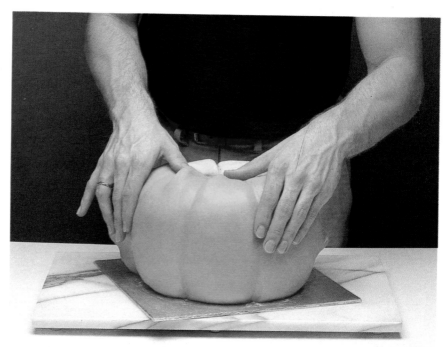

6 Using a food colour pen or a toothpick, mark out the eyes, nose and mouth as illustrated.

7 Using a sharp pointed knife, cut the marzipan and cake through to the hollow centre. If unsure, proceed steadily by removing small pieces one at a time. Do not be afraid that the cake will collapse in on the cut-out detail. If the parkin has been stored for a short time it will have a lovely moist density which makes it perfect for carving in this way.

8 Once again measure the height and circumference of the now marzipanned cake. Take half of the orange fondant icing and roll out on a work surface dusted with cornstarch. Cut out a piece of icing the same height as the cake and as long as *half* its circumference. Moisten the joins between the marzipan segments with water and gently press the icing on to the cake and into the joins (an extra pair of hands can be very useful at this point). Do not be worried if the icing creases at the top of the cake. It is not important to try and flatten out the creases as they add to the natural look of the pumpkin. Trim any excess icing to the hollowed-out centre. Repeat this process with the other half of the cake. Before the icing dries, gently smooth it over the eyes, nose and mouth so that the edges become clearly outlined. Using your kitchen knife, cut out the icing to expose the eyes, nose and mouth.

9 Take the white marzipan and mould the spider as illustrated. Score the details of the eyes and mouth into the marzipan with a toothpick. Allow to dry for several hours before fixing together with a little royal icing. Paint the spider in the colour of your choice, using either food colours and a paintbrush or edible food colour pens.

ASSEMBLY

Secure the candle(s) or nightlight in the centre of the cake. Fix the spider at an angle on top of the cake with royal icing. Light the candles, turn out the lights and Happy Halloween!

BOX OF ROSES

Red roses on St Valentine's Day are the traditional expression of love. Here the romantic theme is presented in a chocolate cake ingeniously concealed in an attractively decorated icing box (see p. 67). The long-stemmed scarlet roses too are moulded from gelatin icing.

To make the cake. First make Mixture 1. Mix the cocoa and sugar in a pan, then beat in the eggs and add the milk. Cook gently, being careful to stir all the time, until the mixture has thickened and starts to bubble gently. Remove the pan from the heat and allow to cool slightly.

For Mixture 2, cream the butter and sugar together until fluffy. Add the eggs and beat vigorously. Sift the flour and baking powder and fold into the mixture, alternating with the milk until combined. Combine mixtures 1 and 2. Grease and line a 12" (30cm) square tin. Pour the mixture into the tin and level off the top. Bake in a preheated oven at 180°C/350°F/Gas mark 4 for about 1 hour 10 minutes. The cake is cooked if it is firm to the touch. Leave in the tin for 5–10 minutes before turning on to a wire rack to cool.

For the filling, break the chocolate into pieces and place in a bowl over a pan of boiling water. When melted, remove the bowl and allow the chocolate to cool. Bring the cream to the boil and add a few drops of vanilla flavouring. Remove the cream from the heat and gradually beat in the melted chocolate. Leave the mixture to cool, then beat again thoroughly. The mixture will almost double in volume and become paler. This process takes a great deal of effort if you are using a hand whisk and is better done in an electric mixer. If you do not have an electric mixer, whisk until the mixture stiffens. If you grow tired before the ganache is of spreading consistency, add a little sifted powdered sugar and fold in. Ganache hardens quite soon after it has been whisked, so use immediately.

(see p. 67)

INGREDIENTS

Cake: Mixture 1
7oz (200g) cocoa powder
12oz (350g) light brown sugar
2 eggs
9 fl oz (250ml) milk

Mixture 2
8oz (225g) butter
12oz (350g) light brown sugar
4 eggs
1lb (450g) all purpose flour
6 teaspoons baking powder
9 fl oz (250ml) milk

Ganache filling
13oz (375g) semi-sweet chocolate
9 fl oz (250ml) heavy cream
a few drops of vanilla extract

Decoration
14" (35cm) square cake board
1lb (450g) fondant icing
1¼lb (565g) marzipan
1½lb (675g) gelatin icing for the box, rose leaves and gift tag
1lb (450g) gelatin or tragacanth icing for the roses
apricot jam
a little royal icing

Equipment
food colour
skewers
modelling wire
white tissue paper
cellophane

TIMESAVERS

TIMESAVER Making the roses takes practice. If you don't have the time to acquire it, a dozen real red roses inside the icing box would make a perfect gift.

TIMESAVER You could leave the box plain white and tie a wide red silk ribbon round it to make a generous bow at the side. Or you could knead red and pink food colours into the icing, mixing them incompletely to create a marbled effect when rolled out.

DECORATION 4 hrs
By using real roses 1 hr 30 mins can be saved
Simplifying box saves 30 mins

ICING 25 mins + drying time

MARZIPAN 25 mins + drying time

COOKING 1 hr 10 mins

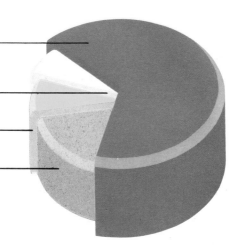

Cut the cake into two 12″ × 6″ (30 × 15cm) rectangles. If flavouring the cake with liqueur, sprinkle the cut surface of both cakes and allow to soak in. Spread the top of one cake with chocolate ganache and sandwich the cakes together.

1 Spread the top and sides of the cake with apricot jam. Roll out the marzipan into a large sheet. Measure the top and sides of the cake and cut out pieces of marzipan to these dimensions. Cover the top and sides of the cake with marzipan. Allow to dry for several hours.

2 Dust a work surface with cornstarch and roll out the fondant icing into a sheet large enough to cover the whole cake. Lay the icing over the cake and smooth over the top and sides. Pinch the icing at the corners to make neat seams. Use scissors to cut the corners and a sharp knife to trim the icing along the edges. Leave the icing to dry for several hours.

3 Roll out the gelatin icing and cut out four pieces to make the box. The sides of the box should be 1½″ (4cm) higher than the iced cake and ½″ (1cm) longer than the length and width of the cake respectively, so that they will fit neatly over it (see step 9) without touching. Let the pieces for the box dry on a flat surface until rigid, turning them over after 4 or 5 hours so that both surfaces come into contact with the air.

4 Using a ruler and a food colour pen, mark the sides of the box to indicate where the stripes should be drawn.

5 Draw the stripes on the box.

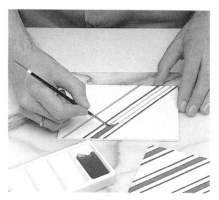

6 Fill in the colour with a paint-brush or food colour pen.

7 Spread the edges of the box pieces with royal icing and press together carefully to make the box. Remove any icing that may squeeze out at the seams with a sharp knife. Once the box is assembled, allow to dry.

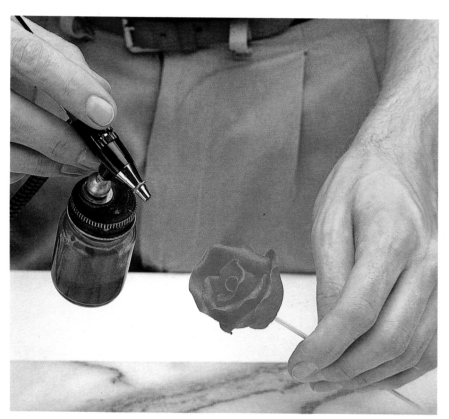

8 The technique of making roses is fully described in the Three-tier Wedding Cake (see p. 125). use the same technique, but make the roses on skewers. A good idea is to secure the skewer in a block of florist's oasis – this will allow you to use both hands to make and shape the rose. A deep red rose is the traditional gift for Valentine's Day, but it is worth noting that it is rather difficult to achieve the depth of colour required by simply adding red to icing. In order to produce a truly deep red it would be necessary to add so much food colour that the texture of the icing would become unmanageable. Another way of achieving a good red is to add a certain amount of red to the icing and then complete the colouring by brushing red on to the dried rose or, as in the photograph, spraying colour on to the flower with an airbrush.

9 To make the rose leaves take a piece of gelatin icing the size of a hazelnut and insert a 3″ (7.5cm) piece of wire through it. Roll out the icing so that the wire runs through its centre. Using a sharp knife, cut out a petal shape, leaving about 1½″ (4cm) wire sticking out of the leaf. Allow the leaf to dry over a rolling pin so that it takes on a gentle curve. Rose petal shapes are available in some shops, and these can be used for cutting round. They also have details of leaf veins, which can be pressed into the soft icing for added authenticity.

10 Once the leaves have dried, paint them green.

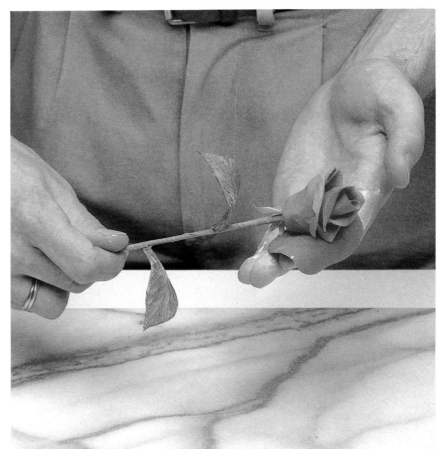

11 To prepare the stem of the rose, cut four 1½″ (4cm) pieces of florists' tape into long slim spear shapes to form the calyx. Gather the four pieces and hold them at the top of the skewer. Secure them to the skewer by wrapping tape around the bottom ½″ (1cm) of the strips. Continue wrapping the skewer for about 2″ (5cm). Take a dried rose leaf and hold the extending wire against the skewer. Continue wrapping the tape over the wire so that the leaf is attached to the skewer. Place another leaf further down the skewer and continue with the tape until the skewer is covered. Bend back the strips of tape at the top of the skewer to form the calyx. This will leave about 1″ (2.5cm) of skewer uncovered.

12 The flower head can be made on the prepared skewer. Here the last petal is being wrapped around the stem.

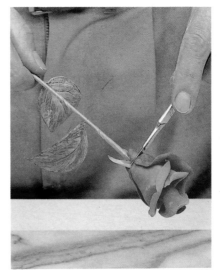

13 Trim the petal level with the calyx using a scalpel or a very sharp knife.

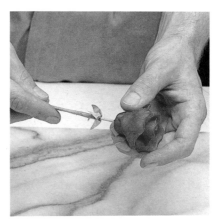

14 Alternatively, flower heads can be made separately and fixed to the skewers once they have dried.

To make an authentic bouquet of roses, at least some of the flowers should be buds, or barely open blooms.

ASSEMBLY

15 Place over the cake.

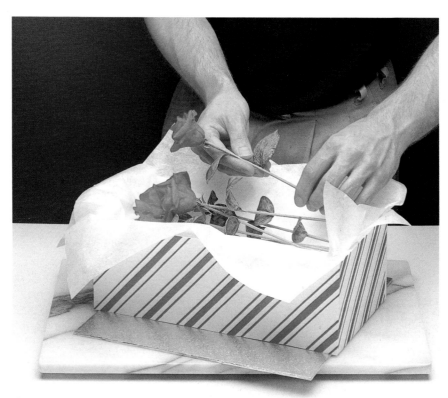

16 Place one or two sheets of cellophane and white tissue paper in the box. Do not press down on the cake more than necessary. Make sure the icing has had time to dry sufficiently, or the paper may stick to it.

Place the roses in the box and gently drape red ribbon tied in a bow over the roses and box.

A gift tag can be added as in the main photograph.

TIPS

This box has been very carefully decorated so that all the stripes match up – the result is smart and professional. A less time-consuming finish can be achieved by printing heart patterns on the box with a sponge or a potato cut to shape.

BIRTHDAY BREAKFAST

Three 12" (30cm) square moist apple cinnamon cakes are transformed by clever sugarwork into a celebration birthday breakfast table. The cake, pictured on p. 73, illustrates the versatility of icing as a modelling medium. The crockery and cutlery is simply moulded by laying gelatin icing over a real table setting. The authentic-looking multi-petalled carnations, on the other hand, may require a little practice to perfect. Delicate brushwork completes the gift and the decorations can be kept as a souvenir of a lovely day.

To make the cake. Grease a 12" (30cm) square cake tin and line with waxed paper. Sift the flour and cinnamon into a bowl and stir in the sugar and raisins. Mix in the melted butter or margarine along with the eggs, milk and apple. Beat until smooth. Transfer the mixture to the tin and bake in a preheated oven at 180°C/350°F/Gas mark 4 for 45–50 minutes. The cake is ready when it springs back when lightly pressed. Remove the cake from the tin and allow to cool on a wire rack.

For the filling, use unsalted ricotta cheese and sweeten with powdered sugar to taste. Stir in the calvados to taste, without making the mixture too runny.

TIMESAVERS

TIMESAVER prefer, use a real cup and saucer, carnation, croissant, birthday card etc. on top of the cake instead of making them from icing.

TIMESAVER We have made a very large cake in order to accomodate all the iced novelties on top. It will serve a sizeable gathering. If you wanted to make a smaller cake, you could change the decoration on top to suit. Mould a large dinner plate and make an icing breakfast of bacon, eggs and mushrooms, or the recipient's favourite meal.

INGREDIENTS
(for one cake)
10oz (300g) self-rising flour
1½ teaspoons ground cinnamon
8oz (225g) light brown sugar
4oz (125g) raisins
4oz (125g) butter or margarine, melted
2 eggs, beaten
6 fl oz (175ml) milk
8oz (225g) eating apples, peeled, cored and chopped

Filling
1½lb (675g) ricotta
powdered sugar to taste
calvados to taste

Decoration
16" (40cm) square cake board
2lb (900g) fondant icing coloured blue for the tablecloth
1lb (450g) fondant icing left white for the overcloth
2lb (900g) marzipan for the cake
12oz (350g) marzipan for the croissant and butter rolls
1¾lb (800g) gelatin icing for the crockery, spoon and vase
1lb (450g) tragacanth or gelatin icing for the carnations
apricot jam
baker's glaze
royal icing

Equipment
food colour
florists' tape
wooden skewers
decorative cutters

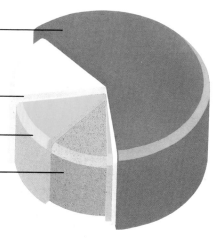

DECORATION 4 hrs + 12 hrs drying time
By cutting down on the crockery up to 2 hrs saved on decoration.
By making a smaller cake up to 2 hrs 30 mins can be saved.

ICING 1 hr + drying time

MARZIPAN 45 mins

COOKING 45 mins per cake

1 Spread the cakes with the filling and sandwich on top of each other. Spread the top of the cake with apricot jam. Roll out half the marzipan. Using the tin in which the cakes were baked as a guide, cut out a square of marzi-pan and place on top of the cake. Measure the length and height of the sides of the cake. Roll out the remaining marzipan and cut 4 pieces to the sizes just noted. Spread the pieces with apricot jam and fix to the sides of the cake.

4 Using colours of your choice, decorate the tablecloth with a bold check. If you like, using a contrasting colour, paint deli-cate brush strokes to emphasize the lace effect and to indicate the stitching around the edge of the cloth.

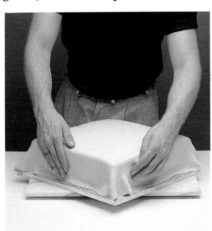

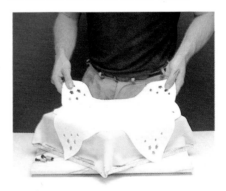

2 On a work surface well dusted with cornstarch, roll out the fondant icing for the tablecloth into a large enough square to drape over the cake. Place over the cake and arrange the decorative folds at the corners and sides. Trim off any excess icing.

3 Roll out the icing for the over-cloth and cut into a decorative shape. If a little unsure about this, simply cut out another but smaller square than before, which looks just as effective. Before placing the second layer of icing on the cake, take small decorative icing cutters and punch out flower shapes in each corner to represent a lace effect. Lay the overcloth on the cake as illustrated. Allow the icing to dry for several hours.

5 A homely touch – a slightly lighter blue gives the effect of a woven check.

TIPS

Painting the checks on the tablecloth is quite time-consuming. Instead you could print a check design using two or more 1″ (2.5cm) squares cut from a kitchen sponge, with one colour on each. The effect will be 'hand-woven' rather than crisp.

6 Take 6oz (175g) gelatin icing and roll out into a circle. Gently ease the icing into a tea cup, pressing gently against the sides and bottom of the cup to smooth out any creases that might form. Trim the excess icing to the top of the cup. Save any leftover icing. Remember that to reconstitute leftover gelatin icing you should simply add a very little water and knead briefly. Let the icing cup dry overnight.

8 Take 12oz (350g) gelatin icing. Roll out and cover a dessert plate and saucer. Gently smooth the icing around the lip of the plate and into the saucer and trim away any excess icing. Leave to dry overnight.

9 Remove the icing crockery from the plate and saucer. Fix the handle to the cup with a little royal icing.

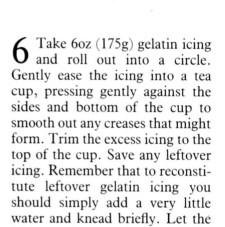

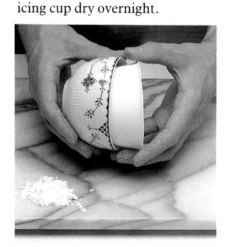

7 Remove the icing cup and using 2oz (50g) gelatin icing roll out a small circle. Take a sharp knife and cut out a handle similar to the one on your teacup. Allow to dry overnight.

10 To make the vase, take a straight-sided drinking glass and measure the height and circumference. Roll out the remaining gelatin icing and cut out a rectangle to the dimension noted. Wrap the icing around the glass. Secure the icing while it dries by wrapping glass and icing in a sheet of parchment paper and securing with sticky tape. Let the icing dry overnight.

11 Once dry, remove the glass and secure the join of the vase by spreading with a little royal icing and pressing gently together. To keep the join closed, wrap the vase in paper again and tape up if necessary.

12 Using colours of your choice, decorate the crockery and vase. For this stage of the operation remember that food colour pens could be very useful.

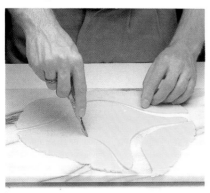

13 To make the croissant, roll out 8oz (225g) of the marzipan on a surface lightly dusted with powdered sugar. Cut out a stylized triangle with somewhat extended points, as in the photograph.

14 Roll up the croissant beginning with the base of the triangle facing you. Complete the croissant by folding the remaining point over. Bend the edges of the croissant round to produce the characteristic shape.

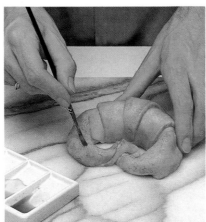

15 Mix up a number of orange, yellow and brown food colours and paint the croissant. Allow to dry and paint over with edible confectioner's or baker's glaze. Use egg white if this is not available.

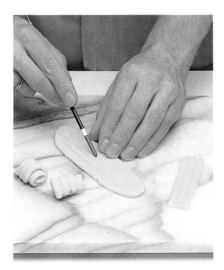

16 To make the butter roll take 4oz (125g) marzipan and roll out. Cut out three 1″ (2.5cm) wide strips. Using the end of a paint brush or skewer, deeply score the marzipan with parallel lines. Turn the strips over and roll up so that the scored lines are on the outside. Leave to dry.

To make a calyx for the carnation (if such authenticity is required), take a small amount of icing and colour it pale green. Shape it into a rounded pyramid. Using a sharp knife, make five small cuts at intervals around the bottom edge of the mound. Moisten the flat end with a little water and thread on to the skewer, pressing the calyx against the base of the flower to secure it. Leave to dry. Wrap the skewer in florists' tape as with the roses in the Valentine's Day cake.

17 To make the carnations, roll out the tragacanth (or gelatin) icing as thinly as possible. With a pastry cutter, cut out a circle of icing. Take a sharp knife and make ¼″ (5mm) cuts into the edge of the icing circle at ½″ (1cm) intervals.

19 Insert a bamboo skewer through the icing into the centre of the flower. Fold the icing circle in half with the point of the skewer inside it. With the skewer lying flat on a work surface fold up one side of the half circle to the centre as illustrated and secure by moistening the icing. Turn the skewer over and repeat so that the half circle has now been folded into an 'S' shape. The flower should dry upside down. To allow it to do this, simply moisten a small piece of icing and stick it to a wall unit above your work surface. Insert the skewer through the icing so that the flower is hanging down below the unit. It is not essential for each stage to be completely dry before continuing. Each flower is made of 4 or 5 iced circles, depending on the fullness of flower required. To add the second layer, moisten the next ruffled circle and thread it on to the skewer allowing it to rest over the shaped centre, then return to the wall unit to dry. When making the flowers it is easier to make all the centres, then all the second layers etc., rather than making one complete flower before going on to the next. This way the various layers have a chance to dry a little before the next layer is applied. Leave the completed flowers to dry overnight.

Additional decorative features in the shape of a birthday card and a folded newspaper can also be made quite easily. To make the newspaper, take 12oz (350g) of gelatin icing and roll out to a rectangle measuring 12″ × 9″ (30 × 23cm). Fold into 3 and allow to dry. To write a newspaper headline, trace letters or words from a real newspaper on to parchment paper. Put a piece of graphite paper on the icing newspaper and lay the tracing over the top. Copy over the tracing and then with black food colour or a colour pen paint over the graphite trace.

To make the card, take 8oz (225g) of gelatin icing and roll out thinly. Cut out 2 rectangles measuring 6″ × 4″ (15 × 10cm). Cut corresponding holes in each rectangle with a small icing cutter, then allow to dry. Tie the pieces together with thin ribbon and make small decorative bows. Decorate the front of the card with a design of your choice. You can sign a greeting inside the card in edible food colour pen, then the card can be kept as a reminder of the celebration.

18 Using the end of a paint brush or skewer, press on to the surface of the icing and roll backwards and forwards to produce a ruffled effect. Moisten the centre of the icing up to the ruffle.

ASSEMBLY

Place all the separate elements on the cake as illustrated. To ensure that the carnations are secure, it is perhaps a good idea to gently push the ends of the taped skewers into the surface of the cake.

TREASURE ISLAND

Three 9" (23cm) shop-bought chocolate sponge layers are sandwiched together with cream filling to make the island and the gelatin icing treasure chest contains gifts for all the guests at the party. The finished cake with its marzipan palm tree and brightly painted icing shells (see p.79) will make a spectacular centrepiece for any children's party.

To make the filling. Cream the butter or margarine with the powdered sugar and add vanilla to taste.

(see p.79)

INGREDIENTS

Filling
6oz (175g) butter or margarine
1lb (450g) powdered sugar
vanilla extract

Decoration
12" (30cm) round cake board
1½lb (675g) marzipan
1½lb (675g) fondant icing
2½lb (1.1kg) gelatin icing
royal icing
apricot jam

Equipment
small gifts
gold chocolate money
food colours
junk jewellery
lustre powder
½" (1cm) ribbon of various
colours
shells

TIMESAVERS

TIMESAVER The treasure chest and its contents are bound to be the main point of interest for the person receiving the cake. Save time on the other decorations by placing real shells on the sand instead of moulding them from icing.

TIMESAVER Instead of making the decorative corner pieces for the chest, you could encrust it with fake jewels and sequins arranged in formation. Go to the notions department of any major store for inspiration.

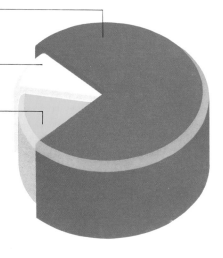

DECORATION 2 hrs 30 mins + 2 hrs drying time for the food colour and a total of 12 hrs drying time for the icing

ICING 25 mins + 2 hrs drying time

MARZIPAN 25 mins

1 Spread the vanilla cream filling between the layers of cake and pile on top of one another.

2 Using a sharp kitchen knife trim off the top edge all round the cake and roughly trim the sides to produce an irregular sloping edge. The treasure chest will measure 6 × 3 × 2½″ (15 × 7.5 × 6.5cm), so when you are trimming the cake make sure you still have enough room on top for the chest.

4 On a work surface lightly dusted with cornstarch roll out the fondant icing into a sheet large enough to cover the cake and board. Lay the icing over the cake and trim to the edge of the board. Let the icing dry for two hours.

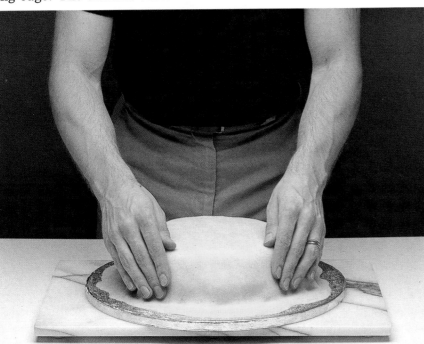

3 Spread the top and sides of the cake with apricot jam. On a work surface lightly dusted with powdered sugar roll out the marzipan into a sheet large enough to cover the cake and the board. Lay it over the cake and gently smooth down. It is not necessary to allow the marzipan to dry before proceeding.

5 Make up yellow and pale blue food colours. With a large paintbrush paint a wash of yellow over the island leaving an irregular strip around the edge of the board. Paint this with a wash of pale blue. Put some more yellow on the brush, pressing the bristles into the colour to splay them out. Gently dab at the surface of the wet yellow wash to produce a stippled effect. Repeat on the blue strip with the brush dipped in blue food colour. Let the colours dry for at least two hours.

6 On a work surface lightly dusted with cornstarch roll out 12oz (350g) gelatin icing and cut out the following shapes: three rectangles measuring 6 × 2½″ (15 × 6.5cm), two rectangles measuring 2½ × 3″ (6.5 × 7.5cm), two narrow strips measuring 6 × ½″ (15 × 1cm) and two measuring 3 × ½″ (7.5 × 1cm). Allow to dry for at least four hours, turning the pieces over at least once to let the air get to both sides. The body of the chest is made by fixing together two of the large rectangles and the two small rectangles into a box shape as illustrated. Fix in place with royal icing, which for this purpose should be quite stiff. The lid is made with the remaining pieces arranged as shown. When fixed together with royal icing, allow the body and lid of the chest to dry overnight.

7 Make up two shades of brown food colour, one quite pale

and one much darker. When the chest and lid are quite dry, brush them all over with the light brown and allow to dry for an hour. Take the paintbrush and dip into the dark brown, pressing the bristles to splay them out. Brush over the pale brown leaving a trace of separate thin dark lines, as in wood grain. To make a knot hole, bend the painted lines above and below the knot, then fill in with a series of circular brush strokes. This adds visual interest. However, the wood grain effect is interesting without the knot holes if you prefer to leave them out.

9 To make a starfish roll out 4oz (125g) gelatin icing into a rough circle about 2½" (6.5cm) in diameter. Trace the starfish shape from the design on *p.189*. Cut out and place the template on the iced circle. Cut round it. Gently press down the edges of the starfish to round them off. With the point of a cocktail stick prick two lines of decorative dots into the icing all around the edge of the starfish. Allow to dry in position on the edge of the cake for at least four hours so that the starfish takes on the curve of the cake before you paint it. To decorate the starfish, brush over with a bright food colour of your choice and leave to dry for an hour.

8 On a work surface lightly dusted with cornstarch roll out 8oz (225g) gelatin icing into a large sheet. Using the illustration on *p.189* trace out the various designs for the chest trimmings on to parchment or tracing paper and cut out. Using the paper templates triangular shapes to be fixed to the corners of the sides and lid of the chest. Also cut out one each of the large and small decorative shapes. Allow to dry for at least four

hours. When dry paint with a number of food colours, or in silver or gold or embellish richly with fake jewels or sequins. Paint a keyhole on the smaller decorative shape if you like. Allow to dry, then fix the large design in the centre of the lid with royal icing and the small one on the front of the chest. Fix the corner pieces at the corners.

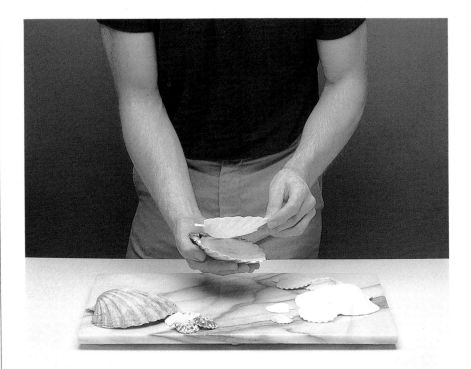

To make the palm leaves roll out 4oz (125g) gelatin icing on a work surface lightly dusted with cornstarch. Cut out about eight spear-shaped leaves about 2½″ (6.5cm) long. With a sharp knife make a series of ¼″ (5mm) cuts all round the edge like a fringe. Let the leaves dry for at least four hours in the bottom and at the side of a round cake tin, so that they are curved along both their length and their width. When dry paint the trunk brown and the leaves green. Allow to dry for a further two hours. To assemble the tree dab about a teaspoon of royal icing on top of the trunk and press the ends of the leaves into it. If any royal icing is visible when the tree has dried, paint it so that it won't show.

Place the body of the chest on the cake and fix in position with a little royal icing. If you want it to look as though it has partly sunk into the sand, put some fairly stiff royal icing under one end to lift it slightly off the cake. Then take some softer royal icing and smooth it up against the raised side of the chest like a drift of sand. Allow to dry and paint yellow. Allow to dry again. Place the gifts inside the chest with the ribbons trailing out on to the sand. Fill the chest up with gold chocolate money and colourful junk jewellery and lay the lid on top. It is not necessary to fix the lid in place as it will be removed when the gifts are taken out. Fix the tree to the cake behind the chest with stiff royal icing. Place the shells and starfish around the base of the cake. For an added magical effect brush the various items of decoration with several shades of lustre powder.

10 To make the shells roll out a further 4oz (125g) gelatin icing. You may want to colour the icing first, or perhaps to give a marbled effect by adding two or more colours and incompletely kneading them in so that swirling patterns are produced when the icing is rolled out. Lay the icing over any shells you may have. If you have none at home, you may find that your local fishmonger will give you a few, or sell them to you for next to nothing. Press the icing into any detail on the shell and trim it to the edge with a sharp knife. Allow to dry for at least four hours and then remove. If you have not already coloured the icing, paint in bright and attractive shades.

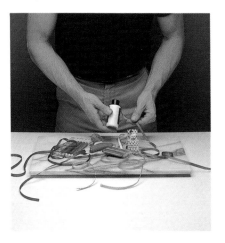

11 Take a number of small gifts, one for each guest at the party, and tie a piece of ribbon round each one, leaving a long tail.

To make the palm tree trunk take 8oz (225g) gelatin icing and roll roughly into a sausage shape about 6″ (7.5cm) long. It should be quite a bit fatter at the bottom than at the top. Using a pointed knife or skewer score 'v' shapes all over the bark of the tree. Leave to dry, for authenticity making a slight bend in the trunk.

CANCER STAR SIGN

This cake is made from a box of yellow cake mix (to make two 8"/20cm round layers) and is therefore very inexpensive, which ties in well with the Cancerian tendency towards frugality. If you prefer you can use a dome-topped bought sponge to avoid the need for carving. The crab's legs are moulded from icing and the body is painted in a good shellfish pink (see p.83) to appeal to Cancer's imagination and well-known sense of fun.

TIMESAVERS

TIMESAVER In this cake you could dispense with the icing altogether, and cover the crab with a layer of white marzipan to provide a sharp background against which to apply colour and decoration. The legs and claws would then also be made out of marzipan.

TIMESAVER A bought sponge cake could be quickly transformed into a crab. Jam sandwich cakes usually come with domed tops, so if you chose to decorate a bought cake you would not have to do any cutting and shaping.

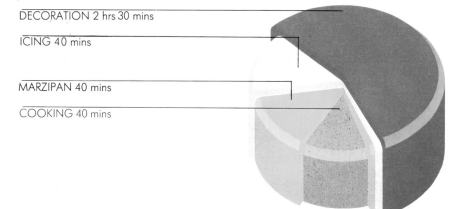

DECORATION 2 hrs 30 mins

ICING 40 mins

MARZIPAN 40 mins

COOKING 40 mins

INGREDIENTS

Decoration
10" (25cm) round cake board
1lb (450g) marzipan
12oz (350g) fondant icing
12oz (350g) gelatin icing
royal icing
apricot jam

Equipment
various food colours
dragees (silvered candy beads) or
fake jewels for eyes

1 Prepare the cake mix and bake in two 8" round pans. Cool on a wire rack. For the filling, use either chocolate fudge filling (*p.18*) or apricot jam.   Split the cakes in half and sandwich together with the filling.

2 Make a pattern for the crab shell by tracing out the shape on *p.182* including the decorative sub-divisions of the shell. Cut the cake into the shape of the crab shell using the pattern. Using a sharp knife, shape the cake so that the centre of the top remains the height of the entire cake but then slopes down to the edge, which is about 1½" (4cm) in height.

3 On a work surface lightly dusted with powdered sugar roll out 4oz (125g) of the marzipan into a strip 1½″ (4cm) wide and long enough to stretch around the cake. To determine the circumference of the shaped cake, wrap a piece of string around the edge and measure its length. Spread the strip with a little apricot jam and fix to the side of the cake. Roll out the remaining 8oz (225g) of marzipan into a circle large enough to cover the cake but extending ¼″ (5mm) beyond the edge. Place the pattern on the marzipan as a guide and using a sharp knife cut out the shape of the shell, but this time cutting ¼″ (5mm) beyond the edge of the pattern all round. It is not necessary to draw a second pattern as cutting free-hand is quite easy with such a simple shape. Spread the top of the cake with a little apricot jam and fix the marzipan to it.

so that it becomes sticky to the touch, and fix the strip of icing to the side of the cake. Take the remaining 8oz (225g) of fondant icing and roll out into a circle large enough to cover the top of the marzipanned cake and extending ¼″ (5mm) beyond the edge of the marzipan. Place the pattern on top of the icing and using a sharp knife cut out the shell shape, but this time cut ½″ (1cm) outside the pattern all round. Lay the piece of icing on top of the cake. By extending the marzipan and icing beyond the edge of the cake you will be creating a shell that covers the body of the crab. Allow the icing to dry for about 4 hours before continuing with the decoration.

4 On a work surface lightly dusted with cornstarch roll out 4oz (125g) of fondant icing 1½″ (4cm) wide and long enough to stretch around the cake. Using a large paintbrush lightly brush the sides of the cake with a little water

5 Take 8oz (225g) gelatin icing and divide into 8 1oz (25g) pieces. For the legs, on a work surface lightly dusted with cornstarch use your hands to roll out each piece to 3″ (7.5cm) long and the thickness of a pencil. With your finger gently roll one end of the piece into a point and cut off the other end neatly. Press into the icing gently with the side of a paintbrush handle or a skewer to divide each leg into 5 sections. Roll the legs back and forth under the paintbrush or skewer to emphasize the divisions and at the same time keep the necessary rounded shape of the leg. Allow the legs to dry in various naturalistic positions as shown for about 4 hours or more if necessary. The painted legs demonstrate the final effect to aim for.

6 Take the remaining 4oz (125g) of gelatin icing and roll out into a sheet about ¼″ (5mm) thick. Cut out two pincer arms as outlined on *p.182*. When each piece has been cut out, gently press on the cut edges to make them slightly rounded. Fix each of the separate pieces together with a little royal icing and allow to dry for 4 hours, or more if necessary.

7 To decorate the cake make up colours of your choice. Take the original pattern as used in step 2 and lay gently on the iced cake. With a toothpick trace lightly over the decorative divisions of the shell, scoring into the icing. Obviously the pattern will fall ½″ (1cm) short of the edge. Score around the edge of the pattern to produce a ½″ (1cm) strip all round the edge of the shell. Pick out the scored lines in silver food colour and allow to dry for about 20 minutes. Using the colours of your choice, paint in the various decorative divisions and allow to dry for an hour or so.

8 Further decorations in either silver or another food colour can be added. When the legs and pincers are dry, paint them with one of your chosen food colours and allow to dry. The ½″ (1cm) strip around the edge of the shell can be painted in a third colour. The eyes can be made using either large dragees, or small dragees mounted on circular pieces of icing cut out from any icing remains. Fix to the cake with royal icing.

9 To assemble the cake take each leg in turn and fix to the side of the cake at the cut-off end with royal icing, positioning them under the shell around the back two thirds of the cake. Fix the pincers in position at the sides of the cake just underneath the shell with royal icing.

LEO

Leo's spirited personality will warm to this lionhearted tribute based on two 10″ (25cm) round spicy ginger cakes with a stem ginger and cream filling. The three-dimensional lion's face and his mane of flames are moulded from marzipan and applied to the cake under the fondant. The design is copied from an outline on p.184 and the various sections can be filled in with vibrant solid colour or delicate brushwork as in the photograph on p.87.

To make the cake. Grease a 10″ (25cm) round cake tin and line with waxed paper. Gently heat the golden syrup, molasses, sugar and butter or margarine in a pan over low heat. Mix well. Sift the flour, spices and bicarbonate of soda into a bowl. Pour the molasses mixture into the flour and mix well. Add the milk and beaten eggs and mix until smooth. Pour into the prepared tin and bake in a preheated oven at 160°C/325°F/Gas mark 3 for 1–1¼ hours. The cake is ready when firm to the touch. A skewer inserted in the centre of the cake should come out clean. Remove the cake from the tin and allow to cool. The cake is best left for 24 hours before being eaten to let the flavours develop.

For the filling, cream the butter or margarine with the sugar and add syrup from the stem ginger to taste.

INGREDIENTS

(for one cake)
6oz (175g) golden syrup
6oz (175g) molasses
4oz (125g) light brown sugar
6oz (175g) butter or margarine
12oz (350g) all purpose flour
4 level teaspoons ground ginger
2 level teaspoons mixed spice
1 level teaspoon bicarbonate of soda
8 fl oz (250ml) milk
4 eggs, beaten

Filling
4oz (125g) butter or margarine
8oz (225g) sifted powdered sugar
syrup from stem ginger to taste
chopped stem ginger

Decoration
12″ (30cm) round cake board
4lb (1.85kg) marzipan
2lb (900g) fondant icing
apricot jam
a little royal icing

Equipment
metallic gold ribbon
food colours
lustre powder

TIMESAVERS

TIMESAVER It is possible to decorate this cake more simply by using the second Leo outline on p 184 and applying the icing like marquetry or a jigsaw. Marzipan the cake in one flat piece. Make up three colours of fondant icing: pale brown, red and orange. Cover the cake with red icing. Using the second Leo design, cut out the lion's face in pale brown and apply to the cake. Cut out the flame shapes from the orange icing and fix around the lion's face. Paint on the details of the face using the first outline as your guide and finish off by outlining the flames and crown in gold food colour. Dust with lustre powder.

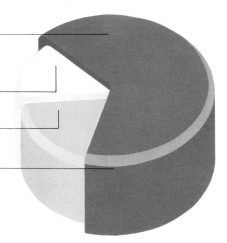

DECORATION 3 hrs
Decoration can be cut to 1 hr 30 mins, see Timesavers

ICING 30 mins + 8 hrs drying time

MARZIPAN I hr + 4 hrs drying time

COOKING 2 hrs 30 mins

1 The design for this cake can be found on *p.184* Trace the complete head and the marzipan cutting guide on to parchment or tracing paper, enlarging the design if necessary to fit your cake.

2 Sandwich the cakes together with a layer of filling and pieces of chopped stem ginger.

3 On a work surface lightly dusted with powdered sugar roll out 12oz (350g) marzipan. Using the tin in which the cake was baked as a guide, cut out a circle of marzipan to fit the top of the cake. Spread the top with apricot jam and fix the marzipan to it. Wrap a piece of string around the cake to measure its circumference and also measure its height. Roll out 12oz (350g) marzipan and cut a piece to the measurements just taken. Spread the side of the cake with apricot jam and fix the marzipan to it, in two pieces if necessary for easier handling. Allow to dry for a couple of hours.

4 Take the tracing for the marzipan cutting. Roll out 12oz (350g) marzipan and cut out the outer sections of the design as shown. Using the first tracing as a guide, position the marzipan on the top of the cake and fix in place with a little apricot jam. Roll out a further 8oz (225g) marzipan, slightly thicker this time, and cut out the middle section of the design. Place in position and fix with apricot jam. Roll out another 12oz (350g) marzipan, slightly thicker again, and cut out the lion's face. Fix in position with jam.

5 For the lion's nose, roll 8oz (225g) marzipan into a ball and flatten the base on your work surface. With a rolling pin, make a slope from the high point of the ball, which should be about 1½″ (4cm) above the work surface. Smooth down the sides so that they slope away from what will become the bridge of the nose. Place your tracing on top of the marzipan and cut out the nose shape as it runs down towards the forehead to include a full eye socket on the left and a part of the eye socket on the right. As the final photograph illustrates, the lion is looking out of the cake at an angle. Take your piece of marzipan and place it in position on the cake. Gently round down the cut edges to blend in with the rest of the face. The slope down from the nose on the right will be sharp as the lion's head is turned to the left. Fix the nose to the cake with apricot jam.

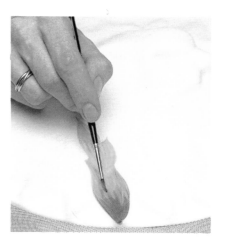

6 On a work surface lightly dusted with cornstarch roll out the fondant icing into a sheet large enough to cover the cake. Drape the sheet over the cake and smooth the icing into the sides. Using a flat-bladed knife held against the side of the cake trim off any excess icing.

7 With fingers lightly coated in cornstarch gently mould the icing into the marzipan features. Allow to dry for eight hours or overnight. The icing needs to be completely dry before it is painted.

8 Make up a series of red, yellow and orange food colours. Paint the tips of the flames red and then gradually brush into orange and then yellow. Apply the colours one after the other so that they can be merged while still wet. Make some of the flames solid red.

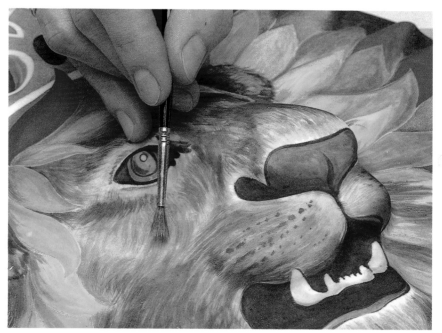

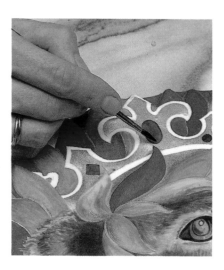

10 Outline the edges of the flames in gold and fill in the gaps between the outer flames in purple. Paint the crown gold, edged with pale yellow.
The jewels are purple, their facets outlined in silver.

ASSEMBLY

When the paint is dry, dust the surface of the cake with gold lustre powder. Wrap the cake in a wide metallic gold ribbon and secure with a little royal icing.

9 Paint the end of the nose and the mouth solid brown, adding a little shading around the lips and on the very tip of the nose. Leave the teeth white, or brush with ivory or palest brown food colour. For the fur, dip a medium paintbrush in brown, splay the bristles out and drag them across the icing. Apply the colour very sparingly, if at all, round the eyes and nose to emphasize these areas. Deeper shades of brown underline the contours of the face and fur merges into flame around it. Pick out the eyes, like the flames, in red, yellow and orange and edge them with a line of unbroken deep brown. Allow the colour to dry completely for several hours.

PISCES

This rich chocolate truffle cake is very quick to make – it needs no cooking. The use of moulds, such as those featured here, opens up an enormous range of possibilities for both cakes and desserts. For a dessert you could leave out the fondant icing and cover the mould instead with a shiny thin layer of chocolate glacé icing. The cakes pictured on p. 91 show the subtle effects that can be achieved with delicate brushwork and a good range of food colours. The two cakes shown here are made from four quantities of chocolate truffle mixture to fill a 9″ mould. The amount of the mixture needed will vary according to the size of the mould used.

To make the cake. Break up the chocolate into pieces and put into a bowl along with the butter or margarine. Place the bowl over a pan of gently boiling water. Leave until the chocolate melts, stirring once or twice. Remove the basin from over the pan and stir in the egg yolks, powdered sugar, cake crumbs and brandy. Mix thoroughly. Leave to cool for a couple of hours. For a less sweet mixture, you could replace some of the powdered sugar with cocoa powder to taste.

TIMESAVERS

TIMESAVER To avoid painting the fish, knead a number of food colours into the icing, mixing them incompletely so as to create a swirled effect when rolled out. When dry, dust the icing with a number of shades of lustre powder.

DECORATION 2 hrs
By not painting an hour can be saved, see timesaver

ICING 40 mins

MARZIPAN 40 mins + 2 hrs drying time

PREPARATION 45 mins

INGREDIENTS

Cake (enough for one quantity of mixture)
4oz (125g) semi-sweet chocolate
2oz (50g) butter or margarine
2 egg yolks
4oz (125g) sifted powdered sugar
4oz (125g) cake crumbs (madeira cake is best)
2 tablespoons brandy (or spirit or liqueur of your choice)

Decoration (for both cakes)
one 18″ (46cm) square cake board or two 10″ (25cm) square boards
2lb (900g) marzipan
8oz (225g) semi-sweet chocolate
1lb (450g) fondant icing
apricot jam

Equipment
fish mould about 9″ (23cm) long
food colour

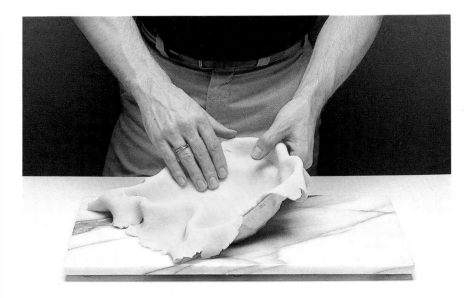

1 Take 8oz (225g) marzipan. Roll out on a work surface lightly dusted with cornstarch into a sheet large enough to line the mould. Place the marzipan inside the mould and gently press into the detail inside. Trim any excess marzipan to the edge of the mould.

3 Spoon the truffle mixture into the mould, gently pressing down to ensure that there are no holes or gaps in the filling, which should be quite solid. Do not press too hard or you may damage the chocolate coating. Level off the mixture leaving the ¼" (5mm) strip of marzipan uncovered.

2 Break the chocolate for the decoration into pieces and place in a bowl. Place the bowl over a pan of gently boiling water. Wait until the chocolate melts. Remove the bowl from over the pan and allow to cool for a few minutes. Using a large paintbrush coat the inside of the marzipanned mould with chocolate leaving a ¼" (5mm) strip of marzipan uncovered round the edge. Allow the chocolate coating to dry and harden completely. The layer of hardened chocolate will prevent the moist truffle mixture from wetting the marzipan and thereby making it impossible to turn the cake out of the mould.

4 Smear the surface of the truffle mixture with apricot jam. Roll out 8oz (225g) marzipan into a sheet large enough to cover the mould. Lay the marzipan over the truffle mixture and trim any excess to the edge of the mould. Seal the edges by pressing the sheet of marzipan against the ¼" (5mm) strip left uncovered by the truffle mixture.

5 Turn the cake out of the mould immediately and allow to dry for a couple of hours.

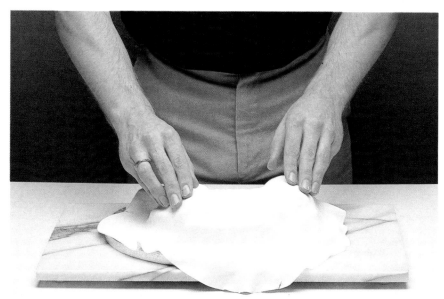

6 On a work surface lightly dusted with cornstarch roll out 8oz (225g) fondant icing as thinly as possible so that the maximum amount of detail from the mould will show through when the icing is applied to the cake. Lay the icing over the cake.

7 Gently smooth the icing into the detail on the cake. Using a sharp knife trim any excess icing to the edge of the cake.

Repeat steps 1 to 6 to make the second fish for the completed Pisces cake.

SPECIAL FINISHES

We have chosen to use subtle shades of blue, green and pink washes to colour the fish. Make up several pale colours. Brush on gently, merging the shades into each other. Add edible lustre powder to emphasize the scales and give the fish a silvery sheen, or if lustre powder is not available emphasize the scales with a darker colour.

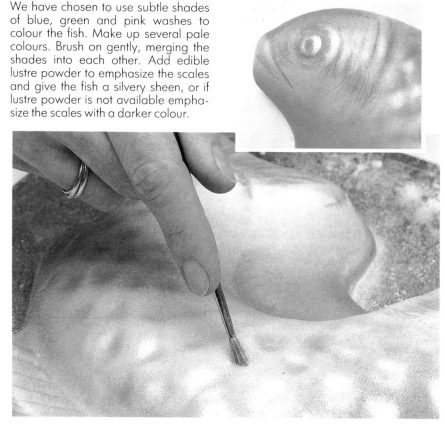

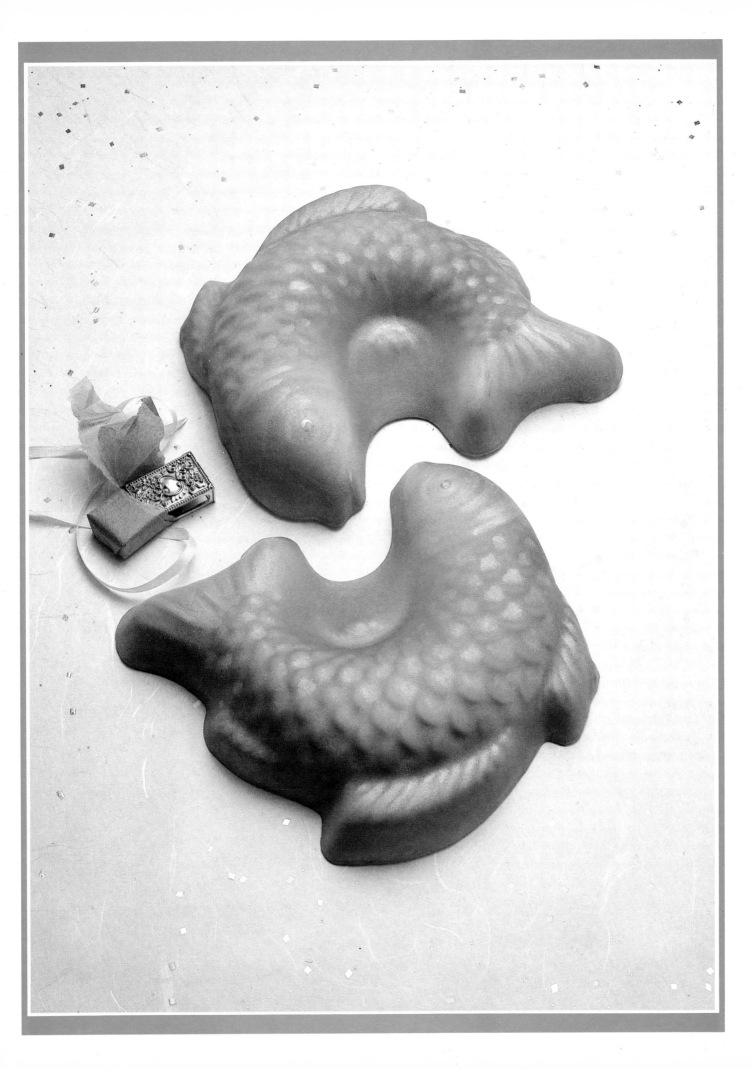

HOT AIR BALLOON

A refreshingly light cake of orange madeira layered with cream and marmalade and flavoured with liqueur forms the basis for this breathtaking wedding centrepiece. You need to make two 12" (32cm) round cakes for this design. The gondola cake requires only basic carving but the balloon, which is hollow, demands a degree of dexterity. It is made in two halves by laying gelatin icing over a mould. The two halves are then fitted together like a box, which could contain small gifts, confetti, orchids or flower petals. Icing shapes supply relief decoration and delicate brushwork provides the finishing touches.

To make the cake. Cream together the butter or margarine and sugar until light and fluffy. Add the eggs two at a time and mix well followed by a tablespoon of flour. Sift the remaining flour together and fold into the mixture followed by the orange rind and juice. Grease a 12" (30cm) round cake tin and line with waxed paper. Spoon the mixture into the prepared tin and level the top. Cook in a preheated oven at 160°C/325°F/Gas mark 3 for the times shown. The cake is ready when risen and firm to the touch. Cool in the tin for 5 minutes. Turn out on to a wire rack to cool completely. Remove the lining paper.

For the filling, cream the butter or margarine into the powdered sugar. Mix in the orange rind and juice.

INGREDIENTS

	12" (30cm) round	8" (20cm) square
butter or margarine	1lb (450g)	8oz (225g)
sugar	1lb (450g)	8oz (225g)
eggs	8	4
self-rising flour	1lb (450g)	8oz (225g)
all purpose flour	8oz (225g)	4oz (125g)
grated orange rind	2 oranges	1 orange
orange juice	3 tablespoons (45ml)	4 tablespoons (20ml)
cooking time	1 hour 15 minutes	1 hour 15 minutes

Filling (for the 12"/30cm cake only)
6oz (175g) butter or margarine
1lb (450g) powdered sugar
1 teaspoon grated orange rind
2 tablespoons (30ml) orange juice
orange marmalade
liqueur of your choice

Decoration
16" (40cm) round cake board
3lb (1.4kg) marzipan
2lb (900g) blue fondant icing
1lb (450g) white fondant icing
3lb (1.4kg) gelatin icing
apricot jam
royal icing

INGREDIENTS

Equipment
miniature silk bridal flowers
baby ribbon
Non-toxic modelling clay (from art shops)
plastic or wood decorative detail (from hardware shops – sold for embellishing cupboard doors etc.)
mould for the balloon
3 yards (3m) small seed pearls
silk rosebuds, baby's breath, honeysuckle
wire lampshade support about 4" (10cm) high★

TIMESAVERS

TIME SAVER Instead of making a gondola for underneath the balloon, you could bake a 4" (10cm) or 6" (15cm) round madeira cake and make the tub shape into a more traditional looking basket.

TIME SAVER Making the decorative icing shapes to surround the monogram and for the swagging is quite time-consuming. You could instead decorate the balloon with small bridal flowers and ribbons.

★ English wire lampshade supports are difficult to find in the U.S. Alternately, have a good lampshade shop make one to your specifications, adding a ring at the bottom as well for extra support.

DECORATION 3 hrs 30 mins + 8 hrs drying time

ICING 1 hr + 4 hrs drying time

MARZIPAN 1 hr 15 mins + 4 hrs drying time

COOKING 1 hr 15 mins per cake

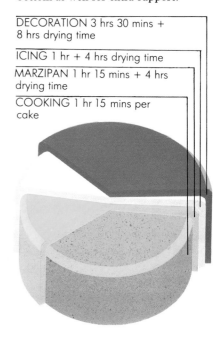

1 Split each cake in half. Sandwich the two halves together with 6oz (175g) orange marmalade. Sprinkle the cakes with the liqueur of your choice. Sandwich the two cakes together with the orange cream filling.

On a work surface lightly dusted with powdered sugar roll out 1lb (450g) marzipan. Using the tin in which the cake was baked as a guide, cut out a 12″ (30cm) circle. Spread the top of the cake with apricot jam and fix the marzipan in position. Measure the depth of the cake. Wrap a piece of string round the edge to measure the circumference. Roll out 1lb (450g) marzipan and cut out a strip to the measurements just noted. For ease of handling cut the strip into two halves. Spread the side of the cake with jam and fix the marzipan in position, making the seams as neat as possible. Leave to dry for four hours.

2 On a work surface lightly dusted with cornstarch roll out the blue fondant icing into a sheet large enough to cover the cake. Lay it over the cake and smooth down the sides, cutting off the excess with a flat-bladed knife held against the cake. Allow to dry for four hours.

3 Trace the designs for the clouds from *p.185* on to parchment paper and cut out. Roll out 1lb (450g) gelatin icing and cut out the cloud shapes in batches of five (see next step).

4 Allow the clouds to dry resting against the outside and inside of the tin in which the cake was baked, so that they take on the same curve. Allow to dry for four hours or until completely hard. Make and dry the clouds in batches of five, as no more will fit on the tin.

5 Once the clouds' have dried and can stand up, they will be placed round the cake.

6 Mix some pale pink food colouring and paint the clouds as illustrated. There are two methods. The first involves painting simple outlines. The second involves using a close-textured sponge as illustrated in the painting techniques on *p.185.* Here the shadows in the clouds are gently sponged on to give a delicate impression of depth. Allow the colours to dry for an hour.

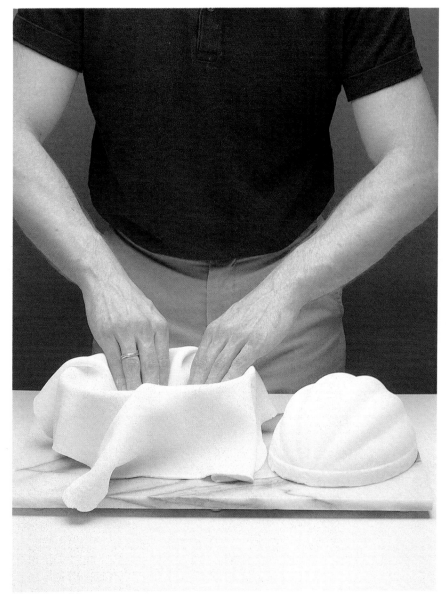

7 To make your balloon, choose a mould from any that you have available or can buy. The mould used here is a melon-shaped mould, which was expensive but ideal for the purpose because it is the perfect shape. You could, however, just as well use an Easter egg mould or even a sieve – preferably a new one with a regular rounded shape.

8 To make the balloon roll out 8oz (225g) gelatin icing and lay over the top half of the mould. Working quickly, smooth the icing over the mould and into any detail on it. Trim off any excess to produce a very neat edge half way round the mould. Ideally there should be no signs of creasing in the finished balloon. However, if your icing persists in creasing, try to confine the creases to the top and bottom of the balloon, which will eventually be covered with decoration. Allow the icing to dry for eight hours or overnight. When dry, take the icing off the mould and leave to dry out completely while you make the second half of the balloon. For the second half, proceed as for the first half, but this time ice the inside of the mould. This may sound a little odd, but it is done for a good reason – to make the two halves fit together by pressing one half just inside the other, like closing a tin. The balloon is thus easier to assemble, and to take apart again, if you should wish. If you are using a sieve, it would be better to make both halves on the outside, and stick them together with royal icing, or one half of the balloon will bear the pattern of the sieve.

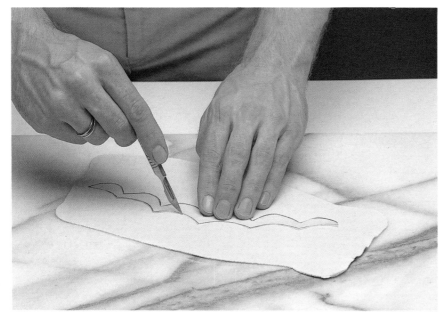

9 Trace the design for the balloon swagging from *p.185* on to a piece of parchment and cut out. Take 6oz (175g) gelatin icing and colour pale blue. Cut out a long piece of swagging to go round the wide part of the mould, and a shorter piece to go round the top. Save the leftover icing to make a second set of swagging.

11 Soften the modelling clay according to package instructions, if necessary, and roll out into a sheet about ½″ (1cm) thick. Take the plastic or wood decorative detail and push firmly into the clay to leave a clear impression. Remove the detail and let the impression or 'mould' dry. The mould in this case was made from a circular flower pattern about 1½″ (4cm) in diameter and another featuring a laurel wreath and ribbons. Details of this sort are ideal for making unusual icing shapes.

10 Place the swagging in position on the mould to dry. While it is still soft, pinch the narrow part of the swagging with the end of a brush to draw it up into gentle folds. Let it dry for about four hours. Repeat with a second set of swagging for the other side of the balloon.

12 To make the wreath and ribbon streamers take 6oz (175g) gelatin icing and colour it pale pink. Dust the mould lightly with cornstarch and press half the icing into it firmly, making sure that the whole mould has been filled with icing. As soon as you have made the shape, tip the icing out – you may need to pull gently so that it will come away cleanly. Trim any excess icing with a sharp knife. Read step 13 before making the other wreath and ribbon streamers.

14 Cut the square madeira cake into two oblongs measuring 8 × 4″ (20 × 10cm). Place one on top of the other. Trace the side of the gondola from *P185* and cut out the pattern. Place the pattern on the side of the cake. Cut a gentle curve at the front and a straight angled line and a step into the back. Finally cut two steps into the top for the seat and trim off any excess cake.

13 Let the icing detail dry for about four hours in position on the centre of the balloon mould. Repeat step 12 once the first iced detail has dried. To make the circular flower detail take 4oz (125g) gelatin icing and divide into four. Lightly brush the circular mould with cornstarch and firmly push the icing into the mould. Immediately remove it and trim off the excess. Allow to dry flat. Repeat to produce four flowers.

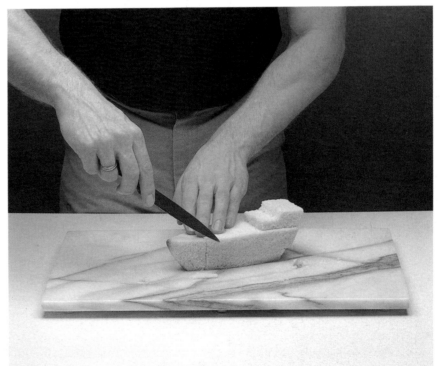

15 Now finish carving the prow of the gondola. Beginning at the front, carve outwards and downwards on both sides, leaving the back of the cake intact. Look closely at the photographs and copy the shape required.

16 To marzipan the gondola make a template of the top of it on tracing paper. Make another template of the side (you may not have followed the tracing you made from *p.185.* very accurately). On a work surface lightly dusted with powdered sugar roll out 8oz (225g) marzipan. Cut out the shape of the top of the gondola, extending it about 6″ (15cm) beyond the pattern at the back, so that you will have enough marzipan to cover the stern. Spread the appropriate parts of the cake with apricot jam and fix on the marzipan. Take the remaining 8oz (225g) marzipan, roll it out and cut two sides. Spread the sides of

the cake with apricot jam and fix the marzipan in position. Allow to dry for two hours.

17 Use the same templates for icing the gondola. On a work surface lightly dusted with cornstarch roll out 8oz (225g) white fondant icing. Cut out the shape for the top of the gondola, again extending it 6″ (15cm) at the back to cover the stern. Moisten the marzipan with a little water and fix the icing in position. Roll out the remaining white fondant and cut out two pieces for the sides. Moisten the sides of the cake and fix them on. Gently press all the seams together to make them as neat as possible.

SPECIAL FINISHES

Purchase an English wire lampshade support, or have one made at a good lampshade shop. If the one you have bought is more than about 4″ high, you can cut it down with wire cutters. Wrap the frame in baby ribbon to cover it completely.

Place the clouds at intervals round the side of the cake, fixing them to the board with dabs of royal icing. Fix the two halves of the balloon together. You could add pink shadows to the balloon with a close textured sponge, from top to bottom, as for the clouds. This will emphasize the segments of the balloon. Allow the colour to dry for an hour. If using a monogram, trace the letters from *p.185.* Transfer to the balloon with graphite paper and paint silver. Allow to dry for an hour. If using, stick the seed pearls to the balloon in lines from top to bottom with dabs of royal icing. Fix the wreath and ribbon streamers around the monogram with royal icing. Fix the swags in position likewise. Fix one of the circular decorations at the top and the other at the bottom. Additional colour can be added to the swags and wreath as shown – this very simple effect is achieved with pink, blue and silver. Fix miniature silk flowers and lengths of baby ribbon at intervals along the swags. Place the gondola on top of the cake. Place the balloon support on top of the gondola and fix it firmly with stiff royal icing – do not stint on the amount, as it will be hidden under silk flowers. Decorate the support with flowers, ribbons and lengths of seed pearls. Fix one circular decoration to each side of the gondola and decorate further with flowers and ribbon.

PANDA

Three 8" (20cm) and one 6" (15cm) round madeira sponges sandwiched with sweetened ricotta cheese and fruit preserve provide an ideal medium for the detailed and careful cutting and shaping this cake requires. The step-by-step photographs illustrate just how well fine, close-textured cake responds to carving. For sculpting you will need a sharp knife, a steady hand and patience. The application of fondant icing to an irregular shape like this requires a deft touch. The picture of the finished cake on p.107 shows how the panda's black markings cunningly hide any visible seams.

To make the cake. Cream the butter or margarine and sugar together until light and fluffy. Add the eggs one at a time and beat into the mixture. Add a spoonful of flour to the mixture after each egg is incorporated and mix again. Sift the remaining flours together and fold into the creamed mixture followed by the lemon juice. Turn the mixture into a greased and lined tin and level the top. Place in a preheated oven set at 160°C/325°F/Gas mark 3 for the times indicated, or until risen and firm to the touch. Turn out on to a wire cooling rack.

For the filling, sweeten the ricotta to taste with powdered sugar. Split the cakes in half and sandwich together with the sweetened cheese mixture and a layer of fruit preserve.

INGREDIENTS

(for one cake)

	8" (20cm)	6" (15cm)
butter or margarine	8oz (225g)	4oz (125g)
sugar	8oz (225g)	4oz (125g)
eggs	4	2
self-rising flour	8oz (225g)	4oz (125g)
all purpose flour	4oz (125g)	2oz (50g)
lemon juice	4 teaspoons	2 teaspoons
cooking time	1 hour 20 minutes	1 hour

Filling
2lb (900g) unsalted ricotta
2lb (900g) fruit preserve
powdered sugar to taste

Equipment
black food colour
twigs (in this case fennel twigs)
wire for wired leaves

Decoration
10" (25cm) round cake board
1½lb (675g) marzipan
1½lb (675g) fondant icing
8oz (225g) gelatin icing
apricot jam
a little royal icing

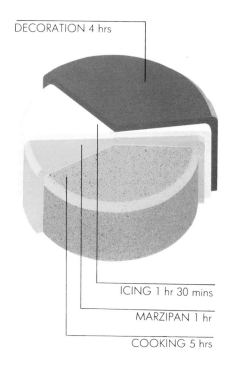

DECORATION 4 hrs

ICING 1 hr 30 mins

MARZIPAN 1 hr

COOKING 5 hrs

1 As this cake requires quite a lot of carving, it is advisable not to overfill each layer. Assemble the cakes as illustrated. Place the 6″ (15cm) cake slightly towards the back of the top 8″ (20cm) cake, so that it is just off-centre. Allow the complete block to rest for 3 or 4 hours before working on it. The separate layers should now not move out of place when handled.

2 Using a sharp kitchen knife, begin carving the panda. Starting at the highest point of the 6″ (15cm) cake, carve a gentle curve from the top to the bottom of the pile of cakes. This curve should be cut into the back of the cakes extending half way round each side. As madeira is quite a close-textured cake it is possible to cut or shave very slim pieces of cake from the block and in this way proceed very slowly until you are satisfied with the shape.

3 At this stage concentrate on carving the general outline of arms, legs and head without being too concerned about the finer details. Use the layers of cake as measures to help you determine the size and position of individual features. For the legs, start at a point half way round each side towards the back of the cake. Take a point at the top of the second layer of cake and with the tip of your knife draw a line down to the top of the first layer in the middle of the front of the cake. Repeat for the other leg. Using the sharp point of the knife cut out a block of cake from the middle of the bottom layer approximately 1½″ (4cm) wide and 1″ (2.5cm)

deep. This is the space between the feet. Take your knife and starting with the line that you have drawn, carve upwards and inwards to produce the rounded shape of the legs. Look at the photographs and note how the leg emerges from the shape of the panda's back, growing thicker towards the front, where it is at its thickest. In this photograph you can see where the original line was cut from the top of the second to the top of the first layer – below the line the cake is the golden brown of the cooked outside, and above the line the carving eats into the pale gold of the inside of the cake. Repeat for the other leg.

5 The second stage of making the panda is to carve in more detail, beginning with the head. From the front, the head is roughly triangular in shape. At the back and sides it is carved to join the curve of the back and shoulders. The muzzle and lower half of the head are carved out of the bottom layer of the top cake. On either side of the broad nose, carve hollows for the eyes.

6 Once the head is shaped, gently curve the arms and legs so that the back and sides of the panda are continuous curves.

4 To carve the arms the process is essentially the same as for the legs. To carve the underside of the arms, once again start at a point half way round the side of the back of the cake. Starting at a point on top of the fourth layer of cake, take your knife and draw a line down to the top of the third layer, ending in the centre of the front. Starting from the line just drawn, carve downwards and in-wards into the cake. This section of carving will meet up with the upwards and inwards carving that produced the leg, leaving the third layer to be shaped gently into the tummy. To produce the upper edge of the arm, take your kitchen knife and draw a line extending from the top of the fifth layer to the top of the fourth layer in the centre of the front of the cake. Cut out a block of cake between the paws 1¼" (3cm) wide and 1" (2.5cm) deep. Take your knife and carve upwards and inwards from the line just drawn. Check in the photographs to see exactly how the arm emerges from the back of the panda. The arm gets thicker towards the front, reaching its maximum extension from the body at the paws. For the head, start at the highest point on the top cake and cut a gentle slope down to the middle of the front of it.

7 The spaces between the arms and legs and down the front of the cake – the panda's tummy – should be shaped to slope down and out from under the chin to the widest point half way between the arms and legs, and then down and inwards to the bottom of the cake between the legs.

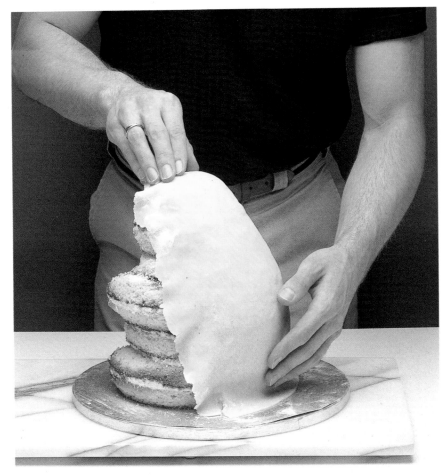

8 Marzipanning the cake is a rather fiddly process and you should not be unduly concerned if the result looks a little untidy. Marzipan is not as malleable as fondant icing, and it is difficult to get it to stretch along two curves at the same time. It is possible to marzipan the panda in three pieces. As illustrated, the first piece should cover the whole of the back and extend half way round each side. Spread the cake with apricot jam. Roll out 12oz (350g) marzipan quite thinly and lay on the cake. Press out as many of the folds and creases as possible and trim the edges with a sharp knife. The second piece of marzipan should be fixed across the panda's chest to meet the first piece at the sides. For this take 8oz (225g) marzipan and roll out thinly. Spread the cake with apricot jam and fix on. Trim the edges with a sharp knife and match the seams as closely as possible. To marzipan the head, spread the remaining cake with apricot jam. Roll out the remaining 4oz (125g) marzipan thinly and apply to the cake. This stage is not straightforward in that the marzipan will fold and crease under the chin. Simply use scissors and a sharp knife to trim away the excess – any slight irregularities will not show in this position. Do not worry if the surface is uneven, or if the marzipan splits a little as it is being smoothed over the carved features. This is almost bound to happen and will not show in the finished panda. Allow to dry for 8 hours.

9 Now is the time to correct any bothersome irregularities in the surface of the cake and to mend the splits in the marzipan. Simply take some of the royal icing and smooth it into the problem areas. When this has dried you will have the smooth surface you need in order to proceed.

10 The icing is applied in three stages, as with the marzipan. Brush the marzipan with a little water to make it sticky before applying the icing. On a work surface lightly dusted with cornstarch roll out 12oz (350g) of the fondant icing. Moisten the back and sides of the cake and drape the icing sheet over it. Gently smooth the icing as far as possible around the sides of the cake. Trim off and keep the excess. Take special care in trimming and neatening the edge across the top of the panda's head. Icing seams on this particular cake can be disguised under the patches of black fur, but bear in mind that the face, which is white, should not have seams running across it. Moisten the panda's front with water, roll out 8oz (225g) icing and fix across the panda's chest and to just below the chin, meeting the first sheet at the sides. Trim the icing carefully to neaten the side seams. Trim neatly under the chin and keep any leftovers. Finally, ice the head. Moisten the rest of the cake with a little water. Take the remaining icing plus any leftovers and roll out. Drape over the panda's head and gently smooth in the facial detail. Using a sharp knife carefully trim off any excess icing and press the seams together to make them as neat as possible. Allow the icing to dry for at least 2 hours before proceeding.

11 To make the ears take 2oz (50g) gelatin icing and roll into a ball. Press your thumb into the centre of the ball, and then cut in half. Fix to the sides of the head with royal icing. If there are any gaps between the ears and the head fill these in with more royal icing so that the ear is continuous with the head.

13 The detail of the eyes and claws is created by leaving white icing uncovered. As far as possible, cover up the icing seams with black food colour. Allow to dry completely.

12 To colour the panda make up some black food colour and apply to the icing in the areas illustrated. Note that the edges of the black areas are feathered to give the impression of fur – do this by splaying out the bristles of the brush when applying the colour at the edges.

14 To make the bamboo leaves take the remaining gelatin icing and roll into balls the size of a hazelnut. Insert a 3″ (7.5cm) length of modelling wire into each ball and roll out so that the wire extends well into the flattened-out piece. Using a sharp knife, cut out spear-shaped leaves. The leaves can either be allowed to dry flat or can be scored down the centre with a toothpick and have each side bent upwards to create a 'v'-shape in cross-section. Allow to dry for about 4 hours, or longer if necessary. Paint them green and allow to dry again. Trim the wire stalks to 1″ (2.5cm) each.

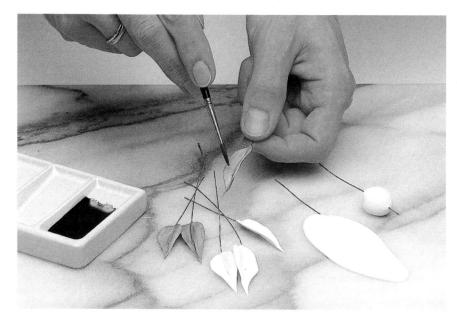

15 Take the fennel twigs (or other twigs you have selected) and glue the wire stalks to them so that the leaves stick out at an angle. This decorative feature is obviously not intended for eating, so this is one instance where glue can safely be used. If you prefer to use royal icing, you will need to colour it once it has dried.

ASSEMBLY

Prop the bamboo between the panda's paws and legs and scatter any remaining twigs and leaves around the base of the cake.

MOUSEHOUSE

The charming mousehouse pictured on p.113 is based on four 9″ (23cm) round chocolate and banana cakes layered with banana cream. The irregular tree trunk is made by moulding tree roots in marzipan and fixing them to the cake before the fondant is added. The figure of the mouse is modelled from white marzipan and the windows are cut from gelatin icing. Anyone who enjoys painting will take great pleasure in decorating this cake. An additional feature of a flowerpot roof can be made by moulding gelatin icing onto a plastic plant pot.

To make the cake. Cream the butter and sugar together until light and fluffy. Beat in the honey, then the eggs one at a time. Mix in the mashed banana. Sift the flour and cocoa together and fold into the mixture. Grease a 9″ (23cm) round cake tin and line with waxed paper. Spoon the mixture into the prepared tin and level the top. Cook in a preheated oven at 160°C/325°F/Gas mark 3 for about 45 minutes or until firm to the touch. Turn out of the tin and allow to cool.

For the filling, cream together the butter or margarine and powdered sugar, adding banana flavoring to taste.

TIMESAVERS

TIMESAVER Wiring the leaves provides you with a better means of displaying them, but if you prefer, you could leave out the wire and just stick the leaves to the cake with dabs of royal icing.

TIMESAVER The windows and window boxes on the mousehouse are charming but quite fiddly to make. To save time, when brushing the tree trunk with brown food colour leave the space for the windows white and then paint on the details of the curtains and the leaded panes later.

TIMESAVER If you have no time to make the wired bunches of flowers, you could use dried flowers, wheat, barley and grasses, which would give an added touch of authenticity.

DECORATION 4 hrs + 8 hrs drying time
Up to 1 hr 30 mins can be saved on decoration, see Timesavers

ICING 1 hr + 4 hrs drying time

MARZIPAN 1 hr + 4 hrs drying time

COOKING 45 mins per cake

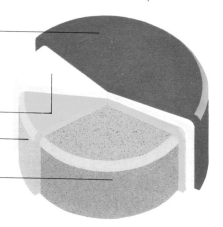

1 Spread the filling on the cakes and pile one on top of the other.

2 Using a long-bladed kitchen knife cut a gentle slope into the top cake. Cut thin irregular slices off the sides of the cake – this will be the basis for the tree trunk. Decide which face of the cake will be the front. Cut a slice off the front of the cake leaving it smooth and vertical so that the door will fit neatly on to it.

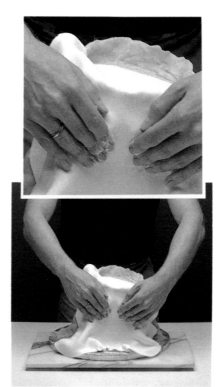

3 Take three separate pieces of yellow marzipan weighing 12oz (350g) each and roll each piece into a rough sausage shape. Press firmly on to the sides of the cake and on to the board to represent the tree's roots.

5 Moisten one third of the side of the cake with water to make the marzipan sticky. On a work surface lightly dusted with cornstarch roll out 1lb (450g) fondant icing into a large sheet. Drape over the moistened section of the cake and press gently onto the marzipan. Cut off excess icing with a sharp knife and keep in cling film. Repeat with the other two thirds. Press the seams together as neatly as possible. It is not essential that they should be vertical. Moisten the top of the cake and roll out the leftover fondant icing into a circle. Drape it over the top of the cake and press down gently so that it covers the top and the collar. Cut off any excess. Allow to dry for four hours.

4 On a work surface lightly dusted with powdered sugar roll out 12oz (350g) yellow marzipan. Spread the sides of the cake not already covered with marzipan with apricot jam. Cut the marzipan into pieces and press into the areas between the roots just applied. It is not necessary to be exact or very neat as the tree trunk should have a rough surface.

Take 8oz (225g) yellow marzipan and roll it into a sausage shape. Spread the edge of the top of the cake with apricot jam and fix the marzipan round it. Pinch the marzipan to create a raised collar effect all round the cake. Roll out a further 8oz (225g) marzipan into a rough circle. Spread the top of the cake with apricot jam and fix on the circle, pressing the edges to join the raised collar. Allow to dry for four hours.

TIPS

If you would prefer not to use the large quantity of marzipan we suggest for this cake, you could make the tree roots and the 'collar' on top of the tree trunk out of the pieces of cake you have carved away. Stick them in position on the tree trunk with apricot jam.

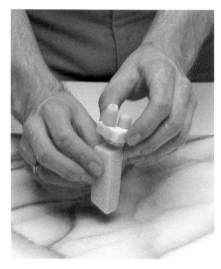

6 Take the plant pot and make a paper pattern to fit it following the instructions in steps 2 and 3 of the Champagne Celebration on *p. 35*. On a work surface lightly dusted with cornstarch roll out 8oz (225g) gelatin icing. Stand the pot on the icing and cut out a circle round the bottom. Place the paper pattern on the icing and cut around. Place the icing shape on top of the pattern and use the paper to wrap the icing round the pot. Tape the paper pattern together to hold the icing in position to dry. Press the icing gently into the pot and leave overnight.

8 To make the chimney take 4oz (125g) yellow marzipan and roll out to a thickness of ½″ (1cm). Cut out a rectangle measuring 2 × ¾″ (5 × 2cm). Cut out a second rectangle measuring 1 × ½″ (2.5 × 1cm). Roll out any marzipan remains into a cylinder of pencil thickness. Cut one piece ¾″ (2cm) long and another ½″ (1cm) long. Fix the chimney together with royal icing as illustrated and allow to dry for two hours. To decorate paint in brown food colour or in several shades to represent brickwork.

9 To make the windows roll out 6oz (175g) gelatin icing and cut out six rectangles 2 × 1½″ (5 × 4cm). Set three aside and cut two smaller rectangles out of each of the other three to make a window frame and two open window panes. Leave the pieces to dry, then assemble as shown, sticking the frames and panes on to the window pieces with royal icing.

To decorate the windows make up brown and blue food colours. Paint the window frames and the leaded panes brown and the curtains inside the windows blue.

7 When dry remove the paper and take off the iced pot. Fix the bottom on the pot with royal icing. Allow to dry. Mix brown and red food colours to make terracotta. Paint the pot all over, splaying out the bristles of the brush to achieve a stippled effect.

10 To make the front doorstep roll out 4oz (125g) yellow marzipan to a thickness of ½″ (1cm) and cut out a circle about 2½″ (6.5cm) in diameter. Cut off a slice from the back of the circle and allow to dry for two hours. Paint all over with brown food colour and allow to dry.

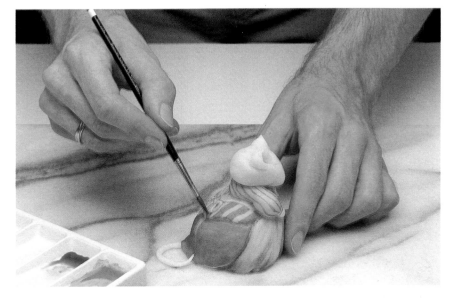

11 To make the skirt for the mouse take 4oz (125g) white marzipan and roll into a rough ball. Press down gently to flatten the bottom of the ball and pinch the back to elongate it slightly. Use the end of a paint-brush to score lines into the marzipan to represent folds in the pinafore and skirt. Allow to dry for one hour. To make the arms take 2oz (50g) white marzipan and roll into a sausage about 2½" (6.5cm) long. Gently pinch the ends and bend down to make paws. Press the middle of the piece to flatten the top and bottom so that it sits comfortably on top of the skirt. Allow to dry for an hour. To make the head take 1oz (25g) white marzipan. Shape to form the nose and pinch to make ears. Hollow out the ears with the end of a paintbrush. Roll the remaining marzipan into a 2" (5cm) tail. Allow to dry for an hour. Assemble the mouse as shown.

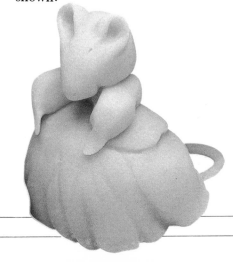

12 To paint the mouse make up a series of food colours of your choice. Paint the pinafore with streaks to represent folds in the material. The blouse is painted in stripes to provide contrast, though a third solid colour would also look good.

13 To achieve the effect of bark on the tree trunk, begin by painting it all over with a wash of mid brown. Paint the detail with a medium brush and a darker brown, splaying out the bristles to leave a trace of fine lines. An additional wash of moss green in places gives a real woodland feel. Paint the top in a series of circles, starting at the centre and working out. Paint a number of fine lines radiating out from the centre and leave to dry for four hours or until completely dry.

14 To make a toadstool take 6oz (175g) gelatin icing and roll into a rough ball shape. On a work surface lightly dusted with cornstarch press the ball gently to flatten the bottom and pinch the top into a good thick stalk. Lay the toadstool upside down and with a sharp knife score fine lines into the underside of the toadstool radiating out from the stalk. Cut small v shapes into the edge of the toadstool at intervals to make a slightly irregular shape. Curve the top upwards as shown and allow to dry for four hours. Make up red and orange food colours and paint the toadstool. Allow to dry.

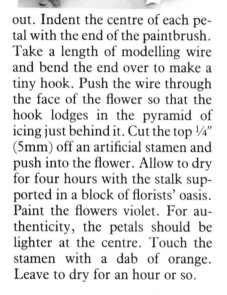

15 To make the violets trace the outline on *p.190.* on to tracing paper and transfer to a piece of thin cardboard with graphite paper. Cut out the shape and cut a hole about ¼" (5mm) in diameter out of the centre. Take 4oz (125g) gelatin icing and break off a piece the size of a hazelnut. Roll into a ball and pinch the centre into a pyramid about ½" (1cm) high. Flatten the icing around the pyramid on to the work surface and put the pattern over it so that the pyramid sticks up through the hole. Cut round the flower pattern and remove the paper. Pinch the petals between thumb and forefinger to make them thin and delicate. Push the end of a medium paintbrush into the centre of the flower to hollow it

out. Indent the centre of each petal with the end of the paintbrush. Take a length of modelling wire and bend the end over to make a tiny hook. Push the wire through the face of the flower so that the hook lodges in the pyramid of icing just behind it. Cut the top ¼" (5mm) off an artificial stamen and push into the flower. Allow to dry for four hours with the stalk supported in a block of florists' oasis. Paint the flowers violet. For authenticity, the petals should be lighter at the centre. Touch the stamen with a dab of orange. Leave to dry for an hour or so.

18 To make the door take 2oz (50g) gelatin icing and roll out on a work surface lightly dusted with cornstarch. The door is 2½" (6.5cm) wide at the bottom and 2½" (6.5cm) tall at its highest point. Cut out the door and allow to dry for four hours. Paint with a wood grain effect as described To make the carpet take 2oz (50g) gelatin icing and roll out. Cut out a rectangle 3" × 2" (7.5 × 5cm). Allow the icing to dry in position over one of the roots of the tree for four hours. Paint with food colours in a bright pattern. Allow to dry. Spread the board with a thin layer of royal icing and roughen the surface a little by pricking it with a toothpick. On the pathway up to the front door, score several irregular squares into the icing to represent paving stones. Allow the icing to dry for an hour. Paint it green for the grass and pick out the paving stones in yellow and orange. Allow to dry.

ASSEMBLY

Stick the doorstep and door in position with royal icing. Fix the plant pot and chimney to the cake in the same way. Stick the ivy leaves to the side of the cake, with one piece growing round the door. Fix the mouse, carpet and toadstool in position. Twist the wires of the violets and primroses together to make small bunches and dot around the base of the tree.

16 To make the primroses, take a further 4oz (125g) gelatin icing and proceed as for the violets, using a primrose cutter. Allow the completed flowers to dry for four hours before painting.

17 Paint the primroses yellow, shading the petals so that they are darker at the edges. Paint the stamens yellow and allow to dry.

SPORTS BAG

This simply decorated cake makes a perfect vehicle for a present of small items of sports equipment such as tennis balls, socks and wristbands. Based on two 10" (25cm) gingerbread cakes with honey cream filling (see the picture on p.119), this design could easily be transformed into a golf bag lying on its side with icing golf club heads on dowelling rods sticking out of it and real golf balls spilling from its mouth.

To make the cake. Grease and line one 10" (25cm) square tin with waxed paper.

Sift the flour and soda into a bowl. Place the butter or margarine, honey, molasses, sugar, syrup, spices and milk in a saucepan and heat gently. Cool slightly and beat in the eggs. Pour the mixture into the flour a little at a time and beat well with each addition. Pour into the tin and bake in a preheated oven at 160°C/325°F/Gas mark 3 for 1 hour to 1 hour 10 minutes or until firm to the touch. Turn out on to a wire rack to cool.

For the filling, cream together the butter or margarine and powdered sugar. Add the honey and mix together.

TIMESAVERS

TIMESAVER Save time here by omitting the marzipan pocket detail on the sides of the bag. The sports logo could also be omitted or replaced with a team logo patch stuck to the side of the cake with royal icing.

DECORATION 1 hr 45 mins +
2 hrs drying time
Up to 45 mins can be cut from
the decoration time, see
Timesavers

ICING 1 hr 30 mins + 1 hr
drying time

MARZIPAN 1 hr + 4 hrs drying
time

COOKING 1 hr 10 mins per cake

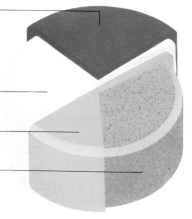

INGREDIENTS

(for one cake)
1lb (450g) all purpose flour
1 teaspoon bicarbonate of soda
8oz (225g) butter or margarine
8 tablespoons honey
8 tablespoons molasses
4oz (125g) light brown sugar
4 tablespoons golden syrup
6 teaspoons ground ginger
1 teaspoon ground cinnamon
8 fl oz (240ml) milk
4 eggs

Filling
1½lb (675g) powdered sugar
10oz (300g) butter or margarine
2 tablespoons honey

Decoration
12" (30cm) round cake board
2¾lb (1.25kg) marzipan
2lb (900g) cream coloured
fondant icing
1½lb (675g) pale blue fondant
icing
1lb (450g) gelatin icing
apricot jam
royal icing

Equipment
food colours
sports equipment such as socks,
wristbands, tennis balls, or
small towel

1 Cut each cake into two rectangles measuring 10″ × 5″ (25 × 13cm). Sandwich the cakes together with the filling.

2 Using a sharp knife, trim off all the corners and edges to produce a shape like a loaf of bread.

3 Measure the height of the cake. On a work surface lightly dusted with powdered sugar roll out 12oz (350g) marzipan and cut out two pieces about 5″ (13cm) wide and to the height of the cake. Spread the ends of the cake with apricot jam and fix on the marzipan. Take a piece of string and wrap over the cake to determine the length of the piece of marzipan needed to cover the rest of the cake. Roll out 1lb (450g) marzipan and cut a piece 10″ (25cm) wide and the length you have measured. Spread the remainder of the cake with jam and fix on the marzipan, pressing it gently on to the cake and getting the seams as neat as possible. Allow to dry for two hours.

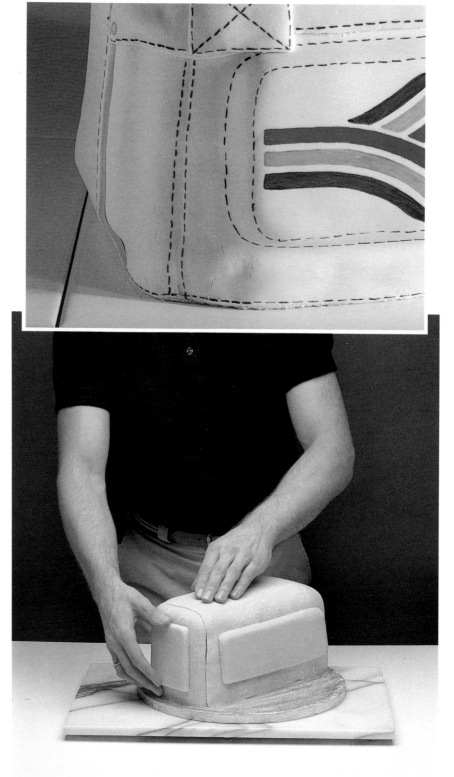

4 To make the side pockets roll out 8oz (225g) marzipan into a sheet about ½″ (1cm) thick. Cut out two rectangles about 3 × 4″ (7.5 × 10cm). Round off the edges by pressing with your fingers. Spread the pieces with jam and fix to each end of the cake.

5 To make the pocket for the front of the bag roll out 8oz (225g) marzipan into a sheet about ½″ (1cm) thick. Cut out a rectangle 8 × 3″ (20 × 7.5cm). Press the edges down to round them off. Spread with apricot jam and fix to the front of the cake. Allow to dry for at least two hours.

6 To ice the cake, measure the width and height of the ends of the cake. Take 12oz (350g) of the cream coloured fondant icing and roll out on a work surface lightly dusted with cornstarch. Cut out two rectangles to the measurements just noted. Moisten the marzipan at the ends of the cake by brushing lightly with water. This will help the icing stick. Gently smooth the icing in place and over the pocket detail. Measure the width of the marzipan piece still to be iced and wrap a piece of string over the cake to determine its length. Roll out 1¼lb (600g) of the cream fondant icing and cut a piece to fit. To make handling easier, you can cut this piece in half so that the seam runs along the centre of the top of the bag (where a zipper would be). Moisten the marzipan as before and fix on the icing, making sure that the seams are neat with edges closely pressed together. Let the icing dry for an hour or so.

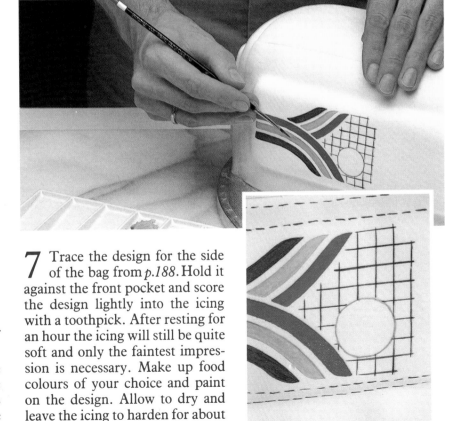

7 Trace the design for the side of the bag from *p.188*. Hold it against the front pocket and score the design lightly into the icing with a toothpick. After resting for an hour the icing will still be quite soft and only the faintest impression is necessary. Make up food colours of your choice and paint on the design. Allow to dry and leave the icing to harden for about four hours.

8 The top of the bag is to be filled with sports equipment such as wristbands, socks and tennis balls. These can be real items (as here), and form part of the gift, or they can be made out of icing. In which case, take 4oz (125g) gelatin icing and roll out. Cut out two sock shapes, fold them up as with a real pair, press indentations into the ankles for the ribbing and allow to dry. Take a further 4oz (125g) gelatin icing and roll into a ball. Allow to dry. The ball will dry with a flat bottom, but this will not be seen inside the bag. When dry paint the ball with the characteristic seam. To make a piece of soap and wristbands, take another 4oz (125g) gelatin icing. Form half of it into the shape of a bar of soap. The wristbands are simply rectangles of icing, though as with the other decorations additional colours and patterns can be added for extra interest. Allow the pieces to dry for two hours. Note that this does not include the towel, which will be made in step 9.

9 Fix the iced or real sports equipment to the top of the cake with a little royal icing. To make the opening of the bag, roll out 12oz (350g) blue fondant icing on a work surface lightly dusted with cornstarch. Cut out two rectangles about 14 × 4″ (35 × 10cm). Take one of these pieces and moisten one of the long edges. Fix to the side of the cake as illustrated, allowing the icing to fall gently against the sports equipment. Fold the top edge back a little so that the things inside can be seen. Now roll out 4oz (125g) gelatin icing for the towel and cut a square as large as possible. Fold it loosely and place on top of the bag, draping it over the opening. Take the second piece of blue icing and apply to the other side of the cake as for the first piece. Take 4oz (125g) blue fondant icing, roll out and cut two rectangles 3 × 2″ (7.5 × 5cm). Moisten and fix these tabs to the ends of the cake.

10 To make the handle, roll out 8oz (225g) blue fondant icing into a long strip and cut out two pieces about 1 × 18″ (46 × 2.5cm). Moisten both ends of each piece and fix in position on the bag, making sure that the handles do not obscure the detail inside. Allow the icing to dry for four hours.

ASSEMBLY
With blue and silver food colour paint the stitching on the sides of the bag and the zipper at the opening.

THREE-TIERED WEDDING CAKE

The classically decorated three-tiered wedding cake pictured on p. 129 would easily serve a party of 200 guests. The soft fondant icing on the rich fruit cake allows for effortless cutting by the bride and groom, and the decoration includes not only delicate icing roses and stephanotis that can be kept as a reminder of a splendid day, but also real flowers to match those chosen for the wedding.

To make the cake. Grease the cake tin and line with a double layer of waxed paper. Mix together the dried fruit, quartered cherries and mixed peel in a bowl or plastic bag. Add the almonds, spices and half the flour. Mix the ingredients in the bowl or toss in the plastic bag to coat the fruit with the flour, spice and almonds. Cream the butter or margarine and sugar until light and fluffy. Do not overbeat or the cake will be heavy. Add the eggs one or two at a time and mix well, adding a tablespoon of flour after each egg. Fold in any flour remaining and then add the dried fruit mixture.

Spread the mixture in the tin and level off the top. Some people advise making a slight hollow in the centre of the cake with the back of a spoon so that when cooked, the top of the cake is flat. However, if it is cooked slowly and gently this is not strictly necessary.

Tie two or three thicknesses of brown paper or newspaper round the tin and bake in a preheated oven at 150°C/300°F/Gas mark 2 for the time shown. For the larger cakes it may be advisable to turn down the oven to 140°C/275°F/Gas mark 1 after half the cooking time, and to cover the tin with a double layer of paper or cooking foil to prevent the surface from overcooking. To test for readiness insert a skewer into the centre of the cake. If it is done, the skewer will come out clean. If it is not ready, the skewer will be sticky and have bits of cake mixture sticking to it. When cooked, allow the cake to cool in the tin.

Turn the cake out of the tin and prick the surface all over with a skewer. Spoon brandy or whisky over the cake and then wrap in a double thickness of waxed paper and cooking foil. The 'feeding' with brandy or whisky can be repeated at intervals until the cake is decorated. Opinions as to the length of time the cake needs to mature differ from three weeks to several months. Generally speaking the cake will improve somewhat if left for a few months in a cool place, but it is not essential to leave it so long.

TIMESAVERS

TIMESAVER To create the three-tiered wedding cake that we have designed will undoubtedly take a considerable amount of time – time well spent for such a special occasion. The cake will provide a centrepiece for the wedding breakfast and the detachable decorations can be kept as a souvenir. If you should want to cut down on the decoration time, instead of moulding the stephanotis and wired rosebuds, use more real flowers in the trailing decoration to reflect those in the bouquets or headdresses. Or, cut down on the decoration for the bottom tier by emphasizing three individual groups of moulded and real flowers to be placed between the ends of the trailing decorations, instead of joining up the flowers round the baseboard to form a wreath.

DECORATION 16 hrs
By using real flowers over 4 hrs can be saved from the decoration time

ICING 1 hr 30 mins + 12 hrs drying time

COOKING 2 hrs 45 mins to 5 hrs 15 mins per cake

MARZIPAN 2 hrs

INGREDIENTS

	8″ (20cm)	10″ (25cm)	12″ (30cm)
mixed dried fruit	1lb 5oz (600g)	2lb 6oz (1kg)	4lb 4oz (1.9kg)
glacé cherries	3oz (75g)	5oz (150g)	10oz (300g)
mixed peel, chopped	2oz (50g)	4oz (125g)	7oz (200g)
ground almonds	2oz (50g)	4oz (125g)	7oz (200g)
ground cinnamon	¾ teaspoon	1½ teaspoons	2½ teaspoons
ground mixed spice	½ teaspoon	1 teaspoon	1½ teaspoons
all purpose flour	7½oz (210g)	14oz (400g)	1½lb (675g)
butter or margarine	6oz (175g)	12oz (350g)	1lb 5oz (600g)
light brown sugar	6oz (175g)	12oz (350g)	1lb 5oz (600g)
eggs	3	6	11
cooking time	2¾ hours	3¾ hours	5¼ hours

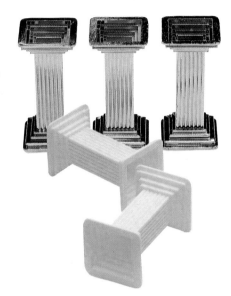

Equipment
8 cake pillars
dowelling
modelling wire
food colour
real or silk flowers:
irises
bluebells
sweet peas
baby's breath
baby ribbon
4m (4 yards) 2″ (5cm) wide
ribbon

Decoration
one 16″ (40cm) round cake
board
one 12″ (30cm) round cake
board
one 10″ (25cm) round cake
board
4lb (1.8kg) tragacanth or gelatin
icing
8lb (3.75kg) marzipan
5lb (2.3kg) cream coloured
fondant icing
apricot jam

1 Steps 1 to 8 are the same for all three tiers of the cake. Turn the cake upside down. Roll out a sausage shape of marzipan. You will need 1lb (450g) for the bottom tier, 12oz (350g) for the middle tier and 8oz (225g) for the top tier. Push the marzipan into the gap between the cake and the board.

2 Using a flat-bladed knife trim the marzipan to the edge of the cake. Smooth the marzipan to ensure that the sides of the cake are completely flat.

3 At this stage it is a good idea to check that the top of the cake is level with a spirit level – you may have made it uneven by forcing marzipan under the bottom of the cake. If there is any irregularity, insert more marzipan to compensate. The use of a spirit level is not essential, but it is worth taking the time to get things right at this stage given all the effort you are going to be putting in.

TIPS

If you don't own a spirit level, shown in the picture above, a simpler method of checking if the top of your cake is level is to place a shallow dish or baking tray on the cake and pour in a small amount of water (enough to cover the bottom). Any deviation in level can be spotted – if the water level is not consistent from one side of the dish to the other, the cake is not level.

4 Spread the top of the cake with apricot jam. On a work surface lightly dusted with powdered sugar roll out the marzipan. You will need 2½lb (1.1kg) for the bottom tier, 2lb (900g) for the middle tier and 1¼lb (575g) for the top tier. Using the tin in which the cake was baked, cut out a circle of marzipan and place on top of the cake. Measure the circumference of the cake with a piece of string. Cut the string in half. Roll out the marzipan left after the top is in position. Measure the depth of the cake and cut out two rectangles of marzipan to the depth of the cake and the length of the pieces of string. Spread the sides of the cake with apricot jam. Apply the marzipan to the sides of the cake. Press the seams gently together to make them as neat as possible. Using a plastic smoother, gently smooth the marzipan on the sides and top of the cake to make all the seams as even as possible.

5 On a work surface lightly dusted with icing sugar roll out the fondant icing. You will need 2½lb (1.1kg) for the bottom tier, 1½lb (675g) for the middle tier and 1lb (450g) for the top tier. Roll the icing into a circle large enough to cover the cake.

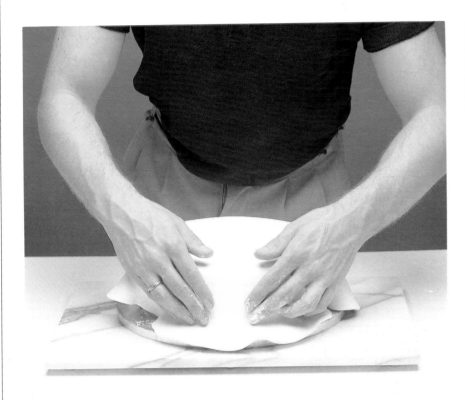

6 With fingers lightly covered in cornstarch smooth the icing into the edges of the cake.

8 Cut a piece of ribbon to go round the side of the cake. Cut the end decoratively as illustrated. Fix the ribbon to the side of the cake with a dab of royal icing.

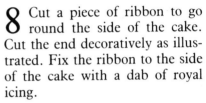

7 Using a flat-bladed knife with the blade lightly pressed against the side of the cake, cut off any excess icing. Leave to dry for 12 hours or overnight.

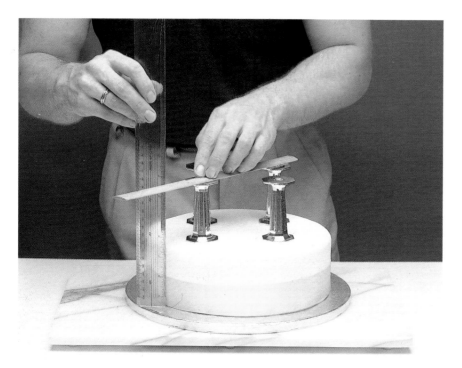

9 For the bottom and middle tiers, place the pillars in position. Lay a piece of wood or a ruler across the top of the pillars. Measure the height from the board to the top of the pillar.

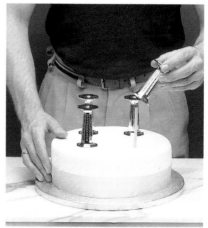

11 With the pillars in position on the surface of the cake, insert the dowelling. If you have miscalculated and the dowelling is too long, take it out and shave off any excess with a sharp knife.

12 Take 1½lb (675g) of the tragacanth or gelatin icing. Roll out half of it and cut out about a dozen ivy leaves. Leave some to dry over a curved surface such as a rolling pin, and allow others to dry flat. Cut the modelling wire into 3″ (7.5cm) lengths. Take the other half of the icing and remove a piece the size of a hazelnut. Insert the wire into it. Roll out the icing leaving the wire running through its centre and cut out an ivy leaf shape. Make about 50 wired leaves. Keep any leftover icing and knead again. Wrap the icing in cling film and use to make more leaves or keep for the rosebuds.

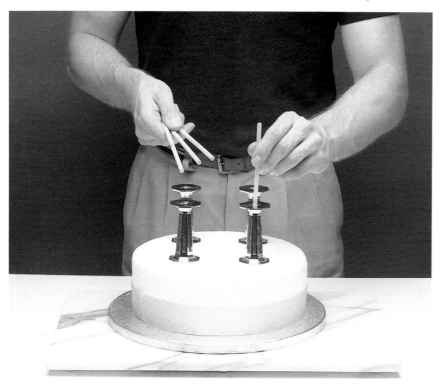

10 Cut four pieces of dowelling to the measurement just taken.

13 Allow the wired leaves to dry over a rolling pin. When dry, paint all the leaves green and allow to dry.

14 Take the flat ivy leaves and place on top of the bottom and middle tiers between the pillars as shown.

15 When making the roses it is helpful to have a real rose to study so that you make the flower as authentic as possible. Take 1lb (450g) of gelatin or tragacanth icing and colour a pale shade of lemon. This amount of icing should produce between 12 and 16 roses. Take a piece of icing the size of a hazelnut and mould into a small elongated pyramid. Take a second piece of icing of similar size and press out as thinly as possible into a petal shape as illustrated. Moisten the bottom half of the petal with a little water and wind it around the pyramid shape. Gently bend back the edge of the petal as illustrated.

16 The next layer of the rose has three petals, each slightly larger than the one before. Moisten the bottom half of the petal and fix on to the bud. Gently curl back the petals.

17 The final layer of the rose has four or five petals depending on the fullness of bloom required. The petals are essentially the same shape as that illustrated in step 15.

19 On the bottom tier fix two roses at four intervals round the board with a little royal icing.

18 Once the petals are attached to the flower, bend them back, or pinch them to a point as illustrated. Leave the completed rose to dry for 12 hours or overnight. Using a sharp knife cut away the base that will have developed on the completed rose.

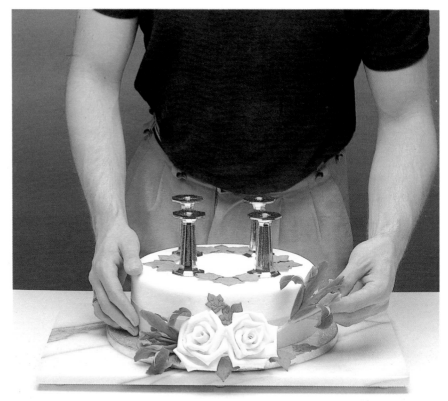

20 Arrange the ivy leaves and iris heads as shown.

21 Fill in the gaps between the roses and irises with sweet peas and bluebells.

22 Take 12oz (350g) tragacanth or gelatin icing. Break off a piece the size of a hazelnut and flatten the edges out on to a work surface leaving a central elongated pyramid or stem extending upwards about 1" (2.5cm).

23 Place a stephanotis or five-point star cutter over the stem and press out the flower head.

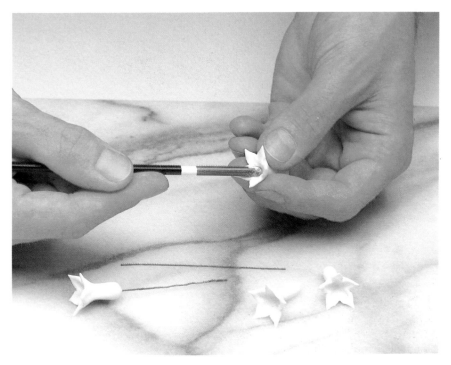

24 Insert the end of a thin paintbrush or skewer into the centre of the flower head and roll backwards and forwards over each petal point to thin it out and produce a curve in the petal. Cut pieces of modelling wire about 3" (7.5cm) long and insert through the flower head and down the stem. Leave about ½" (1cm) wire inside the flower. Leave the stephanotis to dry with the stem pushed into a block of oasis. Make about 36 stephanotis.

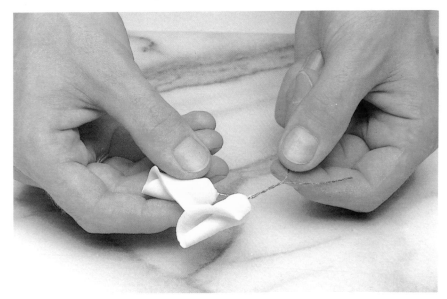

25 To make wired rosebuds use the remaining 12oz (350g) tragacanth or gelatin icing coloured a similar shade to the full-blown roses. Make the buds as for the first stage of the rose, but push a 3" (7.5cm) piece of wire into the central pyramid of icing. Like the stephanotis, the rosebuds are best left to dry with their stems pushed into a block of oasis. Make about 36 rosebuds.

26 To make the three flower garlands, twist the wire stems of the stephanotis, ivy leaves and rosebuds together at intervals.

27 A completed garland should be long enough to stretch from the top of the cake to the bottom. Make the garlands fuller and thicker at the top and more delicate at the bottom.

28 Take the three completed garlands and twist the top ends together to produce one decoration.

29 Make bows as illustrated with baby ribbon, securing the ends with either thread or modelling wire.

ASSEMBLY

Decorate the side of the middle tier as illustrated and arrange three full roses on the top secured with royal icing. Assemble the tiers. Arrange the flower garlands so that one falls between each of the three roses on the top tier. Once the garlands are in position, place a fourth rose on top of the three to form a pyramid. Drape the garlands down the cake as shown. More bluebells can be pushed into the garlands and irises, bluebells and sweet peas added to the flower arrangement on the top tier. If you are using real flowers these should be added only at the last moment. The decoration is completed with sprigs of baby's breath and ribbon bows.

CHRISTMAS TREE

Here is a simple and delicious orange madeira cake that proves it's possible to have your tree and eat it too! The tree (pictured on p. 135) is made from four 8″ (20cm) round cakes and the tub is a 6″ (15cm) cake. It requires only basic carving and shaping. The marzipanning and icing are deliberately left rough to create the illusion of branches and snow. Neither does the brushwork require a delicate hand. The finishing touches to the tree can be left to the children in the last busy days before Christmas.

To make the cake. Cream the butter or margarine and sugar together until light and fluffy. Add the eggs one at a time and beat into the mixture. Add a spoonful of flour to the mixture after each egg is incorporated and mix again. Sift the remaining flours together and fold into the creamed mixture, followed by the orange rind and juice. Turn the mixture into a greased and lined tin and level the top. Place in a preheated oven set at 160°C/325°F/ Gas mark 3 for the time shown and cook until well risen and firm to the touch. Leave for 5–10 minutes then turn out on to a wire cooling rack.

INGREDIENTS

	6″ (15cm)	8″ (20cm)
butter or margarine	4oz (125g)	8oz (225g)
sugar	4oz (125g)	8oz (225g)
eggs	2	4
self-rising flour	4oz (125g)	8oz (225g)
all purpose flour	2oz (50g)	4oz (125g)
grated orange rind	1 orange	1½ oranges
approximate cooking time	1 hour	1 hour 25 minutes

Christmas Tree
Made from four 8″ (20cm) and one 6″ (15cm) orange madeira cakes

Decoration
one 10″ (25cm) round cake board
one 8″ (20cm) thin round cake board
2lb (900g) marzipan
1lb (450g) royal icing
2lb (900g) fondant icing

apricot jam
dragees (silvered candy beads)
small chocolates

Equipment
approx 1′ (30cm) of ¼″ dowelling
food colour
coloured foil
ribbon
candles and holders
heart-shaped cutter
star-shaped cutter

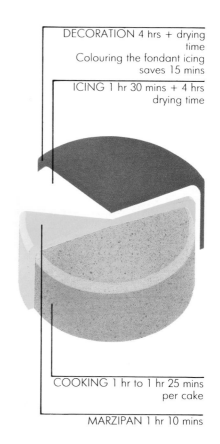

DECORATION 4 hrs + drying time
Colouring the fondant icing saves 15 mins

ICING 1 hr 30 mins + 4 hrs drying time

COOKING 1 hr to 1 hr 25 mins per cake

MARZIPAN 1 hr 10 mins

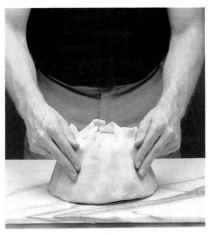

1 Assemble the four 8″ (20cm) madeira cakes on the thin 8″ (20cm) cake board. These cakes will form the carved branches of the tree and the board will eventually be placed on the tub.

3 Marzipan the three sections of the tree individually. For the lower third take 1lb (450g) marzipan. Spread the sides of the cake with apricot jam. Roll out the marzipan in a piece wide enough to reach from top to bottom of the cake and long enough to stretch round it. The measurements need not be precise as in other cakes. As you will see from the photograph it is not necessary to produce a completely flat finish, in fact the creases that form in the marzipan can be accentuated to produce the irregular effect of branches. Continue with the middle and top layers using 8oz (225g) and 4oz (125g) marzipan respectively. Trim off any excess marzipan.

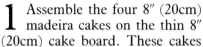

2 To carve the cakes into the tree shape as illustrated, it may be helpful to separate the cakes, and then reassemble them to check for symmetry. The bottom two cakes represent the lower third of the tree, and the other two represent the middle and top sections. If you wish to add further detail at this stage, you could carve irregular ridges running from top to bottom in each section of the cake to represent branches, though this is not essential. To make the tub, take the 6″ (15cm) cake and carve to produce gently sloping sides as illustrated.

4 Take 12oz (350g) fondant icing and on a work surface lightly dusted with cornstarch roll out a circle large enough to cover the top and sides of the bottom third of the cake. Drape it over the cake.

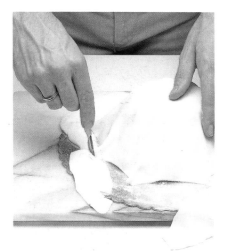

5 Once again, do not try to get rid of the creases, but emphasize them to add to the branch detail. Trim off the excess icing and repeat the process with the middle and top sections using 8oz (225g) and 6oz (175g) fondant icing respectively. Be sure to keep any fondant trimmings and wrap them in cling film as they will be needed to make the decorations for the tree. Allow the icing to dry for 4 hours before proceeding.

6 To ice the tub, spread the top and sides of the cake with apricot jam. Roll out the remaining marzipan with any trimmings that may have been left over. Use the 6″ (15cm) tin in which the cake was baked to cut a circle of marzipan and apply it to the top of the tub. With the remaining marzipan, make a strip long enough to go around the tub and wide enough to cover the sides. Fix to the sides of the tub. Measure and cut 4 pieces of dowelling to the height of the marzipanned tub. Insert into the cake as shown so that they are flush with the surface. This will give extra support to the tree.

TIPS

The tricky part with this cake is placing the fully decorated tree top on the small tub. If you want to avoid using the dowelling supports, you could replace the tub with a decorated plant pot. To prevent the pot tipping over, line it with a polythene bag and fill with flour or rice, which you will be able to use afterwards.

7 Take 4oz (125g) fondant icing and colour it Christmas red. The tub can be iced in one sheet or in strips 1″ (2.5cm) wide to represent wooden slats. Use a cocktail stick or skewer to score lines into the icing to produce or emphasize this effect.

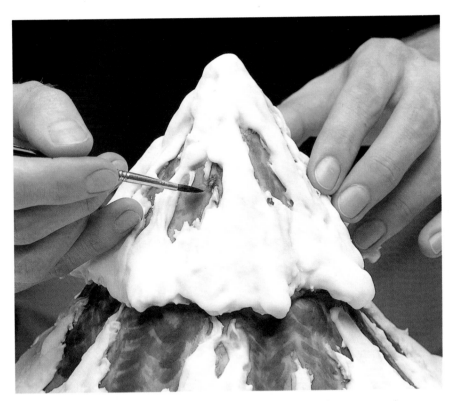

8 Now make up some green food colour and brush over the icing on the tree. The painting need not be completely even. Paint a herringbone pattern in a darker green on top to emphasize the branches. Leave to dry.

9 Take the royal icing and apply roughly to the cake as illustrated. Using either a paintbrush dipped in water or a wetted knife, gently smooth the icing to produce the rounded effect of a fresh and heavy fall of snow. Save a little icing to fix the decorations.

10 Take the chocolates and rewrap them in various coloured foils. Tie each parcel with a bow of narrow ribbon.

11 Take the candle holders and insert into the snow-laden boughs. Fix in the candles.

13 To make the other decorations take the icing trimmings from the tub and roll out again. Using a small heart-shaped cutter, cut out as many hearts as possible and allow to dry on waxed paper or non-stick cooking parchment. When dry, fix dragees in the centre of each heart with a dab of royal icing and fix to the tree. Another decoration that children can help make involves using the remaining 2oz (50g) fondant icing. Colour half the icing and leave the other half white. Roll out both pieces of icing. Cut an equal sized strip from both pieces, making it as wide as possible. Brush the surface of one piece with water and place the other piece on top. Once again brush the surface of the top piece with water and roll up the icing as in a Swiss roll. Cut the roll into thin slices and gently flatten with a rolling pin. This will produce an attractive spiral pattern. Using a small star-shaped cutter, cut out a star from the centre of each piece and allow to dry on waxed paper or non-stick parchment. When dry fix to the cake with a dab of royal icing.

12 Using a dab of royal icing fix the parcels to the tree.

ASSEMBLY

Paint two silver lines around the tub to look like metal hoops. Place the tree on its board on top of the tub. Serve at the table with the candles lit, and have a very Merry Christmas.

SUNDAY TEA CAKE

This Sunday tea cake, made with two airy Genoese sponges sandwiched with strawberries and cream (pictured on p. 139), is decorated colourfully and quickly without being iced. Instead, simply made red marzipan strawberries, each with a realistic green calyx, and green marzipan leaves are arranged attractively on the sugar-dusted top of the cake to complete this luxurious tea-time feast.

To make the cake. Line the bottom and sides of the tin with waxed paper. Brush the lining paper with butter and sprinkle the tin with flour. Tip out the excess flour. Sift the flour and salt together two or three times. If using butter, clarify by melting and skim off any froth. Pour the melted butter out of the pan leaving the milky sediment behind. Put the eggs in a large bowl, copper if possible, and add the sugar. Place the bowl in or over hot but not boiling water. Whisk for about 10 minutes until the mixture is thick enough to leave a trail when the whisk is lifted out of it. Take the bowl from the heat and continue beating until cool. Sift the flour and salt on to the mixture in three batches, folding in each batch as lightly as possible. If using the butter, add after the last batch of flour and fold in. Be careful to fold the butter in as lightly and quickly as possible as the mixture loses volume once the butter is added. Pour the mixture into the prepared tin and bake in a preheated oven set at 180°C/350°F/Gas mark 4 for about 35–40 minutes until the cake shrinks slightly from the sides of the tin and the top springs back when lightly pressed.

INGREDIENTS

Cake (for one sponge)
4 eggs
4oz (125g) sugar
4oz (125g) all purpose flour
pinch of salt
2oz (50g) butter optional

Filling and decoration
10oz (284ml) heavy
whipping cream
strawberries
1¼lb (575g) white marzipan
powdered sugar to dust
a little royal icing

Equipment
food colour
piping bag with ½″ (1cm) star
tip
star-shaped cutter

TIMESAVERS

TIMESAVER Save time and money by making only one sponge and splitting it in half before decorating the top.

TIMESAVER If you have your own strawberry patch, you could use real strawberries and leaves to decorate the cake, extending the decoration on to the cake stand or plate.

DECORATION 1 hr 30 mins
Up to 1 hour can be saved by using real strawberries for decoration

COOKING 40 mins per cake

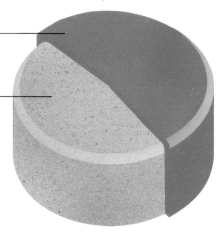

1 Take the two cakes and brush away any loose crumbs from the sides.

2 Whip the cream into soft peaks. Spread half the cream on the surface of one of the cakes and put the other half into a piping bag fitted with a ½″ (1cm) star tip. Pipe swirls of cream all around the edge of the cake.

3 Slice the strawberries in half and place some between the swirls of cream on the edge. Pile the remaining strawberries cut edge down in the centre of the cake.

4 Place the second cake on top of the fruit and dust the surface lightly with powdered sugar.

5 Take 12oz (350g) of the marzipan and colour it red with edible food colour. Cut the marzipan into 1oz (25g) pieces and roll into strawberry shapes. Using a toothpick or skewer, prick the marzipan strawberries at intervals all over the surface.

6 Colour the remaining 8oz (225g) of marzipan green. On a work surface lightly dusted with cornstarch, roll out the marzipan. Using a star-shaped cutter, press out a calyx for each strawberry. Press a skewer or the end of a paintbrush into the centre of the calyx to draw up the points. Fix the calyx to the strawberry with a little royal icing. Gather up the remaining marzipan and roll out. Cut out several leaves and score veins on them with a toothpick. With the marzipan left, roll out four long thin strands about the thickness of a drinking straw. Cut one of them into ¼" (5mm) lengths. Take each of these small pieces and roll one end into a point. Fix to the centre of the calyx on the strawberry with a little royal icing. Take the remaining lengths of marzipan and arrange on the cake.

ASSEMBLY

Place the strawberries and leaves on top of the cake, taking care not to disturb the powdered sugar.

'WINNERS'

The technique of icing marquetry featured here – making pictures with shapes of different coloured icing – can be used to create any bold design and is particularly effective in the portrayal of cartoon characters. The Union Jack with its torch and laurel wreath (p.143) can mark the occasion of any victory from an Olympic medal downwards. The flag itself could be replaced with a club badge or colours. The basic cake is made from two 12" (30cm) square coconut and cherry cakes piled on top of one another.

To make the cake. Grease and line a tin with waxed paper. Mix the butter or margarine with the sugars and beat until light and fluffy. Add the eggs one at a time, followed by a spoonful of flour. Fold in the remaining flour and the salt alternating with some of the milk. Mix the cherries with the coconut and fold into the mixture. Turn the mixture into the tin and bake in a preheated oven set at 180°C/350°F/Gas mark 4 for about 50 minutes until firm to the touch. Turn out on to a wire rack to cool.

Although there is no filling in this cake, you might like to fill it with a cherry, coconut and vanilla cream, made as follows. Take 8oz (225g) butter or margarine and mix in 1lb (450g) powdered sugar. Fold in 4oz (125g) finely chopped glacé cherries and 2oz (50g) desiccated coconut. Use to sandwich the two cakes together.

TIMESAVERS

TIMESAVER If you have decided not to bother cutting an undulating surface to the top of your cake, you will find that you also save time on the decoration. If you decorate the top of the cake alone, wrap the side of the cake in a broad red, white and blue ribbon to complete the decoration.

TIMESAVER You could use real leaves in the laurel crown instead of making them from icing. If you don't have a laurel bush in your garden, ivy leaves would look just as good, and as they are hardy they would keep fresh even if the decoration was made the day before.

INGREDIENTS

(for one cake)
9oz (250g) butter or margarine
8oz (225g) sugar
4oz (125g) dark brown sugar
3 eggs
12oz (350g) self-rising flour
¾ teaspoon salt
9 fl oz (270ml) milk
8oz (225g) glacé cherries, quartered
4oz (125g) desiccated coconut

Decoration
14" (35cm) square cake board
1lb (450g) white fondant icing
8oz (225g) red fondant icing
12oz (350g) blue fondant icing
1lb (450g) gelatin icing
1½lb (675g) marzipan
apricot jam

Equipment
12" (30cm) of thick wire, such as a wire coathanger
modelling wire for leaves and flames
florists' tape

1 Cut the cakes into oblongs 12 × 9" (30 × 23cm). Put the cakes on top of one another and trim the top to make a regular block of cake. Using a kitchen knife carefully cut an undulating surface into the cake as shown.

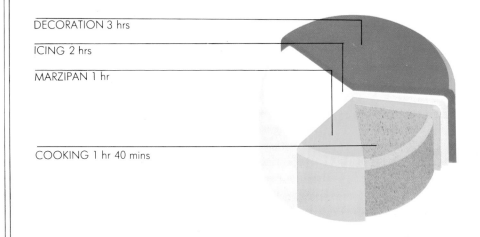

DECORATION 3 hrs

ICING 2 hrs

MARZIPAN 1 hr

COOKING 1 hr 40 mins

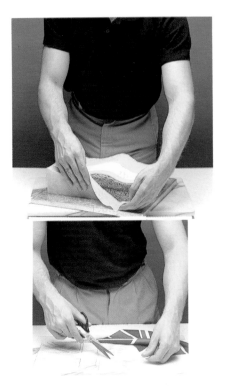

2 Take a piece of parchment paper and lay on the surface of the cake. Trace the outline of the cake. Take more parchment paper and trace the shape of the four sides of the cake. These templates will be used in cutting out the marzipan. Spread the surface of the cake with apricot jam. On a work surface lightly dusted with powdered sugar roll out 12oz (350g) of the marzipan into a sheet large enough to contain the template for the top. Lay the parchment outline on the marzipan and cut round it. Fix the marzipan on top of the cake. Roll out the remaining marzipan and cut out the pieces for the sides of the cake using the templates. Fix them to the cake. Let the marzipan dry for two hours before proceeding. Copy the design on *p.185* onto a piece of parchment. With blue and red crayons or food colour pens, mark out the sections of the design in appropriate colours. Cut out the blue and red sections. Note that the size of the template will vary according to whether or not you intend to continue the flag pattern down the sides of the cake.

3 On a work surface lightly dusted with cornstarch roll out 1lb (450g) of white fondant icing into a sheet large enough to cover the cake. Drape the icing over the cake and smooth over the sides and down the corners. Using a sharp knife trim the icing along the edges of the cake and use scissors to trim the corners. Roll out the red icing and lay the template for the large red cross on top. Cut out the cross and lay in position on the cake. Gather up the red icing remains and roll out again. Take the templates for the smaller red cross running diagonally across the flag and cut out the four pieces. Lay in position on the cake. Take the blue fondant icing and roll out. Cut out the eight blue pieces with the aid of the templates and lay on the cake. Trim the icing to the edge of the cake with a sharp knife, shaping it to continue down the sides.

4 Take 8oz (225g) gelatin icing and divide into balls the size of hazelnuts. Cut the modelling wire into 3″ (7.5cm) lengths and insert into the icing balls. Roll out each piece so that the wire extends well inside it. Using a sharp knife cut out leaves and score veins into them with a toothpick. Allow the leaves to dry flat for about 4 hours. Paint green and allow to dry again.

5 Take the coathanger wire and bend into a horseshoe shape. Wrap florists' tape around it. Place the leaves on the wire as you go and secure by wrapping the tape over the wire stalks of the leaves.

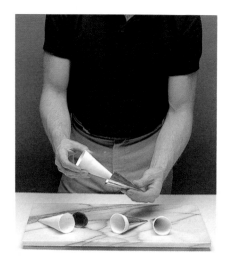

6 To make the cone for the torch, take any mould that is cone-shaped. In this instance a cream horn mould was used, but you could make a mould from stiff cardboard. Wrap the cone in waxed paper, cut to the shape of the cone and secure with sticky tape. Cut down one side and open out to form a template. Roll out 4oz (125g) gelatin icing and lay the template on top. Cut round the paper template. Take the icing piece and carefully make into a cone. Place the icing cone inside the cone mould to dry for at least 4 hours. The flames for the torch are made like leaves for the crown described in step 5. The flames are irregular in shape as illustrated and are cut from the remaining 4oz (125g) gelatin icing. Allow the flames to dry flat.

9 Fill the cone with tissue or a piece of florists' oasis, and insert the wire to fix the flames in position. Take all the flames and fix together.

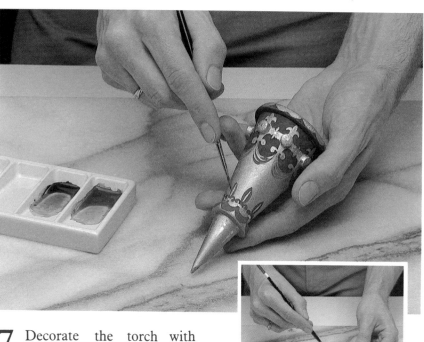

7 Decorate the torch with food colours of your choice. This particular design is quite complex and has been further embellished by the addition of strips of icing around the top edge of the cone and again about two thirds down its length. There are also small cut-out circles of icing studded around the top of the cone. It is not necessary for the cone to be quite so highly decorated, and the use of gold and silver with possibly one other colour could be just as effective.

8 To paint the flames make up several shades of yellow, orange and red with food colours, and either paint individual flames in separate colours or use all the colours on each flame.

10 An alternative and easier way of making the cone would be to buy an ice cream cone and paint it gold with food colour. The flames could then be made from red tissue paper.

ASSEMBLY

Place the torch in the centre of the cake and fix in position with a little royal icing. Place the laurel crown so that it frames the torch in the centre of the cake.

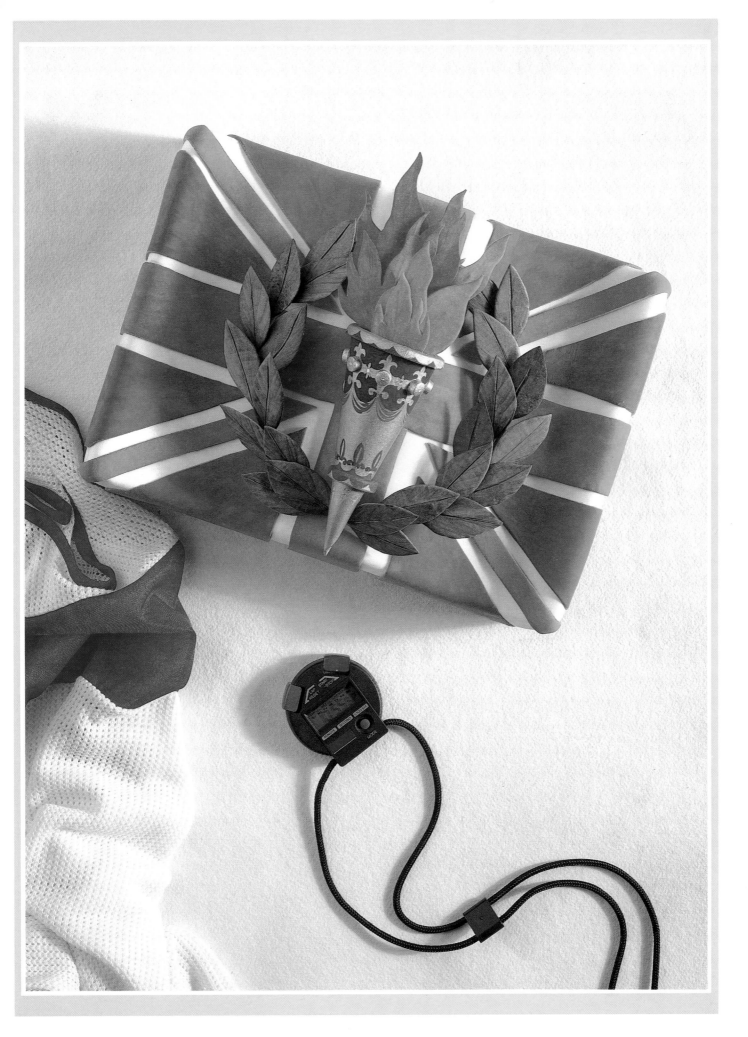

PARTRIDGE IN A PEAR TREE

A partridge in a pear tree may be a traditional Christmas image, but there is nothing traditional about the decoration of the cake pictured on p.147, or indeed about the cake itself, which is two whisky cakes sandwiched together with lemon and honey filling. The bird, fruit and leaves are cut from different thicknesses of marzipan and applied underneath the fondant, giving a three-dimensional effect to the decoration. The deep midnight blue background is a bold move away from the traditional red, green and gold of Christmas time.

To make the cake. Grease and line a 10″ (25cm) round cake tin with waxed paper. Cream the butter and sugar until light and fluffy. Gradually beat in the finely grated rind of half the lemon and the eggs. Fold in half the sifted flour and then add the whisky. Fold in the remaining flour. Spoon into the prepared tin and bake in a preheated oven at 160°C/325°F/Gas mark 3 for about 50 minutes to one hour. Check the cake after about 40 or 45 minutes. If it is getting too brown, cover with a sheet of kitchen foil. The cake is ready when firm to the touch. Remove from the tin and allow to cool.

For the filling, cream the softened butter or margarine with the sugar. Add the honey. If a firmer filling is required, add more powdered sugar. Add the lemon juice and mix together.

INGREDIENTS

Cake
6oz (175g) butter or margarine
6oz (175g) light brown sugar
1 lemon
3 eggs, beaten
6oz (175g) sifted self-rising flour
4 tablespoons (60ml) Scotch

Filling
4oz (125g) butter or margarine
8oz (225g) sifted powdered sugar
4oz (125g) honey
1–2 tablespoons (15–30ml) lemon juice

Decoration
12″ (30cm) round cake board
4½lb (2kg) marzipan
2lb (900g) fondant icing
apricot jam
royal icing

Equipment
food colours
pieces of rhinestone

TIMESAVERS

TIMESAVER Most of the time spent decorating this cake is devoted to moulding the marzipan shapes before icing. You can save a lot of time by moulding decoration for the top only.

TIMESAVER To simplify the decoration on the top of the cake concentrate on cutting out just the partridge and the pears in marzipan. Place these in position as described and then ice over. Make the leaves separately as in the box of roses (p.64)

and fix to the cake with royal icing once the bird and the pears have been painted. You could either use real ribbon or cut thin strips of red fondant icing and drape them over the decoration.

TIMESAVER The midnight blue colouring around the decoration can be left out if you wish. If you decide to leave the icing white, add a ribbon round the side of the cake to introduce depth of colour into your design.

DECORATION 3 hrs + 5 hrs drying time for food colour

ICING 30 mins + 8 hrs drying time

MARZIPAN 1 hr 30 mins + 4 hrs drying time

COOKING 1 hr per cake.

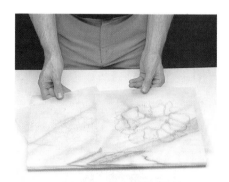

1 The design for the top of this cake can be found on *p.186*. It is a good idea to trace it out twice – use one tracing to position the elements in the design and the other to cut out the pieces of marzipan. Trace the design for the side of the cake.

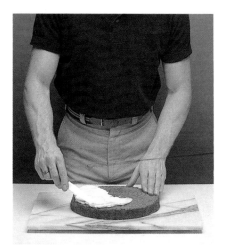

2 Sandwich the cakes together with the filling.

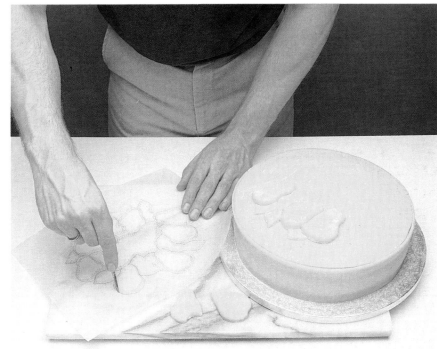

3 On a work surface lightly dusted with powdered sugar roll out 12oz (350g) marzipan. Using the tin in which the cake was baked as a guide, cut out a circle to fit the top of the cake. Spread the top of the cake with apricot jam and fix on the circle. Wrap a piece of string round the cake to measure its circumference, and measure its height. Roll out a further 12oz (350g) marzipan into a strip and cut to the measurements just noted. To make it easier to handle, cut in half. Spread the side of the cake with apricot jam and fix the marzipan to it. Allow to dry for a couple of hours.

4 To decorate the top of the cake, roll out 6oz (175g) marzipan fairly thinly. Place one tracing over the marzipan and cut out the leaves as shown. Place these in position on top of the cake using the other tracing as a guide and fix to the first layer of marzipan with a little apricot jam. Roll out a further 6oz (175g) marzipan into a slightly thicker layer. Cut out the partridge and fix on the cake with apricot jam. Roll out 12oz (350g) marzipan into a still thicker layer and cut out the pears. Round down the edges. Place the pears in position and fix to the cake with jam. To decorate the side of the cake roll out 12oz (350g) marzipan into a strip long enough to stretch half way round the cake and wide enough to contain the decoration on your tracing. Making sure that the tracing will also stretch half way round the cake, lay it on the marzipan and cut out the design. Fix to the side of the cake with jam. Use only

enough jam to make the marzipan stick – too much and the weight of the marzipan will cause it to slip down the side of the cake. Repeat for the other half of the cake. If you would like to add more relief decoration to the side of the cake, cut out more pear shapes from any leftover marzipan and fix in place with jam. Allow to dry for two hours.

5 On a work surface lightly dusted with cornstarch roll out the fondant icing into a sheet large enough to cover the cake. Moisten the side of the cake with water to make it sticky and lay the icing over the cake. Using a flat-bladed knife held against the side trim off any excess icing. With fingers lightly coated in cornstarch gently mould the icing into the marzipan detail on the top and side of the cake. Allow to dry for eight hours or overnight.

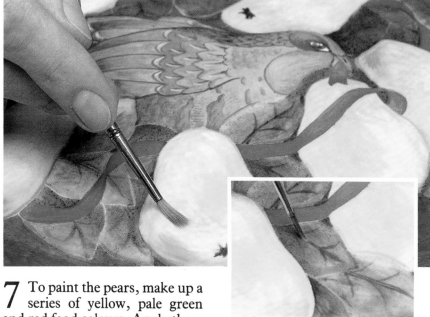

7 To paint the pears, make up a series of yellow, pale green and red food colours. Apply them one after the other while still wet and mix with the brush to create a delicate shaded effect. Leave to dry for an hour.

Paint the ribbon decoration in deep Christmas red food colour. Leave to dry for an hour.

8 To paint the leaves, make up two or three shades of green and apply one after the other, mixing with the brush while still wet. Use a darker shade of green to paint the veins on the leaves. Leave to dry for an hour.

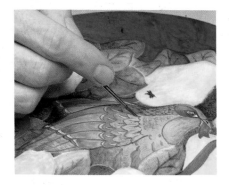

6 To paint the partridge make up a series of brown, red and orange-brown food colours. The bird's markings have been stylized in order to make colouring simpler. Transfer these to the icing from your tracing with a toothpick. Start by outlining the markings with unbroken lines of dark brown. Allow to dry for 20 minutes or so, then continue by filling in the various sections in different shades as shown.

Add gold highlights on the feathers for further effect. Leave to dry for an hour before proceeding.

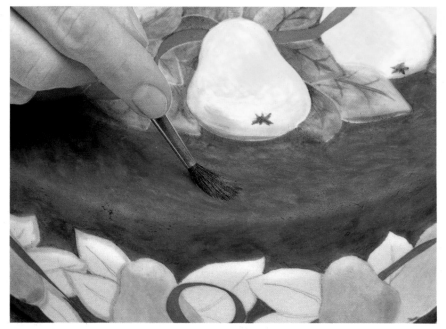

9 To colour the background, make up a rich midnight blue and brush on to the un-coloured icing. Do not worry that you will see the brushstrokes – that the cake is hand-painted is a great part of its charm. Paint on the colour with the bristles splayed out to emphasize this. Gently press the tip of the brush all over the blue icing to produce a stippled effect.

OPENING NIGHT

The Opening Night cake (pictured on p.153) is a wholesome 10" (25cm) fruit cake and its decoration features careful hand painting to create a striking illusion of perspective, and moulded masks of gelatin icing. You can buy masks to take moulds from or make simpler versions with cut-out features. The masks could be decorated to represent specific characters – here they are embellished with gold leaf. The pillar is moulded on a candlestick in two halves, which are then stuck together with royal icing. The dramatic red curtain is made of tragacanth icing.

To make the cake. Mix together the dried fruit, glacé cherries, spices and ground almonds. Cream the butter or margarine until soft, then add the sugar and beat until light and fluffy. Do not overbeat. Add the eggs one at a time, beating well, followed by a spoonful of flour. Fold in the remaining flour, followed by the dried fruit mixture. Add the honey and lemon rind. Grease and double line a 10" (23cm) square cake tin with waxed paper. Level the surface of the cake. Tie two or three thicknesses of brown paper or newspaper around the tin. Bake in a preheated oven at 150°C/300°F/Gas mark 2 for four hours 15 minutes or until cooked. To prevent the cake from burning on top, cover with a double thickness of brown paper after half the cooking time. Test with a toothpick to see if the cake is ready. If the cake is done, the stick will come out clean. Leave to cool in the tin, then turn out.

TIMESAVERS

TIMESAVER The picture frame effect created by the marzipanning of the sides of the cake allows for the continuation of the black and white theme.

An alternative way of decorating the sides would be to drape red fondant icing all the way around the cake like a theatre curtain.

DECORATION 4 hrs and a total of 12 hrs drying time

ICING 45 mins + 8 hrs drying time

MARZIPAN 1 hr 30 mins + 6 hrs drying time

COOKING 4 hrs

INGREDIENTS

Cake
1lb 2oz (500g) currants
13oz (375g) golden raisins
8oz (225g) glacé cherries
2 teaspoons cinnamon
1½ teaspoons mixed spice
5oz (150g) ground almonds
1lb 2oz (500g) butter or margarine
1lb 2oz (500g) light brown sugar
9 eggs
1lb 5oz (600g) wholewheat flour
2 tablespoons honey
grated rind of 1 lemon

Decoration
12" (30cm) square cake board
4½lb (2kg) marzipan
2lb (900g) fondant icing
1lb (450g) Christmas red tragacanth or gelatin icing
2¼lb (1kg) gelatin icing, uncoloured
royal icing
apricot jam

Equipment
dowelling
food colours
baby ribbon
gold size (gold leaf glue, available at art shops)
moulds for masks

1 Prepare the cake for marzipanning as in the instructions for the Three-tiered Wedding Cake on *p.121* Turn the cake upside down on the board. Roll 1lb (450g) marzipan into a long sausage on a work surface lightly dusted with icing sugar. Gently press it into the gap between the cake and the board all round the cake. Hold a flat-bladed knife against the side of the cake and cut off any excess marzipan. Spread

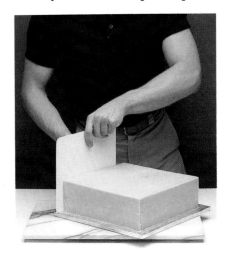

the top of the cake with apricot jam. Roll out 1½lb (675g) marzipan and cut out a square to fit the top using the tin in which the cake was baked as a guide. Fix in position on top of the cake. Measure the depth of the cake. Roll out 12oz (350g) marzipan and cut out two rectangles measuring 10″ (25cm) long by the depth of the cake. Spread opposite sides of the cake with apricot jam and fix the marzipan in position. Measure the length of the other two sides to take into account the depth of the marzipan just applied. Cut out two rectangles to fit from a further 12oz (350g) marzipan, spread the cake with apricot jam and fix the marzipan in position. Carefully smooth the top and sides of the cake with a plastic sheet to ensure that all surfaces are flat and the seams are as neat as possible. Leave to dry for four hours.

2 Roll out 8oz (225g) marzipan and cut out eight strips measuring ½″ (1cm) wide by the length of the sides of the cake. Spread the strips with a little jam and fix to the top and bottom edges of the cake. Do not use too much jam or the weight of the marzipan may cause the top strips to slip down the sides of the cake. When in position take a sharp knife and trim the ends of each strip to an angle of 45°. Take up the marzipan remains and roll out another eight strips ½″ (1cm) wide and to the depth of the cake. Trim the top and bottom of each strip to an angle of 45°. Spread the strips sparingly with apricot jam and fix to the corners so that the angled pieces fit neatly together as shown. The effect created is that of a picture frame on each side of the cake. Allow to dry for two hours.

TIPS

It is particularly important to have a flawlessly smooth finish to this cake. One of the purposes of moistening the marzipan before icing is to ensure against trapping air bubbles between the two layers. Instead of water you could use any alcoholic spirit for this purpose to give a little additional flavour.

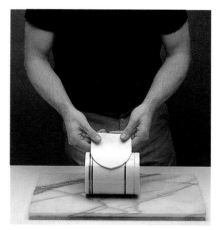

4 Masks to use as moulds can be bought in department stores, or you could use the face of a large doll. You could even cut out a simple mask shape and let it dry over a large tin of beans. Once the icing has dried you can cut details of eyes and mouth in a smile and a grimace to represent comedy and tragedy. In this case, bought masks have been used as moulds and each has been covered with 6oz (175g) gelatin icing. On a work surface lightly dusted with cornstarch roll out the gelatin icing and lay over the mask. Gently press the icing into the detail. Cut around the mask with a sharp knife to trim off excess icing. Leave to dry for at least four hours.

3 Moisten the sides of the cake with a little water to make the marzipan sticky. On a work surface lightly dusted with cornstarch roll out 2lb (900g) fondant icing into a sheet large enough to cover the cake. Place the icing sheet on the cake and gently smooth into the detail on the sides. Press the icing into neat seams at the corners and trim off the excess with sharp scissors. Hold a flat-bladed knife against the side of the cake and trim off any excess icing. Make the seams as neat as possible, smoothing the icing to mould the pieces around the corners into one piece. Allow the icing to dry for eight hours or overnight.

Trace the design for the top of the cake from *p.187* on to a piece of parchment paper. Enlarge the pattern to fit the size of your particular cake. Lay the pattern on top of the cake and secure with small pins. Be sure to remember exactly how many pins you have used. Using a ruler and toothpick gently score along the lines of the pattern so as to leave a faint

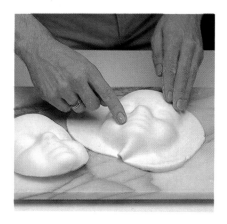

trace of the design on the surface of the icing. Be careful not to move the pattern. When you have finished, remove the pins and pattern and draw over the scored lines with a black food colour pen against a ruler. Be careful not to smudge the colour by dragging the ruler across it. It is a good idea to draw all the lines in one direction, then wait for 10 minutes or so until they have dried before drawing the second set of lines. Take care too not to smudge the colour. Take a medium paintbrush and black food colour and following your pattern paint alternating squares black. Allow the colour to dry for four hours.

5 We have chosen to use genuine English gold leaf to embellish the masks. The effect is quite stunning and the gold leaf is easy to use. Each piece measures 3″ (7.5cm) square and is stuck on a fine tissue backing. To transfer the gold to the mask, first paint the mask with gold size, which will leave it tacky. Place the gold leaf on the tacky surface and gently smooth it down. Pull back the fine tissue, leaving the gold on the mask. Although ordinary gold leaf

is edible, the type requiring the use of gold size is not, so the masks will be purely decorative. As it is not always possible to produce a perfect covering on a curved surface we have added finger gold (used on picture frames) of various shades for an antique effect. Even on the partly decorated mask we have deliberately left the surface looking 'distressed'. Other ways of decorating the masks are with food colours, poster paints, sequins, feathers, fabric, ribbons or jewellery.

When the masks are completed stick a short piece of dowelling to the back of the mask with stiff royal icing or glue. The length of dowelling will depend on how high you want the mask to stand above the cake. Here the prop for one mask is 12″ (30cm) and for the other 9″ (23cm).

6 On a work surface lightly dusted with cornstarch roll out 12oz (350g) gelatin icing and cut out four rectangles 1½″ × 8½″ (4 × 21cm). Allow to dry for four hours, turning the pieces over at least once. The design for the decorative panelling can be found on *p.187*. Trace the design on to parchment paper and enlarge it if necessary to fit your cake. Lay a piece of graphite paper on top of the panel and place the tracing over it. Transfer the design on to the icing and draw over it with black food colour pen. Leave to dry for 10 minutes. Make up black and grey food colours (grey is just watered-down black) and paint the panels as illustrated. Leave to dry for an hour. The small grey geometrics can be further decorated with delicate black lines to produce a marbled effect. When dry fix the panelling to the sides of the cake in the 'picture frames' with a little royal icing.

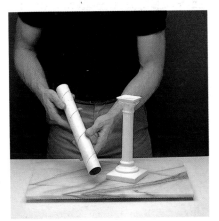

7 The column is modelled on a 9″ (23cm) candlestick. If you do not have a suitable candlestick, you could use the centre of a roll of paper towels to make a simplified column.

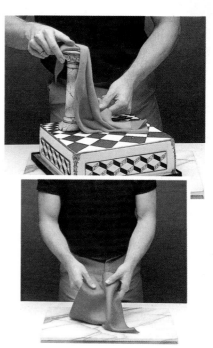

8 On a work surface lightly dusted with cornstarch roll out 6oz (175g) gelatin icing and lay over the candlestick. Gently smooth the icing into the detail. Using a sharp knife, trim away the excess icing from the sides and top, leaving a neat edge at the half-way line. Let the half-iced column dry for several hours or overnight if possible. Repeat the process to make a second half-column and when completely dry stick the two halves together with royal icing. Allow the completed column to dry for four hours.

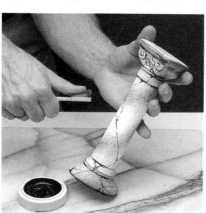

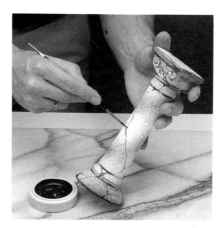

9 To decorate the column make up some fairly thick black food colour. Take a toothbrush and dip the bristles into the colour. Hold the toothbrush as shown and draw your thumb briskly over the bristles to flick a fine mist of colour on to the column. The colour needs to be quite thick to prevent it dripping down the column.

10 With a fine paintbrush, paint a delicate tracing of lines on the column and add decorative lines and swirls at the top and bottom. If you wish, gold highlights could be added too.

11 Fix the column securely in position on top of the cake with stiff royal icing. Allow to dry for an hour. The curtain is made of tragacanth icing – it sets hard when dry but is remarkably elastic while it is being moulded. At a pinch gelatin icing could be used, but this dries out quickly and so might not fold and drape as easily. On a work surface lightly dusted with cornstarch, roll out the tragacanth icing as thinly as possible into a 12″ (30cm) square. Drape it carefully over the column, using royal icing to help stick it to the top. Arrange the curtain decoratively on the surface of the cake. Take care that the weight of the curtain is supported by the cake as well as by the column, or it could split and tear. Once the curtain is safely in position, allow to dry overnight.

ASSEMBLY

Carefully push the dowelling supports on the back of the masks into the surface of the cake and right down to the board. Tie a piece of white baby ribbon round the edge of the cake and secure with a dab of royal icing.

THE TEDDY BEARS' PICNIC

The full range of minute detail can be included in this project when time and patience allow. However, the cake can be simplified in a number of ways without losing the sense of fun. Anyone who receives this cake will have the pleasure of a permanent reminder of the thought you put into it in the shape of a ready-made teddy bears' party to keep.

Cream the butter and sugar together until light and fluffy. Beat in the eggs, one at a time, then a tablespoon of flour. Sift the rest of the flour on to the creamed mixture and fold in using a rubber spatula. Fold in the lemon juice. Turn the mixture into a 9″ (25cm) round greased and lined tin. Bake in a preheated oven at 160°C/325°F/Gas mark 3 for 1½ hours. Cool in a the tin for 5 minutes before turning out on to a wire rack. When it is completely cool remove lining paper.

Slit the cake in half; cover the bottom half with the sweetened ricotta, then with the conserve. Place the top back in position.

TIMESAVERS

TIMESAVER The decoration |in| this particular cake includes all surfaces of the cake and board. To save time it is possible to restrict decoration to the top of the cake. Marzipan and ice the cake as for the three-tiered wedding cake on page 82 and wrap a colourful ribbon round the side.

TIMESAVER Several items on the cake can be replaced with non-edible alternatives. For example, instead of making miniature water lilies, small dried flowerheads can be used, or instead of an umbrella made of icing, a paper cocktail parasol could be included.

TIMESAVER Although the teddy bears are very much a central feature of this cake, it is possible to cut down on the time required to make them. Yellow marzipan is an ideal material in which to mould the bears and they look very good without the addition of swimming costumes and strawhats. In fact by simply decorating the face with black dots for eyes and nose you can make the resulting character just as lovable.

DECORATION: 4 hrs

ICING: 15 mins + 8 hrs drying time

MARZIPAN: 45 mins + 2 hrs drying time

COOKING: 1 hour 45

1 Using a sharp knife, cut a series of steps into the surface and side of the cake to form the waterfall.

2 Spread the top surface of the cake and the waterfall with a thin layer of jam. Roll out 8 oz (225 g) of the marzipan and place on the surface prepared with jam. Mould the marzipan into the steps. Trim the marzipan round the top edge of the cake and the sides of the waterfall. Using a further 8 oz (225 g) of marzipan, cut out a strip to the depth of the cake and place around the side, having first spread the sides of the cake with a thin layer of jam.

TIP BOX

Not everyone is fond of marzipan and it can certainly be rather costly. In order not to waste any of the cake and at the same time cut down on the amount of marzipan used, cut up the cake left after carving the waterfall in step 1 and chop it roughly into blocks. Fix these on to the sides of the cake before marzipanning, using a little jam from the filling, and proceed with step 2, wrapping marzipan over the blocks.

3 Take 6 oz (175 g) of marzipan and mould in a rough crescent shape to form the grassy bank at the back of the cake; spread a little jam on the underside of the marzipan and fix to the surface of the cake. Take 2 oz (50 g) of marzipan and press on to the board to form the bottom of the waterfall. Take 4 oz (125 g) of marzipan and mould into irregular blocks to form the rocks at the side of the waterfall. Fix to the cake with a small amount of jam.

4 Roll out the fondant icing and cover the cake and board. With hands dusted with cornstarch, gently mould the icing to the shape of the cake, emphasizing the details. Trim surplus icing to the edge of the board.

5 Using food colours and paste, mix up a number of shades of blue, adding more water to produce a lighter colour. Take a medium-sized paint brush and, starting near the edge, dab the colour on to the icing to form the lily pond, with darker blue towards the centre to give the impression of depth. Using this same technique, apply the colour to the pool at the base of the waterfall. To achieve the effect of the waterfall, flatten out the bristles of the brush in the food colour, as illustrated, and brush lightly over the steps up the waterfall.

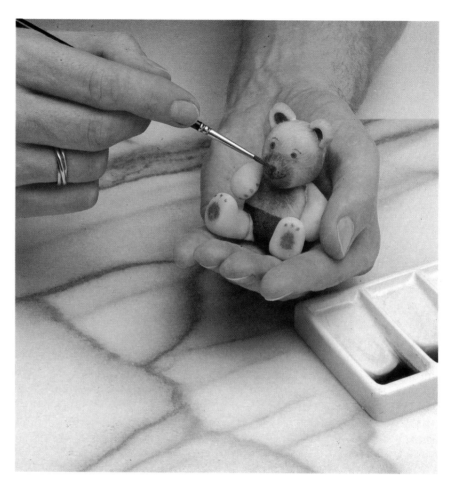

6 To create the grass effect on the bank and around the sides of the waterfall, brush the icing all over with a green food colour. While this is still wet, use a damp paint brush to dab the surface to produce a mottled effect. Paint the stones at the side of the waterfall with a mixture of green and brown food colours.

7 Using 4 oz (125 g) of marzipan for each bear, mould as illustrated. Fix the pieces together in various positions, using a little royal icing.

8 Take a small paint brush and a little brown food colour and paint the features on to the bears. Using one or more bright food colours, add the swimming costumes.

9 Take 4 oz (125 g) of gelatin icing and roll out into a thin sheet. Cut out various sized circles for the plates, cups and lily leaves using a biscuit cutter, or cut around various sizes of coins.

10 To make the straw boaters, once again cut out circles of icing, ensuring that the smaller circle is cut out of a slightly thicker layer of icing. To create the straw effect, while the icing is still damp press gently against the fine wire mesh of a sieve. Lay flat and allow to dry completely. Fix the two circles together, using a little royal icing. Paint and wrap around a short length of narrow ribbon.

11 To form plates, allow the circles of icing to dry in the bottom of a wine glass to produce a slight curve. When dry, paint on a decorative design. To form cups, allow the circles of icing to dry over a thimble. Paint when dry.

13 To make the umbrella, cut out a larger circle of icing, approximately 3″ (7.5 cm) in diameter as illustrated, and allow to dry on a curved surface, such as a ladle. Then paint in bright colours. Attach a thin wooden skewer or toothpick to the underside of the umbrella, using stiff royal icing, and leave to dry.

To make the picnic basket, cut out rectangles of icing. Use a large rectangle at the back to make the lid. Assemble the basket with a little royal icing; paint with food colour to get a straw effect.

To make the tablecloth, cut a square and allow to dry curved over the edge of a square box or cake tin. When dry, paint in a checked pattern with blue food colour.

Attach water lilies, umbrella, straw boaters etc. to the cake with a little royal icing.

12 To make the water lily leaves, cut a narrow wedge from the centre to the edge of a circle of icing, and leave to dry flat. Paint, using green food colour, brushing from the centre to the edge.

To make water lilies, take a small star-shaped flower cutter and press out three stars for each flower. Place one star on top of the other, fixing with a dab of water. Press gently in the centre of the flower. so the petals bend upwards. Allow to dry and paint the centres yellow.

TIPS

Working in miniature and in some detail – for example on the lilies, crockery and parasol – might seem a rather daunting task. A way round this could be to colour the icing before icing and do without the intricate brushwork patterns on the tea service. The parasol could be made from icing in which the colour has been incompletely mixed, producing an attractive marbled effect.

As a special feature, a music box movement has been incorporated into the decoration of the cake in the form of a gramophone. Such music box movements are available in good toy or model shops. To make the gramophone speaker, roll out a thin sheet of gelatin icing and press gently into one of the sections of an egg carton.

Using the remaining gelatin icing, cut out the sides and top of the gramophone, which should be similar in size to a matchbox. Cut a small groove into one side of the box for the winding handle. Fix the box together with a little royal icing. Paint a wood effect with brown food colour. Add the detail of the turntable, record and record arm as illustrated. Using a sharp knife, cut around the top edge leaving a small lip. Allow to dry and paint. Fix on to the gramophone with a small amount of royal icing.

14 Take a small ball of gelatin icing and mould the ducks as illustrated. Score the sides of the duck with a toothpick to produce the impression of wings.

15 Paint as illustrated and attach to cake with a little royal icing.

16 Take a small amount of the remaining gelatin icing and mould fruit, food and bottles as illustrated. Paint with food colours and attach with royal icing.

BODY BEAUTIFUL

A 12″ (30cm) square carrot and fruit cake celebrates health and fitness in the form of the Body Beautiful, pictured on p. 165. achieving a three-dimensional effect without carving or sculpting. Once the first layer of marzipan has been applied to the cake, the muscles and swimming trunks are moulded from different thicknesses of marzipan and fixed in position before the cake is iced.

To make the cake. Mix the sugar, honey, carrots, raisins, dates, nutmeg, butter and water together in a saucepan. Bring to the boil and simmer for 5 minutes. Turn into a mixing bowl and leave to cool. Stir in the beaten eggs. Mix the flours and the baking powder together and sprinkle on to the mixture. Carefully fold in the flour.

Grease and line a 12″ (30cm) square cake tin with waxed paper or cooking parchment. Grease the lined tin and sprinkle with flour. Remove excess flour. Turn the mixture into the prepared tin and bake in a preheated oven at 180°C/350°F/Gas mark 4 for an hour or until firm to the touch. Cool on a wire rack.

TIMESAVERS

TIMESAVER As an alternative to cutting the muscles out of marzipan as described, you could score them into the marzipan covering the cake. Knead it well before applying to make it warm, soft and therefore more pliable. Score the outlines of the muscles with the end of a paintbrush. When the fondant is applied it will settle into the lines and the muscles will become apparent.

TIMESAVER Replace the icing rosette with one that has been won by the recipient of the cake, or tie an extravagant bow at the hip in its place.

INGREDIENTS

Cake
12oz (350g) light brown sugar
1lb (450g) honey
1¼lb (575g) finely grated carrot
12oz (350g) raisins
8oz (225g) chopped dates
2½ teaspoons ground nutmeg
12oz (350g) butter
¾ pint (450ml) water
3 eggs, beaten
12oz (350g) wholewheat flour
12oz (350g) all purpose flour, sifted
6 teaspoons baking powder, sifted

Decoration
16″ (40cm) square cake board
2lb (900g) marzipan
2lb (900g) fondant icing, 1½lb (675g) flesh coloured for the body, 6oz (175g) yellow for the trunks and 2oz (50g) deeper flesh coloured for the nipples
apricot jam
royal icing

Equipment
ribbon for the edge and across the top of the cake

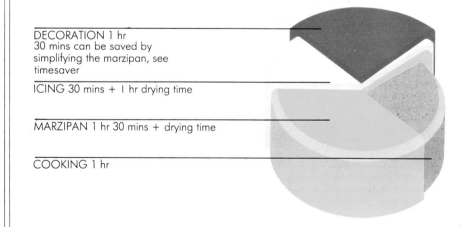

DECORATION 1 hr
30 mins can be saved by simplifying the marzipan, see timesaver

ICING 30 mins + 1 hr drying time

MARZIPAN 1 hr 30 mins + drying time

COOKING 1 hr

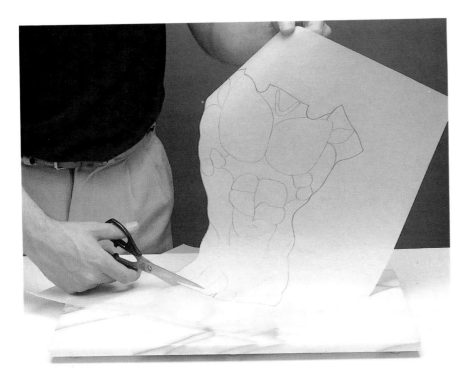

1 Using the design on *p. 188*, trace the outline and details of the muscles on a piece of waxed paper or cooking parchment. Cut out the design.

2 Place the paper outline on top of the cake and cut around.

4 Measure the depth of the cake. Roll out a little of the marzipan and cut out one or more strips to the depth of the cake. Brush the marzipan with apricot jam and fix to the side of the cake. Continue until the sides are completely covered with marzipan. Cut out the chest muscles from the traced design. Roll out a little marzipan fairly thickly and cut around the paper guide.

3 If it is not possible to cut out the entire shape from the cake in one go, simply reassemble the cut-off pieces and complete the cutting as in the illustration.

5 Press the edges of the marzipan pieces to round off the cut edges.

6 Continue cutting individual muscles and the shape of the trunks from the traced design. Roll out the marzipan and continue cutting round the shapes in turn. Gently round off all the cut edges. For complete authenticity, make the chest muscles thicker than the stomach muscles, and the stomach muscles thicker than those around the waist.

7 Reassemble all the prepared pieces as in a jigsaw.

8 Spread the surface of the cake with apricot jam and position the jigsaw of marzipan pieces on the cake. Allow to dry for several hours.

9 Roll out the fondant icing on a work surface lightly dusted with cornstarch. Cover the cake in one piece and gently smooth the icing over the muscles and down around the sides. Trim off the excess icing with a sharp knife. Leave to dry for an hour or so.

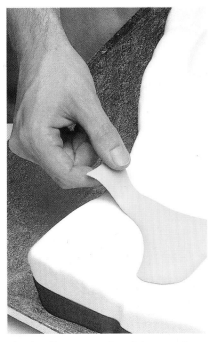

11 Cut out the icing swimming trunks using the appropriate shape on the paper design. Lay them in position on the cake.

10 Take a coloured ribbon and fix to the side of the cake with royal icing at intervals.

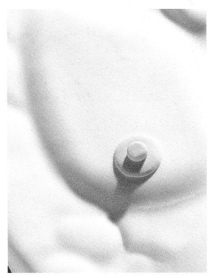

12 Roll out the dark flesh coloured icing and make the nipples. Moisten the icing with a little water and place the nipples on the chest.

13 Roll out the gelatin icing and cut out a circle appropriate to the size of the cake and the required message. Allow to dry. Trace the 'Body Beautiful' lettering or another appropriate message (*see p.185*) on to a piece of parchment or tracing paper. Put a piece of graphite paper over the icing disc and lay the tracing paper on top of it. Write over the top of the lettering to leave a trace on the disc. A number can be added to the decoration if the cake is being given to celebrate a birthday, or the recipient's placing in an athletics, fitness or body-building event. Paint over the design on the disc, which can eventually be kept as a reminder of the event.

15 Fix the icing disc to the ribbon at the hip of the body with a little royal icing.

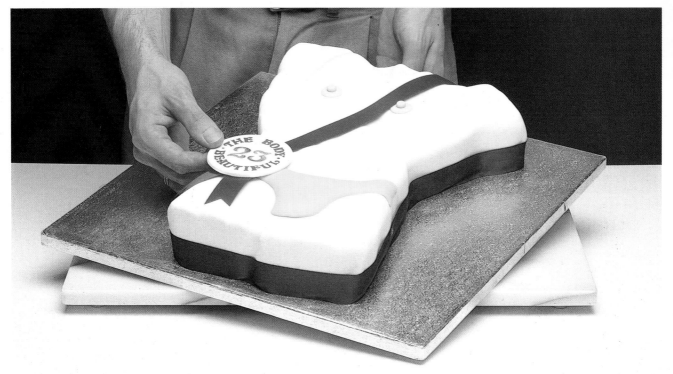

14 Cut a length of ribbon and two shorter pieces as shown and fix across the cake with a little royal icing.

TEAM COLOURS

A 9" (23cm) round carrot cake has been transformed into a prize-winner's ribbon (see p. 169). This bold design is one of the simplest in the book, with the ribbon pieces cut individually from coloured icing. They can be taken off the cake before it is cut and reassembled to be kept as a reminder of the occasion. The colours of the ribbon can be chosen to match those of the recipient's school, college or team.

To make the cake. Sift together the flour, baking powder, bicarbonate of soda, salt and cinnamon. Combine the walnuts and sugar in a bowl and add the eggs. Mix well. Add the melted butter and gently fold in the flour mixture until well incorporated. Mix in the grated carrot. Grease a 9" (23cm) round cake tin and line with waxed paper. Pour the mixture into the tin and level off the surface. Bake in a preheated oven at 180°C/350°F/Gas mark 4 for approximately 1 hour or until firm to the touch. Turn out on to a wire rack to cool.

For the filling, sweeten the ricotta to taste, flavour with the vanilla and spread on the split cake.

INGREDIENTS

Cake
9oz (250g) all purpose flour
2 teaspoons baking powder
1 teaspoon bicarbonate of soda
½ teaspoon salt
1 teaspoon cinnamon
4oz (125g) chopped walnuts
8oz (225g) light brown sugar
3 eggs
4oz (125g) melted butter or margarine
8oz (225g) grated raw carrot

Filling
12oz (350g) unsalted ricotta cheese
powdered sugar to taste
vanilla extract

Decoration
one 12" (30cm) round cake board
1lb (450g) marzipan
1lb (450g) fondant icing
1¼lb (575g) gelatin icing
apricot jam
a little royal icing

Equipment
food colour
ribbon

TIMESAVERS

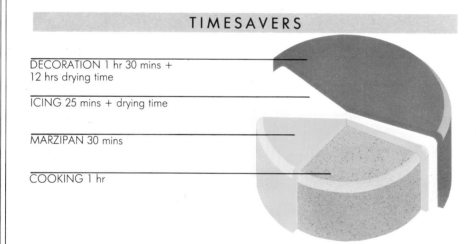

DECORATION 1 hr 30 mins + 12 hrs drying time

ICING 25 mins + drying time

MARZIPAN 30 mins

COOKING 1 hr

1 Cut the cake in half and sandwich together with the filling.

3 On a work surface lightly dusted with cornstarch roll out the fondant icing into a circle

large enough to cover the cake. Lay the icing over the cake and press into the edges. Using a large

2 On a work surface lightly dusted with powdered sugar, roll out 8oz (225g) of the marzipan. Take the tin in which the cake was baked and using the base as a guide cut out a circle of marzipan. Spread the top of the cake with apricot jam and fix the marzipan to the top of the cake. Using

a piece of string measure the circumference of the cake, and also measure its depth. Roll out the remaining 8oz (225g) marzipan and cut out one or two strips according to the measurements taken. Spread the sides of the cake with apricot jam and fix the marzipan on to the cake.

flat-bladed knife held against the sides of the cake, trim off any excess icing and allow to dry for several hours.

6 When the icing is dry trace out the '21' using the numbers on *p. 185*. Transfer the number to the centre of the rosette using graphite paper. Paint the number blue and leave to dry.

4 Take the gelatin icing and colour half of it blue and the other half yellow. Using the designs on *p. 189* trace out the shapes that make up the ribbon to go round the top of the cake and the tail pieces that extend from its edge. Roll out the blue icing and cut out 8 of the ribbon sections.

ASSEMBLY

Wrap the silk ribbon round the edge of the cake and fix with a little royal icing. Place the icing ribbon sections around the top of the cake, alternating the blue and yellow pieces. When evenly spaced, place the rosette centre in the middle. Finally, insert the two tail pieces under the ribbon edging. If the cake is to be transported any distance the individual pieces can be fixed to it with royal icing. Otherwise the pieces are best left loose so that they can be removed and the cake evenly sliced.

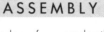

5 Cut out one tail piece in blue. Repeat using the yellow icing and cut an additional circular piece for the centre of the rosette measuring about 4" (10cm) in diameter – a saucer will provide a good cutting guide. Allow the pieces to dry for about 12 hours. Turn each piece over after several hours so that the air gets to both sides.

THATCHED COTTAGE

Four 8" (20cm) square fruit cakes need only simple carving to transform them into a charming country cottage (see p.173). We have used royal icing here instead of fondant, just to show how simply a professional finish can be achieved. The finishing touches are provided by careful hand painting of the thatch and brickwork and a colourful display of country garden flowers.

To make the cake. Mix together the flour, cake crumbs, baking powder and sugar. Rub in the butter or margarine. Beat the eggs with 6floz (180ml) milk. Add to the flour mixture with the fruit and beat thoroughly until mixed. The mixture should be of soft dropping consistency. Add the remaining milk if necessary. Turn the mixture into a greased and lined 8" (20cm) square cake tin and bake in a preheated oven at 180°C/350°F/Gas mark 4 for 1 hour 15 minutes or until golden and firm to the touch. Turn out and allow to cool on a wire rack.

INGREDIENTS

(for one cake)
8oz (225g) wholewheat flour
8oz (225g) cake crumbs
4 teaspoons baking powder
8oz (225g) light brown sugar
4oz (125g) butter or margarine
4 eggs
8floz (240ml) milk
12oz (350g) raisins and/or currants

Decoration
12" (30cm) square cake board
royal icing made with 4 egg whites
2lb (900g) marzipan
apricot jam

Equipment
food colour
lustre powder

TIMESAVERS

DECORATION 1 hr 30 mins +
1 hr for food colour to dry

ICING 1 hr 30 mins + 2 hrs
drying time

MARZIPAN 1 hr 30 mins + 8 hrs
drying time

COOKING 1 hr 15 mins per cake

1 Pile the cakes on top of each other.

2 Use the layers of cake to help you plan the carving of the cottage. Look at all the illustrations before you begin and study the relationship of the individual features to each other and their position on the block of cake. To start carving the roof take a sharp kitchen knife and draw a line across the top of the cake to divide it in half. This line will be the highest point of the roof. Note that the front of the roof features a window extending out from under the thatch. You will need to mark out the window before you cut the roof. Take a knife and draw a 2″ (5cm) square on the third layer beginning 2″ (5cm) in from the right wall. On the right-hand wall mark a line with the knife from the mid-point line drawn on the top cake, to the top of the second layer. Begin cutting the top cake 2″ (5cm) in from the right wall using the slanting line just drawn as a guide, thereby shaping the roof up to the edge of the window. Returning to the top of the cake, cut another 2″ (5cm) section fol-

lowing the same slanting line as before, but this time stopping half way down the roof. Moving to the front of the cake, cut a line into the cake along the top of the square that marks out the window, cutting about 1½″ (4cm) back into the cake. This line should meet up with the slanting line just carved and expose the top of the window. Before carving out the remaining section of the front of the thatched roof, it is important to mark out the chimney.

3 The chimney is 2″ (5cm) wide and is carved into the left wall. With the point of the knife, score two vertical lines 2″ (5cm) apart into the end of the cake, that is one line 3″ (7.5cm) in from each corner. Leave this 2″ (5cm) piece intact but cut ¾″ (2cm) into the wall on either side to expose the chimney. Returning to the top of the cake, take a point 2″ (5cm) in from the outside wall of the chimney and cut a slanting line down towards the left wall ending at the top of the second layer. Obviously you will have to cut around the chimney in order to leave it intact. Cut the remaining section of the front of the roof to expose the window completely. Cut the roof at the back of the cottage to match the angle of the front roof – there is no window here.

4 One additional feature needs to be carved before continuing. Cut out a 1″ (2.5cm) square block from the front left-hand corner of the cake from the board up to the top of the second layer under the roof. This will eventually be the log stove. To produce an overhanging thatched roof, carefully trim away about ¼″ (5mm) from all the walls. Trim away all straight lines and edges on the roof to produce a rounded thatch.

5 Any irregularities in the marzipanning of this cake will be hidden under the royal icing. However, try to be as neat as possible. Before marzipanning each section measure it and cut a piece of marzipan to fit. Spread the cake with apricot jam and fix on the marzipan.

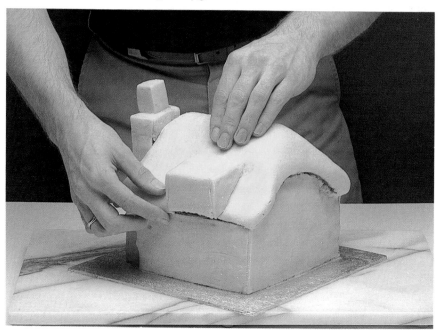

6 Cut a block of marzipan about 1″ (2.5cm) high to stick on top of the chimney for extra height. Stick it on with royal icing. Smooth the surfaces and press the seams together with your fingers to give the cake a rounded appearance. Allow to dry for eight hours or overnight.

7 The royal icing used to cover this cake should be stiff but spreadable. If the icing is too soft, the detail you score into the surface will not hold. Moisten the marzipan with water to make it sticky. Smooth the icing on to the cake with an ordinary kitchen knife or a small spatula. It is a good idea to ice the cake one section at a time, beginning with the roof. The detail should be scored into the wet icing and then left to dry. Make the surface of the icing as regular as possible. If it is not smooth, try dipping your knife into lukewarm water and smoothing it again. You could also do this with a wet finger – in fact all the icing could be applied by hand if you prefer.

8 When one section is completely iced take a bamboo skewer or toothpick and score in the detail. On the roof, score fine vertical lines from top to bottom of the thatch except for two decorative bands as illustrated. Elsewhere, score in details on the windows, door, log stove and beams. When the cake is fully iced allow to dry for two hours.

ASSEMBLY

To make bushes and climbing flowers around the cottage, pile royal icing on the board and against the walls and prick all over with a skewer to make the surface rough. Leave to dry for an hour, then paint in various shades of green, leaving white spaces for the flowers that can be touched in with colour later, as it is difficult to apply colour effectively to a dark green surface. The flowers on the bushes were dabbed thickly with lustre powder. (Note that lustre powder does not stick evenly to vertical surfaces.) Finally, if you wish, lightly dust the thatched roof with gold lustre powder for a magical finish.

9 Paint the cake with a number of food colours. The colour will collect in the scored lines, giving the illusion of texture and depth.

10 Several shades can be brushed into each other on the chimney and the thatch to produce a weathered effect. Do not overload your brush when painting the beams in case the colour drips down and spoils the effect.

LADY LIBERTY

The jaded figure of beautiful Lady Liberty reclines after a gruelling night on the town on a couch of orange marmalade cake (made out of a 12"/30cm square) draped in the Stars and Stripes. Liberty's body is sculpted out of white marzipan and her shades are made of stiff paper. Her jewels are diamanté. *This cake is bound to inspire you with other ideas for portraying the famous at leisure.*

To make the cake. Grease a 12" (30cm) square tin and line with waxed paper. Sift the flour and spices together. Cream the butter or margarine with the sugar and orange rind until light and fluffy. Beat in the eggs two at a time followed by one tablespoon flour after each addition. Fold in the marmalade followed by the remaining flour, orange juice and milk. Spoon the mixture into the prepared tin and level the top. Bake in a preheated oven at 160°C/325°F/Gas mark 3 for 1¼–1½ hours. The cake is ready when risen and firm to the touch. Leave it in the tin for a few minutes, then turn out to cool on a wire rack.

For the filling, cream the butter or margarine and powdered sugar. Mix in the marmalade and orange juice and use to sandwich the pieces of cake together.

TIMESAVERS

DECORATION 3 hrs + 6 hrs drying time
45 mins can be cut from the decoration time by using the Timesavers

ICING 30 mins + 6 hrs drying time

MARZIPAN 40 mins + 1 hr drying time

COOKING 1 hr 30 mins

INGREDIENTS

Cake
1lb (450g) self-rising flour
2 teaspoons ground mixed spice
12oz (350g) butter or margarine
12oz (350g) light brown sugar
grated rind and juice of 2 oranges
6 eggs
4 tablespoons chunky orange marmalade
4 tablespoons milk

Filling
4oz (125g) butter or margarine
12oz (350g) sifted powdered sugar
2 tablespoons marmalade
1 tablespoon orange juice

Decoration
14" (35cm) round cake board
1½lb (675g) yellow marzipan
1 ¼lb (575g) white marzipan
2lb (900g) fondant icing
apricot jam
royal icing

Equipment
food colour
thin stiff paper (an index card is ideal)
diamanté (tiny fake jewels)

2 Using a sharp kitchen knife cut the smaller piece of cake in half on the diagonal. Enjoy the offcut of cake with a cup of tea.

1 Cut the cake into three rectangles 12″ × 4″ (30 × 10cm). Using three quarters of the filling, sandwich two of the pieces together. Cut the remaining piece into two rectangles 4″ × 3″ (10 × 7.5cm). Use the remaining filling to sandwich these two pieces together as illustrated.

3 The front edge, top and back of the cake form three rectangles each measuring 4″ (10cm) in width. To marzipan the cake measure the length of each of these three rectangles. Spread the surfaces with apricot jam. Roll out half the yellow marzipan and cut out three pieces to the measurements just noted. Fix the first piece to the front of the cake. The second covers the top of the lounger and extends up the inclined back. The third piece covers the back of the lounger. To marzipan the sides, hold a piece of parchment or tracing paper against the cake and lightly trace out the shape. Cut a rectangle and a triangle of marzipan to fit. Spread the sides of the cake with apricot jam and fix the pieces in position. Allow the marzipan to dry for an hour or so before proceeding.

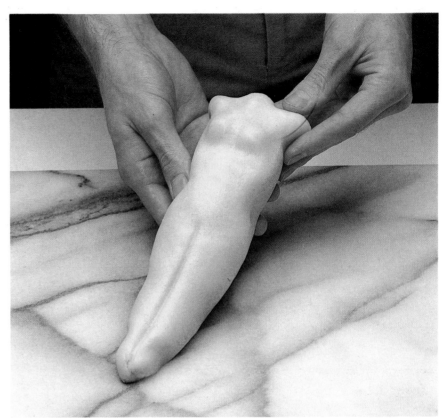

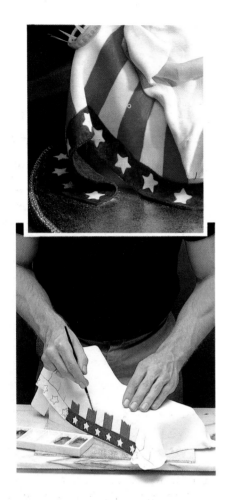

4 Setting 4oz (125g) fondant icing aside, roll out the rest into a large rectangle on a work surface lightly dusted with cornstarch. The piece should be large enough to cover the whole cake and drape decoratively at the corners. Lay the icing over the cake and arrange the folds. Allow to dry for six hours. Trace the design for the stars and stripes from *p.190*. Hold the tracing against the side of the cake and gently score the pattern into the icing. Be very careful not to press too hard, or you could break the icing sheet or the folds. Draw the stars freehand to prevent this if necessary. Paint the background stripe midnight blue, leaving the stars white. Let the blue colour dry for an hour, then paint the Christmas red stripes. Leave to dry while moulding Lady Liberty.

5 To mould the body roll out 1lb (450g) white marzipan into a cylindrical shape tapering slightly towards one end. Pinch the wide end of the piece to make a neck and shoulders. Gently pinch the cylinder a third of the way along to make a waist, then begin to mould the hips, thighs, calves and ankles. Mould the breasts. It is not necessary to mould detail for the feet as Liberty is wearing shoes. Score a line into the marzipan to indicate the separation of the two legs.

TIPS

Painting the stars and stripes on the flag is quite time-consuming. You could colour the icing by kneading red into it before you roll it out and buy a small paper or silk Stars and Stripes — perhaps even two of them — to anchor in the cake above the lady's head.

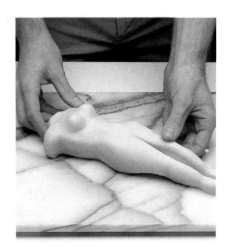

6 With a sharp knife, cut along the line dividing the legs, then round off the cut edges to make them shapely. Put the finishing touches to the body moulding and lay the body in position on the surface of the cake, taking care to leave enough room for the head. If you want one knee bent, support it underneath with the end of a pencil until the marzipan has dried in position, then remove it.

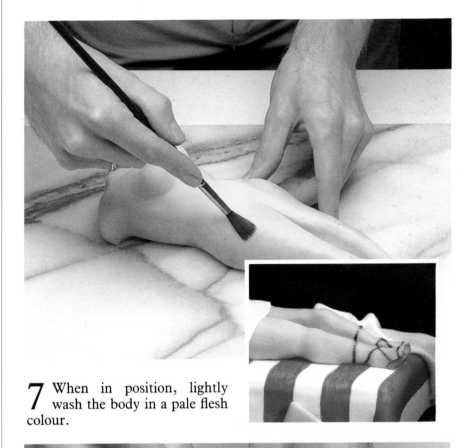

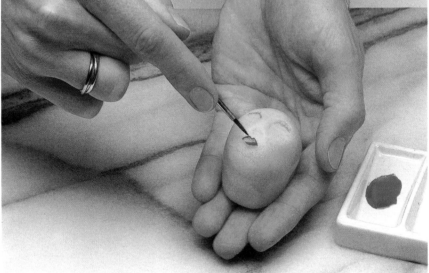

7 When in position, lightly wash the body in a pale flesh colour.

9 To make the arms take 1oz (25g) white marzipan and roll into two sausage shapes about 2½″ (6.5cm) long. Bend in two places for the elbow and wrist and pinch to make a hand. Wash in pale flesh colour and pick out the nails in Christmas red. Allow to dry for an hour. When dry, fix the arm that stretches up and behind the head in position, fixing it to the body with a dab of royal icing. Do not place the other arm in position yet.

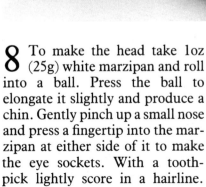

8 To make the head take 1oz (25g) white marzipan and roll into a ball. Press the ball to elongate it slightly and produce a chin. Gently pinch up a small nose and press a fingertip into the marzipan at either side of it to make the eye sockets. With a toothpick lightly score in a hairline. Lightly wash the head in a pale flesh colour except for the hair, which should be golden. If you wish, add a little more colour at the cheekbones for emphasis. When the wash is dry, paint in the eyebrows and lips. Place the head in position on the body, fixing the two parts together with royal icing.

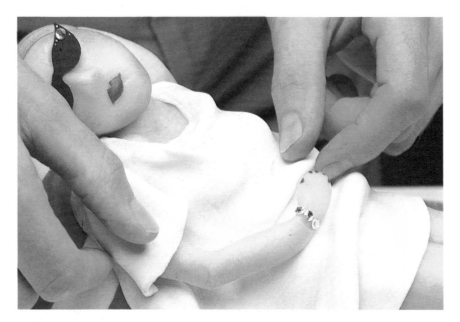

12 To make the regalia take 2oz (50g) white marzipan and mould as illustrated. The points of the crown are made from thin pieces of the card. Brush with peppermint food colour to match the clothing.

10 Take the remaining 4oz (125g) fondant icing and colour a pale peppermint shade. Roll out thinly and cut out a 3″ (7.5cm) square. Arrange the icing round the neck of the statue and drape decoratively over the body. When this piece of icing is in position fix the second arm across the body with a dab of royal icing at the shoulder. Cut out a small triangular piece from the leftover peppermint icing and arrange over the shoulder to make a sleeve. Keep any leftovers. Cut the sunglasses from the card and paint with black food colour. Add tiny pieces of *diamanté* and silver food colour for further effect. Use *diamanté* too to make a bracelet.

ASSEMBLY

Paint further washes of peppermint on to the clothing to add more definition if you wish. Roll out any peppermint icing leftovers and drape over the corner of the lounger to represent discarded layers of clothing. Arrange the regalia. For a truly glamorous effect decorate the edge of the board with *diamanté*.

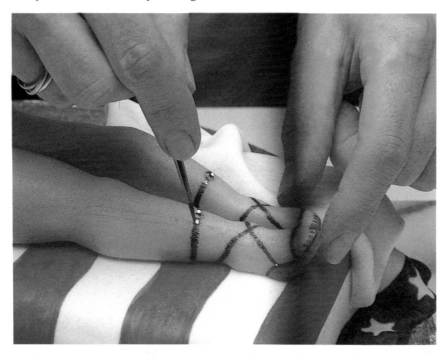

11 To finish the feet, paint on the detail of the shoes and paint the toenails Christmas red. Add small pieces of *diamanté* for glamour.

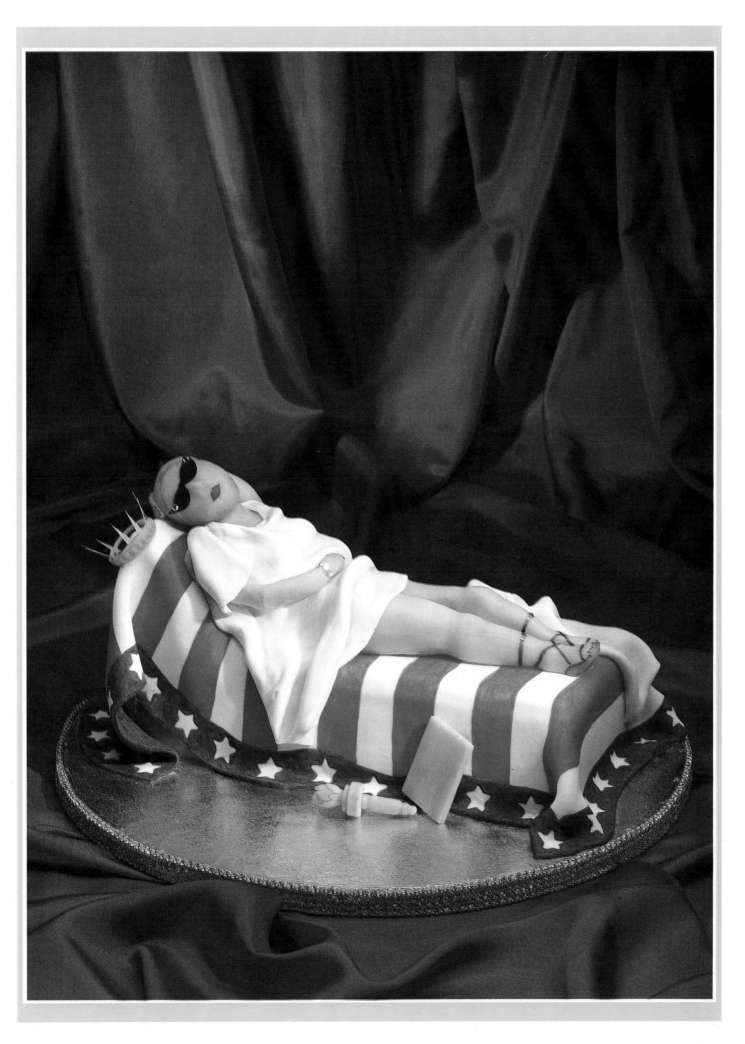

ABCDEFGHIJKLMNOPQRSTUVWXYZ

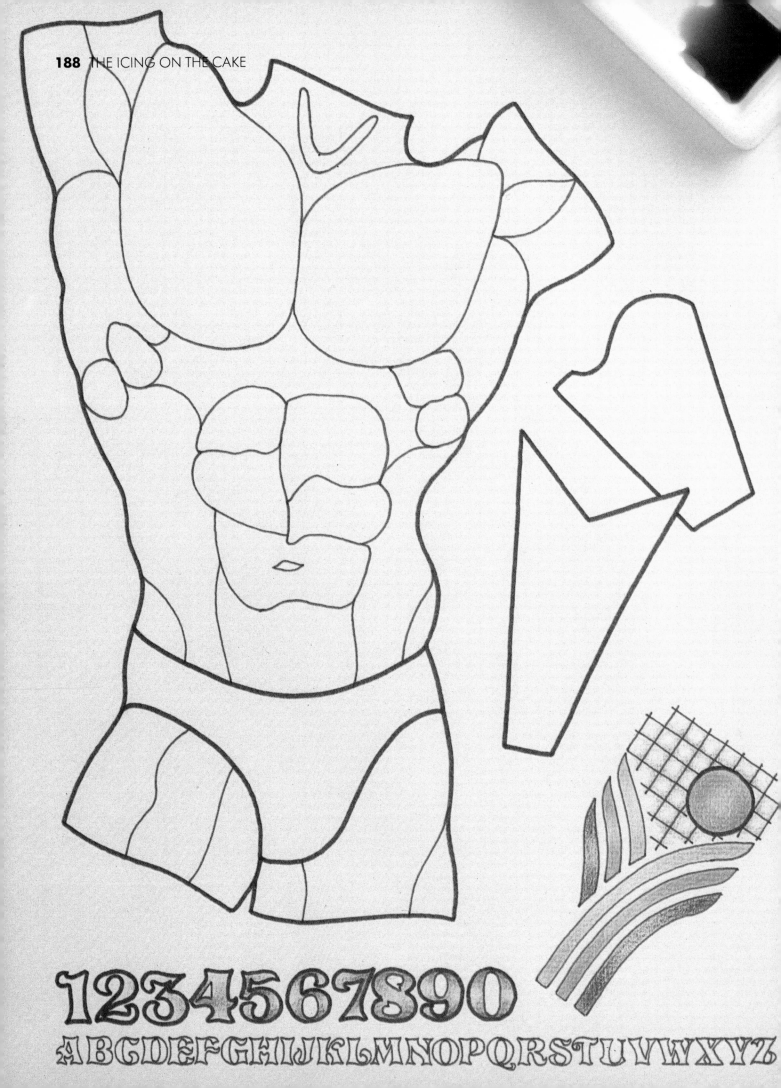

FINE STRUCTURE
OF CELLS
AND TISSUES

By KEITH R. PORTER, Ph.D.

and MARY A. BONNEVILLE, Ph.D.

Department of Biology, Harvard University
Cambridge, Massachusetts

with the collaboration of
SUSAN A. BADENHAUSEN
in electron microscopy

Third Edition

66 Illustrations

Lea & Febiger

Philadelphia · 1968

Third Edition

Copyright © 1968 by Lea & Febiger

All Rights Reserved

First Edition, 1963

Second Edition, September, 1964

Reprinted, October, 1964

Reprinted, January, 1966

Published in Great Britain
by Henry Kimpton, London

German Translation
Springer-Verlag, Berlin

Spanish Translation
El Ateneo, Buenos Aires

Italian Translation
Piccin Editore, Padova

Japanese Translation
Homeido Shoten, Tokyo, 1966

Library of Congress Catalog Card Number: 68–55359

Printed in the United States of America

Preface

This book, a limited collection of micrographs and associated legends, is designed to give the student of histology and cell biology a compact account of the more significant information currently available on cell and tissue fine structure. In this edition we have expanded the collection to include additional cell and tissue types that are exciting for the student and the investigator alike. Moreover, the text of the second edition has been largely rewritten. This was done primarily because the rapid accumulation of information on functional-structural relationship has made obsolete some of the earlier narratives. The objective, then, in this edition has been to provide information at the level required by the more sophisticated student now studying cell biology.

As we have worked on this edition, we have become aware, as have others interested in histology, that the microscopic anatomy of cells and tissues emerging from electron microscopy is rapidly gaining independent status and is superseding much of the older information from light microscopy. The latter, valuable in its time, is being pushed aside by this relatively recent accumulation of knowledge; many of the old questions and problems of thirty years ago have been solved, and entirely new ones are now being investigated. In what manner this shift of emphasis will influence the design of textbooks in cell biology and histology is not a subject for this limited preface except to note that it stimulates one to experiment with various ways of presenting structural information. The textbooks that will evolve will doubtless be different from those written during the first fifty years of this century.

It is our hope, of course, that this book will prove valuable to teachers and students of this subject. They may recognize that the atlas is, in a way, analogous to the classical slide collection, so much a part of past and current education in histology. It may indeed come to be used as a companion to conventional light microscope study. It also represents, we think, a body of information that can be used as a base on which to construct a more advanced course of study for cell and tissue fine structure. For this reason, we encourage reading in the current literature by including after each legend a short bibliography of significant papers.

To a very large extent, the pictures reproduced in this atlas originated in the Laboratory for Cell Biology at Harvard University and have not been published elsewhere. The authors are pleased to acknowledge the assistance of Robert Dell and Rick Stafford in the preparation of the photographic reproductions. To Helen Lyman we owe thanks for the line drawings and the cover design. Pamela Pettingill, our secretary, has dealt patiently and superbly with numerous drafts. Supplementary micrographs of special interest have been generously provided by investigators in other laboratories, and acknowledgments to them are made in the text. Finally, we are indebted to several friends who have contributed criticism and advice, and most especially to Helen Padykula, Geraldine Gautier, and A. Kent Christensen.

Keith R. Porter
Mary A. Bonneville

Cambridge, Massachusetts

iii

Contents

List of Abbreviations and Symbols

A	A Band	Lu	Lumen
a, b, c, d	Regions of Intercalated Disk	Ly	Lysosome
Ac	Acrosome	M	M Line
Ar	Arteriole	M	Mitochondrion
AS	Alveolar Sac	Mb	Microbody
BB	Basal Body	MD	Mucous Droplet
BC	Bile Canaliculus	Mt	Microtubule
BM	Basement Membrane (Basal Lamina)	Mv	Microvillus
C	Cilium	My	Myelin
Ca	Canaliculus	N	Nucleus
Ce	Centriole	NE	Nerve Ending
CeS	Centriolar Satellite	Nf	Neurofilaments
Ch	Chromatin	NF	Nerve Fiber
Chr	Chromosome	Ng	Neuroglial Cell
Co	Collagen	Ni	Nissl Body
Col	Collecting Tubule	Nu	Nucleolus
Cor	Stratum Corneum	NuE	Nuclear Envelope
Cp	Capillary	O	Oocyte
Cr	Crista	OR	Olfactory Rod
CT	Connective Tissue	OV	Olfactory Vesicle
D	Desmosome	P	Pore
DB	Dense Body	PC	Pigment Cell
E	Erythrocyte	PM	Plasma Membrane
El	Elastic Fibers	Pr	Process
Ell	Ellipsoid	Pt	Pit
En	Endothelium	R	Ribosome
Ep	Epithelium	RB	Residual Body
ER	Endoplasmic Reticulum	SC	Schwann Cell
F	Fibrocyte or Fibroblast	SD	Secretion Droplet
Fe	Ferritin	SER	Smooth Endoplasmic Reticulum
Fl	Filament	Sl	Slit
FP	Foot Process	SM	Smooth Muscle
FS	Fibrous Sheath	Sn	Sinusoid
FV	Fusiform Vesicle	Sp	Stratum Spinosum
FZ	Fibrillar Zone	SR	Sarcoplasmic Reticulum
G	Golgi Complex	St	Stalk
Ge	Stratum Germinativum	T	Tonofilaments and Tonofibrils
Gl	Glycogen	TB	Terminal Bar
Gr	Granule	Tc	Thrombocyte
Gra	Stratum Granulosum	Th	Thymocyte or Platelet
Gu	Gutter	TS	Tubular System
GZ	Granular Zone	Tu	Tubule
H	H Band	TW	Terminal Web
H	Hemoglobin	UM	Unit Membrane
HD	Hemosiderin Deposits	US	Urinary Space
I	I Band	V	Vesicle
JF	Junctional Fold	Z	Z Line
L	Lipid	Z	Zymogen Granule
Lc	Lymphocyte	ZA	Zonula Adhaerens
LF	Liquor Folliculi	ZO	Zonula Occludens
LH	Loop of Henle	ZP	Zona Pellucida

FINE STRUCTURE
OF CELLS
AND TISSUES

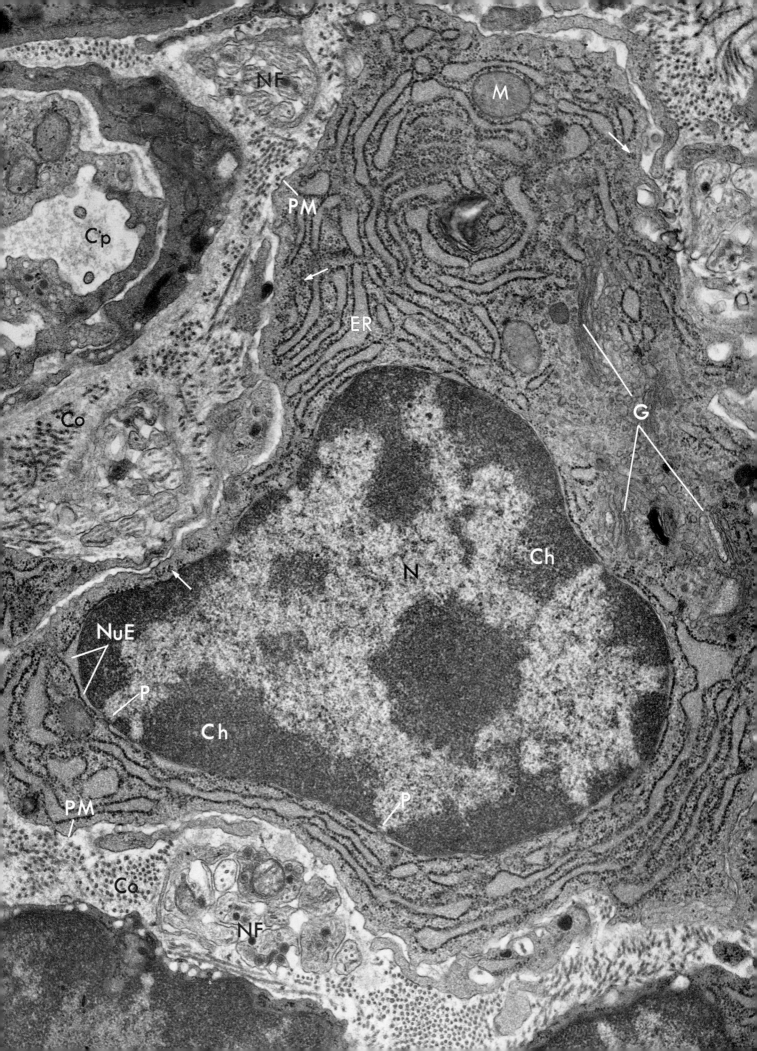

PLATE 1
The Plasma Cell

This micrograph of a plasma cell illustrates some of the structural detail revealed by electron microscopy and serves to introduce several of the systems and organelles repeatedly observed in most cell types. The clarity and richness of detail, especially of cytoplasmic structures, when observed even at relatively low magnifications, are a product of the resolving power of the electron optical system.

The plasma cell is readily identified under the light microscope by a combination of almost unmistakable features that are also easily recognized in electron micrographs. Following most fixation procedures (in this case glutaraldehyde followed by osmium[1]) the nucleus (N) takes on a "cartwheel" appearance due to the prominent clumping of dense granular chromatin (Ch) at its center and around its periphery. The chromatin, named because of its affinity for certain dyes, is the nuclear component richest in deoxyribonucleic acid or DNA. This is, of course, the material within which is coded the information necessary for maintenance of the cell's life and the determination of its special functions. In this dense form the chromatin is referred to by cytologists as heterochromatin and is believed to be in a relatively inactive state (see Plate 4). We might presume that information in the heterochromatin, while perhaps not functional in the plasma cell, had previously been decoded and used in some earlier cell generation. The less dense nuclear material, which displays little affinity for dyes in light microscope preparations, is called euchromatin. It is now thought that only in such regions is genetic information being transcribed for a particular cell. Note that the zones of euchromatin extend to the pores (P) in the nuclear envelope (NuE), while the heterochromatin is confined to the interpore areas. To reach the cytoplasm, information in the form of messenger RNA (one type of ribonucleic acid) must traverse the nuclear envelope, probably in the pore regions. (The nuclear envelope is discussed more fully in Plate 2, and details of nuclear structure are given in Plate 4.)

The appearance of the cytoplasm suggests to the experienced cell biologist that intense synthetic activity is occurring, since two systems known to be associated with the production of protein

for export from the cell, the rough-surfaced endoplasmic reticulum (ER) and the Golgi region (G), are both extensively developed. The markedly basophilic regions of plasma cell cytoplasm that characterize its light microscope image are now known with certainty (see Plate 2) to correspond to piles of large flattened sacs (cisternae) studded on their outer surfaces with ribosomes, particles of ribonucleoprotein. It is these that give the cytoplasm its special affinity for basic dyes. The cisternae shown here represent one structural form adopted by the endoplasmic reticulum, a membranous intracellular system that serves somewhat different functions in different cell types (see, for example, Plates 7, 11, 12, 14, 15, 18, 19, 38). The ribosomes are the sites of protein synthesis. In the plasma cell much of the protein product formed is sequestered within the cisternae and is seen in this micrograph as finely particulate material of medium density present within the sacs (see below).

The second cytoplasmic organelle of special prominence in the plasma cell is, as just mentioned, the Golgi complex (G). In the plasma cell it occupies an extensive juxtanuclear region and displays its typical configuration, i.e., stacks of flattened sacs and associated vesicles. Both are delimited by smooth-surfaced membranes. The Golgi, which appears under the light microscope as an unstained area when basic dyes are applied, was for many years the subject of controversy and discussion among light microscopists, many of whom regarded it as an artifact. At present not only is its morphology well established, but its several functions are being revealed. Prominent among these is the role of the Golgi in packaging protein and complex carbohydrate products of the cell into membrane-bounded granules, which are subsequently secreted (see Plates 11 and 12).

The mitochondria (M), although not particularly numerous in plasma cells, are easily identified by their size and general structural plan (described in connection with Plate 2). They are well known as organelles active in the production of energy-rich compounds by aerobic metabolic pathways.

The organelles described above are embedded in a cytoplasmic ground substance. Among its several functions it serves as a reservoir for compounds that will be needed to produce secretory

---

[1] See page 189 for general description of techniques.

products (the major activity of the plasma cell) and to repair the structural components of the organelles themselves. Free ribosomes (arrows) are included in the ground substance and in this location are thought to participate in the formation of proteins that are retained within the cell as part of the cytoplasmic machinery.

The plasma cell—and indeed all cells—is enclosed in a plasma membrane (PM), which in transverse sections appears as a thin dense line. This lipoprotein structure is semipermeable; that is, it acts as a selective barrier, exerting control over the passage of ions and small molecules into and out of the cell. Certain molecules are prevented from entering, but others are taken in or expelled preferentially by "active" transport. The latter term implies that energy is expended to overcome adverse concentration gradients and to "pump" essential substances across the membrane. The basic substructure common to plasma membranes and to cytoplasmic membranes is discussed in Plate 2.

The highly ordered and complex cytoplasmic organization of the plasma cell is a manifestation of its mature or differentiated state, in which it performs special functions. Several lines of evidence indicate that this cell, which is found in certain areas of connective tissue, is most important in the formation of circulating antibodies. By this, of course, is meant that in response to a number of foreign materials (called antigens) these cells produce proteins (antibodies), which combine specifically with the foreign antigens. The animal containing the responding plasma cells is then said to be immunized. This highly specific reaction serves to protect the organism against the harmful effects of extraneous substances.

Direct evidence of plasma cell involvement in the synthesis of antibodies and information on the precise localization of the sites of synthesis within the cell can now be obtained by electron microscopy. If, for example, the plasma cells from an animal immunized against horse ferritin (an iron-rich protein) are appropriately fixed, exposed to ferritin, and then prepared for electron microscopy, it is found, as illustrated in the accompanying text figure 1a, that the ferritin

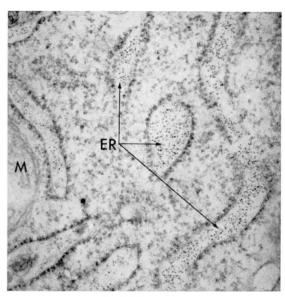

Text Figure 1a

This electron micrograph, kindly supplied by S. de Petris, shows a part of a plasma cell from a rabbit hyperimmunized against ferritin. This cell and others were fixed with formalin, frozen, thawed twice (to open the cells), and then exposed to the antigen. The dense particles in the ER cisternae (ER) represent ferritin in combination with antibody. A mitochondrion (M) is included in part at the left.

Magnification × 61,000

molecules can be visualized as dense particles (because of their iron cores) and that they are associated specifically with the contents of the ER cisternae. This reaction marks the location of the antibody and shows that, like other proteins, it is segregated in these cavities after synthesis.

4

Similar observations have been made using other proteins as antigens and then linking these to ferritin as a marker. These experiments stem in turn from earlier fundamental studies in which antigen or antigen-antibody complexes were localized in tissues with the aid of fluorescent dyes and light microscopy.

The plasma cell in this micrograph lies within a connective tissue ground substance rich in collagen fibers (Co). Bundles of thin unmyelinated nerve fibers (NF) and the cross section of a small blood vessel (Cp) may also be identified.

In the plasma cell and in other cells and tissues presented in this atlas are found homologous structures that occur almost universally in living cells; these are the structures concerned with maintaining processes vital to the life of the individual cell. In addition, these same components show great diversity and specialization related to the performance of specific functions, i.e., functions peculiar to each of the wide variety of cell and tissue types characteristic of multicellular organisms. The correlation of this diversity in form at the fine structural level with diversity in function, which is the current interest of many investigators, makes this period one of the more exciting in the history of cell biology.

From the submucosa of the rat (*Mus norvegicus*)
Magnification × 29,000

References

Note: The first five plates of this edition of the atlas serve as a general introduction to the concepts of cell structure in accord with current knowledge, especially that derived from electron microscopy. Descriptions of cell organelles touched on briefly in Plate 1 are referred to in greater detail in Plates 2-5, where pertinent references to each are given. The student may find it helpful to read introductory chapters in standard textbooks of histology before studying original research papers. The article by Brachet, cited below, will also be helpful. The remaining three references given here deal with the specific function of the plasma cell.

BRACHET, J. The living cell. *Sci. Amer., 205:*51 (September, 1961).

COONS, A. H., LEDUC, E. H., and CONNOLLY, J. M. Studies on antibody production. I. A method for the histochemical demonstration of specific antibody and its application to a study of the hyperimmune rabbit. *J. Exp. Med., 102:*49 (1955).

DE PETRIS, S., KARLSBAD, G., and PERNIS, B. Localization of antibodies in plasma cells by electron microscopy. *J. Exp. Med., 117:*849 (1963).

RIFKIND, R. A., OSSERMAN, E. F., HSU, K. C., and MORGAN, C. The intracellular distribution of gamma globulin in a mouse plasma cell tumor (X5563) as revealed by fluorescence and electron microscopy. *J. Exp. Med., 116:*423 (1962).

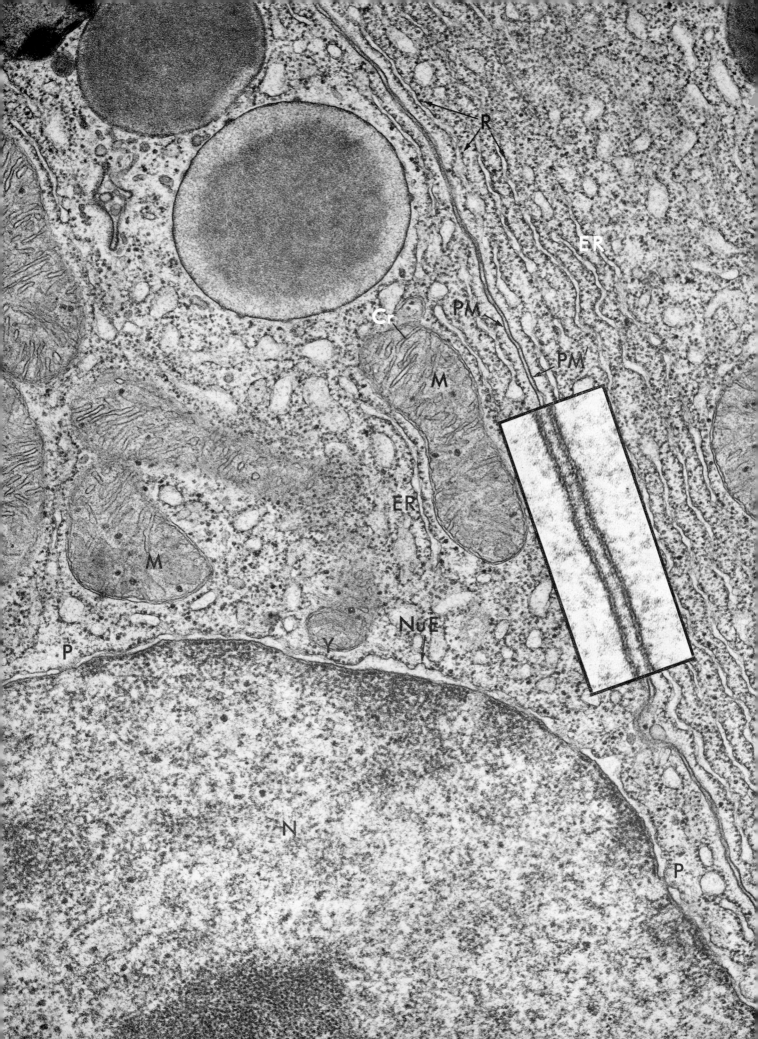

PLATE 2

Cell Systems and Organelles:
Endoplasmic Reticulum, Nuclear Envelope,
Plasma Membrane, and Mitochondria

From viewing this and the preceding plate one may reasonably gain the impression that the cytoplasm of cells is a confusion of membranes and particles so complex as to defy understanding. Though quite justified, this first impression has not apparently discouraged attempts to unravel the obvious complexities; instead, it has probably served to stimulate their investigation. Thus some cell biologists have undertaken widely ranging comparative studies of different cell types to determine how commonly the observed structures occur and to note any constant correlation between form and known functional specialization. Others have essentially disassembled the cell and isolated by centrifugation fractions rich in one or the other of the cytoplasmic substructures. Straightforward analyses of these fractions for their composition and enzymic properties have given valuable information as to the intracellular distribution of biochemical processes and clues to the significance of various structural features. It is now realized, for example, that membranes, which occur in such great profusion in some cytoplasmic systems and organelles, provide relatively large surfaces upon which packets of enzymes and genetic information may be distributed according to a functionally important plan. The spaces limited by such membranes serve as sites for the sequestration of products of the cell's synthetic activity. The organized and frequently patterned distribution of finely divided substructures and surfaces seems designed to bring enzyme and source of substrate closer together or energy-rich compound closer to where it is needed. Diffusion distances, which could be rate limiting for physiological processes, are thus made less significant.

One of the more remarkable of the systems involved in these several roles is called the endoplasmic reticulum (ER). This complex of membrane-limited spaces extends to nearly all parts of the cytoplasm and thus endows the cell with an extensive intracytoplasmic compartment, separate from the cytoplasmic ground substance. In a thin section of a fully differentiated cell of the pancreas, shown here and also in the plasma cell shown in Plate 1, the ER is constructed in large part of thin flattened sacs, or cisternae, which appear in section profile as long, slender, membrane-limited spaces of homogeneous content suspended in a particle-rich matrix. Many of the 100 to 150 A particles, the ribosomes (R), are attached to the outer surfaces of the cisternae—an association that is universal in cells manufacturing proteins for export. Visualization of the entire system as it exists in a cell is, of course, impossible from a single thin section, but from the study of many sections cut at different angles and planes through the cell the total form can be reconstructed. Actually the existence of this system, as well as its spatial arrangement, was first observed in electron micrographs of thinly spread whole cells, where it could be seen *in toto*.

Our concepts of the endoplasmic reticulum, which have greatly expanded in recent years, are actually based on observations going back to the beginning of the century. In 1899, Garnier and Matthews independently described the basophilic properties of certain regions of the cytoplasm, called the ergastoplasm, and pointed out that this basophilic component is prominently developed in certain secretory cells. Several decades passed before the distribution of this component in the cytoplasm was shown to coincide with the distribution of ribonucleic acid (RNA). This discovery rested mainly on two observations, namely that the property of basophilia could be destroyed by the enzyme ribonuclease (which hydrolyzes RNA) and that the ergastoplasm, like RNA, strongly absorbs ultraviolet light in the wavelength of about 260 mμ.

Another exciting phase of this work began in the late 1940's, when correlative experiments involving electron microscopy and differential centrifugation resolved, with a wealth of detail formerly impossible, the structure and function of the ergastoplasm. A tiny vesicular element, the microsome of cell fractions, was identified as a fragment of the rough-surfaced endoplasmic reticulum. And labeled amino acids, provided experimentally to an animal's circulation, quickly became part of proteins in the microsomes. For the first time, then, the investigator could identify the rough-surfaced endoplasmic reticulum with protein synthesis. Experiments of a similar kind later narrowed this function to the RNA-rich ribosomes. Further reference to this provocative work is given in the text for Plate 11.

Little concrete information is available concerning the function of the ER membranes. When high resolution micrographs are obtained, these membranes can be shown to share a common

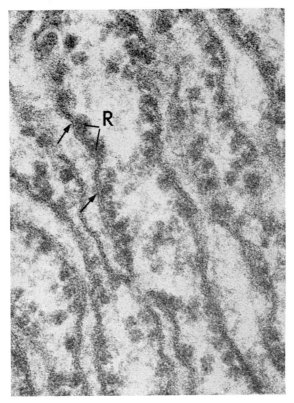

Text Figure 2a

In this high resolution electron micrograph, the ribosomes (R) and their relation to the ER membranes are particularly well shown. Like other cytoplasmic membranes, those of the ER are trilaminar (arrows). The ribosomes are closely adherent to the membrane, but whether at the zone of contact they are structurally integrated with the outer leaflet of the membrane cannot be easily decided. It is pertinent in this regard that the attachment is not a permanent one, inasmuch as the ribosomes are known to dissociate from the membrane surface. (This micrograph has been kindly provided by E. De Harven and is reproduced from *Methods in Cancer Research*, vol. I, H. Busch, editor, New York, Academic Press, 1967.)

From the liver of the mouse (*Mus musculus*)
Magnification × 150,000

structure with other cytoplasmic membranes (see below and also text figure 2a). That they have special permeabilities is manifest in their ability to sequester within the cavities they limit products synthesized by the ribosomes on their surfaces. Furthermore, in the living cell the membranes seem extraordinarily labile and lend themselves to the remodeling that the ER constantly undergoes in response to shifts in physiological conditions. The remodeling may involve changes in area, modification from rough to smooth form and from lamellar cisternae to reticular, as well as changes in location relative to the mitochondria, the Golgi, and the cell surface.

Thin sections of the kind depicted here also reveal a close relationship between the ER and the membrane system surrounding the nucleus (the nuclear membrane of classical cytology). As can be seen, the nucleus (N) is enclosed by a system of two membranes, aptly named the nuclear envelope (NuE). The space enclosed by these membranes has been repeatedly observed to be continuous with that within the membranes of the endoplasmic reticulum. As a consequence the envelope can be regarded as a special portion of the ER, or, if one prefers, the cytoplasmic ER is an outgrowth of the envelope that is ever present in nucleated cells. Its outer surface at least is like ER membranes, studded with ribosomes (as at Y); its inner membrane is in close contact with the heterochromatin (see Plates 1 and 4).

The nuclear envelope has a few other interesting properties. It is, for example, interrupted by pores (P). Moreover, the inner and outer membranes are continuous around the rim of the pore. In spite of this arrangement it seems unlikely that there is free passage for large molecules between the interphase nucleus and the cytoplasm of most cell types, for in micrographs of excellent quality a diaphragm of dense material is often found filling each gap in the envelope. At least one investigator has shown that this constitutes a barrier for macromolecules like ferritin. These observations have aroused interest because the currently accepted theory of protein synthesis requires movement of RNA molecules (e.g., messenger, transfer, and ribosomal RNA's) between nucleus and cytoplasm.

Different sorts of membranes are distinguishable in electron micrographs. For instance, the plasma membranes (PM) and (PM') of the two adjacent secretory cells differ from the cytoplasmic membranes in several respects: they are without attached ribosomes, and they are slightly thicker (100 A) than those of the ER (70 A). Except at isolated and special sites, the surface membrane of one cell never fuses with its neighbor's. Instead, it is usual for the plasma membrane of adjacent cells to be separated by a distance of at least 200 A, a fact taken to indicate the presence of a thin layer of material (a mucopolysaccharide-rich layer called the glycocalyx) on the outer surface of each membrane. As apparent in the inset on this figure, each plasma membrane can be resolved at high magnifications into two dense layers (protein) and an intermediate layer of lower density (lipid). This trilaminar structure has been called the unit membrane, and it seems to represent a universally occurring organization in plasma membranes and cytoplasmic membranes alike (see text figure 2a).

Maintaining complex cell structure and carrying out various physiological processes impose a constant need for energy on living cells. Living systems as we know them utilize as an immediate source of energy the compound adenosine triphosphate (ATP), which they are able to manufacture and to some degree store. Both aerobic and nonaerobic (anaerobic) processes can produce ATP, but in the cells of vertebrates the former is the more efficient and important. By again exploiting the techniques of cell fractionation, biologists showed some twenty years ago that cytoplasmic particles with certain sedimentation properties were capable of oxidizing fatty acids and producing ATP aerobically. Microscopic examination of the granules established that they were mitochondria, structures long recognized as an almost universal component of cytoplasm.

Once techniques for thin sectioning of cells were developed, it was found that mitochondria (M) possess a common structural plan. Their identification in sections is thus assured. Variations in their morphology exist from cell type to cell type, but they are always seen to be limited by two lines that represent the two membranes constituting the wall of these tiny organelles. As revealed at the higher magnification shown in text figure 2b,

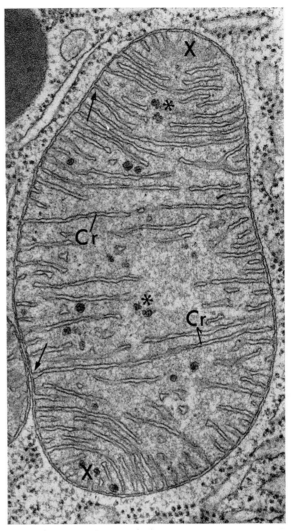

Text Figure 2b

A longitudinal section of a mitochondrion from the pancreas of the bat exemplifies the basic structural plan common to all these organelles. The arrows indicate places at which the inner of the two membranes limiting the mitochondrion is clearly continuous with that forming the cristae (Cr). Dense granules (*) are suspended in a relatively less dense matrix. Mitochondria are known to grow in length, and growing points of this organelle are perhaps represented by areas (X) at either end of it.

From the pancreas of the bat
Magnification × 64,000

9

the inner of the two membranes is folded into shelf-like structures, the cristae (Cr), which project into the homogeneous matrix that fills the cavity of the mitochondrion. Where the energy requirements of the cell are greater, as in heart muscle (Plate 39), the mitochondria are more numerous, and the number of cristae is greater, presumably to provide a larger surface area for the organized distribution of the resident enzymes. Dense granules, 20–30 mμ in diameter, also evident in the matrix, are now known to represent accumulations of bound divalent metallic ions (Ca^{++} and Mg^{++}) required for mitochondrial enzyme systems.

Electron micrographs, of course, present a completely static picture, but in time-lapse cinematography of living cells it is strikingly apparent that mitochondria stretch and contract, move about in the cell, and seem to coalesce and divide. Such properties as growth and division suggest a measure of autonomy or semi-autonomy for mitochondria, and a number of recent studies of them are consistent with this notion. For example, contractile protein, as well as specific nucleic acids (both RNA and DNA), has been found within them. There has also been advanced more sophisticated evidence that new mitochondria arise only by division of pre-existing mitochondria.

From the pancreas of the frog (*Rana pipiens pipiens*)
Magnification $\times$ 43,000
Inset $\times$ 216,000

References

Bennett, H. S. Morphological aspects of extracellular polysaccharides. *J. Histochem. Cytochem., 11*:14 (1963).

Claude, A. Fractionation of mammalian liver cells by differential centrifugation. I. Problems, methods, and preparation of extract. *J. Exp. Med., 84*:51 (1946).

————. Fractionation of mammalian liver cells by differential centrifugation. II. Experimental procedures and results. *J. Exp. Med., 84*:61 (1946).

Feldherr, C. M. Binding within the nuclear annuli and its possible effect on nucleocytoplasmic exchanges. *J. Cell Biol., 20*:188 (1964).

Lehninger, A. L. The Mitochondrion. Molecular Basis of Structure and Function. New York, W. A. Benjamin, Inc. (1964).

Littlefield, J. W., Keller, E. B., Gross, J., and Zamecnik, P. C. Studies on cytoplasmic ribonucleoprotein particles from the liver of the rat. *J. Biol. Chem., 217*:111 (1955).

Palade, G. E. A small particulate component of the cytoplasm. *J. Biophysic. and Biochem. Cytol., 1*:59 (1955).

————. An electron microscope study of the mitochondrial structure. *J. Histochem. Cytochem., 1*:188 (1953).

————, and Siekevitz, P. Liver microsomes: an integrated morphological and biochemical study. *J. Biophysic. and Biochem. Cytol., 2*:171 (1956).

Porter, K. R. The endoplasmic reticulum: some current interpretations of its forms and functions. *In* Biological Structure and Function. T. W. Goodwin and O. Lind-berg, editors. New York, Academic Press, vol. I (1961) p. 127.

————. Observations on a submicroscopic basophilic component of cytoplasm. *J. Exp. Med., 97*:727 (1953).

Redman, C. M., Siekevitz, P., and Palade, G. E. Synthesis and transfer of amylase in pigeon pancreatic microsomes. *J. Biol. Chem., 241*:1150 (1966).

Robertson, J. D. Design principles of the unit membrane. *In* Principles of Biomolecular Organization. Ciba Foundation Symposium, G. E. W. Wolstenholme and M. O'Connor, editors. London, J. and A. Churchill Ltd. (1966) p. 357.

Sabatini, D. D., Tashiro, Y., and Palade, G. E. On the attachment of ribosomes to microsomal membranes. *J. Molec. Biol., 19*:503 (1966).

Siekevitz, P., and Palade, G. E. A cytochemical study on the pancreas of the guinea pig. V. *In vivo* incorporation of leucine-1-C[14] into the chymotrypsinogen of various cell fractions. *J. Biophysic. and Biochem. Cytol., 7*:619 (1960).

Sjöstrand, F. S., and Elfvin, L.-G. The layered, asymmetric structure of the plasma membrane in the exocrine pancreas cells of the cat. *J. Ultrastruct. Res., 7*:504 (1962).

Stoeckenius, W. Structure of the plasma membrane. *Circulation, 26*:1066 (1962).

Watson, M. L. Further observations on the nuclear envelope of the animal cell. *J. Biophysic. and Biochem. Cytol., 6*:147 (1959).

Yamamoto, T. On the thickness of the unit membrane. *J. Cell Biol., 17*:413 (1963).

10

PLATE 3

Cell Systems and Organelles:
The Cell Center with Centriole and Golgi Complex

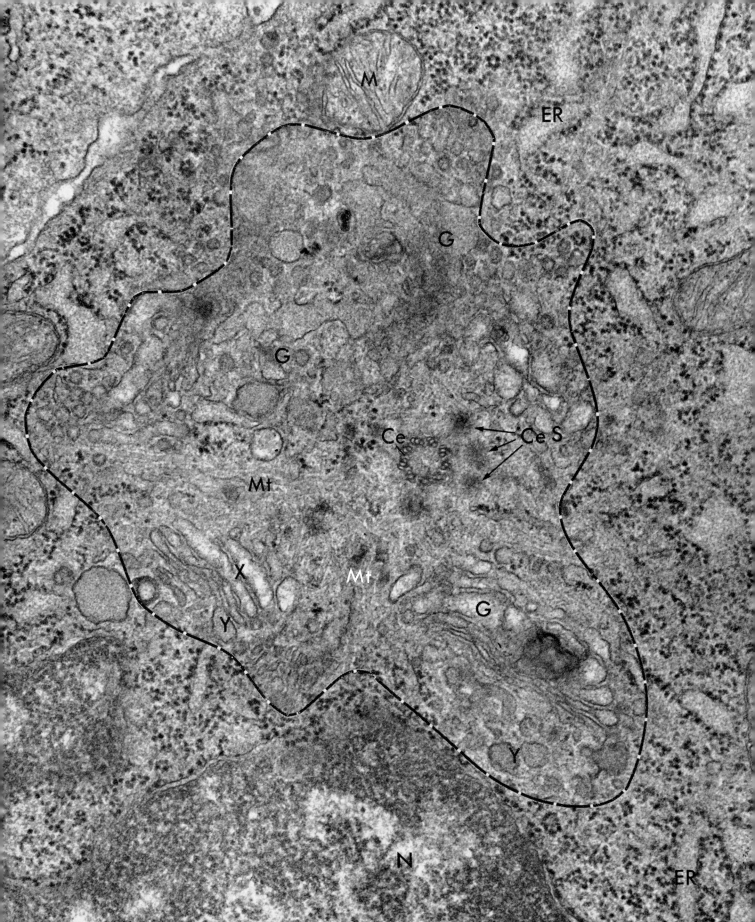

PLATE 3

Cell Systems and Organelles:
The Cell Center with Centriole and Golgi Complex

It is common for tissue cells to show evidence of polarity or a roughly radial organization around a center called the cytocentrum or centrosphere. In animal cells two paired structures of unique design, the centrioles, generally reside at the focal point of this organization. In order to discover the nature of the influence (structural or physiological) that emanates from this point, investigators must apply a variety of techniques in addition to electron microscopy. It must be admitted, however, that even now no completely clear understanding of the basis for cell polarity and organization has been achieved.

The cytocentrum depicted here within the broken line lies near one pole of the nucleus (N). Most of the larger cell organelles, such as the mitochondria (M) and rough-surfaced endoplasmic reticulum (ER), are excluded from it. Micromanipulation studies reveal the centrosphere to be more gelatinous than other parts of the cytoplasm, so that free movement of organelles into the region may be prevented. The central zone of this region is occupied by the paired cylindrical centrioles ($0.2\ \mu$ in diameter), of which one is shown here in cross section (Ce), together with closely associated centriolar satellites (CeS). (The second centriole, if evident in the section, would be oriented with its long axis at $90°$ to that of the one shown.) A myriad of microtubules (Mt), quite closely packed, radiate from this central zone. These are slender (240 A diameter) rods, viewed here for the most part as running obliquely through the section.

In its fine structure, as shown here in cross section, the centriole is made up of nine triplets consisting of small, tubular structures (microtubules). The triplets are equidistant from one another and from the central axis of the bundle. It is evident as well that this precise organization extends to the small masses of dense material, the satellites, for they too are radially arranged about the centriolar axis at a uniform distance. Occasionally a second or even a third order of these bodies can be identified.

Near the margins of the cytocentrum in this plasma cell one observes elements of the Golgi complex (G). As mentioned in the text of Plate 1, this is a major intracellular system of membrane-limited sacs, which can now be easily identified in a wide variety of cell types and which frequently exists in the shape of a basket around the central pair of centrioles. Though not displayed here with diagrammatic clarity, some features of the Golgi morphology can be discerned. These will be found repeatedly in other displays of the complex included in this collection of micrographs (see Plates 11, 12, 17 and 23).

The aspect of the Golgi most easily recognized is that shown at X. It represents a section cut transversely through a bundle of cisternae. These take the form of flattened sacs, which here number four to eight but vary in number within the Golgi complexes of different kinds of cells. They have associated with them the profiles of various smaller and larger rounded vesicles. The stacks of cisternal elements are usually curved and therefore have a concave and convex side. This configuration imparts a polarity to the stacks. In this micrograph vesicles enclosing material of low density are adjacent to the convex surface (as at X). Other vesicles on the concave side show more extensive size variation, with the larger ones (Y) containing a homogeneous substance of medium density.

The possible structural relationship between the membranous Golgi components has been deduced from clues gleaned from electron micrographs. It is certain that the system is a dynamic one, and images have been seen indicating that the small vesicles pinch off the margins of the flattened sacs. Once formed, the vesicles seem capable of growing or coalescing to form larger membrane-bounded bodies that may then move into other areas of the cytoplasm or even to the cell surface. It is also generally accepted that vesicular derivatives of ribosome-free surfaces of the endoplasmic reticulum are fed into the convex pole and integrated into the Golgi complex. Therefore, while a permanent connection between these two major membrane systems is not present, the contents and membranes of one may be transferred to the other.

The characteristics of the Golgi complex are sufficiently constant and well enough known to make certain its identification in electron micrographs. This is, however, a relatively recent capability. In fact, for several decades microscopists were not convinced even of the reality of this cell system. This uncertainty resulted from the apparent variability of form displayed by the Golgi and the limited resolving power of the light microscope. As originally described by Golgi (in 1898), it appeared as a reticular structure stained black by its ability to reduce silver or osmium to metallic form. In spite of careful light microscope studies, especially those of Bowen, on the formation of the acrosome in sperm (see Plate 23), unbelievers persisted. Finally evidence from electron microscopy provided convincing identification and a relatively complete description. The Golgi is now accepted as a major membrane-limited system of both plant and animal cells, and evidence is accumulating to indicate that, like several other cell components, it possesses the capacity to grow and duplicate.

For several decades those cytologists willing to accept the existence of the Golgi believed it to be related in some way to secretion. This role has now been investigated extensively, particularly in the exocrine cells of the pancreas (see Plate 11). In those cells, as well as in other protein-secreting cells, it is thought that specific cell products, synthesized by the ribosomes and sequestered within the membranes of the ER, are transferred into the Golgi spaces and there packaged into membrane-bounded secretory droplets, to be ejected later from the cell. The Golgi is also known to participate in the production of specific enzyme-containing vesicles which fuse with and contribute hydrolytic enzymes to lysosomes (see Plate 15). In addition it also brings about the sulfation of mucopolysaccharides within cells that produce mucus (Plate 12) and extracellular ground substance (Plates 28 and 29). It may therefore be regarded in general as a site of assembly and production of cell products that may be stored in membrane-bounded granules before their use within or secretion from the cell.

From a plasma cell in the intestinal submucosa of the rat
Magnification × 67,000

References

BAINTON, D. F., and FARQUHAR, M. G. Origin of granules in polymorphonuclear leukocytes. *J. Cell Biol.,* 28:277 (1966).

BERNHARD, W., and DE HARVEN, E. L'ultrastructure du centriole et d'autres éléments de l'appareil achromatique. *In* Proceedings of the Fourth International Conference on Electron Microscopy, Berlin, 1958. W. Bargmann, D. Peters, and C. Wolpers, editors. Berlin, Springer, vol. II (1960) p. 217.

CUNNINGHAM, W. P., MORRÉ, J. D., and MOLLENHAUER, H. H. Structure of isolated plant Golgi apparatus revealed by negative staining. *J. Cell Biol.,* 28:169 (1966).

DALTON, A. J., and FELIX, M. D. Cytological and cytochemical characteristics of the Golgi substance of epithelial cells of the epididymis—in situ, in homogenates, and after isolation. *Amer. J. Anat.,* 94:171 (1954).

FRIEND, D. S., and FARQUHAR, M. G. Functions of coated vesicles during protein absorption in the rat vas deferens. *J. Cell Biol.,* 35:357 (1967).

FRIEND, D. S. and MURRAY, M. J. Osmium impregnation of the Golgi apparatus. *Amer. J. Anat.,* 117:135 (1965).

GALL, J. G. Centriole replication. A study of spermatogenesis in the snail *Viviparus. J. Biophysic. and Biochem. Cytol.,* 10:163 (1961).

MIZUKAMI, I., and GALL, J. Centriole replication. II. Sperm formation in the fern, *Marsilea,* and the cycad, *Zamia. J. Cell Biol.,* 29:97 (1966).

MURRAY, R. G., MURRAY, A. S., and PIZZO, A. The fine structure of mitosis in rat thymic lymphocytes. *J. Cell Biol.,* 26:601 (1965).

ROBBINS, E., and GONATAS, N. K. The ultrastructure of a mammalian cell during the mitotic cycle. *J. Cell Biol.,* 21:429 (1964).

SZOLLOSI, D. The structure and function of centrioles and their satellites in the jellyfish *Phialidium gregarium. J. Cell Biol.,* 21:465 (1964).

PLATE 4

The Interphase Nucleus and Nucleolus

PLATE 4

The Interphase Nucleus and Nucleolus

The interphase nucleus gives little morphological evidence of the important activities occurring within it. It was once called the "resting" nucleus, but this name is highly unsuitable, because it is now known that during the periods between cell divisions the nucleus is exerting its greatest influence on events occurring in the cytoplasm. Furthermore, it is during the interphase period that the genetic material in the chromosomes is duplicated in preparation for the next cell division.

Electron microscope images have added surprisingly little to our knowledge of nuclear substructure apart from what they reveal regarding the nature of the nuclear envelope (NuE) and its pores (P), both discussed in Plate 2. Light microscope stains, combined with specific enzyme digestion, have localized deoxyribonucleic acid (DNA) in the chromatinic substance lying at the periphery of the nucleus as well as in the nucleolus, and they have further shown that the latter structure contains ribonucleic acid (RNA) as well. Careful comparison of light and electron micrographs established that DNA is localized in the central fibrillar zone (FZ) of the nucleolus, surrounded by a coarser granular zone (GZ) that is rich in RNA. The DNA-containing chromatin (the heterochromatin), or the bulk of it, appears as peripheral clumps of material (Ch) possessing a relatively uniform granular texture. Some also occurs near the nucleolus.

In cells such as the one shown here, in which synthetic activity in the cytoplasm is high, most of the nucleoplasm (the euchromatin) appears as fine granules and delicate filaments. These components are not detected with the light microscope because they are not sufficiently aggregated to be resolved or to combine with a noticeable amount of stain.

The functions of the interphase nucleus have been variously investigated. Certain large unicellular organisms, particularly amebae and the alga, *Acetabularia,* allow enucleation and nuclear transplantation experiments to be carried out. From such studies it has become clear that cells lacking a nucleus are unable to assimilate nutrients or to build and repair protoplasm. Furthermore, interspecific transfers of nuclei have shown that the nucleus soon exerts an influence on the cytoplasmic characteristics of the host cell.

This influence of the nucleus on the cytoplasm is demonstrably due to its control over the production of various kinds of RNA, which eventually reach the cytoplasm. As evidence of this, when cells are exposed to isotopically labeled precursors of RNA, the nuclei are labeled first and after only a short interval, whereas the cytoplasmic label appears much later. Moreover, destruction of RNA by the enzyme ribonuclease prevents regeneration of surgically excised parts of the cytoplasm.

The nuclear-derived RNA is not all of one type but consists rather of transfer, messenger, and ribosomal RNA's. Of these, ribosomal RNA is now known to be produced in the nucleolus. Treating cells with the antibiotic actinomycin D in low dosages has been found to interfere with the formation of DNA-dependent RNA, and when cells so treated are exposed to radioactive labeled precursors of RNA, no nucleolar labeling is observed. This result is in contrast to the marked nucleolar labeling in untreated cells. Dramatic confirmation of the role of the nucleolus in the production of RNA has been obtained also from the study of offspring from *Xenopus* (toad) parents each possessing only one of the normal pair of nucleoli. One quarter of the resulting embryos begin development without nucleoli. They live only a short time, but analysis of their RNA is possible, and, as expected, they lack ribosomal RNA.

This evidence correlates well with earlier observations that nucleoli undergo hypertrophy when cells are stimulated to greater protein synthesis, an event now equated with increased ribosomal activity. Thus when a nerve cell, as after nerve resection, is stimulated to regenerate a new axonal process and hence a large amount of cytoplasm, its nucleolus undergoes a 7- to 8-fold increase in volume (see text figure 4a).

In spite of this knowledge that the nucleolus produces ribosomal RNA, the RNA-rich granules of the nucleolus have not been shown to be equivalent to cytoplasmic ribosomes. As a matter of fact, the form in which various kinds of RNA are transferred to the cytoplasm is unknown.

The fibrillar zone of the nucleolus, where DNA

17

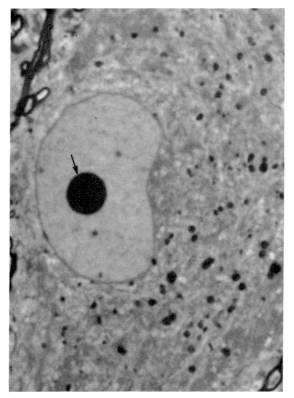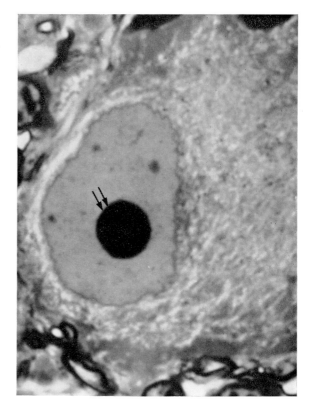

Text Figure 4a

Nuclei of neurons from the spinal cord of the frog are shown in two light micrographs at the same magnification. At left, a normal neuron displays the large dense nucleolus (arrow) characteristically present. At right, marked enlargement of the nucleolus (double arrow) is easily observed. The hypertrophy occurred after the surgical removal of the long axonal process of the cell. During the period of axonal regeneration that followed, the nucleolus was presumably stimulated to produce an extraordinary amount of ribosomal RNA, which would later have played a role in building up new protoplasmic proteins for the growing axon.

From the spinal cord of the frog
Magnification × 1,000

is located, represents part of one chromosome, a region known as the nucleolar organizer. In telophase, the last stage of cell division, the nucleus resumes synthesis of RNA and protein, i.e., processes interrupted at the beginning of the division cycle. Simultaneously some prenucleolar materials may be detected in the interchromosomal spaces. Subsequently these condense and associate with a specific chromosomal region, the nucleolar organizer. As a rule one organizer occurs in each haploid set of chromosomes, so that two nucleoli are formed in each somatic cell.

Concepts of chromosomal organization have depended primarily on studies of special cases in which interphase chromosomes retain at least a partially compact structure characteristic of mitotic chromosomes. The compact areas (e.g., in giant salivary gland chromosomes of dipterans; "lamp-brush" chromosomes of amphibian oocytes) stain positively for DNA and are con-

sidered to be regions where the chromonemata, the filamentous threads of genetic material, have remained tightly coiled. Such areas are equated with heterochromatin and are regarded as relatively inactive regions of the genome. Less densely staining regions of the chromosomes (called euchromatin), which appear under the light microscope as "puffs" or "loops," contain some RNA, as evidenced by their staining properties. These are believed to be areas in which the chromonemata are uncoiled and where the genetic information is being transcribed, probably in the production of messenger RNA.

In the more common appearance of the interphase nucleus, such as that shown here, individual chromosomes lose their identity, and the peripheral clumps of material (Ch) associated with the interpore regions of the nuclear envelope probably correspond to the densely coiled regions of the salivary gland chromosome. Less dense

18

regions of the nucleoplasm, on the other hand, may be regarded as representing the uncoiled regions (euchromatin) where messenger RNA is being actively synthesized.

During cell division, the entire chromosome becomes a compact structure, and it is during that state that attempts have been made to determine how the nucleoprotein is arranged. Although the details are far from clear, it is evident that long threads of nucleoprotein are coiled in a complex way and that several orders of coiling exist. Apparently the very small dense granules and strands in the denser chromatin (Ch) shown in this micrograph represent portions of the fundamental thread included in the section. Since interpretation of chromosomal structure from thin sections is far from simple, it is not surprising that the observed details have brought forth diverse interpretations.

From the pancreas of the frog
Magnification × 40,000

References

GALL, J. G., and CALLEN, H. G. H[3] uridine incorporation in lampbrush chromosomes. *Proc. Nat. Acad. Sci. U.S.A., 48:*562 (1962).

GOLDSTEIN, L., and PLAUT, W. Direct evidence for nuclear synthesis of cytoplasmic ribose nucleic acid. *In* Cell Biology. L. Goldstein, editor. Dubuque, W. C. Brown (1966) p. 104.

GRANBOULAN, N., and GRANBOULAN, P. Cytochimie ultrastructurale du nucléole. II. Etude des sites de synthèse du RNA dans le nucléole et le noyau. *Exp. Cell Res., 38:*604 (1965).

GURDON, J. B., and BROWN, D. D. Cytoplasmic regulation of RNA synthesis and nucleolus formation in developing embryos of *Xenopus laevis. J. Molec. Biol., 12:*27 (1965).

HÄMMERLING, J. Nucleo-cytoplasmic relationships in the development of *Acetabularia. Int. Rev. Cytol., 2:*475 (1953).

HARRIS, H. The reactivation of the red cell nucleus. *J. Cell Sci., 2:*23 (1967).

Jones, K. W. The role of the nucleolus in the formation of ribosomes. *J. Ultrastruct. Res., 13:*257 (1965).

LAFONTAINE, J. G., and CHOUINARD, L. A. A correlated light and electron microscope study of the nucleolar material during mitosis in *Vicia faba. J. Cell Biol., 17:* 167 (1963).

LITTAU, V. C., ALLFREY, V. G., FRENSTER, J. H., and MIRSKY, A. E. Active and inactive regions of nuclear chromatin as revealed by electron microscope autoradiography. *Proc. Nat. Acad. Sci. U.S.A., 52:*93 (1963).

MAGGIO, R., SIEKEVITZ P., and PALADE, G. E. Studies on isolated nuclei. II. Isolation and chemical characterization of nucleolar and nucleoplasm subfractions. *J. Cell Biol., 18:*293 (1963).

MARINOZZI, V. Cytochimie ultrastructurale du nucléole—RNA et protéines intranucléolaires. *J. Ultrastruct. Res., 10:*433 (1964).

McCONKEY, E. H., and HOPKINS, J. W. The relationship of the nucleolus to the synthesis of ribosomal RNA in Hela cells. *Proc. Nat. Acad. Sci. U.S.A., 51:*1197 (1964).

PRESCOTT, D. M. RNA synthesis in the nucleus and RNA transfer to the cytoplasm in *Tetrahymena pyriformis. In* Biological Structure and Function. T. W. Goodwin and O. Lindberg, editors. New York, Academic Press, vol. II (1961) p. 527.

REICH, E., FRANKLIN, R. M., SHATKIN, A. J., and TATUM, E. L. Effect of actinomycin D on cellular nucleic acid synthesis and virus production. *Science, 134:*556 (1961).

RIS, H. Ultra structure and molecular organization of genetic systems. *Canad. J. Genet. Cytol., 3:*95 (1961).

SWIFT, H. Nucleic acids and cell morphology in dipteran salivary glands. *In* Molecular Control of Cellular Activity. J. M. Allen, editor. New York, McGraw-Hill (1962) p. 73.

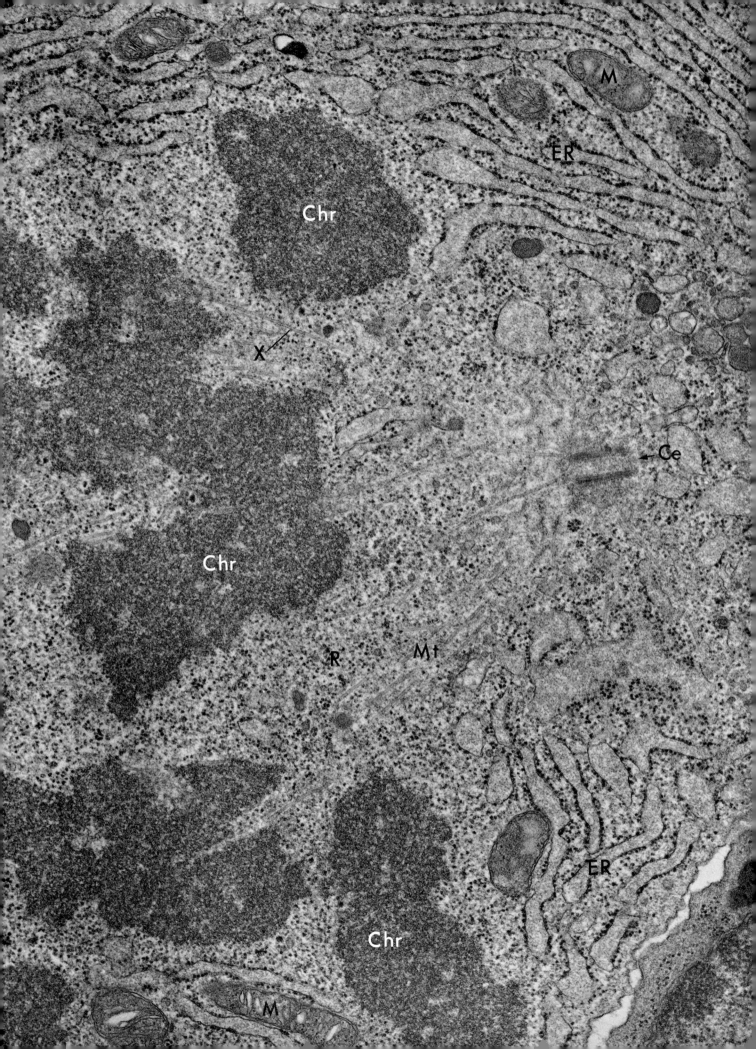

PLATE 5
The Mitotic Spindle

The spindle is a transient structure, yet one which is of prime importance in maintaining the continuity of genetic information from one cell generation to the next. It provides the mechanism that guides the chromosomes into ordered positions on the metaphase plate and normally effects the separation and movement of the daughter chromatids during anaphase. If spindle formation is prevented, as with the drug colchicine, or if the spindle is caused to disassemble, as with low temperatures, mitosis is blocked.

Normally the mitotic (or meiotic) movements occur only after complex preparatory changes have taken place in both the chromosomes and the centrioles. The latter changes are involved in the formation of the spindle apparatus.

The micrograph presented here has captured only a moment in cell division, and one during which chromosomes are united with the spindle in carrying out the characteristic mitotic movements best visualized by time-lapse cinematography. We can, however, see in this static picture evidence of earlier events as well as the structures involved in this dynamic process. The chromosomes (Chr) are now in a condensed state. Although one may assume that the essential genetic material is arranged in a compact and orderly way in these bodies, it remains extremely difficult from these images (as noted in Plate 4) to arrive at an exact description of their structure. Understanding the relationship among the minute components—described by some workers as 100 A filaments—presents a special challenge, because one is able to examine in thin sections only a small volume of the bulky chromosome.

A second important nuclear change is evident: the continuous envelope of the interphase nucleus (see also Plate 4) has disappeared, and the chromosomes are no longer "isolated" from the cytoplasm. Although remnants of the envelope have been followed through mitosis, none is clearly identifiable here. Only elements of the endoplasmic reticulum (ER), interspersed with mitochondria (M), lie at the perpihery of the cell. Near the end of mitosis, when the chromosomes of the daughter nuclei have aggregated at the poles of the spindles (telophase), a new envelope forms, apparently arising from cisternae of the adjacent ER. Thus the concept of the nuclear envelope as a specialized portion of the endoplasmic reticulum is given added credence.

While chromosomal movements are in progress, as at early anaphase shown here, the spindle plasm contains ribosome-like particles (R) intermingled with spindle microtubules (Mt). The particles are probably derived from the nucleoli, which disassembled in late prophase. The tubules, which are long, straight structures of uniform diameter, can be traced for a considerable distance in longitudinal section (as at X) and can also be identified as tiny rings in cross section (text figure 5a, arrowheads).

The existence of fibers within the spindle, as well as their function, is indicated by observations with the light microscope, especially in studies using polarized light. The form birefringence of the spindle points to the existence of asymmetric structural units oriented parallel to the spindle axis. When the changes in birefringence are observed during division, the distribution of these fibers in the spindle and the kinds of movements occurring can be analyzed.

Two kinds of fibers can be described, using light microscopy. The first appears to extend from one pole of the spindle to the other and is most properly referred to as a spindle fiber. A second kind reaches from the pole to the chromosome, to which it is attached at a special structure called a kinetochore; this is called a chromosomal fiber. The poles of the spindle are established during prophase when the centrioles in the cell center (cytocentrum) separate and migrate to antipodal positions with respect to the nucleus. It is from these poles that the spindle originates and becomes organized.

Although it is impossible to examine spindle fibers over their entire length in electron micrographs, short lengths of both types described above have been identified in thin sections, and the disposition of microtubules in them has been studied. Longitudinal sections of tubules have been found passing between the chromosomes at anaphase and have been located centrally between the chromosomal masses at telophase. In addition, spindle microtubules have been seen radiating from each polar centriole, as they do from the one (Ce) shown in this micro-

21

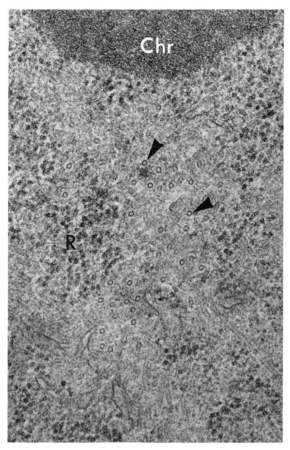

Text Figure 5a

When the mitotic spindle is cut in an equatorial section, cross sections of the spindle fibers (arrowheads) that run from the pole to the equator include circular profiles 240 A in diameter. The birefringent fibers of the spindle comprise then in part microtubules displaying a structural similarity to ciliary fibers (Plate 8) and neurotubules (text figure 45a). Part of a mitotic chromosome (Chr) and ribosome-like particles (R) may also be seen.

From the bone marrow of the rat
Magnification × 64,000

graph. It is probable that the microtubules do not extend without interruption from pole to pole within the spindle but rather consist of two sets that overlap in the fibers at the spindle equator. These are thought to be involved in spindle elongation, observed as an increase in the distance between the poles during anaphase and telophase. The attachment of microtubules to the chromosomes at the kinetochore has also been observed. These, along with spindle fibers, are believed to be instrumental in moving the chromosomes toward the poles. The mechanism involved in the earlier distribution of the chromosomes on the equatorial plate in metaphase is not in the least understood. Electron microscope studies have therefore demonstrated that both spindle and chromosomal fibers comprise microtubules. It does not follow that the spindle fibers of classical light microscopy consist only of microtubules, for, in fact, they probably include adjacent spindle plasm as well. However, it seems appropriate to assign to the microtubules a central role in determining the form and functional characteristics of the spindle (see below).

Microtubules are so named because in cross section they appear as dense rings around less dense centers (text figure 5a, arrowheads). Similar structures (long, straight, slender rods, ca. 240 A in diameter) have now been described in a wide variety of cells and seem to be among the regularly occurring cell structures. Though they may often be found in orderly array, as in cilia (see Plate 8), they may assume a more random distribution. Their association with the cell center has been confirmed in a number of instances in which one end of a microtubule has been seen embedded in a centriole or a centriolar satellite. The spindle therefore appears to be a special arrangment of a cytoplasmic element that is widely, if not universally, present in cells. In this instance the microtubules assemble out of monomeric tubule protein within the nucleoplasm to form the spindle, and after mitosis they apparently disassemble to become part of the cytoplasmic ground substance.

The occurrence of microtubules in motile cell organelles, such as cilia, and at sites where other cytoplasmic movements take place suggests that they play a significant role in protoplasmic movements in general. How they do this is the critical but unanswered question. One hypothesis currently in vogue is that they provide an elastic frame along which the motile force is exerted.

Isolation of large numbers of mitotic spindles from synchronously dividing populations of sea urchin eggs has provided sufficient material for biochemical analysis of spindle components. An important constituent is a protein that bears some similarity to actin of muscle (see Plate 38) and a close identity with a protein that has been isolated from cilia (see Plate 8) and identified with the microtubules. There is in the spindle, as in muscle and cilia, a protein possessing the ability to split enzymatically the high energy bond of adenosine triphosphate (ATP). This ATP-ase, located in some instances in small condensations in the tubule surface (see also Plate 8), would seem to be strategically placed either for the bending motion of cilia or for the gliding movements of cell organelles relative to stationary microtubules. Although the process by which chemical energy is transformed into mechanical energy is not understood in any of these cases, the investigator may expect that the movement of the chromosomes conforms to a pattern common to other types of cell movements.

From the submucosa of the rat intestine
Magnification $\times$ 40,000

References

BAJER, A. Notes on ultrastructure and some properties of transport within the living mitotic spindle. *J. Cell Biol., 33:*713 (1967).

BEHNKE, O. A preliminary report on "microtubules" in undifferentiated and differentiated vertebrate cells. *J. Ultrastruct. Res., 11:*139 (1964).

BORISY, G. G., and TAYLOR, E. W. The mechanism of action of colchicine. Binding of colchicine-^{3}H to cellular protein. *J. Cell Biol., 34:*525 (1967).

———. The mechanism of action of colchicine. Colchicine binding to sea urchin eggs and the mitotic apparatus. *J. Cell Biol., 34:*535 (1967).

HARRIS, P. Some observations concerning metakinesis in sea urchin eggs. *J. Cell Biol., 25* (No. 1, part 2): 73 (1965).

INOUÉ, S. Organization and function of the mitotic spindle. *In* Primitive Motile Systems in Cell Biology. R. D. Allen and N. Kamiya, editors. New York, Academic Press (1964) p. 549.

———, and BAJER, A. Birefringence in endosperm mitosis. *Chromosoma, 12:*48 (1961).

MAZIA, D. How cells divide. *Sci. Amer., 205:*101 (September, 1961).

PORTER, K. R. Cytoplasmic microtubules and their functions. *In* Principles of Biomolecular Organization. Ciba Foundation Symposium. G. E. W. Wolstenholme and M. O'Connor, editors. London, J. and A. Churchill, Ltd. (1966) p. 308.

———, and MACHADO, R. D. Studies on the endoplasmic reticulum. IV. Its form and distribution during mitosis in cells of onion root tip. *J. Biophysic. and Biochem. Cytol., 7:*167 (1960).

ROTH, L. E., and DANIELS, E. W. Electron microscopic studies of mitosis in amebae. *J. Cell Biol., 12:*57 (1962).

SAKAI, H. Studies on sulfhydryl groups during cell division of sea urchin eggs. VIII. Some properties of mitotic apparatus proteins. *Biochim. Biophys. Acta, 112:*132 (1966).

SHELANSKI, M. L., and TAYLOR, E. W. Isolation of a protein subunit from microtubules. *J. Cell Biol., 34:*549 (1967).

SLAUTTERBACK, D. B. Cytoplasmic microtubules. I. Hydra. *J. Cell Biol., 18:*367 (1963).

STEPHENS, R. E. On the structural protein of flagellar outer fibers. *J. Molec. Biol., 32:*277 (1968).

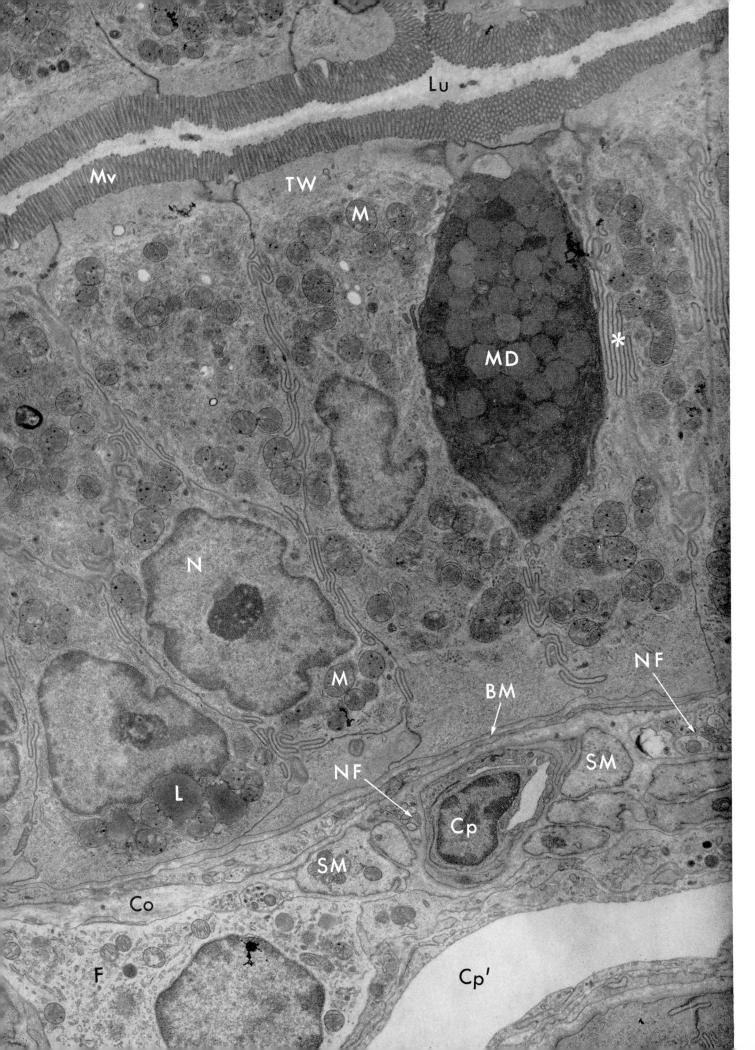

PLATE 6
The Intestinal Epithelium

In multicellular animals the association of cell units into tissues is the rule. Epithelia, in general, form the covering and lining tissues of the animal body. One type, a simple columnar epithelium, can be examined in this plate, and several of its characteristics noted. The individual cells, which are here roughly cylindrical units, are so closely packed together in hexagonal array that little intercellular space occurs between the plasma membranes of adjacent lateral cell surfaces. Instead the epithelial cells at their lateral surfaces are attached to each other by means of certain specializations of the cortex and the plasma membrane. These take the form of interdigitating folds of adjacent cell surfaces (*) or appear as specialized adhesion areas, called tight junctions, terminal bars, and desmosomes (see Plates 7 and 9). Together these structures form the junctional complexes, which seal off the intestinal lumen from the intercellular spaces within and beneath the epithelium.

Two cell types, each performing its special function, have differentiated within this epithelium, the predominant one being the columnar absorptive cell. This tall cell extends from the basement membrane (BM)[1] to the lumen of the gut (Lu). It has long been recognized that the apical surfaces of the absorptive cells have a specialized structure, called the striated border, but the nature of this specialization was not clear until the tissue was examined under the electron microscope. Then this striated border of the light micrographs was resolved into a series of finger-like cytoplasmic projections or microvilli (Mv), each limited by the plasma membrane of the absorptive cell (see Plate 7). The material within the microvilli is continuous with that of a fibrillar ectoplasmic zone, the so-called terminal web (TW), from which the common cytoplasmic organelles are excluded. The cytoplasm subjacent to the terminal web is, in contrast, crowded with the usual cytoplasmic constituents, such as mitochondria (M). The region below the nucleus (N),

though less extensive, is also populated by mitochondria (M) and by lipid droplets (L).

The intestinal epithelium also includes mucus-secreting goblet cells. The "goblet" portion of one of these, which appears in this micrograph, is crowded with numerous mucous droplets (MD). The formation and discharge of mucus, a complex polysaccharide that coats and protects the surface of the epithelium, is considered in Plate 12.

Nutrient materials from the lumen of the gut do not pass between the cells of the epithelium, but rather through their apical surfaces and are transported thence to their basal or lateral surfaces. Both the physical process of diffusion and chemical reactions governed by enzymes (active transport) are important in moving nutrients from the lumen to the underlying tissues.

The basement membrane (also called the basal lamina) forms a barrier between the epithelium and the supporting tissue beneath it. Such an arrangement, that is, the presence of a thin amorphous polysaccharide-rich layer between different types of tissues, is almost universal. It seems likely that the basement membrane is formed by or at least with the participation of the epithelium itself. A more complete discussion of this structure is provided in the legend of Plate 28.

The lamina propria, the supporting layer underlying the intestinal epithelium, is a pliable yet strong layer of connective tissue within which are embedded blood and lymph vessels, nerves, and muscles. Connective tissues, in contrast to epithelia, are characterized by the presence of substantial amounts of various intercellular substances. The latter consist primarily of collagen fibrils (Co), forming a flexible and tough supporting element, together with an amorphous ground substance rich in mucopolysaccharide. The ground substance holds the fibrous elements in place and is the medium of the intercellular spaces through which metabolites diffuse. Fibrils and ground substance are produced by fibroblasts (F). Basement membranes seem, on the other hand, to be produced by the cells they surround or underlie.

The lamina propria is heavily vascularized. Blood capillaries, both in cross section (Cp) and

---

[1] The term *basement membrane,* which was used in the second edition of this book, is now being replaced in histological literature by *basal lamina.* These two terms will be used interchangeably in this edition, since both occur in the literature cited.

ın longitudinal section (Cp′), are evident. They are lined by a thin epithelium, called an endothelium, which is underlain in turn by a basement membrane. Details of capillary structure and examples of their structural diversity may be found in a number of tissues illustrated in this collection, especially Plates 10, 24, 25, 26, 36, and 39. A second type of vessel, quite similar to a blood capillary, occurs in the lamina propria. This is the lacteal, a lymph capillary, which carries away absorbed fat in the form of small droplets, the chylomicrons.

The intestinal epithelium and lamina propria are molded into cylindrical or club-shaped projections, the villi, which impart a velvety appearance to the luminal lining when viewed with the low power of a hand lens. These villi are able to move slowly, due to the presence within them of smooth muscle cells (SM). Such involuntary movements aid in exposing the intestinal surface to hydrolyzed food substances and in moving circulating fluids away from the intestine.

Minute autonomic nerve fibers (NF) are frequently seen coursing through the lamina propria. These are extremely slender processes (~ 0.2–0.5μ in diameter) of nerve cells located elsewhere in aggregations called ganglia.

This micrograph illustrates the nature of cell associations in epithelial and connective tissues. Both types of tissue, and especially the connective tissue, are a composite of various kinds of cells, each specialized for particular function, yet both tissues as such possess easily recognizable properties that permit their classification and identification.

From the duodenum of the bat (*Myotis lucifigus*)
Magnification $\times$ 7,500

References

DEANE, H. W. Some electron microscopic observations on the lamina propria of the gut, with comments on the close association of macrophages, plasma cells, and eosinophils. *Anat. Rec., 149:*453 (1964).

LEBLOND, C. P., and MESSIER, B. Renewal of chief cells and goblet cells in the small intestine as shown by radioautography after injection of thymidine-H[3] into mice. *Anat. Rec., 132:*247 (1958).

NEUTRA, M., and LEBLOND, C. P. Radioautographic comparison of the uptake of galactose-H[3] and glucose-H[3] in the Golgi region of various cells secreting glycoproteins or mucopolysaccharides. *J. Cell Biol., 30:*137 (1966).

PALAY, S. L., and KARLIN, L. J. An electron microscopic study of the intestinal villus. I. The fasting animal. *J. Biophysic. and Biochem. Cytol., 5:*363 (1959).

PLATE 7
Columnar Absorptive Cells

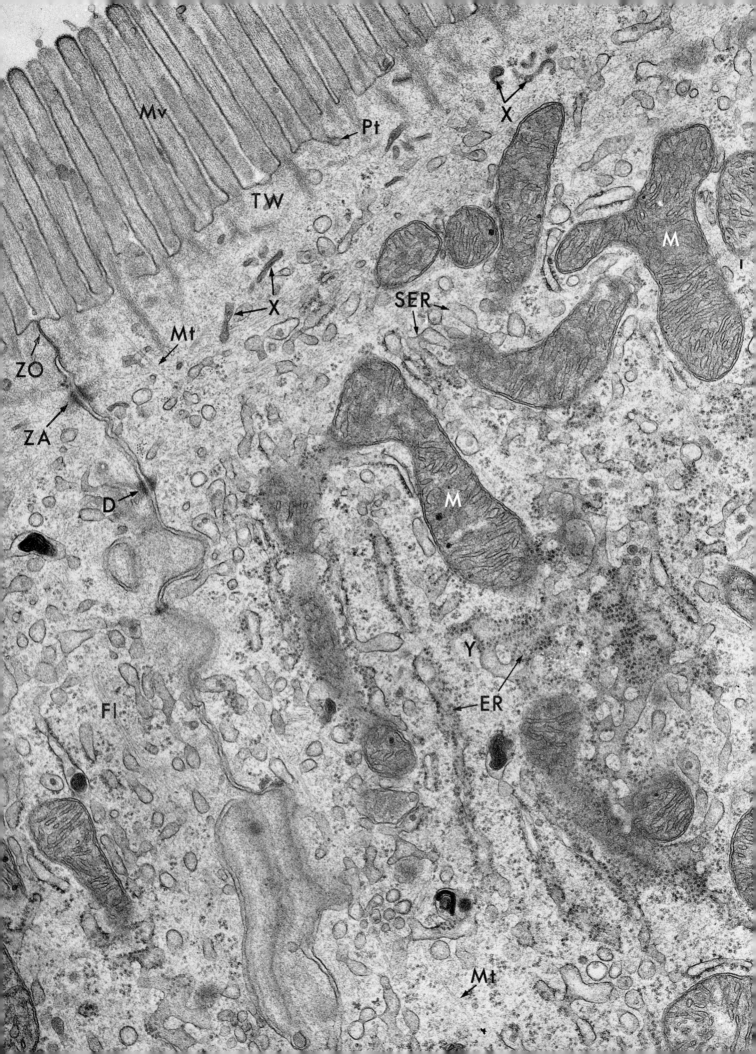

PLATE 7
Columnar Absorptive Cells

The apical surface of columnar absorptive cells is an important area of contact between the organism and its environment. It is here that food materials, after undergoing extracellular digestion (hydrolysis), really enter the organism.

The absorbing surface is enlarged by folds, both macroscopic and microscopic, and, as already shown in Plate 6, studies of this tissue by electron microscopy have revealed the presence here of numerous fingerlike projections, the microvilli (Mv). Fine filaments constitute the cores of these projections and extend into the terminal web (TW) area. A close examination of the microvillar profiles demonstrates the existence of a filamentous enteric surface coat external to, but intimately associated with, the plasma membrane (text figure 7a). This layer, which consists of mucopolysaccharide, is believed to be produced by the absorptive cell itself and to be an integral part of the cell surface. The coat probably functions as a trap that can concentrate ions and other charged particles to be absorbed by the cells (see also Plate 13).

Far down between the microvilli the plasma membrane can form pits (Pt) that penetrate the terminal web. Irregular profiles of pits or apical vesicles (X) derived from them are easily identified within the web. Dense material of unknown nature is frequently found within these vesicles.

The lateral surfaces of the absorptive cells are closely united by components of the junctional complex. The tight junction (or *zonula occludens,* ZO), involving fusion between adjacent plasma membranes, is located closest to the free surface of the epithelium. Its structure is seen more clearly in text figure 7a. Beneath it may be seen the terminal bar (or *zonula adhaerens,* ZA). Each of these constitutes a continuous ring encircling each cell of the epithelium at this level. In profile the terminal bar appears somewhat similar to the desmosome (D) or *macula adhaerens.* The latter, however, is only a small disk-shaped area where adjacent plasma membranes adhere. It is described in detail in the legend of Plate 9. Where they are not joined by specialized structures, the plasma membranes of adjacent cells are separated by a zone of constant width and low density. Although no material is discerned within this gap, it is demonstrably a layer of material rich in polysaccharides.

The cytoplasm of absorptive cells subjacent to the terminal web is the site of great activity in the uptake and transport of metabolites. The fine filaments (Fl) and microtubules (Mt) present in the ground substance of the cytoplasm are probably visible manifestations of a cytoskeletal organization influential in maintaining the elongated shape of the cells and in facilitating diffusion. Mitochondria (M) packed with cristae are numerous. Their prominence is to be expected, since energy is required for transporting foodstuffs across the epithelium.

Also conspicuous in this region is a well-developed endoplasmic reticulum. Here the ER is quite different in form from that seen in the plasma and pancreas cells (Plates 1, 2, and 11). Some portions of this system are studded with ribosomes (ER), but the membranes, rather than appearing as flattened cisternae, display a reticulate structure of anastomosing tubules. The ER membranes are also found free of ribosomes (SER), and in such regions are more vesicular in nature. It is usually a simple matter, as in this micrograph, to find places where rough- and smooth-surfaced membranes are continuous (Y). This is taken as evidence that the two forms are part of the same intracellular membrane system and suggests that one may transform into the other.

In studying this micrograph we see then a number of specialized structures associated with the cell surface and the apical cytoplasm. The extent and manner in which each may play a role in absorption and transport of molecules become now subjects of some interest. In the investigation of these phenomena it is rewarding to study the movement of emulsified fat across the columnar epithelial cells, because fat droplets are preserved and can be readily identified in electron micrographs when osmium tetroxide is used as a fixative.

In such investigations it has been observed that when emulsified corn oil is introduced into the lumen of the rat digestive tract, small droplets of fat appear soon afterward, mainly within the cavities of the smooth-surfaced endoplasmic reticulum (text figure 7b). With time the droplets

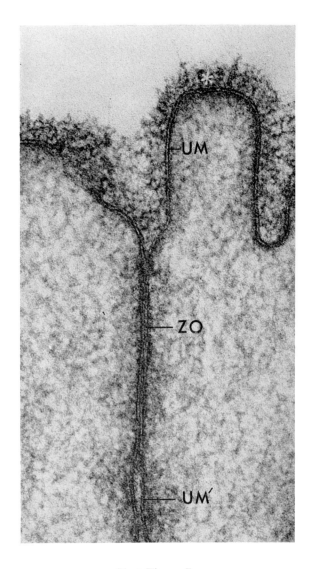

Text Figure 7a

The surfaces of absorptive cells are limited by a trilaminar unit membrane both at their free (UM) and on their lateral (UM′) surfaces. An enteric surface coat (*) of polysaccharide material covers the microvilli that project into the lumen of the digestive tract. At the lateral cell surfaces, the outer dense lamellae of the plasma membranes of adjacent cells are united to form a tight junction or *zonula occludens* (ZO). This structure is believed to act as a seal, preventing the diffusion of even small molecules through the epithelium by an intercellular route.

From the stomach of the bat
Magnification × 180,000

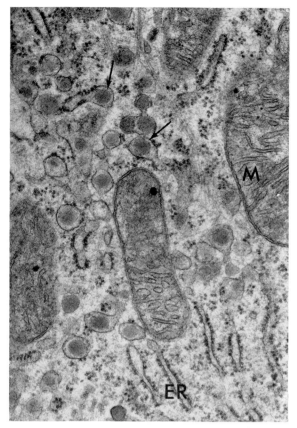

Text Figure 7b

The supranuclear cytoplasm of the columnar absorptive cell depicted here was fixed following injection of emulsified corn oil into the lumen of the intestine. Vesicles of the endoplasmic reticulum contain fat droplets (arrows) resynthesized from monoglycerides and fatty acids absorbed from the gut lumen. Tubules of rough-surfaced endoplasmic reticulum (ER) give rise to the vesicles, which are largely free of ribosomes. Mitochondria (M) are numerous.

From the intestine of the rat
Magnification × 36,000

become larger and increase in number as more and more of the rough ER is transformed into the smooth form. There is now convincing evidence that the membranes of the SER are the sites at which triglycerides (fats) are synthesized from monoglycerides and fatty acids that have diffused the cell from the gut lumen. The droplets coated with protein and surrounded by a membrane seem then to move toward the basilateral surfaces of the columnar cells, where they are ejected, free of membrane, into the intercellular spaces. Their elimination from the cell is believed to involve momentary union of their surrounding membrane with the plasma membrane and the opening of the vesicle so that its inner cavity is for a brief time continuous with the intercellular space.

The pits (Pt) and the apical vesicles (X) derived from them constitute a system that apparently functions in the uptake and destruction of miscellaneous particulate materials that find their way into the deep recesses between the microvilli. When electron dense markers are added to corn oil in the form of fine colloidal suspensions, they are detected in pits and apical vesicles but never reach the internal phase of the SER. In time the apical vesicles are transformed into lysosomes, within which the intruding material is hydrolyzed or otherwise rendered harmless. A similar mechanism for dealing with large foreign molecules has been observed in the absorbing cells of the kidney (see Plate 25).

While diffusion processes adequately account for movement across the brush border (microvilli and terminal web) of digested fats in the form of monoglycerides, absorption of proteins and sugars requires energy and is therefore said to involve "active" transport processes. Specific knowledge of the molecular architecture: that is, the complex lipoprotein plasma membrane of the cell surface is required to understand such processes (text figure 7a). It is thought that carrier molecules exist and that their properties account for the selectivity shown by the membrane in its ability to distinguish between quite similar molecular species.

From the jejunum of the rat
Magnification × 42,000

References

CARDELL, R. R., JR., BADENHAUSEN, S., and PORTER, K. R. Intestinal triglyceride absorption in the rat. *J. Cell Biol., 34:*123 (1967).

FARQUHAR, M. G., and PALADE, G. E. Junctional complexes in various epithelia. *J. Cell Biol., 17:*375 (1963).

ISSELBACHER, K. J. Biochemical aspects of fat absorption. *Gastroenterology, 50:*78 (1966).

ITO, S. The enteric surface coat on cat intestinal microvilli. *J. Cell Biol., 27:*475 (1965).

PALAY, S. L., and KARLIN, L. J. An electron microscopic study of the intestinal villus. II. The pathway of fat absorption. *J. Biophysic. and Biochem. Cytol., 5:*373 (1959).

REVEL, J.-P., and ITO, S. The surface components of cells. *In* The Specificity of Cell Surfaces. B. Davis and L. Warren, editors. Englewood Cliffs, New Jersey, Prentice-Hall (1967) p. 211.

SENIOR, J. R. Intestinal absorption of fats. *J. Lipid Res., 4:*495 (1964).

STRAUSS, E. W. Electron microscopic study of intestinal fat absorption in vitro from mixed micelles containing linolenic acid, monoolein, and bile salt. *J. Lipid Res., 7:*307 (1966).

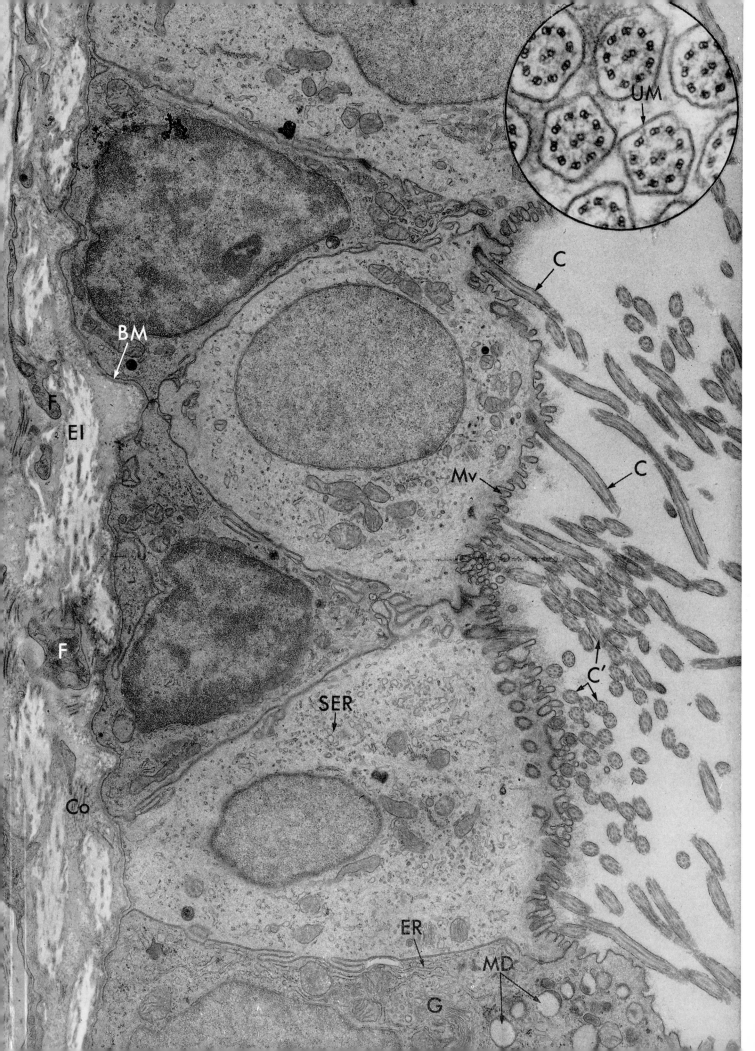

PLATE 8

The Ciliated Epithelium of the Trachea

The removal of foreign particles from the trachea is accomplished by the lashing motion of cilia, which are long, motile extensions from the free surfaces of certain epithelial cells. In this micrograph a few cilia (C) are seen in longitudinal section extending from the apical pole of epithelial cells. Because of their length, slenderness (250 mμ in diameter), and contorted form, most of the cilia are included only in part in the section and so appear variously in oblique and cross section (C′). Like the short microvilli (Mv), which also project from the tracheal cells, cilia are covered by the three-layered unit membrane (UM, inset). Unlike the microvilli, however, cilia have a complex inner organization which is shared in common by all cilia and flagella, whether from plant or animal cells. The nature of this organization is shown best in cross sections (inset). Thus one sees the "figure-8" profiles of nine double filaments or microtubules in a peripheral ring enclosing a central pair. This entire array of microtubules constitutes what has come to be known as the 9 + 2 complex or axoneme. The filamentous nature of these structural units is deduced from longitudinal sections. At the base of each cilium is a basal body, which closely resembles a centriole. Since the 9 + 2 complex was first discovered, more detailed descriptions of the various ciliary components have been published, and several mechanisms of ciliary motion have been proposed, based on the structural features revealed by the electron microscope. As yet, however, the mechanism of movement and the manner in which the movements are coordinated into wave forms have not been fully explained.

Progress has been made, however, in isolating cilia in quantities that allow physical and chemical analysis of their components. By "chemical dissection" it has been possible to isolate the axoneme free of the limiting plasma membrane and relatively free of its surrounding matrix. Further extraction of the axoneme has led to isolation of a protein, dynein, which possesses ATP-ase activity. This fraction and its activity are of special interest because it is believed that splitting of the high energy phosphate bond of ATP provides energy for the movement of cilia as it does for the contraction of muscle (see Plates 38–40).

Electron microscopic examination of the axonemes following extraction of dynein reveals that the "arms" of the outer nine fibrils have disappeared. Normally the "arms," extending like prongs from the side of each doublet toward the one next, are responsible for the assymetry of the nine doublets. (The arms may be detected on close inspection of the inset.) If subsequently the dynein is recombined with the extracted axonemes, the "arms" are restored to their normal positions. It appears then that energy for ciliary movement is released near the nine double tubules, which probably serve simply as an elastic frame for the cylindrical shape of the cilium. How this energy acts to distort or bend this frame has yet to be discovered.

Further study of the nine outer doublets has shown that they are made up of a protein that resembles in a number of ways the protein actin, known to play an important role in the contraction of muscle. Although it is certain that the mechanisms of movement in muscle and cilia are not homologous, it seems likely that fundamental similarities exist.

In the tracheal epithelium the ciliated cells alternate with nonciliated, mucus-secreting cells, in the apical zones of which secretion droplets (MD) may be observed. The cytoplasm of the mucous cells is closely packed with organelles—mitochondria, endoplasmic reticulum (ER)—whereas in that of the ciliated cells, from which no product is exported, components other than mitochondria are rather sparsely represented. For example, the endoplasmic reticulum of the latter cells consists in the main of small smooth-walled vesicles (SER), and the Golgi complex (next to letters ER) is not as extensive as that which characterizes the secretory cells (G).

Although both ciliated and mucous cells extend the full height of the epithelium, slightly oblique sections may obscure this fact. In this micrograph some of the cells appear to be arranged in layers, while others are clearly part of a simple epithelium. The disposition of the nuclei at two or more levels within epithelia in which all components are in contact with the basement membrane accounts for use of the adjective "pseudostratified" to describe this epithelium.

Beneath this epithelium, as is true for epithelia in general, there is a thin basement membrane (BM), now more commonly called the basal lamina, which is supported in turn by rather substantial layers of fibrous connective tissue. Portions of fibrocytes (F) lie among collagenous (Co) and elastic (El) fiber bundles abundant in the connective tissue ground substance. It is this layer of connective tissue that is the major component of the thick basement lamella evident in the light microscope image of tracheal tissue.

From the trachea of the bat
Magnification × 13,000
Inset from the trachea of the rat
Magnification × 97,000

References

Fawcett, D. W. Cilia and flagella. *In* The Cell. J. Brachet and A. E. Mirsky, editors. New York, Academic Press, vol. II (1961) p. 217.
———, and Porter, K. R. A study of the fine structure of ciliated epithelia. *J. Morph., 94:*221 (1954).
Gibbons, I. R. The relationship between the fine structure and direction of beat in gill cilia of a lamellibranch mollusc. *J. Biophysic. and Biochem. Cytol., 11:*179 (1961).

———. Studies on the protein components of cilia from *Tetrahymena pyriformis. Proc. Nat. Acad. Sci. USA, 50:*1002 (1963).
———, and Rowe, A. J. Dynein: a protein with adenosine triphosphatase activity from cilia. *Science, 149:* 424 (1965).
Renaud, F. L., Rowe, A. J., and Gibbons, I. R. Some properties of the protein forming the outer fibers of cilia. *J. Cell Biol., 36:*79 (1968).

PLATE 9

The Germinal Layer of the Epidermis

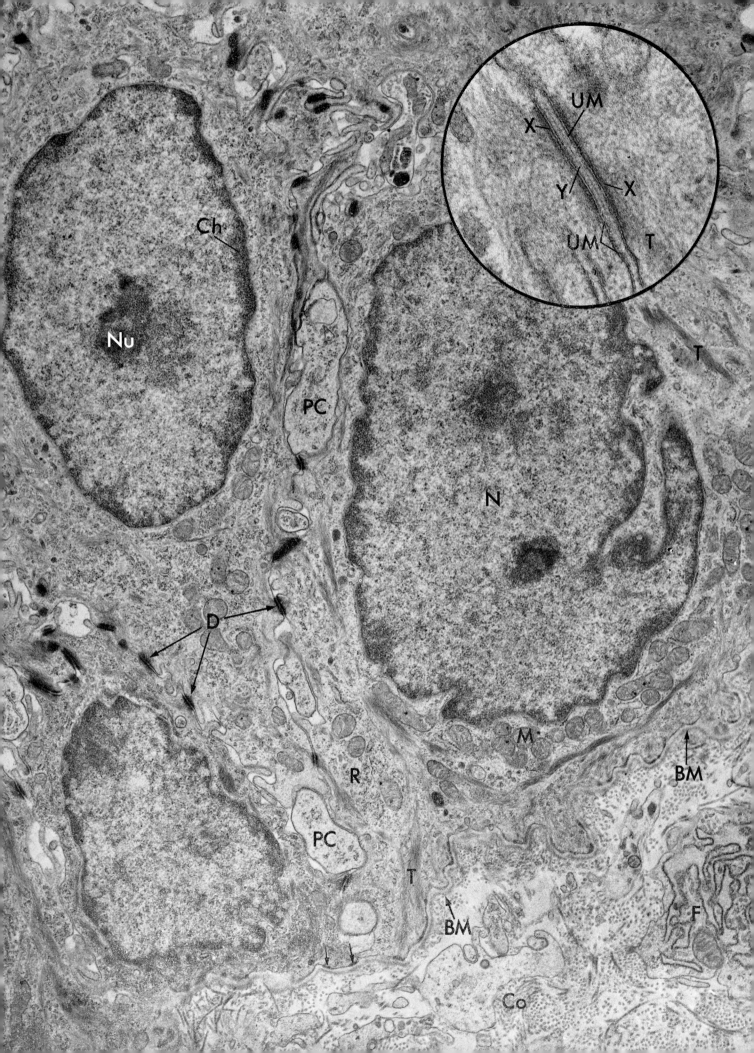

PLATE 9

The Germinal Layer of the Epidermis

The exposed body surfaces of mammals are covered by a specialized stratified squamous epithelium, the epidermis, which protects the animal from mechanical injury, invasion by foreign organisms, and loss of body fluids. The epidermis together with an underlying layer of connective tissue, the dermis, and specialized cutaneous appendages—hair, sweat, and sebaceous glands—form the mammalian skin.

The basal cell layer of the epidermis, the stratum germinativum, shown in this electron micrograph, provides cells for renewal of the epidermal population throughout life. Cells are pushed out from this layer, and only when they become part of the overlying layer, the stratum spinosum, do they begin to differentiate. As they develop, they move toward the surface of the epidermis, and by the time they have reached the uppermost layer, the stratum corneum, they have become lifeless scales, filled with horny material. Some of the features of this process, which is called keratinization, are illustrated in the text figure 9a.

Turning our attention to the germinative cells themselves, we may note that they rest on the connective tissue of the dermis, within which collagen fibers (Co) and fibroblasts (F) may be identified. A thin basal lamina (BM) separates the dermis from the cells of the stratum germinativum. The basal surfaces of the epithelial cells display irregular folds and are probably anchored to the basement membrane by the so-called "half" desmosomes (arrows). (For a description of desmosomal structure, see below.)

The nuclei (N) of the germinative cells usually have prominent nucleoli (Nu) and a thin peripheral layer of chromatin (Ch). Clusters of mitochondria (M) occur in the perinuclear cytoplasm. Strands of tonofilaments making up tonofibrils (T) are the most salient cytoplasmic feature. The fibrils, which are found generally in columnar epithelial cells, are regarded as a structural protein, giving strength to the epidermis without sacrificing permeability. Although elements of the endoplasmic reticulum are scant, free ribosomes are abundant. They are probably involved in the production of the proteins, as, for example, the tonofilaments and later during differentiation in the formation of keratohyalin granules (see Plate 9a) that are retained within the cells.

Continuity and integrity of the epidermis is assured by adhesion plaques, called desmosomes (D), which bind the cells together. The light microscope image of these structures led to the belief that they represented intercellular bridges, through which the cytoplasm of one cell might be continuous with the next. Now, however, electron micrographs have demonstrated that there are no open channels. Rather, as shown in the inset, dense plates (X) are aligned at opposite areas near the cell surface but within the cytoplasm of each cell. The plasma membranes that mark the limits of each cell show the trilaminar structure characteristic of the unit membrane (UM) (see Plate 2). In the region of the desmosome the innermost of the two dense lines is closely associated with the dense material of the plate (X). Usually the space between adjacent epithelial cells lacks evident content or structure, but in the region of the demosome this space is occupied by a material (Y) having, presumably, some cementing properties. As in this case the cementing material is bisected by a thin dense central lamina, seen here in cross section as a fine dense line equidistant between the two cell membranes. The intracellular side of the desmosome has attached to it tonofilaments (T) which are, in many instances, continuous with those in the fiber bundles.

The basal layer of the epidermis also contains a cell type quite different from that already described. This is the melanocyte or pigment cell, which does not begin its development within the epidermis. Instead, at an early stage in embryonic life, precursor pigment cells migrate from an area of tissue near the developing central nervous system and finally enter the epidermis. There is no difficulty involved in distinguishing these cells because they lack the tonofibrils of their neighbors and are not anchored into position by desmosomes. *Dendritic* is the adjective often applied to them, and their endings are wedged in among the more regularly arranged cells around them. Several thin processes of pigment cell cytoplasm (PC) are seen in this micrograph. Because this tissue was taken from an albino rat, the dense

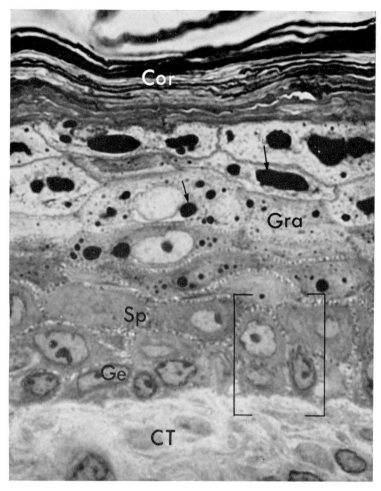

Text Figure 9a

The epidermis of a newborn rat is shown in cross section in this light micrograph, and important features of the mammalian keratinizing epithelium can be seen. An area such as that discussed in the text of Plate 9 is indicated within the brackets. It includes primarily cells of the stratum germinativum (Ge) together with some of the connective tissue (CT) of the dermis. The larger, round cells of the stratum spinosum (Sp) were derived from the basal cells and have begun to differentiate. The "prickles" on their surfaces are due to the many desmosomes that attach them to one another. As the cells are pushed toward the surface by the proliferating germinativum, differentiation continues. Dense granules (arrows) appear and increase in size as the cells near the free surface of the epidermis. Therefore in the granular layer or the stratum granulosum (Gra) production of horny material, that is, the keratinization process, begins. Eventually, in the stratum corneum (Cor) the cells become lifeless scales, filled with a tough proteinaceous material but devoid of organelles that are necessary for synthetic and metabolic activities. Finally, the horny cells at the free surface are shed as new scales are formed.

From the skin of the newborn rat
Magnification × 2,000

pigment granules are not evident. In normal skin the melanoblasts or melanocytes are the only sites of pigment formation. Once formed, the pigment granules can be transferred from the melanocytes to other epidermal cells and to dermal phagocytes.

From the skin of the newborn rat
Magnification × 12,500
Inset from the esophagus of the bat
Magnification × 124,000

38

BIRBECK, M. S., BREATHNACH, A. S., and EVERALL, J. D. An electron microscope study of basal melanocytes and high-level clear cells (Langerhans cells) in vitiligo. *J. Invest. Derm., 37:*51 (1961).

BONNEVILLE, M. A. Observations on epidermal differentiation in the fetal rat. *Amer. J. Anat., 123:* in press (1968).

BRODY, I., The keratinization of epidermal cells of normal guinea pig skin as revealed by electron microscopy. *J. Ultrastruct. Res., 2:*482 (1959).

CHARLES, A., and INGRAM, J. T. Electron microscope observations of the melanocyte of the human epidermis. *J. Biophysic. and Biochem. Cytol., 6:*41 (1959).

FARBMAN, A. I. Plasma membrane changes during keratinization. *Anat. Rec., 156:*269 (1966).

GIROUD, A., and LEBLOND, C. P. The keratinization of epidermis and its derivatives, especially the hair, as shown by x-ray diffraction and histochemical studies. *Ann. N. Y. Acad., Sci., 53:*613 (1951).

MARQUES-PEREIRA, J. P., and LEBLOND, C. P. Mitosis and differentiation in the stratified squamous epithelium of the rat esophagus. *Amer. J. Anat., 117:*73 (1965).

MATOLTSY, A. G. Mechanism of keratinization. *In* Fundamentals of Keratinization. E. O. Butcher and R. F. Sognnaes, editors. AAAS, Publication No. 70, Washington, D.C. (1962) p. 1.

————, and PARAKKAL, P. F. Membrane-coating granules of keratinizing epithelia. *J. Cell Biol., 24:*297 (1965).

RAWLES, M. E. Origin of pigment cells from the neural crest in the mouse embryo. *Physiol. Zool., 20:*248 (1947).

RHODIN, J. A. G., and REITH, E. J. Ultrastructure of keratin in oral mucosa, skin, esophagus, claw, and hair. *In* Fundamentals of Keratinization. E. O. Butcher and R. F. Sognnaes, editors. AAAS, Publication No. 70, Washington, D.C. (1962) p. 61.

39

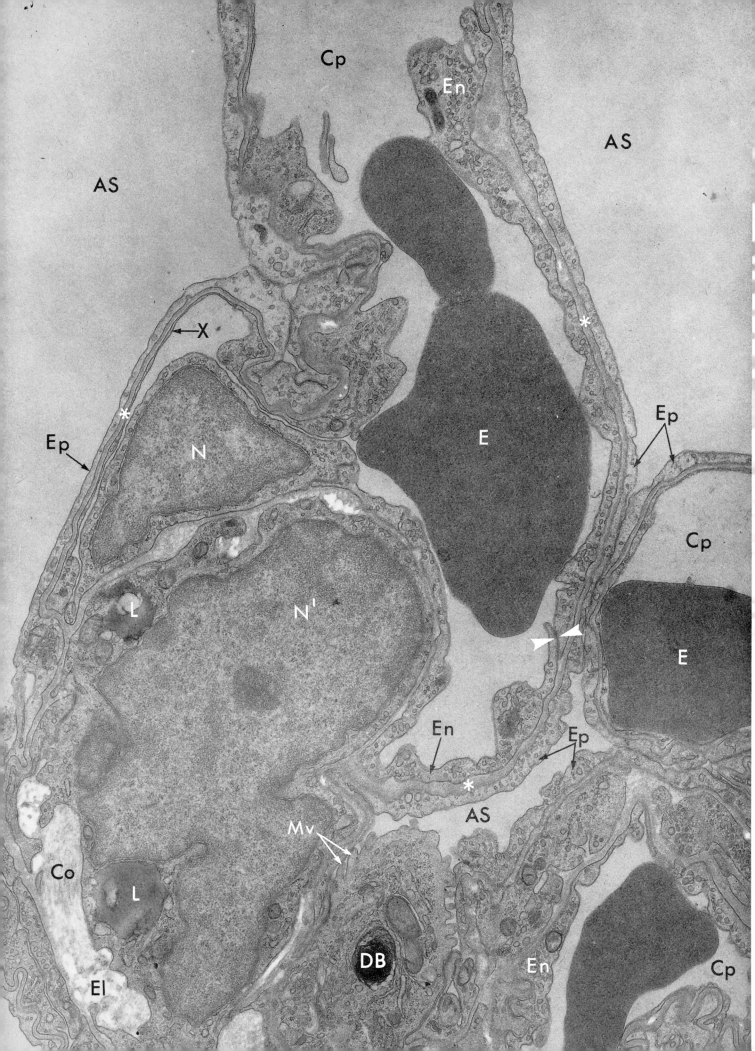

PLATE 10

The Interalveolar Septum
of the Lung and Capillary Structure

Interalveolar septa are partitions separating the alveolar sacs or air spaces of the lung. They constitute the respiratory tissue; that is, the site of gaseous exchanges between air and blood. They are so thin that it was only after examination with the electron microscope that their structure became clear. Portions of several alveolar sacs (AS), each lined by an extremely attenuated squamous epithelium (Ep), are included in this micrograph. The lining, which can be examined quite critically and over several microns in this micrograph, shows no evidence of any interruptions in its continuity.

The septum is, of course, highly vascularized. Here the thin endothelial cell linings (En) of three capillaries (Cp), each containing an erythrocyte (E), can be examined. The large irregularly shaped vessel in the upper portion of the picture has a lining that is characteristically thin and in places extremely so (X). Yet, like the alveolar epithelium, the capillary endothelium forms a complete lining. Neighboring cells are closely apposed (arrows), and no intercellular gaps of appreciable size or fenestrae within the cells themselves are found. Only in the region accommodating the nucleus (N) is the endothelial wall substantially thickened.

Each of these squamous epithelia has its own basement membrane, but where apposed to one another they seem to fuse into a common layer (∗). In such cases the resulting wall—alveolar epithelium, basement membrane, and capillary endothelium—may together be only 100 mμ thick; that is, below the resolving power of the light microscope. In other areas the basement membrane of each epithelium is separated by bundles of collagen fibrils (Co) and also occasional elastic fibers (El), which play an important role in the recoil of the lung during expiration. Such fibers may be produced by septal cells, which are connective tissue elements lying among the capillaries. In this micrograph, the cell having an irregularly shaped nucleus (N′) and possessing cytoplasmic lipid droplets (L) may be of this type.

A striking feature of the endothelial cells is the small membrane-bounded pits and vesicles (∼50mμ in diameter), which populate the two surfaces of each cell and its intervening cytoplasm. The frequency and distribution of these structures has led some students of capillary permeability to the supposition that these structures might be involved in the transport of lipid-insoluble molecules across the endothelium. The distribution of electron opaque markers following their injection into the vascular system has in fact indicated that transport of packets (quanta) of material within vesicles may occur in the case of large molecules such as plasma proteins or antibodies. However, for the bulk transport demonstrable in physiological studies the pits and vesicles are patently inadequate, and recent investigations with the enzyme peroxidase as a marker make it clear that molecules of relatively low molecular weight pass between rather than through the endothelial cells. This conclusion is strengthened by careful examinations of contact zones between endothelial cells. Such studies reveal that in this case tight junctions occur as discrete plaques and that no continuous intercellular band-like seal exists. (Compare the tight junction uniting intestinal epithelial cells, Plate 7). Rather, thin slitlike passages, probably containing polysaccharide "cementing" substances, seem to exist and are in all likelihood the chief route for transport across endothelia. The endothelium of the capillaries in the brain constitutes a notable exception, however, in that in those vessels continuous tight junctions do seal off the capillary lumen so that intercellular transport of molecules is prevented.

Air drawn into the lungs reaches the alveolar sacs only after traveling through the nasal passages and bronchial tree, where it is warmed, moistened, and to some extent cleaned. Yet foreign organisms and contaminating material do penetrate into these deepest recesses of the tissue. Indeed lungs of city dwellers, for example, are commonly blackened by accumulated carbon particles that alveolar macrophages ingest and retain. These phagocytes are able to wander freely in the interstitium of the septum and to move over the surface of the epithelium lining the air sacs.

Recently it has become known that the alveolar

epithelium is coated on its free surface by a fatty substance (a surfactant), which reduces the surface tension at the interface between the epithelium and air. Theoretically, without this provision, the surface tension at this interface would be in aggregate forceful enough to collapse the alveoli. The lipid is believed to originate from the great alveolar cell, which constitutes a second cell type within the alveolar epithelium. Such cells have small microvilli (Mv) projecting into the air space and typically contain dense bodies (DB) that are believed to be precursors of the lipid coat. The intensely osmiophilic lamellae characteristics of these inclusions have been observed apparently emerging from the great alveolar cells and are thought to spread from this source over the surfaces of the entire squamous alveolar epithelium.

From the lung of the mouse
Magnification $\times$ 18,000

References

BALIS, J. U., and CONEN, P. E. The role of alveolar inclusion bodies in the developing lung. *Lab. Invest., 13:* 1215 (1964).

BENNETT, H. S., LUFT, J. H., and HAMPTON, J. C. Morphological classifications of vertebrate blood capillaries. *Amer. J. Physiol., 196:*381 (1959).

BERTALANFFY, F. D. Respiratory tissue: structure, histophysiology, cytodynamics. I. Review and basic cytomorphology. *Int. Rev. Cytol., 16:*233 (1964).

BUCKINGHAM, S., HEINEMANN, H. O., SOMMERS, S. C., and McNARY, W. F. Phospholipid synthesis in the large pulmonary alveolar cell. *Amer. J. Path., 48:*1027 (1966).

CLEMENTS, J. A. Surface tension in the lungs. *Sci. Amer. 207:*120 (December, 1962).

KARNOVSKY, M. J. The ultrastructural basis of capillary permeability studied with peroxidase as a tracer. *J. Cell Biol., 35:*213 (1967).

KARRER, H. E. The ultrastructure of mouse lung. General architecture of capillary and alveolar walls. *J. Biophysic. and Biochem. Cytol., 2:*241 (1956).

KISTLER, G. S., CALDWELL, P., and WEIBEL, E. R. Development of fine structural damage to alveolar and capillary lining cells in oxygen-poisoned rat lungs. *J. Cell Biol., 32:*605 (1967).

LOW, F. N. The pulmonary alveolar epithelium of laboratory mammals and man. *Anat. Rec., 117:*241 (1953).

LUFT, J. H. Fine structure of capillary and endocapillary layer as revealed by ruthenium red. *Fed. Proc., 25:*1771 (1966).

PLATE 11

Pancreatic Exocrine Cells

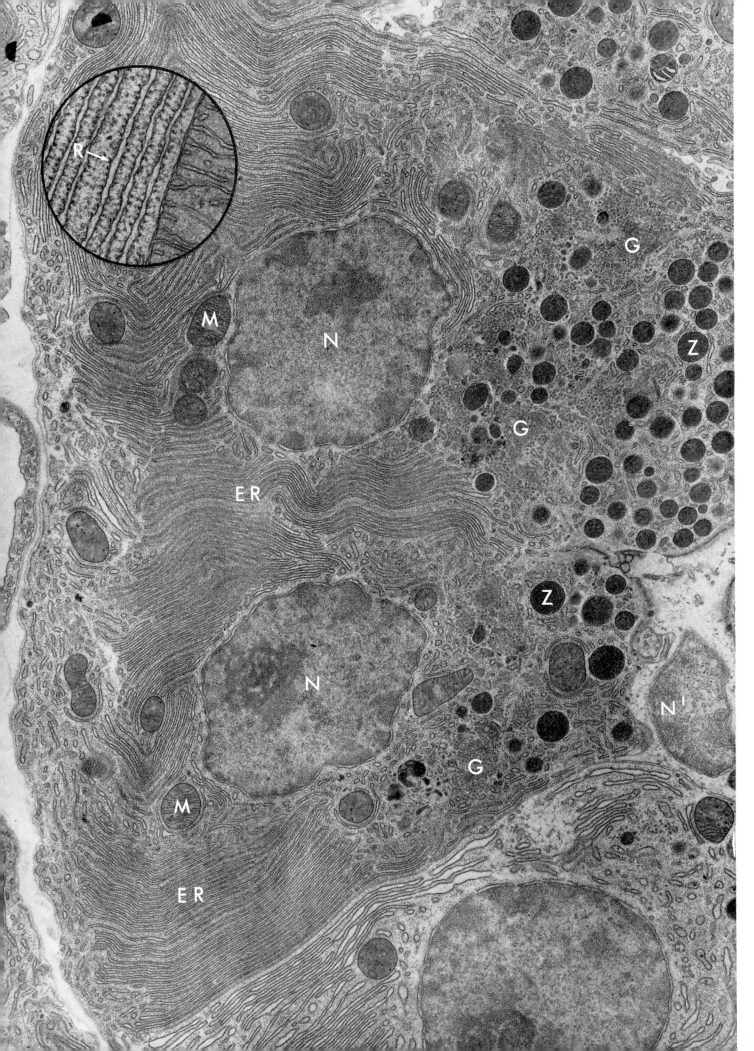

PLATE 11

Pancreatic Exocrine Cells

Secretion is one of the major activities of epithelial tissues. Toward this end the cytological machinery of glandular tissues is specialized to produce a product for export. The pancreatic exocrine cells are really a developmental derivative of the intestinal epithelium, differentiated to produce digestive enzymes, which are poured into ducts and thence reach a section of the intestine called the duodenum. The homogeneity of the tissue in terms of cell type has allowed useful cell fractionation and correlative biochemical experiments, which together have revealed roles of the cytoplasmic organelles in secretion. Thus we have come to know specific details of protein synthesis in the pancreas as well as to recognize important generalizations regarding secretory activities.

In this micrograph two pyramidal-shaped pancreatic acinar cells with centrally located nuclei (N) are shown in a fairly inactive state. Their lateral and basal cytoplasm contains relatively few mitochondria (M) and many large flattened cisternae of the endoplasmic reticulum (ER). Ribosomes in tremendous numbers (see inset, R) encrust the outer surfaces of the cisternal membranes. The ribonucleic acid of these small dense particles accounts for the well-known affinity of these cells for basic dyes. The apical ends of the cells are filled primarily by an extensive Golgi region (G) and by zymogen granules (Z), the enzyme-containing secretion droplets.

The cycle of synthesis and secretion of proteolytic enzymes is conveniently followed in these cells. After the animal has been fed, zymogen granules are discharged from the cell, and their regeneration begins anew. If one examines these cells at suitable time intervals during this period, one can observe the steps in the process and the involvement of various cytoplasmic organelles. Furthermore, if one feeds isotopically labeled amino acids, one can follow their incorporation into proteins (enzymes) and their movements as the proteins are condensed into droplets.

The labeled compounds are identified in two ways. By means of differential centrifugation the cellular organelles are segregated according to density following their release into a suitable medium upon disruption of the cell membranes. At earliest time periods the label is found asso-ciated with the "microsome" fraction, a small particulate fraction containing ribosomes and ER membranes. If now the membranes of the microsomes are destroyed with detergent, a fraction of labeled ribosomes alone is obtained. Intensive experimentation with this system has led to the concepts that the ribosomes are the sites of protein synthesis and that the newly formed enzymes are segregated within the cisternae of the endoplasmic reticulum. Subsequent to these events the radioactivity appears in the zymogen granules, and the pathway by which it reaches the droplets may be inferred from the study of electron micrographs. Small droplets resembling incomplete zymogen granules are found in the Golgi region, and the images suggest that the protein has become secondarily segregated within special smooth-surfaced vesicles and packaged into droplets in preparation for secretion. Before their release from the cell the droplets become larger, and the secretion within them becomes more concentrated.

This sequence of events has been confirmed by experiments in which autoradiographic techniques were adapted for use on electron microscope preparations. After appearing initially in association with the rough-surfaced endoplasmic reticulum (as would be expected from previous results with biochemical methods), the radioactivity becomes concentrated in the Golgi region before appearing in the zymogen granules (see also text figure 11a). In fasting animals, the granules are retained in the apical cytoplasm, but with feeding they are released, free of their membranous covering, into the ducts of the gland.

The pathway of protein synthesis, segregation, concentration, and eventual transport characteristic of the pancreatic acinar cell may be common to a wide variety of cells engaged in protein synthesis. Such variations on this theme as are displayed by other cell types active in protein synthesis involve mostly the use of other routes in the transport and release of the proteins. It is with regard to intracellular transport and to the extent and mechanics of Golgi involvement that the major questions still persist. There is, for example, accumulating evidence that fibroblasts, active in the synthesis of collagen, discharge their product directly from ER cisternae into the en-

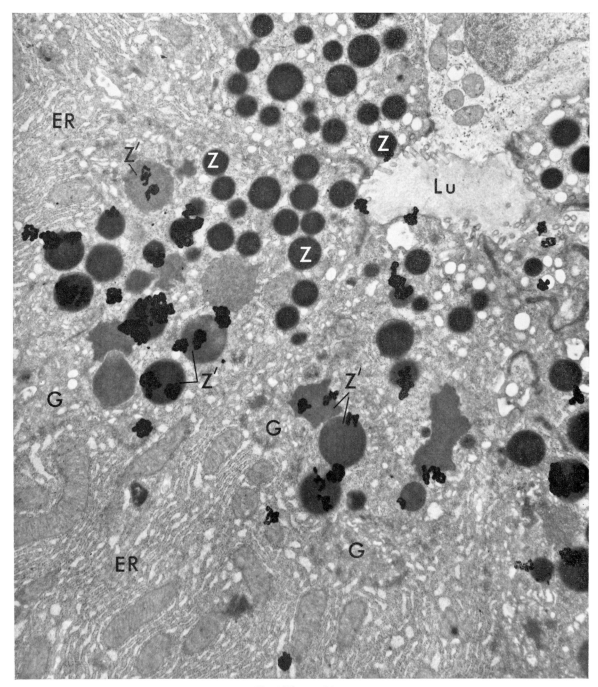

Text Figure 11a

This electron microscope autoradiograph demonstrates the localization of radioactive leucine in specific granules of pancreatic acinar cells 37 minutes after a pulse label had been administered to a slice of tissue incubated in physiological salt solution containing the labeled amino acid. Grains of reduced silver in the overlying photographic emulsion appear as irregular inklike markings near the sites from which radioactive energy was emitted. The apices of several cells bordering on the acinar lumen (Lu) each have a considerable number of secretory granules. The latter are of two types. One type, the smaller, denser round granules (Z) nearest the cell

apex, consist of mature granules that are ready to be ejected into the lumen. Larger, less dense granules (Z′), which often have a serrated border, are the precursors of the former type and are called condensing vacuoles. At the moment when this tissue sample was fixed, the radioactive protein was chiefly in the condensing vacuoles. Some labeling of the more mature vacuoles had already occurred, and, if more time had been allowed between the exposure to label and fixation, these would have been the principal sites of radioactivity. It is to be noted that the rough-surfaced endoplasmic reticulum (ER), where synthesis of the zymogen proteins occurred,

46

no longer contains any of the pulse label so prominent in it immediately after exposure. In the same way the Golgi regions (G), which are involved in transfer of the proteins from the ER into the condensing vacuoles, are not labeled, although they are heavily marked when tissue is fixed only 7 minutes after administration of label. A series of autoradiographs can thus afford a kind of time-lapse movie,

revealing the progress of labeled protein through the cell and the sequential involvement of the ER, Golgi, and condensing vacuoles in the formation of the zymogen granules. We are indebted to J. D. Jamieson and G. E. Palade for this micrograph.

From the pancreas of the guinea pig (*Cavia porcellus*)
Magnification × 13,000

vironment, thus bypassing the Golgi (see Plate 28). Plasma cells may use the same route in the secretion of gamma globulins. But additional variations on the mechanism of cell secretion are recognized and are mentioned in the texts of Plates 12, 16–19, and 35.

The cells lining the ducts of the exocrine pancreas seem relatively inactive when compared

to the secretory cells. In this micrograph one such cell with nucleus marked N′ lies near the apices of the glandular cells. It is evident that this cell type contains only a few organelles and no complex membranous systems.

From the pancreas of the bat (*Myotis lucifigus*)
Magnification × 13,500
Inset × 62,000

References

Caro, L. G., and Palade, G. E. Protein synthesis, storage, and discharge in the pancreatic exocrine cell. *J. Cell Biol., 20:*473 (1964).

Fedorko, M. E., and Hirsch, J. G. Cytoplasmic granule formation in myelocytes. *J. Cell Biol., 29:*307 (1966).

Jamieson, J. D., and Palade, G. E. Intercellular transport of secretory proteins in the pancreatic exocrine cell. I. Role of the peripheral elements of the Golgi complex. *J. Cell Biol., 34:*577 (1967).

————. Intercellular transport of secretory proteins in the pancreatic exocrine cell. II. Transport to condensing vacuoles and zymogen granules. *J. Cell Biol., 34:*597 (1967).

Parks, H. F. Morphological study of the extrusion of secretory materials by the parotid glands of mouse and rat. *J. Ultrastruct. Res., 6:*449 (1962).

Ross, R., and Benditt, E. P. Wound healing and collagen formation. V. Quantitative electron microscope radioautographic observations of proline-H[3] utilization by fibroblasts. *J. Cell Biol., 27:*83 (1965).

Siekevitz, P., and Palade, G. E. A cytochemical study on the pancreas of the guinea pig. V. *In vivo* incorporation of leucine-1-C[14] into the chymotrypsinogen of various cell fractions. *J. Biophysic. and Biochem. Cytol., 7:*619 (1960).

Sjöstrand, F. S., and Hanzon, V. Membrane structures of cytoplasm and mitochondria in exocrine cells of mouse pancreas as revealed by high resolution electron microscopy. *Exp. Cell Res., 7:*393 (1954).

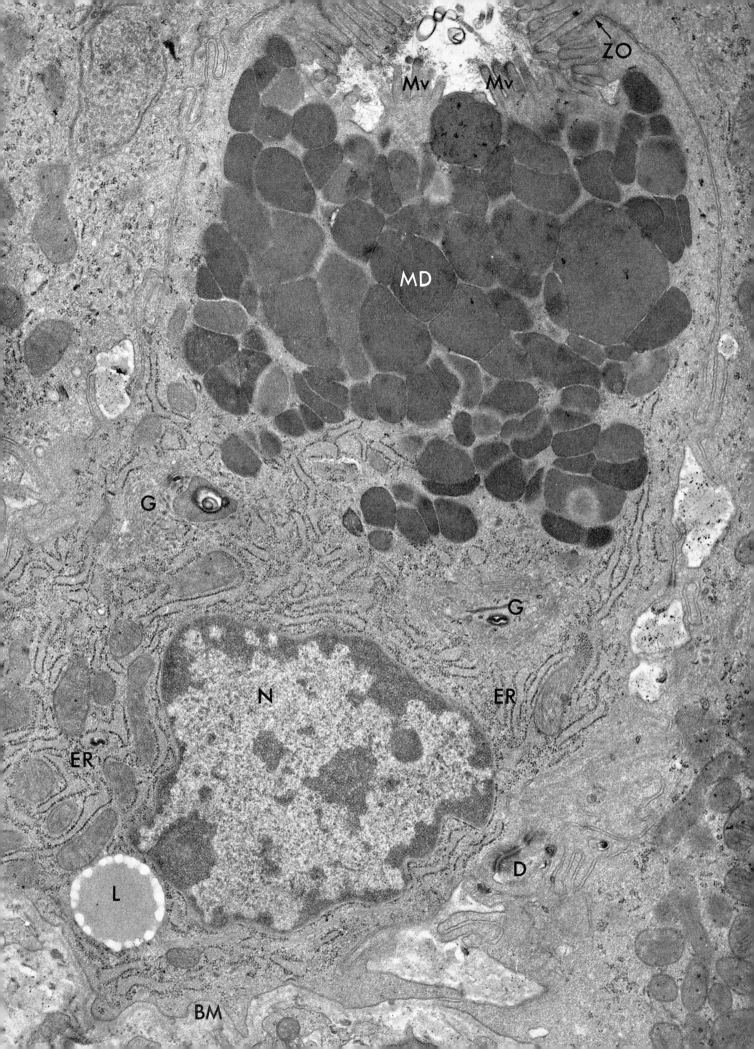

PLATE 12

The Goblet Cell

The epithelial lining of the gastrointestinal tract has among its components cells that secrete mucus, a viscous lubricating substance. Closely packed mucigen granules or mucous droplets (MD) often cause a bulging expansion of the apical cytoplasm above the narrower nucleus-containing "stem," hence the name *goblet cell*. The granules or droplets have been shown by their staining properties to contain polysaccharides, and analysis of mucous secretion has revealed it to be a complex carbohydrate, that is, a carbohydrate bound to protein, in this instance of the type referred to as glycoprotein.

The extensive knowledge of the cytological events in the production of protein secretion (see Plate 11) demands a comparison of the fine structure of the goblet cell with the pancreatic acinar cell in the hope of revealing similarities and differences in their secretory processes. In the basal cytoplasm surrounding the nucleus (N) of the columnar goblet cells, the rough-surfaced endoplasmic reticulum (ER) abounds, as one would expect in a protein secreting cell (see also Plates 1 and 2). Lipid inclusions (L) are common. Near the apical pole of the nucleus a large Golgi complex (G) underlies the mass of mucous droplets (MD). The Golgi has been described in this instance as a cup-shaped structure with its base oriented toward the nucleus. Within the cup the cavities of the Golgi saccules become distended and in the central region approach the size of smaller mucigen granules. Furthermore the contents of saccules and granules are quite similar. This observation reinforces the suggestion that the membranous Golgi saccules transform into mucous droplets.

As new droplets form, they push older ones toward the apical surface of the cell. There seems to be relatively little increase in the size of the droplets once they leave the Golgi region, and contrary to earlier electron microscope studies, recent examination of well-preserved cells indicates that the droplets are encased by a membrane during their intracellular existence and are still so enclosed as they emerge from the apical surface through gaps in the plasma membrane. In this micrograph a mucous droplet lies close to the apical membrane between two groups of microvilli (Mv). Once free in the lumen of the

intestine the membrane breaks down, and the mucus is released.

Microscopic examination therefore reveals a pattern of droplet formation in many ways similar to that of protein secretion. Yet there may be essential differences between protein and mucous secretion, especially in the nature of Golgi involvement. Because goblet cells do not aggregate to form homogeneous cell populations, they are not amenable to analysis by differential centrifugation. Autoradiography, however, has proved an effective tool for studying the assembly of mucous droplets (compare Plate 11). Following the intraperitoneal injection of tritiated glucose into young rats, samples of tissue can be taken after suitable intervals. In intestinal epithelium fixed only minutes after injection, silver grains can be detected over the Golgi saccules, but the ER remains essentially unlabeled. With time, the label appears associated with mucous droplets in the Golgi "cup"; later it is found near the apical granules, and eventually it can be detected over the mucus in the intestinal lumen. These observations have led to the conclusion that the labeled glucose is incorporated into the carbohydrate component of mucus that is being synthesized within the Golgi saccules.

Chemical characterizations of the mucus presents some technical difficulties when only small amounts are available. Treatment of tissue sections with enzymes of varying specificity suggests that the cell product is a glycoprotein, since it is removed by treatment known to break down this sort of compound. When sufficient amounts of mucus can be obtained, as from the surface of the epithelium of the colon (which contains numerous goblet cells), this product, too, has been identified as glycoprotein.

Fine structural and autoradiographic studies have focused attention on the importance of the Golgi region in the production of epithelial glycoprotein. Supporting biochemical evidence from studies on liver cells indicates that the protein moiety is synthesized by the ribosomes associated with ER membranes and that the enzymes that link simple sugars to polysaccharides are to be found in a cytoplasmic membrane fraction. It seems reasonable to expect on the basis of this evidence and autoradiographic information that the

Golgi is the site where carbohydrate and protein are combined to form the glycoprotein of mucus.

The polarization and dynamic activity of the Golgi are in evidence in goblet cells. Although saccules within the cup-shaped Golgi are transformed into mucous droplets, the number of Golgi saccules does not become depleted. This indicates a constant renewal, probably at the periphery of the region. Furthermore, the production of droplets does not seem to be part of a secretory cycle, but rather is a continuous activity of the functioning goblet cell.

Goblet cells are clearly integral units of the intestinal epithelium as demonstrated by their close attachment to absorbing cells. A *zonula occludens* (ZO) is evident laterally near the apical surface, and desmosomes (D) occur at the basilateral surface. These cells have a basement membrane (BM) in common with absorbing cells of the epithelium.

From the intestine of the bat
Magnification × 23,000

References

Freeman, J. A. Goblet cell fine structure. *Anat. Rec., 154:* 121 (1966).
Hollmann, K. H. The fine structure of the goblet cells in the rat intestine. *Ann. N. Y. Acad. Sci., 106:*545 (1963).
Lane, N., Caro, L., Otero-Vilardebó, L. R., and Godman, G. C. On the site of sulfation in colonic goblet cells. *J. Cell Biol., 21:*339 (1964).

Neutra, M., and Leblond, C. P. Synthesis of the carbohydrate of mucus in the Golgi complex as shown by electron microscope radioautography of goblet cells from rats injected with glucose-H[3]. *J. Cell Biol., 30:*119 (1966).
Sarcione, E. J. The initial subcellular site of incorporation of hexoses into liver protein. *J. Biol. Chem., 239:*1686 (1964).

PLATE 13
Gastric Parietal Cells

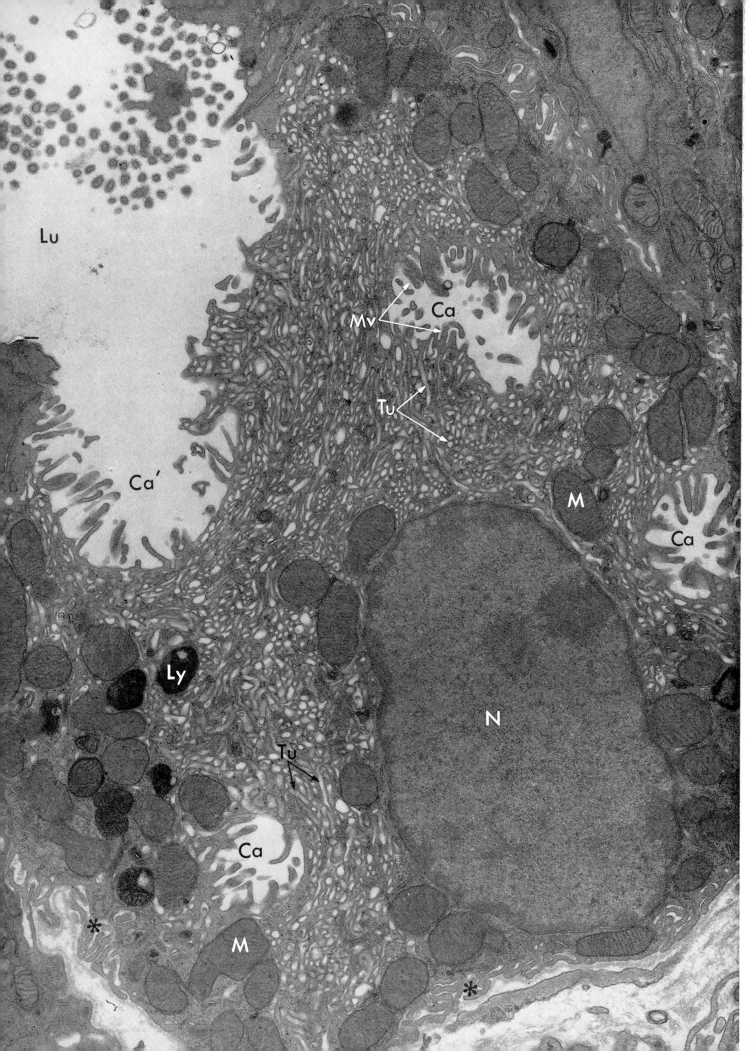

PLATE 13

Gastric Parietal Cells

Nearly one hundred years ago, the parietal cells of the gastric gland were designated as the probable sites of hydrochloric acid secretion, and this interpretation of their function continues to be generally accepted. The production of an HCl solution, approximately 0.15 N, a concentration lethal to many cells, is certainly an intriguing phenomenon, and much effort has been spent in discovering how this is accomplished. Since complete understanding still eludes us, it is not surprising that electron microscopists have been seeking clues in the fine structure of parietal cells.

A striking feature of these cells is the elaborate system of surface invaginations, or secretory canaliculi (Ca), which penetrate the cytoplasm lateral to the nucleus (N) of the cell. These passageways are connected by a common outlet (Ca′) to the lumen (Lu) of the gastric gland. While light microscopists knew about this complex system, they were unaware that the canaliculi were covered with microvilli (Mv). These latter obviously increase the area of the free surface of these cells over that provided by the surface invaginations themselves. Observations on the fate of indicator substances presented to the basal surface of parietal cells have shown that, while the cytoplasm of the cells remains slightly alkaline, the canaliculi are acid. These experiments support the theory that the parietal cells produce acid, and they seem furthermore to localize the site of secretion at the free surfaces of the canaliculi.

In addition to these labyrinthine invaginations, parietal cells possess an extensive cytoplasmic membrane system consisting of tubules (Tu) limited by smooth-surfaced membranes. The tubules have been reported on occasion to open into the canaliculi. In this micrograph, the tubular system is so extensive that other cytoplasmic organelles such as mitochondria (M) and lysosomes (Ly) are crowded laterally or toward the folded basal surface (*) of the cell. On the assumption that such a complex system might be involved in acid secretion, comparisons have been made between cells in stomachs active and inactive with regard to this secretion. In the active state, a concentration of smooth-surfaced tubular profiles near the canaliculi was observed. Simultaneously, the smooth-surfaced elements of the cytoplasm showed a general decrease, and the secretory canaliculi became more extensive. The inference is that the former tubules move to the surface, open to release H^+, and indeed become part of the free surface of the cell. Such observations indicate that the intracellular system of smooth-surfaced membranes performs essential functions in acid secretion.

Similar tubular cytoplasmic membrane systems apparently exist in other cells that secrete ions. In this group are included "chloride" cells that help rid certain marine fishes of excess salt. Observations on these cells have shown that the cavities of their tubular systems are continuous with the extracellular space. If, for example, electron opaque markers that cannot penetrate the plasma membrane are added to the cell's environment, they find their way into this system but are not found within the endoplasmic reticulum, the nuclear envelope, or the Golgi vesicles. These results argue that ion-secreting cells possess a unique system of plasma membrane invaginations that greatly expands the area of the cell surface. Furthermore, there seems to be no reason to suppose that the system, in spite of its superficial resemblance to the ER, is a variant of that system or that the Golgi is involved in its formation.

It is tempting to speculate on the role of this intracellular membrane system in acid secretion by the gastric parietal cell. Physiologists have discovered that while acid is secreted into the lumen of the gastric gland, an equal amount of base is formed and liberated into the blood stream. The bicarbonate ion released is believed to be formed from hydrated carbon dioxide through the mediation of the enzyme, carbonic anhydrase, which is apparently abundant in parietal cells. Just how the hydrogen ion that is secreted is formed and transported out of the apical pole of the cell is unknown, but it is known to depend on oxidative metabolic processes. It is reasonable to assume that its formation must occur at a site that is separate spatially from available hydroxyl ion and that it must be trapped in some way in order to prevent the water formation that would normally be expected. One may suppose in this regard that the system of tubules within the parietal cell could represent the separate surfaces and compartments for this segregation. There is, in fact, accumulating evidence that mucopolysaccharides reside in the cavities of similar systems in other ion-secreting cells and are capable of binding per unit weight relatively large quantities of hydrogen or other ions. As we have noted, this system is continuous with the cell surface and thus contributes to the total surface area where ion concentration apparently occurs. Upon stimulation the intracellular membrane system with its ion load can become externalized and thus achieve the secretion of hydrochloric acid.

From the stomach of the mouse
Magnification $\times$ 17,000

References

BRADFORD, N. M., and DAVIES, R. E. The site of hydrochloric acid production in stomach as determined by indicators. *Biochem. J., 46:*414 (1950).

DAVIES, R. E. Gastric hydrochloric acid production—the present position. *In* Metabolic Aspects of Transport Across Cell Membranes. Q. R. Murphy, editor. Madison, The University of Wisconsin Press (1957) p. 277.

ELLIS, R. A., and ABEL, J. H., JR. Intercellular channels in the salt-secreting glands of marine turtles. *Science, 144:* 1340 (1964).

ITO, S., and WINCHESTER, R. J. The fine structure of the gastric mucosa in the bat. *J. Cell Biol., 16:*541 (1963).

PHILPOTT, C. W. The specialized surface of a cell specialized for electrolyte transport. *J. Cell Biol., 35:*104A (1967).

———, and COPELAND, D. E. Fine structure of chloride cells from three species of *Fundulus. J. Cell Biol., 18:* 389 (1963).

ROBERTSON, R. N. The separation of protons and electrons as a fundamental biological process. *Endeavour, 26:*134 (1967).

SEDAR, A. W. Fine structure of the stimulated oxyntic cell. *Fed. Proc., 24:*1360 (1965).

VIAL, J. D., and ORREGO, H. Electron microscope observations on the fine structure of parietal cells. *J. Biophysic. and Biochem. Cytol., 7:*367 (1960).

PLATE 14

The Hepatic Parenchymal Cell

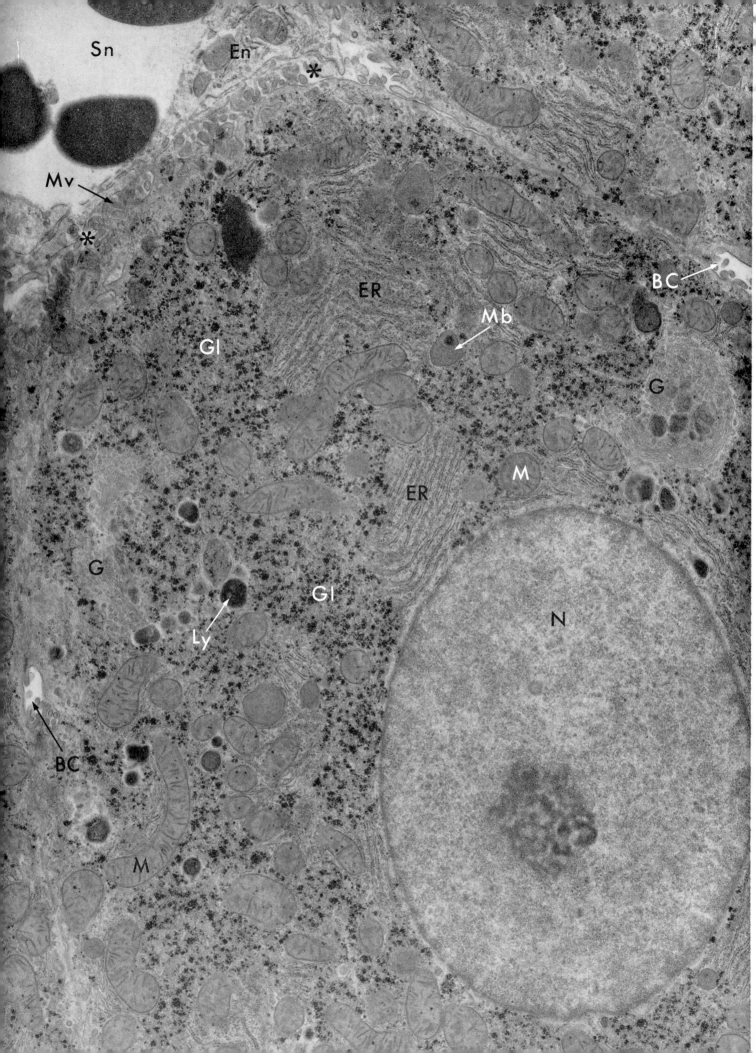

PLATE 14
The Hepatic Parenchymal Cell

The liver cell or hepatocyte is one of the most essential cells in the animal body. It is the unit of structure in a vast organ (1.5 kgs in man) which, like other glands of the gastrointestinal tract, develops from a small outpocketing of the primitive gut wall. During its growth and differentiation it takes on a variety of functions; and, though it retains only part of these in the adult, it still performs a number that are of great importance to the whole animal. It is interesting to see how the fine structure of this cell is adapted to the performance of these several roles.

Histologically, this complex epithelial tissue mingles intimately with a finely divided vascular portal system through which the blood from the intestine and spleen percolates slowly in humans but still at a total volume rate of better than one liter per minute. During its passage carbohydrates and especially glucose are removed and stored as glycogen. Amino acids are taken up for protein synthesis. One product of this synthesis, serum albumin, is manufactured in a few minutes and eventually secreted into the blood stream. Globulins, fibrinogen, and other proteins as well as lipoproteins are made in smaller amounts. Toxic agents of a wide variety, which find their way into the circulation, are removed and in most cases detoxified.

In addition to absorbing materials for storage and synthesis, the liver cell responds to circulating hormones such as epinephrine, insulin, and glucagon by secreting as an endocrine gland. For example, glucose may be mobilized from stored glycogen and put into the circulation. As an exocrine gland, the liver secretes bile salts derived from the catabolism of blood pigments. Amino acids are deaminated and thus made available to carbohydrate metabolism, while the ammonia formed is detoxified by incorporation into relatively harmless urea. These and other functions of lesser significance contribute to making the liver cell one of the most diversely active in the body.

It is not surprising to find the cytoplasm of this cell (shown here surrounding the nucleus N) morphologically one of the most complicated. No single organelle or system seems to dominate in its substructure. The rough endoplasmic reticulum, for example, does not constitute the major part of the cytoplasm as in the cells of the exocrine pancreas (Plate 11). Instead, the thin flattened cisternae (ER) are assembled into several bundles or stacks of eight to ten parallel units, which are distributed widely in the cytoplasm. In the normal, relatively quiescent cell the mitochondria (M) are located around the margins of these stacks, presumably making ATP available as a source of energy for the synthesis of plasma proteins (see Plate 2).

But these are only two of this cell's components. Marginal to these stacks of cisternae, the cytoplasm takes on a darkly speckled appearance due to dense granules of glycogen (Gl). These are regions of storage, which naturally change in appearance with time in respect to the feeding cycle. Shortly after the animal eats, they fill up with glycogen and appear very dense, whereas toward the end of the fasting period only relatively few granules remain. Scattered among these are small tubules and vesicles, whose profiles can just be detected at this magnification, representing a so-called smooth form of the ER (see Plates 7 and 15 and text figure 15a).

Like other cells, the hepatocyte possesses a Golgi complex or component (G). This tends to become localized in the cell in the vicinity of the bile canaliculi (BC) and consists, as it does in other cells (see Plates 3 and 12), of several flattened vesicles arranged in a parallel, cup-shaped array. Near its concave side there are usually juxtaposed some granule-filled and dilated vesicles (see also Plate 15).

Though the pattern is not evident in this or any single micrograph of a liver cell, examination of many pictures can demonstrate that the distribution of these membrane systems and organelles follows a pattern that brings one margin of the rough-surfaced ER stacks into apposition with glycogen-rich cytoplasm and the opposite margin close to a Golgi complex. These and other aspects of this organization are evident in the liver cell diagram (text figure 15b).

A number of dense masses, appearing round in outline and polymorphic in content, can be identified in the vicinity of the Golgi. These structures are called lysosomes (Ly) because they have been shown to contain a number of hydrolytic enzymes. Within their enclosing membranes small packets of liver cell cytoplasm are walled off and set apart for digestion. Through this device, the liver cell may destroy parts of its machinery that may have been damaged or have ceased to function normally. The products of this digestion are available to the cell for gluconeogenesis (new production of glucose) or regeneration of structure. Another type of enzyme-rich granule, called the microbody or peroxisome (Mb), is characterized by the presence within it of a dense nucleoid. A further examination and discussion of the organelles (apart from the nucleus, N) occurring in hepatic parenchymal cells will be found in the text for Plate 15.

The parenchymal cells of the liver associate to form a cuboidal epithelium that possesses some unusual characteristics. The basal surface of the tissue is exposed to the vascular supply, represented by the blood sinusoids (Sn), a special type of capillary. The usual tissue relationship would place (a) the capillary endothelium, (b) its basement membrane, (c) an interstitial connective tissue matrix, and (d) the epithelial basement membrane between the epithelial cell and the circulating tissue or blood (see Plates 6, 17, and 26). But in the case of the liver these barriers are reduced to remnants at most, so that the blood plasma may come into direct contact with the hepatocyte, thus facilitating rapid exchanges between the two. The sinusoidal endothelium (En) is discontinuous, and the pores (fenestrae) in the sieve, though not large enough to pass erythrocytes, certainly provide for free movement of plasma. Only insignificant bits of the basement membrane are evident, and the inter-

stitium has only occasional bundles of collagen fibrils. The basal surface of the liver cell is covered by microvilli (Mv), which increase its surface area and thus constitute another specialization that aids in rapid exchange of metabolites. These short microvilli project into a space (*) called the space of Disse, which is limited on the opposite side by the sinusoidal endothelium (En). This space is continuous with the narrower ones between the cells and eventually with a system of lymph channels designed to return the extravascular plasma to the circulation. These features of liver tissue fine structure are illustrated only in part by the sinusoid (Sn) containing dense erythrocytes (upper left in this micrograph).

The apical or free surface of the hepatic epithelium is as unusual as the basal surface just described. It is represented by the relatively small surface of the liver cell that faces on and limits the bile canaliculi (BC). Only two contiguous hepatocytes are involved in forming the capillary, and their free surfaces exposed to the lumen of this tiny duct are joined at their edges by relatively tight junctions. The junctions are similar, though not identical, to those which are normally found joining intestinal epithelial cells (Plate 7). One of these attachment devices can be seen just above the arrow to the bile capillary at the right. It can be noted as well that the liver cell surfaces bordering the capillary show a few short microvilli.

From the liver of the rat
Magnification $\times$ 13,000

References

BRUNI, C., and PORTER, K. R. The fine structure of the parenchymal cell of the normal rat liver. *Amer. J. Path.,* 46:691 (1965).

DEANE, H. W. The basophilic bodies in hepatic cells. *Amer. J. Anat.,* 78:227 (1946).

DE DUVE, C. The lysosome concept. *In* Ciba Foundation Symposium on Lysosomes. A. V. S. de Reuck and M. P. Cameron, editors. London, J. and A. Churchill, Ltd. (1963) p. 1.

FAWCETT, D. W. Observations on the cytology and electron microscopy of hepatic cells. *J. Nat. Cancer Inst.,* 15:1475 (1955).

HEATH, T., and WISSIG, S. L. Fine structure of the surface of mouse hepatic cells. *Amer. J. Anat.,* 119:97 (1966).

NOVIKOFF, A. B., and ESSNER, E. The liver cell. *Amer. J. Med.,* 29:102 (1960).

PETERS, T., JR. The biosynthesis of rat serum albumin. II. Intracellular phenomena in the secretion of newly formed albumin. *J. Biol. Chem.,* 237:1186 (1962).

PLATE 15

Hepatic Cell Cytoplasm

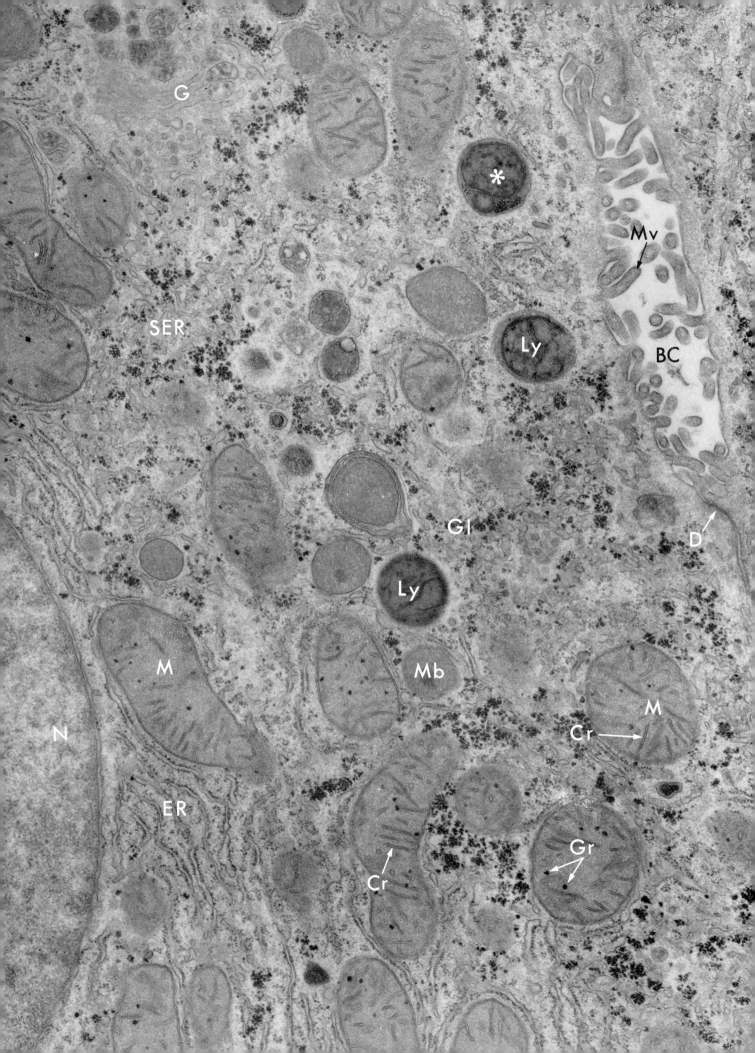

PLATE 15

Hepatic Cell Cytoplasm

Among the many cell types of the vertebrate animal none has been more extensively studied with the combined techniques of cytochemistry and electron microscopy than that of the liver. The reason resides mainly in the fact that liver as a tissue is made up very largely of one kind of cell, the hepatocyte, shown in Plate 14. It follows that any isolated cell fraction (e.g., mitochondria) does not include in important amounts contaminants from other cell types. This favorable feature of liver and the vastly improved techniques for obtaining single element fractions have contributed to the growth of a very rich literature concerning liver cell components. All of this compels one to consider separately some of their features and functions.

This electron micrograph, which shows part of a liver parenchymal cell or hepatocyte, is reproduced at a magnification sufficiently high ($\times$ 30,000) to show the fine structural details of several liver cell components. Additional details are depicted in text figures 15a and 15b.

A small part of the cell nucleus (N) is included at the lower left in the picture. It is limited by the usual two-membrane envelope, appearing quite similar in profile to the cisternae of the endoplasmic reticulum (ER) in the adjacent cytoplasm. Though not shown in this micrograph, continuities between the outer membrane of the envelope and those of the ER are frequently encountered in these cells.

In the cytoplasm of the hepatocyte two forms of this membranous reticulate system are regularly observed. In one (ER) the cisternal membranes have ribosomes on their outer surfaces. This form was discussed in the text of Plate 2, and, as mentioned there, it is the form found in cells in which protein is synthesized for secretion. Experimental studies have shown that when the amino acid leucine (radioactive) is made available to liver cells, it is, within 2 to 3 minutes, incorporated into the protein albumin. When albumin is isolated from the cell within this short period, the labeled protein is attached to microsomes derived from the rough-surfaced endoplasmic reticulum. This shows that at least for this particular protein the ribosome-rich ER is the site of synthesis.

The second form of the ER in liver cells is made up of branching tubular elements constituting a compact three-dimensional lattice. The membrane surfaces here are particle-free or smooth, hence the appellation *smooth endoplasmic reticulum* (SER). This form of the ER (better seen in text figure 15b) is continuous with the rough, and on the basis of experiments in which ^{14}C-labeled membrane components have been followed, it is known that this smooth form is derived from the rough.

In the hepatic parenchymal cell the SER shows a specific (selective) association with glycogen granules (Gl). The latter are enmeshed in the lattice spaces of the reticulum (see text figure 15b). Because of this intimate relationship and also the observed fact that the SER increases in amount during glycogen mobilization and depletion, it was proposed that the system is involved in glycogenolysis and glucose transport. In part this interpretation has been strengthened by discoveries that the SER vesicles and membranes are rich in the enzyme glucose-6-phosphatase. However, the evident mobilization of glycogen can occur in non-hepatic cells without obvious SER intervention, and the absence from the SER of phosphorylases important in the early stages of glycogen breakdown suggests now a more limited role for the SER in its liver-glycogen association. Presumably the glucose-6-phosphate as a product of glycogenolysis is picked up by the SER and dephosphorylated. The glucose then enclosed in SER vesicles is transported to the cell surface and secreted. This, at very least, is a working hypothesis.

The large membrane surfaces that the SER presents to the cytoplasmic ground substance are apparently used for other important functions of the liver cell. Some time ago it was observed that severely toxic carcinogenic agents induced a large increase in the amount of SER. The reason for this was not at once apparent but has since been clarified in discoveries that this is a general response to toxic agents. Such drugs as phenobarbital, when administered repeatedly, induce a pronounced development of the SER and simultaneously a drug-hydroxylating enzyme associated with the ER membranes. The synthesis of the detoxifying enzyme is in turn dependent on

(*Continued on page 63*)

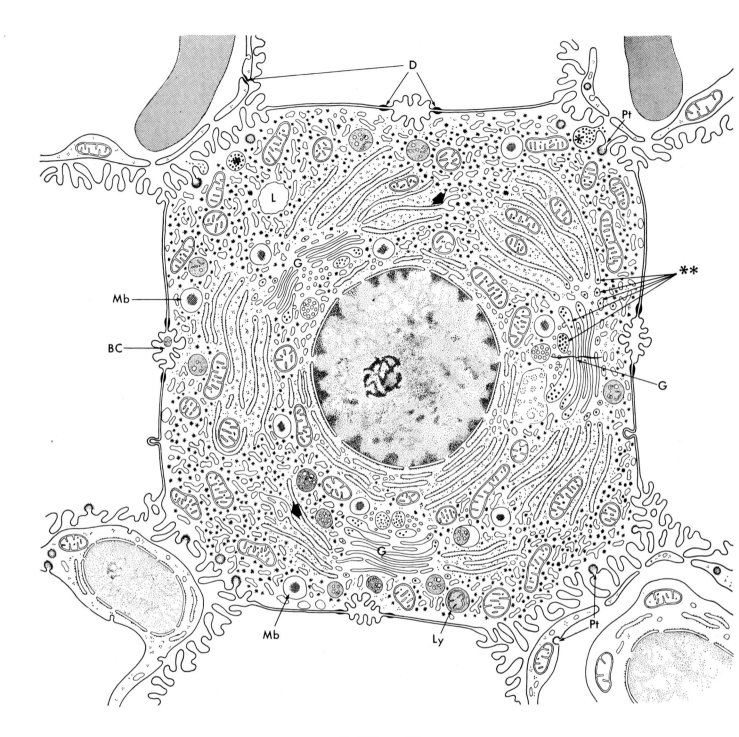

Text Figure 15a

The fine structure of a cell or tissue is frequently clarified by the construction of a diagram of the whole or its parts. Such constructed images represent distillations of the information gathered from the study of many micrographs. As such they are important for the student and even more important for the investigator, who is obliged in making the diagram to clarify his concepts of structural relationships, which might otherwise remain confused. In representing interpretations of observations, diagrams are seldom absolutely correct in all they show and are therefore valuable only as temporary aids to understanding.

This drawing represents a single parenchymal cell of the rat liver. It is surrounded by and closely contiguous with four other hepatic cells (which are not drawn in) and four sinusoids or capillaries of the blood supply. The surfaces of the hepatocyte adjacent to the sinusoids possess many microvilli and are equivalent to the basal poles or surfaces of this epithelial cell, unusual in this instance in not being

(Continued)

62

(*Text figure 15a Continued*)
underlain by a basement membrane. The sinusoids are limited by thin endothelial cells with fenestrae as illustrated. Red blood cells are represented in the two at the upper right and left corners of the picture; a white cell is in that at the lower right.

After examining Plates 1 through 4, 14, and 15 the student should have no difficulty in recognizing such prominent constituents of the cell as nucleus, mitochondria, and the long slender profiles of cisternae belonging to the endoplasmic reticulum or ER. Small particles or ribosomes are abundant on the surfaces of the latter and in the ground substance between them. The cisternae are ordinarily arranged in stacks of 6 to 12 units. One margin of such an assemblage frequently lies adjacent to a Golgi region. It also will be noted that small granules of a particular type occupy the ends of these cisternae and the vesicles intervening between ER and Golgi as well as the expanded ends of cisternae and spherical vesicles belonging to the Golgi proper (G). These images (**) are designed to show the mechanism of protein transport from ER to Golgi, where packaging for export from the cell takes place. The product is subsequently released from the secretion granule into the space of Disse (as shown at *). The opposite margin of the stacks of ER cisternae borders on masses of glycogen and asso-

ciated vesicles belonging to the smooth endoplasmic reticulum or SER. These two forms are often continuous as though the smooth form may develop from the rough. Such continuities are indicated by thick arrows. It is thought that the smooth ER is involved in the transport of glucose from the liver cell during glycogenolysis. Other prominent components of the hepatic cell cytoplasm include lysosomes (Ly), containing remnants of organelles and ground substance apparently set aside for hydrolysis, and microbodies or peroxisomes (Mb). A single lipid granule is indicated at L.

Various differentiations of the cell surface are shown, though their full functional meaning is not completely clarified as yet. The surface adjacent to and limiting the bile canaliculus (BC) is increased in area by many microvilli. This represents the free surface of this cell, and as is common in epithelial cells it is limited by close junctions and desmosomes (D). Besides showing numerous microvilli on its sinusoidal surface, the liver cell possesses peculiar pits (Pt) or spherical depressions with what appear as short bristles on their cytoplasmic surfaces. These same structures are present on the endothelial cells and Kupffer cells lining the sinusoids. They are thought to be involved in the selective uptake of proteins and possibly other macromolecules from the circulating blood plasma.

(*Text Continued*)

the production of a rather short-lived messenger RNA (see Plate 4). Thus the liver cell has evolved a remarkable device for the rapid detoxification of otherwise destructive foreign agents that find their way into the body.

The Golgi complex (G) of the hepatocyte is similar in its major characteristics to that in other cells (see Plates 3 and 12). In this micrograph it appears as a stack of 4 or 5 flattened cisternae limited by smooth-surfaced membranes. That the outlines of these are not more distinctly shown here is due to the somewhat oblique orientation of the section relative to the vertical axis of the stack. At their margins it is common for the Golgi cisternae to be inflated and to contain small dense granules about 500 Å in diameter and currently interpreted as lipoprotein. The presence of similar granules in vesicles of the Golgi-associated ER and on the concave side of the Golgi complex in large spherical vesicles (see top left in micrograph) has been taken to mean that ER-sequestered materials are fed into one pole of the Golgi region to emerge from the other face packaged (and possibly refined) into larger quantities for transport thence to the cell surface. This is only one of several activities that have been postulated for the hepatocyte Golgi. For it,

as for the others, the information yet available is meager and largely morphological.

The dense bodies (Ly) usually located near the surfaces of the hepatocyte bordering the bile canaliculi are representative of lysosomes. It is characteristic for them to contain recognizable portions of cytoplasmic components (*), such as glycogen, mitochondria, or cisternae of the ER. These contents show in turn varying degrees of disintegration, and this morphological picture fits the well-established functional concept that hydrolytic enzymes (phosphatases and proteases) are active within these tiny vesicles. Experiments have demonstrated that in starvation or under other pathological conditions cells possess a mechanism for self-consumption. Small packets of cytoplasm are walled off and digested. Apparently the products of digestion are in part reassimilated. The vesicles involved in this kind of controlled autolysis have been variously called cytolysosomes or autophagic vesicles. Remnants of digestion have been found in the bile canaliculi, suggesting that lysosomes discharge their residual contents from the cell and animal by this route.

Other granular components of the liver cell are reminiscent of secretory granules found in other cell types, such as eosinophils (Plate 34). In the hepatocyte they are called microbodies or peroxi-

(*Continued on page 65*)

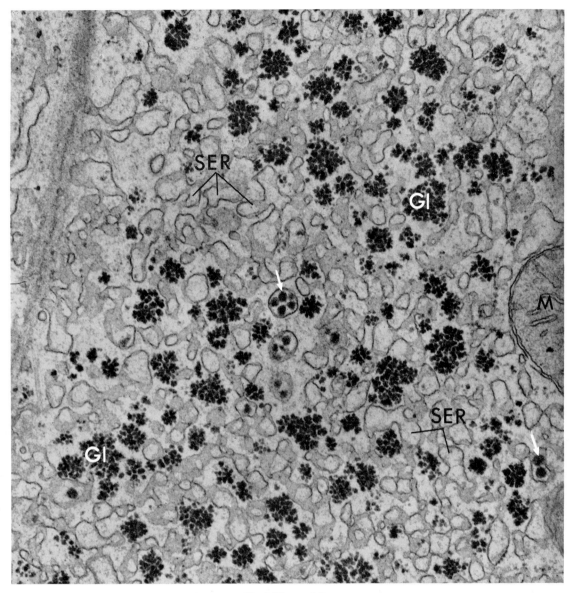

Text Figure 15b

This superb micrograph depicts the form of the smooth-surfaced endoplasmic reticulum in a hepatocyte and its relation to glycogen. The profiles of vesicles and tubules (SER) caught in this thin section show the system to be a tridimensional lattice. The spaces between the tubules and vesicles contain the dense glycogen particles (Gl) and make the relationship between ER and glycogen a very intimate one. Obviously, exchanges between the smooth ER with its large membrane surfaces and products of glycogenolysis would be easily achieved by this close association.

The small granules within some of the vesicles (arrows) are similar in size and density to granules of lipoprotein noted in Plate 15. A mitochondrion (M) enters the picture at the right, and a tangential section through the cell surface is included at the upper left.

We are indebted to G. Dallner, P. Siekevitz, and G. E. Palade for the micrograph, which is reprinted from the *J. Cell Biol., 30:*73 (1966).

From the liver of a three-day-old rat
Magnification $\times$ 48,000

somes (Mb). It may be observed from studying them in this micrograph that they are smaller than mitochondria (M) and that they are limited by a single membrane. Their contents consist of a homogeneous matrix enclosing a nucleoid, which at higher resolutions would appear crystalline. Furthermore, cytochemical techniques applied to the isolation and study of peroxisomes have shown them to be rich in uricase, catalase, and D-amino acid oxidase. Just where the peroxisomes arise is still in doubt, but their content of pure enzyme would implicate the rough ER in their synthesis. It is generally thought that they fuse with or otherwise become part of autophagic vesicles.

Other details of hepatocyte structure may be noted in this micrograph. The bile canaliculus (BC), which is formed by the apical surfaces of two liver cells, is sealed off from intercellular spaces by close junctions, which were earlier interpreted as desmosomes (D). Microvilli (Mv) extend into the lumen of this small duct. Liver cell mitochondria (M), so often isolated and examined, are characterized by a dense matrix, relatively few cristae (Cr), and a goodly number of mitochondrial granules (Gr).

From the liver of the rat
Magnification $\times$ 30,000

References

ASHFORD, T. P., and PORTER, K. R. Cytoplasmic components in hepatic cell lysosomes. *J. Cell Biol., 12:*198 (1962).

ASHWORTH, C. T., LEONARD, J. S., EIGENBRODT, E. H., and WRIGHTSMAN, F. J. Hepatic intracellular osmiophilic droplets. Effect of lipid solvents during tissue preparation. *J. Cell Biol., 31:*301 (1966).

BAUDHUIN, P., BEAUFAY, H., and DE DUVE, C. Combined biochemical and morphological study of particulate fractions from rat liver. *J. Cell Biol., 26:*219 (1965).

COIMBRA, A., and LEBLOND, C. P. Sites of glycogen synthesis in rat liver cells as shown by electron microscope radioautography after administration of glucose-H³. *J. Cell Biol., 30:*151 (1966).

DALLNER, G., SIEKEVITZ, P., and PALADE, G. E. Biogenesis of endoplasmic reticulum membranes. II. Synthesis of constitutive microsomal enzymes in developing rat hepatocyte. *J. Cell Biol., 30:*97 (1966).

DE DUVE, C. The lysosome. *Sci. Amer., 208:*64 (May, 1963).

DROCHMANS, P. Morphologie du glycogène. *J. Ultrastruct. Res., 6:*141 (1962).

HOLT, S. J., and HICKS, R. M. The localization of acid phosphatase in rat liver cells as revealed by combined cytochemical staining and electron microscopy. *J. Biophysic. and Biochem. Cystol., 11:*47 (1961).

HRUBAN, Z., and SWIFT, H. Uricase: localization in hepatic microbodies. *Science, 146:*1316 (1964).

JONES, A. L., and FAWCETT, D. W. Hypertrophy of the agranular endoplasmic reticulum in hamster liver induced by phenobarbital. *J. Histochem. Cytochem., 14:*215 (1966).

JONES, A. L., RUDERMAN, N. B., and HERRERA, M. G. An electron microscopic study of lipoprotein production and release by isolated perfused rat liver. *Proc. Soc. Exp. Biol. Med., 123:*4 (1966).

MILLONIG, G., and PORTER, K. R. Structural elements of rat liver cells involved in glycogen metabolism. *In* Proceedings of the European Regional Conference on Electron Microscopy, Delft, 1960. A. L. Houwink and B. J. Spit, editors. Delft, De Nederlandse Vereniging voor Electronenmicroscopie (1960) p. 655.

NOVIKOFF, A. B., ESSNER, E., and QUINTANA, N. Golgi apparatus and lysosomes. *Fed. Proc., 23:*1010 (1964).

ORRENIUS, S., ERICSSON, J. L. E., and ERNSTER, L. Phenobarbital-induced synthesis of the microsomal drug-metabolizing enzyme system and its relationship to the proliferation of endoplasmic membranes. A morphological and biochemical study. *J. Cell Biol., 25* (no. 3, part 1):627 (1965).

PORTER, K. R., and BRUNI, C. An electron microscope study of the early effects of 3'-Me-DAB on rat liver cells. *Cancer Res., 19:*997 (1959).

ROSEN, S. I., KELLY, G. W., and PETERS, V. B. Glucose-6-phosphatase in tubular endoplasmic reticulum of hepatocytes. *Science, 152:*352 (1966).

SHNITKA, T. K. Comparative ultrastructure of hepatic microbodies in some mammals and birds in relation to species differences in uricase activity. *J. Ultrastruct. Res., 16:*598 (1966).

SWIFT, H., and HRUBAN, Z. Focal degradation as a biological process. *Fed. Proc., 23:*1026 (1964).

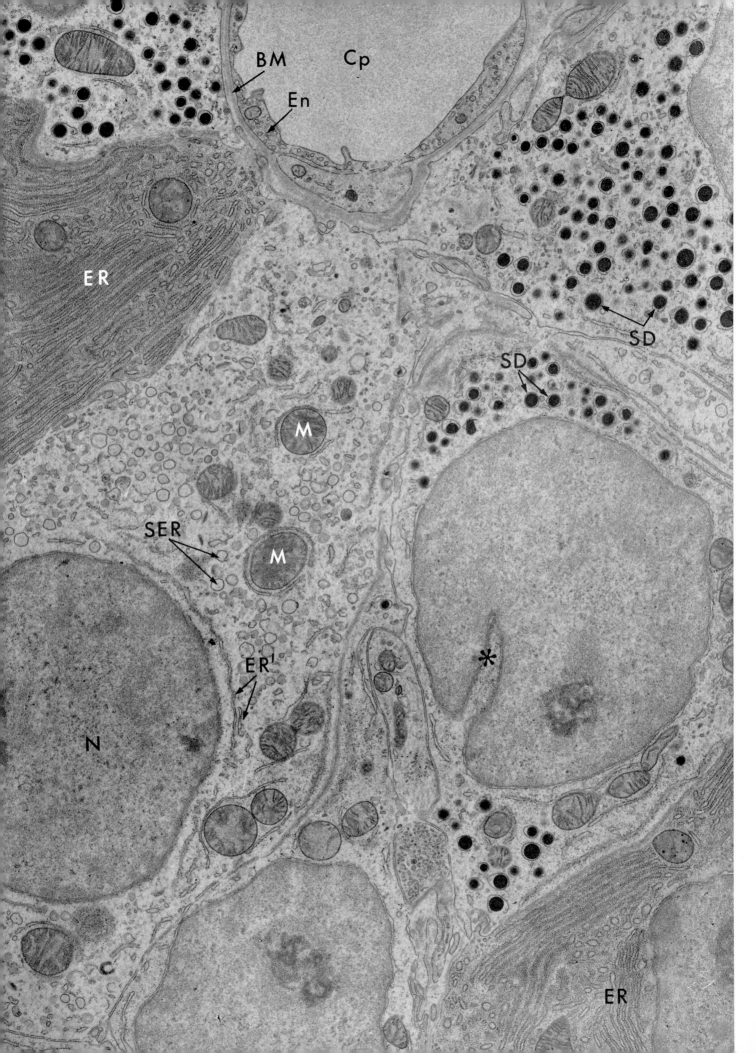

PLATE 16
Pancreatic Endocrine Cells

The pancreatic endocrine tissue, called the islets of Langerhans, differs markedly in fine structure from the exocrine tissue of that gland (see Plate 11). In this micrograph portions of two acinar cells, dense with intracellular membrane systems (ER) and associated ribosomes, may be compared with light-staining cytoplasm of the islet tissue. Characteristically, as here, endocrine cells are always close to blood capillaries (Cp) that carry away their secretory products. The endothelium (En) of this vascular tissue forms a thin but complete cell layer. It rests on a basement membrane (BM) that always constitutes part of the barrier between blood and endocrine tissue.

Several cell types are found in the islets of Langerhans, and differences in morphology suggest that they differ in function as well. The much-studied hormone, insulin, is now known to be a product of the beta cells, which have numerous dense, membrane-bounded secretory granules throughout their cytoplasm. The portions of three granule-containing cells seen in this micrograph—one with a nuclear cleft (∗)—probably belong to beta cells. To be certain of this identification one should prepare an adjacent serial section for light microscopy and determine whether the granules stain with aldehyde fuchsin. This dye is believed to combine with the sulfide groups of the insulin molecule. In electron micrographs, beta cell granules (SD) are usually separated from the membranes that enclose them by a clear halo, supposed to be an artifact.

There is abundant evidence now that beta cells are the source of insulin. Originally this insight resulted from cytological studies of pancreatic islets from humans or experimental animals suffering from diabetes. Although three types of islet cells can be differentiated by their tinctorial properties, of these three it is the beta cell that degenerates in animals with diabetes and exhibits degranulation when exposed to substances that bring about insulin release. The availability of purified insulin at present allows preparation of fluorescent-labeled antibody that reacts specifically with the hormone. The fluorescent label may be detected within beta cells stained with such antibody preparations.

When insulin-producing cells are filled with cytoplasmic secretion droplets (SD), elements of the rough-surfaced endoplasmic reticulum and free ribosomes are reduced in number. When, however, the granules are few, as they are after active secretion, the rough-surfaced ER and free ribosomes are proportionally increased, presumably in response to a stimulus bringing about increased protein synthesis. The morphological events occurring during the formation of secretory droplets are not entirely clear. While some observers believe that the Golgi complex may be involved in formation of the droplets as it is in the exocrine pancreas (see Plate 11), others suggest that the droplets arise solely within the endoplasmic reticulum. The secretory product would, in this second interpretation, be assembled into granules within the cisternae of the ER, and from these, vesicles enclosing the dense granules would pinch off after first becoming free of ribosomes.

Secretion of insulin from beta cells is believed to be initiated by entrance of sodium ion into the cells, but release of granules into the extracellular space has not been detected microscopically. Indeed it has been suggested that the membranes surrounding the granules open into the cytoplasmic ground substance and that the granules dissolve intracellularly. The secretory products would then be free to diffuse out of the cell and into the circulatory system.

Alpha cells are a second type of secretory cell occurring in the islets of Langerhans. Like the beta cells, they contain within their cytoplasm numerous dense secretory granules enclosed by membranes. Although the two types generally resemble each other in their cytoarchitecture, a distinction may be made on the basis of subtle fine structural differences. Alpha cells correspond to those cells that in preparations for the light microscope are stained positively by the phosphotungstic acid hematoxylin method. It is believed that alpha cells secrete glucagon, the glycogenolytic hormone. The production of the small protein molecule, insulin, and the polypeptide, glucagon, are therefore believed to occur in different cells. It is interesting to note in contrast that several different enzymes are produced by a single type of pancreatic acinar cell (see Plate 11).

Cells that lack cytoplasmic secretion droplets

are also present in the pancreatic islets. These have often been called chromophobic or by other names such as c cells, and one appears at the lower left in this micrograph. In the cytoplasm surrounding the spherical nucleus (N) there are a few rough-surfaced cisternae of the endoplasmic reticulum (ER'), a considerable number of smooth-walled vesicles (SER), also parts of the endoplasmic reticulum, and globular mitochondria (M). The function of this type of cell is unknown. As yet no one can say whether it represents a completely different cell type or illustrates simply one stage in the secretory cycle of either of the granule-producing cells.

From the pancreas of the bat
Magnification × 10,500

References

LACY, P. E. Electron microscopy of the beta cell of the pancreas. *Amer. J. Med., 31:*851 (1961).

LAZAROW, A. Cell types of the islets of Langerhans and the hormones they produce. *Diabetes, 6:*222 (1957).

LEVER, J. D., and FINDLAY, J. A. Similar structural bases for the storage and release of secretory material in adreno-medullary and β pancreatic cells. *Z. Zellforsch., 74:*317 (1966).

MILNER, R. D. G., and HALES, C. N. The sodium pump and insulin secretion. *Biochim. Biophys. Acta, 135:*375 (1967).

MUNGER, B. L. The secretory cycle of the pancreatic islet α-cell *Lab. Invest., 11:*885 (1962).

OPIE, E. L. Cytology of the pancreas. *In* Special Cytology, second edition. E. V. Cowdry, editor. New York, Paul B. Hoeber, Inc., vol. I (1932) p. 375.

SATO, T., HERMAN, L., and FITZGERALD, P. J. The comparative ultra-structure of the pancreatic islet of Langerhans. *Gen. Comp. Endocr., 7:*132 (1966).

WILLIAMSON, J. R., LACY, P. E., and GRISHAM, J. W. Ultrastructural changes in islets of the rat produced by tolbutamide. *Diabetes, 10:*460 (1961).

PLATE 17

The Anterior Lobe of the Pituitary: Somatotrophs and Gonadotrophs

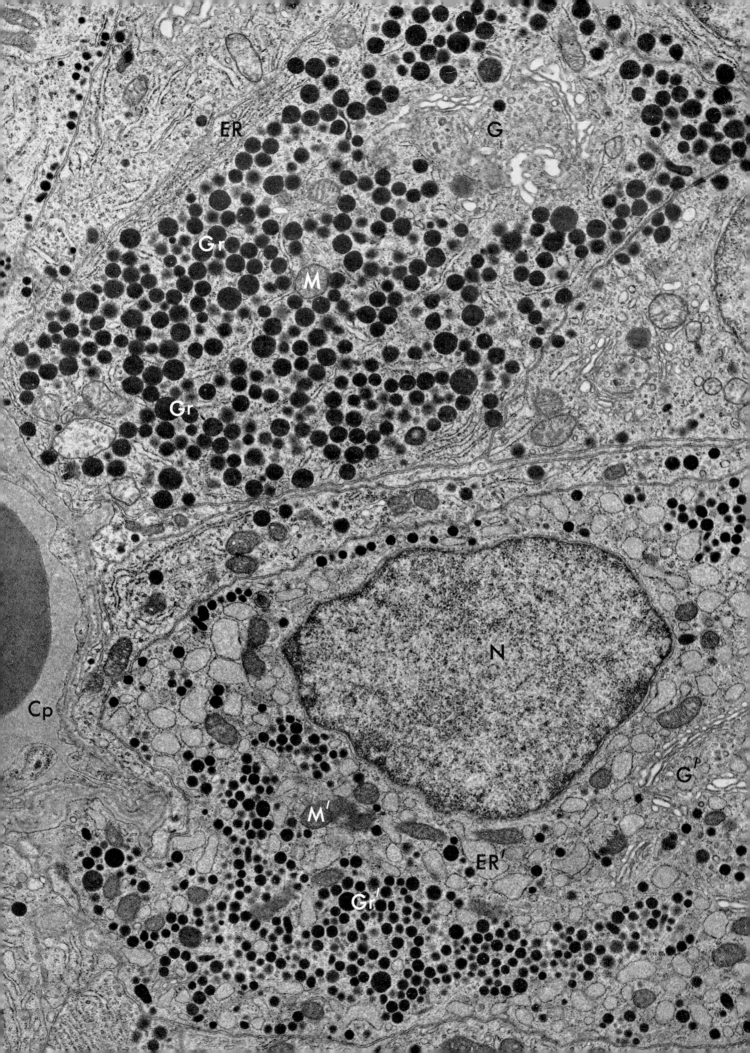

PLATE 17

The Anterior Lobe of the Pituitary: Somatotrophs and Gonadotrophs

Complexity of origin, structure, and function is characteristic of the pituitary gland, and chief among the puzzles to be solved has been the identification of the cell types that produce the multiplicity of hormones discovered through classical physiological experiments. The problem is illustrated by this micrograph. Six hormones are known to arise in the pars distalis or anterior lobe of the adenohypophysis, that portion of the pituitary arising during embryonic life from an outpocketing of the roof of the oral cavity. Distinction of cell types by their staining properties seemed at first to provide only three sorts of cells, named in regard to their affinities for dyes, i.e., acidophils, basophils, and chromophobes. The acidophils, which make up 30 to 45 per cent of the cells of the anterior lobe of the rat, form proteinaceous secretion droplets large enough to be resolved easily in the light microscope. The majority of acidophils produce growth hormone—somatotrophic hormone or STH—and are therefore called somatotrophs. One of these granule-filled somatotrophs may be seen in profile in the upper part of this micrograph. The second less numerous acidophil secretes prolactin, which promotes lactation.

Basophils, which produce glycoprotein secretions (PAS positive), include the thyrotrophs, the producers of thyroid stimulating hormone or TSH, and the gonadotrophs, which produce FSH or follicle-stimulating hormone (an activator of spermatogenesis in the male) and LH, luteinizing hormone, which is also called ICSH or interstitial cell-stimulating hormone in the male. The profile of a gonadotroph appears in the lower part of this micrograph (nucleus, N).

The cell type responsible for production of adrenocorticotrophic hormone or ACTH has not yet been positively identified, but basophils and chromophobes have been implicated as the source of this hormone. In electron micrographs the chromophobe appears as a cell with a very irregular outline and few secretory granules.

Nature performed the earliest experiments that pinpointed the acidophils as the site of growth hormone production. By 1903, acromegaly, the condition characterized by distorted overgrowth of the skeleton, was associated with the presence of pituitary tumors made up of acidophils. In subsequent investigations, extracts made from the lateral regions of the bovine adenohypophysis—areas rich in acidophils—were found superior in growth promoting properties to extracts made from median regions of the gland where acidophils are less numerous. When the pituitaries of dwarf mice were examined, acidophils were almost entirely lacking. Confirmation that the source of growth hormone has been correctly identified has come from the use of fluorescent labeled antibodies to growth hormone used as an antigen. When used to stain anterior pituitary glands, the antibody is, as one would expect, localized in the cells previously designated as somatotrophs.

Somatotrophs are easily identified in electron micrographs because they contain many dense cytoplasmic granules (Gr) that are of fairly uniform size and have a maximum diameter of about 350 mμ. Isolation of protein-containing granules of this size by means of differential centrifugation has shown that they are rich in growth hormone. This evidence therefore supports the reasonable assumption that the granules are secretion droplets.

Cisternae of rough-surfaced endoplasmic reticulum (ER) are present in moderate numbers as are mitochondria (M). Under experimental conditions, however, in which the somatotrophs are stimulated, the ER increases in prominence. A large Golgi complex (G) is a constant feature of these cells. Certain of the secretory granules found within the Golgi area are clearly surrounded by a membrane (see also text figure 17a). The formation of protein secretory granules in the pituitary is believed to involve synthesis by ribosomes of the rough-surfaced ER and assembly of the product in the Golgi complex. After assembly, the secretory granules move out of the Golgi area and may be found throughout the cytoplasm.

Release of secretory product from the cell is difficult to detect morphologically. However, in text figure 17a, secretory product lying outside the cell and free of its membranous covering may

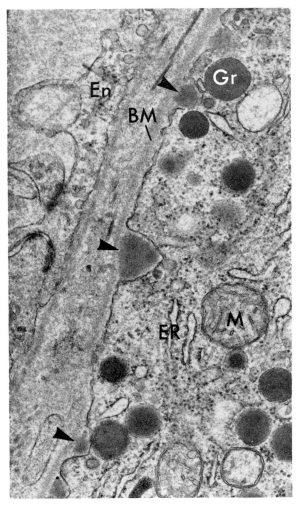

Text Figure 17a

Profiles of mitochondria (M), elements of the endoplasmic reticulum (ER), and secretion droplets (Gr) as present in the peripheral cytoplasm of a somatotroph are depicted in this micrograph. Secretory product (arrows), free of membrane covering, lies extracellularly but within small cavities in the cell surface. The extruded material has not yet penetrated the basement membrane (BM) that underlies the glandular epithelium. The endothelium (En) of an adjacent capillary, together with its basement membrane, is separated from the somatotroph by a thin layer of connective tissue. This micrograph was generously provided by Dr. Robert Cardell.

From the pituitary of the rat
Magnification × 30,000

be identified within small concavities of the plasma membrane of a somatotroph. One can easily postulate that a process of "reverse pinocytosis" could place the contents of the granule outside the cell. The extracellular material always

seems less dense than that in the intracellular granules. Furthermore, it can be detected only between the plasma membrane of the somatotroph and its closely adhering basal lamina. As soon as it leaves this area, its identity as a granule ceases, and the microscopist cannot detect the hormone after it enters the connective tissue that separates the secretory cell from nearby capillaries (Cp).

Identification of the other prominent group of cells of the anterior lobe, the gonadotrophs, in EM preparations has depended on comparison of tissues from normal and castrate animals. Castration results in accumulation of gonadotrophic hormones in the pituitary. Histologically, an increase in basophilic granules and an intensification of PAS staining (for glycoprotein) results. Careful observation has further shown that two types of gonadotrophs may be distinguished. In one, which occurs primarily at the periphery of the adenohypophysis, the response to castration is prompt, while in the second type, located in the central region of the gland, a response is noted only several weeks after castration. Histological studies of normal glands in correlation with the physiological state of the reproductive organs in the female rat reaching maturity have led to the belief that the first type, the gonadotroph lying in the peripheral region of the gland, secretes follicle-stimulating hormone or FSH and that the second type, the one slow to respond to castration, is responsible for the production of luteinizing hormone or LH.

The gonadotroph seen in this micrograph displays several features characteristic of the cell that produces FSH. Mitochondria (M') containing a rather dense matrix material are scattered among distended vesicular elements of the endoplasmic reticulum (ER') with associated ribosomes. As in other cells secreting glycoproteins, the Golgi (G') is large. Secretory granules (Gr') lie near the Golgi and accumulate in the peripheral cytoplasm. The basophilic granules, which are smaller than those of the acidophils, have been isolated and shown to contain gonadotrophic activity. The processes of hormone production and secretion are believed to be in general similar to those of the somatotroph.

From the pituitary of the rat
Magnification × 16,000

72

PLATE 19
Interstitial Cells

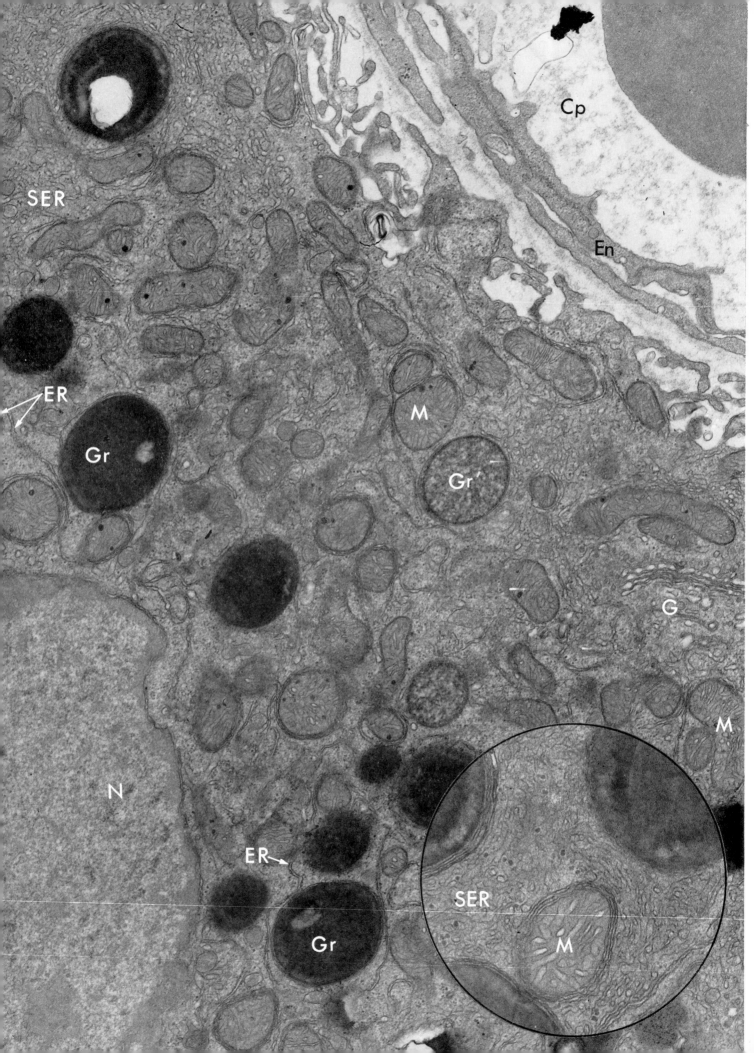

PLATE 19

Interstitial Cells

The testes have been known since ancient times to govern the development of secondary sexual characteristics of the male, an influence now known to be due to the production of the steroid, testosterone. Evidence available indicates that this hormone is secreted by the so-called interstitial cells, which are scattered among the connective tissue elements between the seminiferous tubules (see Plate 22) and which empty their secretion into nearby capillaries. This function of interstitial cells has been inferred from the observation that in certain individuals who produce no sperm both interstitial cells and secondary sexual characteristics remain normal.

A part of one interstitial cell is shown in this micrograph. At the lower left the nucleus (N) is surrounded by cytoplasm containing a Golgi region (G), mitochondria (M), and a highly developed endoplasmic reticulum. The latter two structures each display a particular morphology in steroid-secreting cells. As in the present example, examination of mitochondria frequently reveals their cristae to have a tubular rather than the more familiar shelflike form. The tubular cristae appear during functional differentiation of the tissue, and their number shows a positive correlation with the activity of the gland. Although the profiles of the ER in the perinuclear cytoplasm (ER) are long and slender and have associated ribosomes, the dominant elements of the ER in the more peripheral cytoplasm are without granules (SER) and seem to form a complex latticework of tubules (see inset, SER). This latter form of the ER is often extensively developed in steroid-secreting cells. Frequently, too, the smooth-surfaced cytoplasmic membranes are closely associated with mitochondria (see inset).

Cell fractionation studies have implicated the smooth-surfaced, tubular form of the endoplasmic reticulum in the elaboration of testosterone. Interstitial cells may possess SER in great abundance, and the membranes of this system are the chief component of the microsome fraction isolated from these cells. It is in this fraction that some of the enzymes taking part in the synthesis of cholesterol, a precursor of testosterone, are located. The testis is known to synthesize most of the cholesterol it requires (unlike adrenal cortical cells of the rat, Plate 18), so that there is a good correlation between biochemical and morphological observations on this point. As in the synthesis of the adrenal cortical hormones, the mitochondria are the site of conversion of cholesterol into pregnenolone. This steroid is then converted into testosterone in a series of enzymic reactions occurring in the microsome fraction. The participation of both SER and, as already mentioned, mitochondria is therefore essential, and the close association of these two membranous structures is a special feature of interstitial cells (see inset).

Large spherical granules (Gr), which stain strongly with osmium and lead, are also prominent components of the cytoplasm. Another type of large granule (Gr′), also displayed here, is probably a variant form of the denser ones. It is thought that the granules all contain cholesterol and other lipids that represent stored hormonal precursors. In contrast, the final secretory product, the hormone, is not stored within such granules or indeed in any other kind of granule prior to secretion. Instead the hormone probably diffuses from the cell in molecular form. Once in the intercellular spaces, the testosterone must penetrate the basement membrane and thin endothelium (En) of neighboring capillaries (Cp) to be carried to target organs in other parts of the body.

From the testis of the mouse
Magnification × 29,000
Inset × 55,000

79

BAILLIE, A. H. Further observations on the growth and histochemistry of the Leydig tissue in the postnatal prepubertal mouse testis. *J. Anat., 98:*403 (1964).

CHRISTENSEN, A. K. The fine structure of testicular interstitial cells in guinea pigs. *J. Cell Biol., 26:*911 (1965).

———, and FAWCETT, D. W. The fine structure of testicular interstitial cells in mice. *Amer. J. Anat., 118:*551 (1966).

DE KRETSER, D. M. The fine structure of the interstitial cells in men of normal androgenic status. *Z. Zellforsch., 80:*594 (1967).

———. Changes in the fine structure of the human testicular interstitial cells after treatment with human gonadotrophins. *Z. Zellforsch., 83:*344 (1967).

FRANK, A. L., and CHRISTENSEN, A. K. Localization of acid phosphatase in lipofuscin granules and possible autophagic vacuoles in interstitial cells of guinea pig testis. *J. Cell Biol., 36:*1 (1968).

MUROTA, S., SHIKITA, M., and TAMAOKI, B. Intracellular distribution of the enzymes related to androgen formation in mouse testes. *Steroids, 5:*409 (1965).

PLATE 20
The Follicular Epithelium of the Thyroid

tribute to the formation of the corpus luteum. The latter exists for a limited time as an endocrine organ secreting progesterone, the steroid hormone that is essential in the preparation of the uterus for the implantation of the fertilized ovum.

From the ovary of the mouse
Magnification × 8,000

References

ADAMS, E. C., and HERTIG, A. T. Studies on guinea pig oocytes. I. Electron microscopic observations on the development of cytoplasmic organelles in oocytes of primordial and primary follicles. *J. Cell Biol., 21:397* (1964).

ANDERSON, E. The formation of the primary envelope during oocyte differentiation in teleosts. *J. Cell Biol., 35:193* (1967).

————, and BEAMS, H. W. Cytological observations on the fine structure of the guinea pig ovary with special reference to the oogonium, primary oocyte and associated follicle cells. *J. Ultrastruct. Res., 3:432* (1960).

BARKER, W. L. A cytochemical study of lipids in sows' ovaries during the estrous cycle. *Endocrinology, 48:772* (1951).

DEANE, H. W. Histochemical observations on the ovary and oviduct of the albino rat during the estrous cycle. *Amer. J. Anat., 91:363* (1952).

HERTIG, A. T., and ADAMS, E. C. Studies on the human oocyte and its follicle. I. Ultrastructural and histochemical observations on the primordial follicle stage. *J. Cell Biol., 34:647* (1967).

KNIGHT, P. F., and SCHECHTMAN, A. M. The passage of heterologous serum proteins from the circulation into the ovum of the fowl. *J. Exp. Zool., 127:271* (1954).

ROTH, T. F., and PORTER, K. R. Yolk protein uptake in the oocyte of the mosquito *Aedes aegypti* L. *J. Cell Biol., 20:313* (1964).

SOTELO, J. R., and PORTER, K. R. An electron microscope study of the rat ovum. *J. Biophysic. and Biochem. Cytol., 5:327* (1959).

PLATE 22
The Germinal Epithelium of the Male

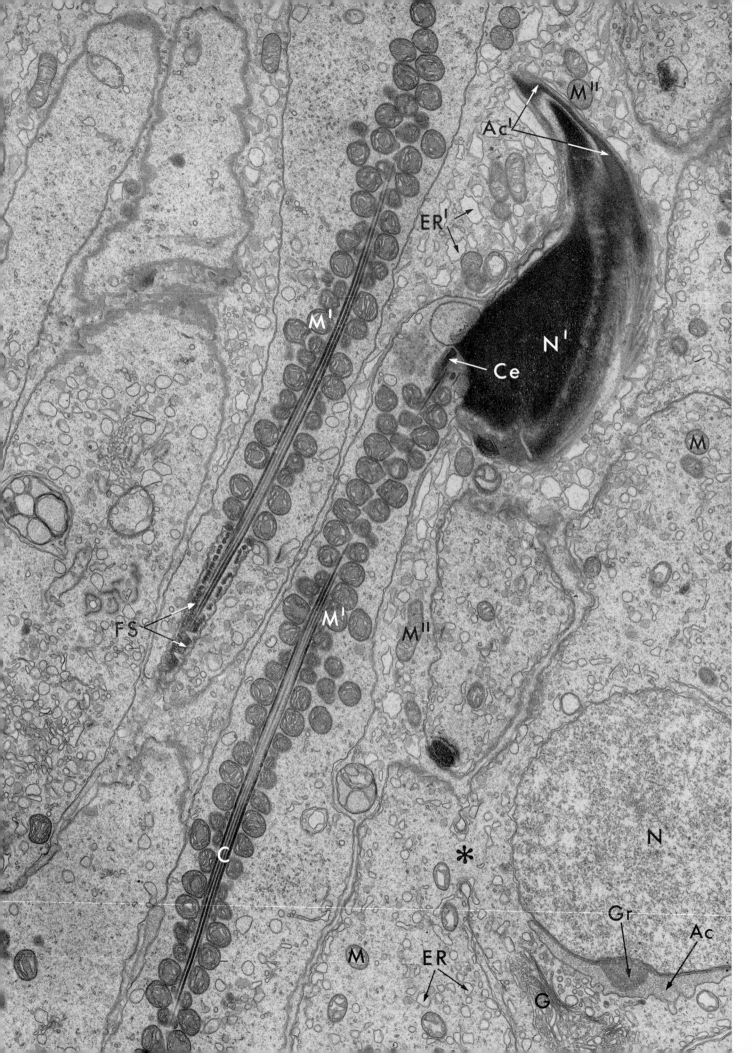

PLATE 22

The Germinal Epithelium of the Male

The male germ cells are produced in the testis by the epithelium of the seminiferous tubules. Undifferentiated spermatogonia, which form part of the basal cell layer of this epithelium, undergo repeated mitotic divisions. After a period of growth, each resulting spermatocyte enlarges and then divides meiotically to produce four spermatids. These in turn pass through a complex metamorphosis during which, by a process called spermiogenesis, they are transformed into mature sperm. It is, of course, impossible to document this intricate life history with one micrograph. However, the present illustration does show two stages in spermatid development and, by illustrating extremes, demonstrates how drastic this transformation is. At lower right one observes the profile of a spherical nucleus (N) that belongs to a fairly early spermatid. At one pole it is covered by a flattened vesicle, the developing acrosome (Ac), which contains a dense granule (Gr), the proacrosomal granule. The cap and the granule arise from the Golgi complex (G), and together they form the anterior tip of the mature sperm (see Plate 23). Early in spermiogenesis the cytoplasm is extensive. Within its irregular outline, mitochondria (M) and vesicles of the endoplasmic reticulum (ER) may be seen. At this point in development, the four spermatids remain linked by cytoplasmic bridges, one of which appears in this micrograph (*).

The appearance of a nearly mature sperm is illustrated at the center of the micrograph. The head, which is hook-shaped in the mouse, contains within its nucleus (N′) the hereditary material in dense, compact form. The anterior tip of the nucleus is covered by the acrosome cap (Ac′), which lies just beneath the plasma membrane. The cap is believed to contain the enzyme hyaluronidase, which may aid the penetration of the egg by the sperm during fertilization.

No less remarkable in this metamorphosis are the changes in the spermatid cytoplasm, which essentially transforms into an elongate motile appendage with which the sperm can swim. Two centrioles are involved in the formation of the neck region, and of these one (Ce) initiates the development of the long bundle of filaments (C) that is the core of the middle piece and tail. This core comprises a 9 + 2 array of microtubules and so, in its internal structure, is very similar to the cilium (see Plate 8). In the middle piece the core of the flagellum is spirally wrapped by a sheath constructed of mitochondria. Oblique sections (M′) of the spiral reveal the mitochondrial nature of this structure.

Posterior to the middle piece, in the tail proper, a fibrous sheath, a portion of which may be examined in this micrograph (FS), is wound around the axial filamenture. Only at its distal end does the flagellum lack a special covering. Although a sheath of cytoplasm covers the middle piece as it develops, this sheath is later lost, so that at maturity the plasma membrane is closely applied to the axial structures.

In the final stages of spermiogenesis, the spermatids become embedded in the Sertoli cells. Many germ cells, each with its anterior tip oriented toward the periphery of the seminiferous tubule, are thus anchored to the epithelium, while their tails lie free in the lumen. Around the dense sperm head and middle pieces shown in this plate there are portions of a Sertoli cell, which contain mitochondria (M″) and dilated vesicles of the endoplasmic reticulum (ER′). No protoplasmic continuity between the Sertoli cell and the germ cells has been observed: each cell type is surrounded by an uninterrupted plasma membrane. Sertoli cells are often called nurse cells, but though they support the developing sperm, it is not really known what additional functions they perform.

From the testis of the mouse
Magnification × 13,500

BURGOS, M. H., and FAWCETT, D. W. Studies on the fine structure of the mammalian testis. I. Differentiation of the spermatids in the cat (*Felis domestica*). *J. Biophysic. and Biochem. Cytol., 1:*287 (1955).

FAWCETT, D. W. Sperm tail structure in relation to the mechanism of movement. *In* Spermatozoan motility. D. W. Bishop, editor. Washington, D. C., AAAS Publication No. 72 (1962) p. 147.

————, and ITO, S. The fine structure of bat spermatozoa. *Amer. J. Anat., 116:*567 (1965).

HORSTMANN, E. Elektronmikroscopische Untersuchungen zur Spermiohistogenese beim Menschen. *Z. Zellforsch., 54:*68 (1961).

YASUZUMI, G., TANAKA, H., and TEZUKA, O. Spermatogenesis in animals as revealed by electron microscopy. VIII. Relation between the nutritive cells and the developing spermatids in a pond snail, *Cipangopaludina malleata* Reeve. *J. Biophysic. and Biochem. Cytol., 7:*499 (1960).

PLATE 26

The Renal Medulla

In birds and mammals the nephrons of the kidney each include a segment that bends back on itself and is called the loop of Henle (LH). The filtrate formed in the glomerulus (Plate 24) is reduced in volume by reabsorption in the proximal tubule (Plate 25) and then enters the descending limb of this segment. The adjective *descending* is used to indicate that the tubule extends from the cortical region of the kidney into the deeper inner region called the medulla. The other arm of the loop, the ascending limb, extends toward the cortex and leads into the thicker walled distal tubule. The two arms of the loop lie near each other, separated by connective tissue, the interstitium (CT) of the renal medulla. In addition, the medulla contains numerous collecting tubules (Col) that open into the renal pelvis. As their name suggests, each of the latter tubules drains urine from a number of nephrons.

The length of the loop of Henle varies from species to species, and it was noted over fifty years ago that its length shows a positive correlation with the ability of the kidney to produce a concentrated urine. Thus it was realized that the loops must contribute to the vital functioning of the kidney, effecting elimination of waste metabolites while conserving water needed especially by land-dwelling vertebrates.

It is only relatively recently, after painstaking study, that the way in which the loops function to accomplish this task has begun to be understood. First it was important to learn by freezing-point determinations, both of the filtrate within the nephrons and of the extracellular fluid, that as samples are taken at levels closer to the tips of the loops and therefore nearer to the tip of the renal papilla, the concentration of salt increases both in the loops and in the extracellular fluids around them. Thus there exists in the medulla a steep gradient of salt concentration, which is thought to be maintained by a salt-pumping segment of the loop. As pointed out above, the collecting tubules also traverse this region and extend toward the renal pelvis. They therefore pass through a zone in which the surrounding medium is increasingly hypertonic. As a result, water moves out of the tubules into the interstitium, and the urine becomes more concentrated. This interesting device for conserving water and salts for the animal's

repeated use while simultaneously eliminating metabolic wastes is considered further below.

Before describing loop function in more detail, however, we should discuss the structure and arrangement of the loop and other medullary tissues. Cross sections of the thin segments of the loops of Henle (LH) differ significantly from adjacent capillaries (Cp) lying near them. The simple squamous epithelium (Ep) lining the loops is slightly thicker than the fenestrated capillary endothelium (En) (which in places is extremely attenuated), and its surface may be somewhat irregular, with small projections extending into the lumens. Its basal surface is also fairly uneven. Since adjacent cells in this epithelium interdigitate in a complex manner, the micrograph shows numerous junctions (arrows) between them. No evidence of pinocytosis has been observed in the tubular epithelium, although machinery for such activity is frequently present in endothelia. The presence in the capillary lumens (Cp) of erythrocytes (E) and coagulated plasma proteins contrasts with the apparently empty thin segments. A basement membrane underlies both the capillary endothelium (BM) and the tubular epithelium (BM′). In the latter, however, this layer is unusually thick and often consists of several lamellae (X). It may be noted in passing that the interstitial spaces contain remarkably little collagen (Co) but an abundance of basement membrane material and ground substance.

As it reaches the outer zone of the renal medulla (nearer the cortex) the ascending limb of the loop of Henle becomes thicker. This thicker portion joins the distal convoluted tubule, which lies within the kidney cortex. Although the thick region of the loop resembles the distal tubule in structure, its special functions as part of the loop have not yet been distinguished physiologically. Therefore it is treated with the loop as a whole in the discussion of loop function given below.

The collecting tubules (Col) are lined by cuboidal epithelial cells. Their basal surfaces, resting on a thin basement membrane (BM″), are highly folded, although the folds are much less deep than those of the cells in the proximal tubule (see Plate 25). Their lateral surfaces are also highly folded and interdigitate with folds of adjacent cells (Y). Irregular, short, villuslike projections are found on their free surfaces. The transport of water through the walls of the collecting tubules is under control of the antidiuretic hormone (ADH), a polypeptide secreted via the neurohypophysis. Within certain limits more water may be conserved and the urine made more concentrated as the hormone acts to make the epithelium increasingly permeable to water.

We can now return to a consideration of how the loops of Henle bring about a hypertonic condition in the interstitium. To account for this function it is assumed that the ascending limbs actively pump out sodium into the extracellular spaces and that they themselves are impermeable to water. Thus filtrate flowing in the descending limbs progressively loses water to the hypertonic interstitium and becomes more concentrated. On entering the ascending limb, sodium is actively removed, and, although the amount is relatively small at any one point along the limb (because the difference in solute concentration between the inside and the outside of the ascending limb is never greater than ~ 200 mOsm/L), it is enough to maintain the gradient. Water, however, is unable to penetrate this side of the loop. The filtrate in losing salt but not water therefore decreases in tonicity and finally becomes hypotonic before reaching the distal tubule. Thus the hairpin-like tubules constitute a kind of countercurrent multiplier system. It is the nature of such a system that the longer the loops the more concentrated will be the tubular filtrate at the point where the tubule turns back on itself. In the kidney, it would follow that the longer the loops, the more hypertonic the interstitium at the tip of the renal popilla and therefore the more concentrated will the urine become because of water removal as it flows through the collecting tubules.

The capillaries of the medulla are also arranged in loops and constitute a second countercurrent multiplier system. They are intimately associated with the loops of Henle, as shown in this image. It is a result of this arrangement that the hypertonic gradient of the medulla is maintained while water and salt are being removed from the kidney. The blood, flowing slowly into descending capillary loops, loses water and gains solutes, chiefly sodium, as the gradient of the interstitium increases around it. At the apex of the loop, deep in the medulla, the tonicity of the blood equilibrates with the surrounding medium, so that the blood as well as the urine becomes concentrated. The crenated appearance of the erythrocytes in this micrograph attests to the hypertonicity of the plasma. However, instead of leaving the kidney at the papilla, the capillary bends back upon itself. Thus on its course toward the renal cortex, the blood loses solutes and regains water without markedly disturbing the gradient. Any salt and water carried away in excess of that brought to the medulla by the capillaries are compensated for by the pumping action of the ascending limbs mentioned above.

Satisfactory preparation of the renal medulla for electron microscopy has proved to be difficult. This is doubtless due to the impossibility of finding a single fixative suitable to the varied tonicities in the tissue. Those who have studied its fine structure, however, have been somewhat dismayed to discover the "simple" structure, especially of the thin segment of the ascending loops, which are thought to be highly active physiologically. Indeed, when the two thin limbs have been identified with certainty in thin sections, even the epithelium of the descending limb appears more complex in structure. The correlation between structure and function in the case of the loop of Henle is therefore less than satisfactory. To some investigators this finding has suggested that the countercurrent theory of loop function may require modification. To others, it seems likely that the morphologists' concept of the fine structural features necessarily associated with actively transporting epithelia should be modified.

From the kidney of the rat
Magnification $\times$ 11,000

BERLINER, R. W. Some aspects of the function of the renal medulla. *In* Progress in Pyelonephritis. E. H. Kass, editor. Philadelphia, F. A. Davis Company (1965) p. 417.

BULGER, R. E., TISHER, C. C., MYERS, C. H., and TRUMP, B. F. Human renal ultrastructure. II. The thin limb of Henle's loop and the interstitium in healthy individuals. *Lab. Invest., 16:*124 (1967).

GOTTSCHALK, C. W. Osmotic concentration and dilution of the urine. *Amer. J. Med., 36:*670 (1964).

MARSH, D. J., and SOLOMON, S. Analysis of electrolyte movement in thin Henle's loops of hamster papilla. *Amer. J. Physiol., 208:*1119 (1965).

OSVALDO, L., and LATTA, H. The thin limbs of the loop of Henle. *J. Ultrastruct. Res., 15:*144 (1966).

PITTS, R. F. Physiology of the Kidney and Body Fluids. Chicago, Year Book Medical Publishers Incorporated (1963).

SCHMIDT-NIELSEN, B., and O'DELL, R. Structure and concentrating mechanism in the mammalian kidney. *Amer. J. Physiol., 200:*1119 (1961).

ULLRICH, K. J., and MARSH, D. J. Kidney, water, and electrolyte metabolism. *Ann. Rev. Physiol., 25:*91 (1963).

YOUNG, D., and WISSIG, S. L. A histologic description of certain epithelial and vascular structures in the kidney of the normal rat. *Amer. J. Anat., 115:*43 (1964).

107

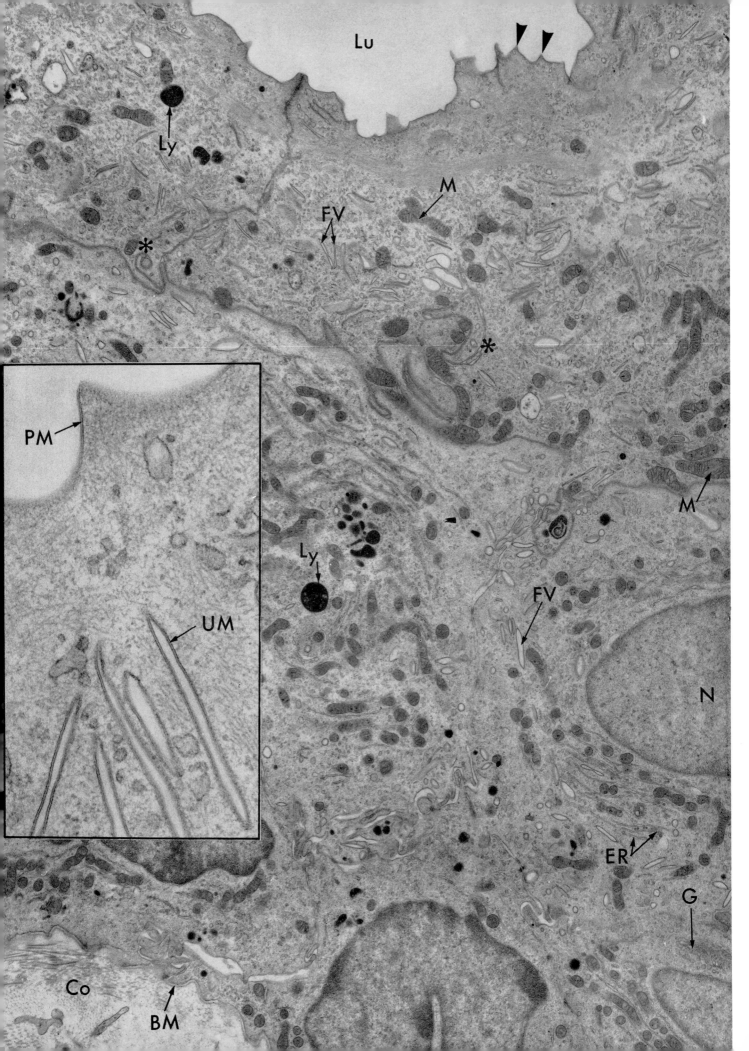

PLATE 32

The Mast Cell

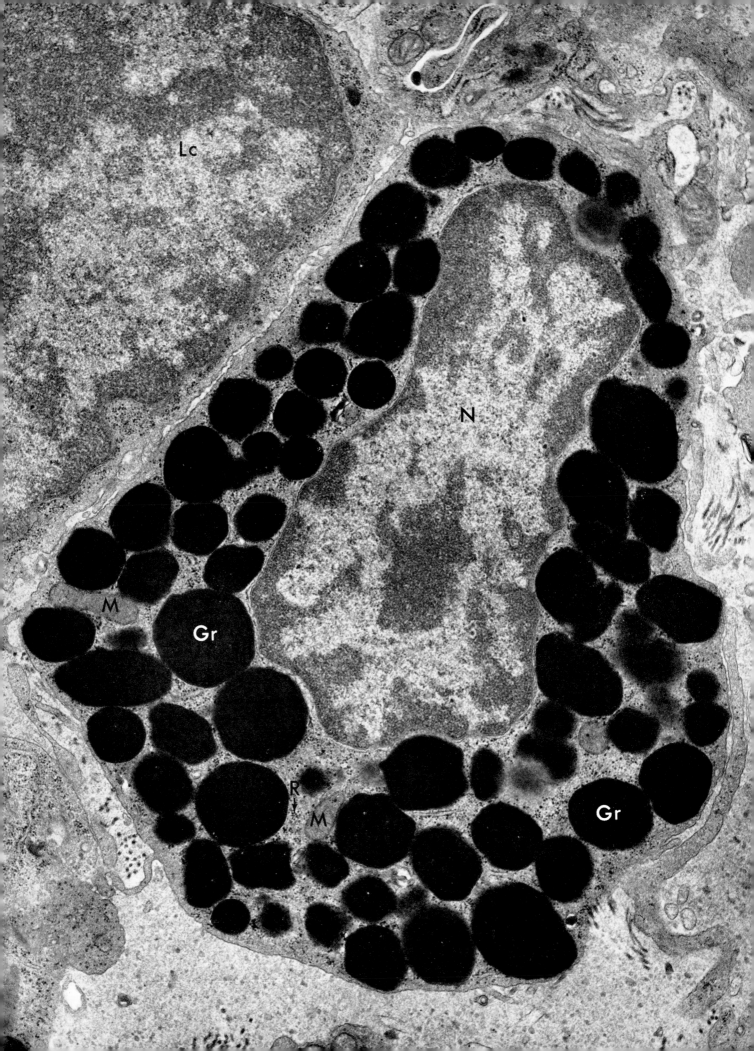

PLATE 32

The Mast Cell

THE mast cells were named about ninety years ago by Ehrlich, who had the impression that their numerous cytoplasmic granules gave them a well-nourished appearance. He designated them as a distinct type of connective tissue cell and noted that their granules stained metachromatically. When toluidine blue is applied to them, the granules assume a purplish-red hue rather than the normal blue color of the dye. This property, now known to be due to the presence of sulfated mucopolysaccharide within the granule, has been used to reveal the widespread distribution of mast cells both in individual animals and in many vertebrate species.

The electron microscope image of the mast cell has confirmed that the numerous granules (Gr) nearly fill the cytoplasm. The mitochondria (M), small and few, were not detected by the light microscope, nor could mitochondrial respiratory enzymes be found in mast cells isolated from fluid of the peritoneal cavity. Free ribosomes (R) may be seen in the cytoplasmic ground substance and along a few profiles of the endoplasmic reticulum. The nucleus (N) displays marginal and central clumping of chromatin material. In brief, these features suggest a fully differentiated cell in which little active synthesis or energy expenditure is occurring. Exposure of mast cells to tritiated thymidine results in only a small amount of labeling, an indication that fully differentiated mast cells are probably not able to divide. The complement of granules is stored, ready to perform its function.

The mast cell depicted here resides in the loose connective tissue of the submucosa. Like other wandering cells it is devoid of a basal lamina. This is especially evident where the mast cell is contiguous with a lymphocyte, shown in part at the upper left (Lc).

Biologists are still uncertain as to the exact function of the mast cell. Since a good deal of information is available concerning the nature of the contents of the granules, speculation on mast cell function centers around the chemical properties of substances localized in them. The main components of mast cell granules are heparin and histamine, both discussed below. In addition, proteases have been found within the granules, and in a few species the vasoconstrictor serotonin

(5-hydroxytryptamine) is also present within them.

The mast cell was first suspected of being the source of heparin, a powerful anticoagulant isolated first from the livers of dogs, when it was noted that heparin content and mast cell number exhibited a positive correlation in a number of tissues. Isolation of mast cells from the peritoneal cavity and the discovery of mast cell tumors provided opportunities for testing directly and thereby confirming that heparin, a sulfated mucopolysaccharide, is indeed contained in the mast cell granules.

The normal function of heparin is less clear than its origins. Its pharmacological effect, that is, its action as an anticoagulant administered clinically in large doses, may not, and probably does not, correspond to its physiological function. Indeed, its anticoagulating ability depends upon its source, and heparin from certain species of animals may show little of this property. In the mast cell granule, heparin seems to be bound to a structural protein, and this association survives during normal functioning of the cell (see below).

Mast cell granules also contain histamine (4-imidazolyethylamine), although this compound is not localized in them exclusively. Release of histamine leads to increased permeability of the capillaries with consequent flow of plasma proteins into the intercellular space. The resulting edema is characteristic of allergic reactions, including anaphylactic shock. As a further consequence of histamine release, leukocytes invade the edematous zone, and phagocytosis is stimulated.

In order to determine the fate of mast cell granules the histological effects of substances known to release histamine from tissues have been studied. One of these releasers—compound 48/80—first reduces the density of mast cell granules. A halolike space appears, separating the granule from the membrane that encloses it. The staining properties of granules altered in this manner indicate that heparin is still present within them. It has been proposed, therefore, that the heparin with its high electronegative charge may function in holding histamine within the granule. At any rate, histamine release does occur without complete disruption of mast cell granules, although with high enough doses of histamine releaser the granules may be ejected from the cell, free of their membranous coverings.

The origin of the mast cell granules relative to the cell's fine structure holds some interest, for it seemingly correlates with the known presence of heparin, histamine, and protein in the mature granules. Early in the morphogenesis of these cells, small dense granules appear in vesicles of the Golgi zone. Later these appear to combine with larger vesicles of ER origin suspected of containing protein. Such observations are consistent with the accepted view of the Golgi as the site of mucopolysaccharide formation (heparin) and the ER as the source of protein (cf. Plates 12, 28, and 29).

From the intestinal submucosa of the rat
Magnification × 27,400

References

BENDITT, E. P., HOLCENBERG, J., and LAGUNOFF, D. The role of serotonin (5-hydroxytryptamine) in mast cells. *Ann. N. Y. Acad. Sci., 103* (Article 1):179 (1963).

BLOOM, G. D., and HAEGERMARK, O. A study on morphological changes and histamine release induced by compound 48/80 in rat peritoneal mast cells. *Exp. Cell Res., 40:*637 (1965).

COMBS, J. W. Maturation of rat mast cells. An electron microscope study. *J. Cell Biol., 31:*563 (1966).

LAGUNOFF, D., PHILLIPS, M., ISERI, O. A., and BENDITT, E. P. Isolation and preliminary characterization of rat mast cell granules. *Lab. Invest., 13:*1331 (1964).

RILEY, J. F. Functional significance of histamine and heparin in tissue mast cells. *Ann. N. Y. Acad. Sci., 103* (Article 1):151 (1963).

SCHILLER, S. Mucopolysaccharides of normal mast cells. *Ann. N. Y. Acad. Sci., 103* (Article 1):199 (1963).

SMITH, D. E. Electron microscopy of normal mast cells under various experimental conditions. *Ann. N. Y. Acad. Sci., 103* (Article 1):40 (1963).

THIÉRY, J. P. Etude au microscope électronique de la maturation et de l'excrétion des granules des mastocytes. *J. Microscopie, 2:*549 (1963).

PLATE 33
The Erythroblast and Erythrocyte

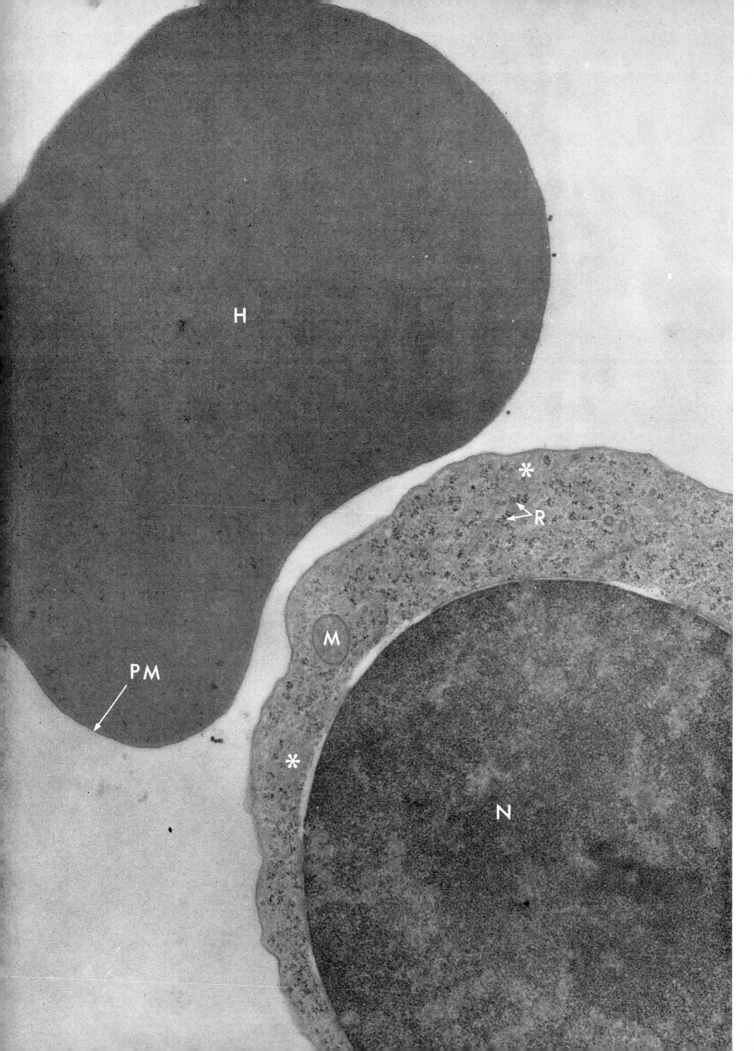

PLATE 33

The Erythroblast and Erythrocyte

THE mammalian erythrocyte or red blood corpuscle is a striking example of a specialized cell. The differentiated form, shown in the upper left-hand portion of this figure, develops in hematopoietic tissue. The limiting membrane (PM), seen as a line, encloses a mass of material (H) consisting mainly of hemoglobin. This respiratory pigment is notable in electron micrographs for its denseness, which is largely due to its iron content. The nucleus has already been extruded from this red cell, and cytoplasmic organelles have disintegrated so that the differentiated unit contains very little except the characteristic respiratory pigment. In the image shown here, a few particles, probably ribosomes, persist, indicating that protein synthesis may still be continuing. In completely mature forms circulating in the blood stream, even these particles disappear, and all the synthetic machinery of the cell is closed down.

An earlier stage in this differentiation is shown by the erythroblast present at the lower right. This cell, which is probably a polychromatophilic erythroblast and which is common in hematopoietic tissue, has ceased to divide; but unlike the mature erythrocyte, it still possesses a nucleus (N) with nuclear envelope, a few mitochondria (M), and small groups of ribosomes (R) separated from each other by a cytoplasmic ground substance or stroma already accumulating hemoglobin (*). Such groups of ribosomes, referred to as polysomes, represent the assembling unit in protein synthesis. It is noteworthy that in the differentiation of this cell the production of protein for intracellular storage does not involve the membranous systems; that is, the endoplasmic reticulum and the Golgi complex, normally present in the cytoplasm of most cells (see Plates 2 and 11). Free or unattached ribosomes are commonly found in embryonic cells and are uniformly associated with the processes of cellular growth and differentiation in which the products of synthesis are retained.

During the course of red cell differentiation, as already indicated above, ribosomes and elements of the ER gradually disappear from the cytoplasm as hemoglobin increases in prominence. Disappearance of ribosomes is correlated with termination of their role in hemoglobin synthesis. Simultaneously, and possibly in relation to these events, the nucleoli fragment and essentially fade from view. Marked clumping of heterochromatic material also occurs as differentiation progresses, and this change is assumed to reflect a cessation in chromosomal production of messenger RNA (cf. Plate 4). Nuclear pores, which normally open into zones of the nucleoplasm between masses of heterochromatin, become less numerous as the cell matures.

Thus micrographs of differentiating erythroblasts provide several signs consistent with the general atrophy of nuclear activity. In mammalian erythroblasts extrusion of the nucleus follows, occurring as one of the last steps in differentiation. First the erythroblast becomes highly polarized as the future cytoplasm of the red cell and the nucleus move into separate parts of the cell. Then vesicles assemble near the neck or isthmus connecting the two parts. Next the vesicles coalesce to form cisternal structures that unite with the plasma membrane of the cell so as to separate the nuclear-containing portion from the young red cell. This sequence of events is reminiscent of those shown by the megakaryocyte in the formation of blood platelets (see Plate 35). It is to be noted that the extruded red cell nucleus retains a thin layer of cytoplasm, including mitochondria, and remains enclosed by the plasma membrane. The potentialities of this attenuated cell have not been tested, so that it is not known whether it may continue to form additional erythrocytes. Probably its usual fate is to be engulfed and broken down by reticuloendothelial cells, a kind of phagocyte found in hematopoietic tissue (cf. Plate 37).

Sinusoids are characteristic of hematopoietic tissue. These are wide bore capillaries with thin endothelial linings. Usually gaps are observed between endothelial cells. After completing their maturation, red cells are able to slip through these interruptions in the vascular lining and join circulating blood cells.

From the liver of a rat embryo
Magnification × 30,000

References

BERMAN, I. The ultrastructure of erythroblastic islands and reticular cells in mouse bone marrow. *J. Ultrastruct. Res., 17:*291 (1967).

GRASSO, J. A., SWIFT, H., and ACKERMAN, G. A. Observations on the development of erythrocytes in mammalian fetal liver. *J. Cell Biol., 14:*235 (1962).

ORLIC, D., GORDON, A. S., and RHODIN, J. A. G. An ultrastructural study of erythropoietin-induced red cell formation in mouse spleen. *J. Ultrastruct. Res., 13:*516 (1965).

SIMPSON, C. F., and KLING, J. M. The mechanism of denucleation in circulating erythroblasts. *J. Cell Biol., 35:*237 (1967).

WARNER, J. R., RICH, A., and HALL, C. E. Electron microscope studies of ribosomal clusters synthesizing hemoglobin. *Science, 138:*1399 (1962).

WEISS, L. The structure of bone marrow. Functional interrelationships of vascular and hematopoietic compartments in experimental hemolytic anemia. *J. Morph., 117:*467 (1965).

ZAMBONI, L. Electron microscopic studies of blood embryogenesis in humans. II. The hemopoietic activity in in the fetal liver. *J. Ultrastruct. Res., 12:*525 (1965).

PLATE 34

The Eosinophilic Leukocyte

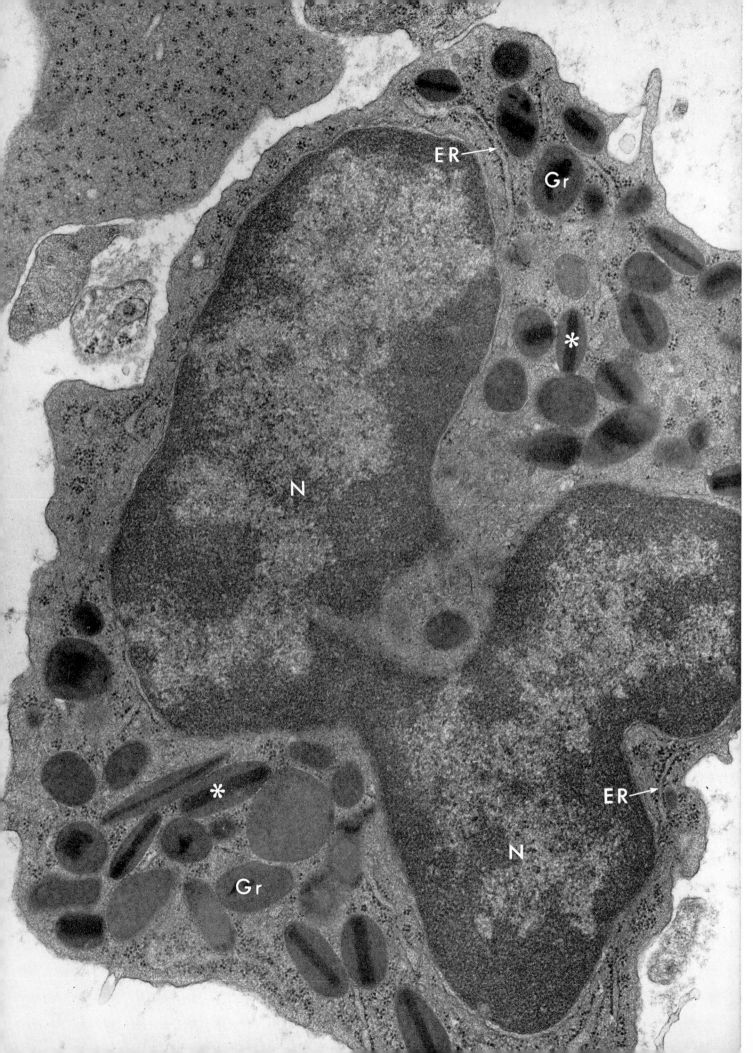

PLATE 34

The Eosinophilic Leukocyte

THE eosinophils with their many cytoplasmic granules have long attracted the eye of the microscopist, but only recently has some progress been made in understanding their function. This electron micrograph shows the structure of an eosinophil, which although still in the bone marrow is in the final stages of its development. This section includes a large part of the prominent bilobed nucleus (N). In the peripheral cytoplasm there are several cisternae of the endoplasmic reticulum (ER), which enclose an amorphous material of low density and support numerous ribosomes on their surfaces. These leukocytes have a large Golgi complex close to the nucleus, but in this section it happens not to be included.

The outstanding components of the cell are the numerous granules (Gr) characteristic of this leukocyte. These are biconvex disks surrounded by a thin membrane and composed of a matrix material of medium density. In favorable sections one or more rods of dense, crystalline material (∗) lie in the equatorial region of the granules. Recently the structure of the crystal has been identified as a cubic lattice, but as yet its composition has not been determined. A peroxidase peculiar to eosinophils, and the lysosomal enzyme, acid phosphatase, have been localized in the matrix of the granule. The matrix also contains an array of other enzymes typical of lysosomes found in various other cells, including neutrophils. However, unlike granules of neutrophils, they seem to lack specific bacteriocidal agents.

The formation of the specific granules of eosinophils closely resembles that of other secretory granules. Early forms appear as condensation vacuoles in the Golgi zone and develop into mature granules as materials are added to them from both the ER and Golgi sources.

Eosinophils are found in considerable numbers in skin, as well as in the tissues of the respiratory and digestive tracts. They are therefore in a suitable position to play a role in defense of the organism against various pathogenic agents. It has been shown that under certain conditions eosinophils become phagocytic and that granules adjacent to the ingested material burst. The hydrolytic enzymes within the granules are thought to enter the phagocytic vacuoles, there to break down the ingested material. This chain of events, as well as the attraction of eosinophils to specific locations in tissues, is apparently stimulated by antigen-antibody reactions.

From the bone marrow of the rat
Magnification × 37,000

References

ARCHER, G. T., AIR, G., JACKAS, M., and MORELL, D. B. Studies on rat eosinophil peroxidase. *Biochim. Biophys. Acta,* 99:96 (1965).

ARCHER, G. T., and HIRSCH, J. G. Isolation of granules from eosinophil leucocytes and study of their enzyme content. *J. Exp. Med.,* 118:227 (1963).

———. Motion picture studies on degranulation of horse eosinophils during phagocytosis. *J. Exp. Med.,* 118:287 (1963).

MILLER, F., DEHARVEN, E., and PALADE, G. E. The structure of eosinophil leucocyte granules in rodents and in man. *J. Cell Biol.,* 31:349 (1966).

SEEMAN, P. M., and PALADE, G. E. Acid phosphatase localization in rabbit eosinophils. *J. Cell Biol., 34:*745 (1967).

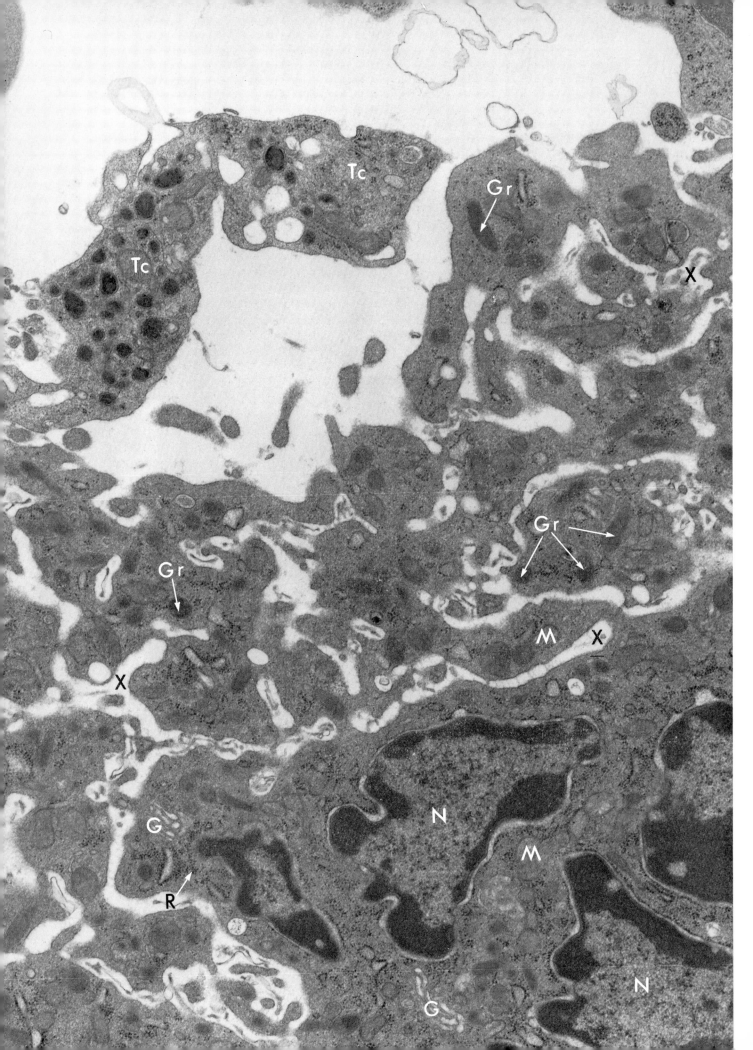

PLATE 35

The Megakaryocyte

THE megakaryocyte is easily identified in the blood-forming tissue of mammals because of its large multilobular nucleus, from which its name is derived, and its extensive cytoplasm, which makes it a giant among myeloid elements. Early in this century careful examinations by light microscopy indicated that this cell gives rise to the blood platelets or thrombocytes, which take part in the formation of blood clots. More recently further information on the manner of their production has come from studies with the electron microscope.

Only isolated portions of the nucleus (N) are evident in this micrograph of a megakaryocyte, and the cytoplasm, though abundant, is only partially included. The latter especially possesses unusual structural features. In addition to mitochondria (M), Golgi regions (G), and ribosomes (R) the cytoplasm is dotted with spherical-to-oblong granules of moderate density (Gr), which are apparently membrane limited. Evidence from electron micrographs suggests that these granules are formed in the Golgi region.

Individual platelets are, however, small cells devoid of nuclei. They contain within a plasma membrane such cytoplasmic components as mitochondria, ribosomes, and vesicles of the endoplasmic reticulum in addition to the characteristic granules just mentioned. Two such cells are seen at Tc, upper left.

Platelets are believed to form from the megakaryocyte by a process in which the cytoplasm of the parent cell is first partitioned and then fragmented along the partitions. Initially in this process curtains of "platelet demarcation vesicles" form. In thin sections these appear as strings of membrane-bounded elements. Later the vesicles coalesce, and become tubular; still later they form large flattened cisternae, the "platelet demarcation membranes" (X). Thus a system of vesicular septa develops, and each separated area is eventually completely detached from the megakaryocyte (see upper left in micrograph). This is essentially a process of secretion similar to that involved in red cell formation (see Plate 33).

The partitions or "platelet demarcation membranes" obviously become the limiting membrane of the platelet after it is freed from the megakaryocyte. This membrane holds more than the usual interest, for it seems to contain a factor (thromboplastin) that activates prothrombin and thus sets the stage for fibrin clot formation. The tendency of platelets to clump is due to a layer of fibrinogen adsorbed on their surfaces.

The dense granules within the platelets (Gr) are membrane limited and slightly smaller than mitochondria. When isolated by the techniques of cell fractionation, they have been shown to be rich in acid phosphatase and β-glucuronidase, facts which probably indicate their similarity to lysosomal granules of other cells (see Plate 15). Though the granules are released during clot formation and appear to disintegrate at that time, their function has not been established. Other compounds, such as serotonin and histamine, are also released from platelets during clot formation, but their localization in the cells remains obscure. For some unexplained reason platelets not involved in clotting may be active in the phagocytosis of foreign bodies such as viruses.

From the bone marrow of the rat
Magnification $\times$ 30,000

References

CRONKITE, E. P., BOND, V. P., FLIEDNER, T. M., PAGLIA, D. A., and ADAMIK, E. R. Studies on the origin, production and destruction of platelets. *In* Blood Platelets. S. A. Johnson, R. Monto, J. Rebuck, and R. C. Horn, editors. Boston, Little, Brown and Company (1961) p. 595.

HAN, S. S., and BAKER, B. L. The ultrastructure of megakaryocytes and blood platelets in the rat spleen. *Anat. Rec., 149:*251 (1964).

MARCUS, A. J., and ZUCKER-FRANKLIN, D. Enzyme and coagulation activity of subcellular platelet fractions. *J. Clin. Invest., 43:*1241 (Abstract) (1964).

MOVAT, H. Z., MUSTARD, J. F., TAICHMAN, N. S., and URIUHARA, T. Platelet aggregation and release of ADP, serotonin and histamine associated with phagocytosis of antigen-antibody complexes. *Proc. Soc. Exp. Biol. Med., 120:*232 (1965).

MOVAT, H. Z., WEISER, W. J., GLYNN, M. F., and MUSTARD, J. F. Platelet phagocytosis and aggregation. *J. Cell Biol., 27:*531 (1965).

RODMAN, N. F., JR., PAINTER, J. C., and McDEVITT, N. B. Platelet disintegration during clotting. *J. Cell Biol., 16:*225 (1963).

SCHMID, H. J., JACKSON, D. P., and CONLEY, C. L. Mechanism of action of thrombin on platelets. *J. Clin. Invest., 41:*543 (1962).

THIÉRY, J. P., and BESSIS, M. Mécanisme de la plaquettogénèse: étude *in vitro* par la microcinématographie. *Rev. hémat., 11:*162 (1956).

VASSALLI, P., SIMON, G., and ROUILLER, C. Ultrastructural study of platelet changes initiated *in vivo* by thrombin. *J. Ultrastruct. Res., 11:*374 (1964).

YAMADA, E. The fine structure of the megakaryocyte in the mouse spleen. *Acta Anat., 29:*267 (1957).

PLATE 36
The Thymus

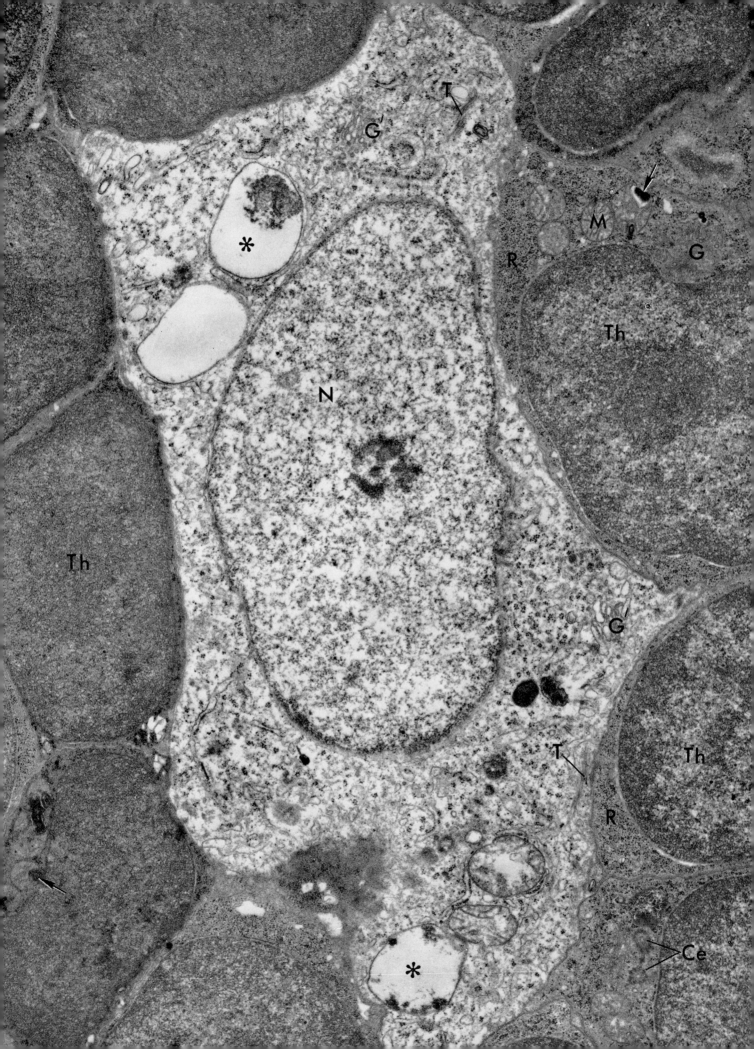

PLATE 36

The Thymus

THE thymus, an organ that is well developed in young animals but that decreases greatly in size at the time the animal becomes sexually mature, has only recently been divested of some of the mystery regarding its function. Noticing its dense aggregations of cells resembling lymphocytes, earlier investigators believed it might be an important source of these cells. Now, however, it is known to exert control over the development of immunological defense mechanisms that lead to rejection of antigenic molecules as well as cells and tissues not derived from the animal itself.

Removal of the thymus from mice on the day of their birth has remarkable effects on the health and life of the animal. Once the technical skill for this delicate operation was acquired, it was shown that the resulting "wasting disease" stemmed from inability of the animal to make antibody and to reject foreign cells and tissues. Invasion by foreign organisms led to the early death of the defenseless animals.

Thymectomized animals never develop plasma cells, which produce antibody (see Plate 1), and they lack circulating lymphocytes as well as aggregations of lymphocytes characteristic of normal lymph nodes and spleen. The lymphocytes are probably responsible for the phenomenon of "delayed hypersensitivity." A good example of this is the inevitable rejection of tissue grafts derived from all other individuals except from an identical twin. The fetal thymus is therefore said to "seed" the tissues where immunologically reactive cells are produced.

In the thymus prior to involution the most numerous cell type is the thymocyte (Th). These cells closely resemble lymphocytes in that the chromatin in their nuclei is densely clumped. The cytoplasm is rich in ribosomes (R), and its volume is small relative to that of the nucleus. Golgi regions (G), centrioles (Ce), and mitochondria (M) may be aggregated at one pole of the nucleus. Small myelin figures (arrows) are frequently enclosed within the mitochondria.

Initially, thymocytes are produced in the thymus at a high rate. Cells that are destined to proliferate enlarge before dividing, and a series of mitotic divisions follows, leading to the production of the small thymocytes. After the seeding of other lymphoid tissues, lymphocytes no longer leave the thymus in appreciable numbers. It seems that the lymphoid organs, especially the spleen and lymph nodes, once having acquired lymphocytes, are immunologically competent.

Interest in the thymus was greatly stimulated by the initial discovery of its importance, and the ensuing investigations revealed an additional function; namely, that it serves as an endocrine organ. As evidence of this, it has been found that transplants of thymus tissue are adequate replacement for glands removed surgically soon after birth. This holds true even when the thymus transplant is enclosed in a porous chamber that allows exchange of body fluids but prevents escape of thymus cells into the host. The convincing test for hormonal involvement is that animals with such transplants respond normally when their immunological defense mechanisms are challenged. Therefore one can conclude that the mammalian thymus behaves as if it were secreting a hormone or hormones that stimulate plasma cells and lymphocytes to proliferate and to form antibody when antigens are introduced.

The thymus hormone is now being isolated and characterized, and examination of the thymus does disclose the existence of cells that may be secretory. One such cell is seen in this micrograph (N). Its nuclear content is thinly dispersed, and there is notably little clumping of chromatinic material. The cytoplasm, also of low density, extends into long processes that attach to other cells of the same nature by means of desmosomes to form a reticular framework within which the lymphocytes are held. Bundles of tonofilaments (T) lie in the cytoplasm. Because of these features and also because they may possess cilia and have one surface resting on a basement membrane, these cells are considered to be epithelial. Vesicular and granular inclusions of the epithelial cells have been examined in regard to their staining properties and their ability to incorporate isotopically labeled metabolites. Such studies have demonstrated that these structures contain sulfated acid mucopolysaccharides, and cytological observations suggest that the vesicles are formed within the Golgi regions (G') and may contain the secretory product of these cells, that is, the thymus hormone.

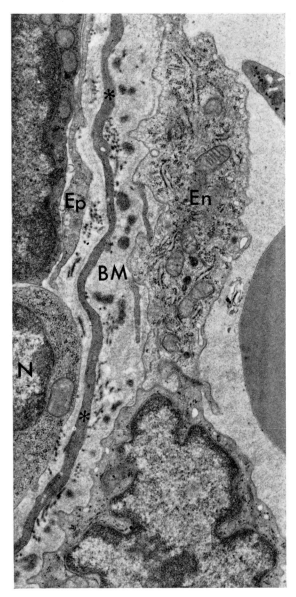

Text Figure 36a

The capillary endothelium (En) of thymus vessels is relatively thick (compare Plates 10 and 24) and lacks obvious fenestrae. An extensive layer of basement membrane material (BM) supports the endothelial cells and encompasses pericytes (*). Processes of thymus epithelial cells (Ep) and lymphocytes (nucleus, N) border the capillary wall.

From the thymus of the newborn rat
Magnification × 9000

While the thymus stimulates lymphopoiesis, it does not itself normally produce any antibody-forming cells. Indeed it lacks germinal centers, present in lymph nodes and the white pulp of the spleen, in which immunologically competent cells are produced in response to suitable stimuli. The lack of response by the thymus may perhaps be related to the fact that little stimulating antigenic material can traverse the "blood-thymus barrier." This barrier in the newborn rats has been found to be only partially effective, whereas in adults it is well established.

Thus it would appear that the capillaries of the thymus are the sites at which substances entering the gland may be monitored. In text figure 36a, included to illustrate this barrier, the capillary endothelium (En) proves to be one of considerable thickness when compared to many other endothelia (cf. Plates 10 and 24). Furthermore it lacks fenestrae and is supported by a thickened layer of basement membrane material (BM), which encloses collagen fibrils. Pericytes (*) are surrounded by this material and may form an almost complete cellular wrapping around the vessel. Processes of epithelial cells (Ep) often extend along the connective tissue of the capillary wall, but lymphocytes (nucleus, N) may abut on it as well. It seems likely that the unusual and rather elaborate structure of this blood vessel and supporting tissues constitutes the physical basis of the "blood-thymus barrier."

Germinal centers appear in the thymus in a certain few of the autoimmune diseases (e.g., hemolytic anemia and myasthenia gravis). These disorders belong to a large group of diseases that are characterized by production of antibodies against the individual's own antigens. The abnormality of the thymus suggests that its control over immunological responses has broken down. Production of "forbidden clones" of cells that are unable to distinguish foreign from "self" antigens may become possible, and normal tissues may then be destroyed. Although this concept of thymus malfunction remains for the moment only a stimulating hypothesis, it does acknowledge the central role of the thymus in the development of immune responses.

From the thymus of the newborn rat
Magnification × 18,400

142

BURNET, M. The thymus gland. *Sci. Amer., 207*:50 (November, 1962).

CLARK, S. L., JR. Cytological evidences of secretion in the thymus. *In* The Thymus: Experimental and Clinical Studies. Ciba Foundation Symposium. G. E. W. Wolstenholme and R. Porter, editors. Boston, Little, Brown and Company (1966) p. 3.

———. The thymus in mice of strain 129/J studied with the electron microscope. *Amer. J. Anat., 112*:1 (1963).

ITO, T., and HOSHINO, T. Fine structure of the epithelial reticular cells of the medulla of the thymus in the golden hamster. *Z. Zellforsch., 69*:311 (1966).

LEVEY, R. H. The thymus hormone. *Sci. Amer., 211*:66 (July, 1964).

MILLER, J. F. A. P. The thymus in relation to the development of immunological capacity. *In* The Thymus: Experimental and Clinical Studies. Ciba Foundation Symposium. G. E. W. Wolstenholme and R. Porter, editors. Boston, Little, Brown and Company (1966) p. 153.

OSOBA, D., and MILLER, J. F. A. P. The lymphoid tissues and immune responses of neonatally thymectomized mice bearing thymus tissue in millipore diffusion chambers. *J. Exp. Med., 119*:177 (1964).

WEISS, L. Electron microscopic observations on the vascular barrier in the cortex of the thymus of the mouse. *Anat. Rec., 145*:413 (1963).

143

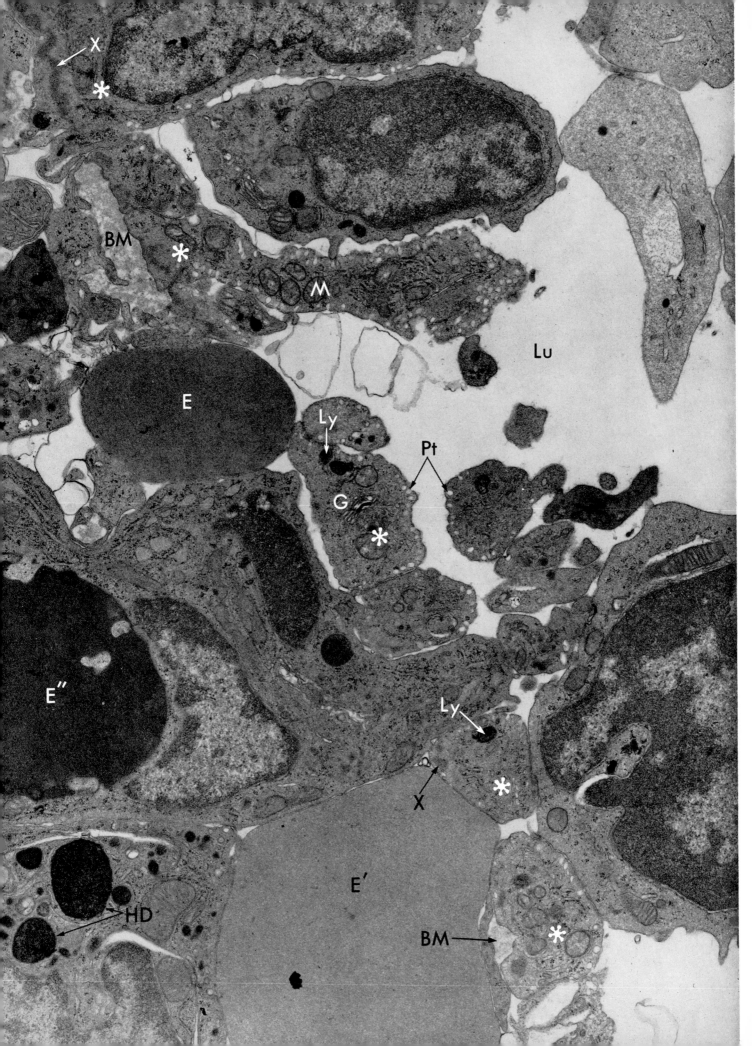

PLATE 37
Sinusoids of the Spleen

IN the spleen the blood is filtered by exposure to cells belonging to the reticuloendothelial system. These are phagocytes or potential phagocytes embedded in a fine fibrous meshwork. Under the light microscope the meshwork, or reticulin, may be visualized by means of silver staining or the PAS reaction. Under the electron microscope, this extracellular material (BM) is amorphous and of medium density, and it bears a striking resemblance to the thin basement membranes underlying the various epithelia illustrated in this atlas (see, for example, Plates 10, 24–26, and 28). Occasionally fine collagen fibrils are found associated with the reticulin. As in other lymphoid tissue, such as that of the lymph nodes, this supporting network contains centers where lymphocytes and plasma cells mature. These areas in the spleen are called the white pulp. But unlike certain other lymphoid tissue, the splenic reticular tissue is infiltrated by the blood vascular system. The presence of numerous erythrocytes accounts for the appearance of the areas known as the red pulp.

While circulation in the spleen has been carefully studied, it is still uncertain just how the blood gains entrance to the reticular tissue surrounding the sinuses, the so-called cords of Billroth. It is evident that there is a complicated system of small arteries and that prominent venous sinuses are the primary collecting vessels. But it is not known whether the arteries empty into the interstices of the reticular tissue or directly into the sinuses through a closed vascular system. In any case, there are openings in the walls of the sinuses so that the movement of cells both into and out of the vascular system in these regions is a definite possibility.

In this micrograph, the wall of a venous sinus may be examined. At the right is the lumen (Lu), and portions of its lining or littoral cells (∗) are arrayed diagonally across the field. These cells differ in several respects from endothelia that line much of the vascular system. They are, first of all, much thicker (see Plates 10 and 24) and may attain a columnar shape in the region containing the nucleus (top of the plate). Their cytoplasm is rich in mitochondria (M), ribosomes are abundant, and a few Golgi regions may be identified (G). Pits (Pt) and small vesicles, like those commonly found in endothelial cells, are especially abundant at or near the free surfaces of these sinusoidal lining cells. In addition, they contain lysosomes (Ly).

The littoral cells are supported by reticulin (BM), which forms an incomplete basement membrane. An irregular band of dense material (X) lies in the basal region of the cytoplasm, facing the underlying membrane. It seems most probable that this material aids in supporting the littoral cells.

Perhaps the most striking feature of the venous sinus is the large gaps that may exist between cells. In this instance an erythrocyte (E) lies near one of these openings. In the lower part of the field, another erythrocyte (E′) seems to have passed completely out of the vascular system.

The reticuloendothelial cells have the extraordinary ability to inspect red cells and to recognize worn or damaged individuals, which they engulf and destroy. Such a red cell (E″) is present within a large reticular cell, a portion of which projects between two littoral cells. After being phagocytized, the red cell increases in density and is eroded away at the surface. As erythrocytes are broken down, bilirubin, a pigment derived from hemoglobin, is released into the blood stream. Residual matter from the red cell breakdown in the form of dense granules called hemosiderin deposits (HD) remains in the cells. The hemosiderin contains an iron-protein complex called ferritin. The iron is conserved and eventually finds its way into the hemoglobin of erythroblasts (see Plate 33).

The conditions which make worn or damaged cells subject to destruction by phagocytes are not entirely known. In the disease called hereditary spherocytosis the red cells are abnormal and are rapidly destroyed by the spleens of individuals suffering from the disease and by spleens of normal individuals receiving injections of the spherotic cells. However, in persons without spleens, the life span of the abnormal spherotic red cells is nearly normal (120 days). More recent work indicates that excessively high permeability of the red cell to sodium ion may be the primary defect in this disease.

From the spleen of the guinea pig
Magnification ×17,000

145

CROSBY, W. H. Normal functions of the spleen relative to red blood cells: A review. *Blood, 14:*399 (1959).

FELDMAN, J. D. Ultrastructure of immunologic processes. *Advances Immun., 4:*175 (1964).

JACOB, H. S., and JANDL, J. H. Increased cell membrane permeability in the pathogenesis of hereditary spherocytosis. *J. Clin. Invest., 43:*1704 (1964).

SIMON, G., and PICTET, R. Étude au microscope électronique des sinus splénique et des cordons de Billroth chez le rat. *Acta Anat., 57:*163 (1964).

THOMAS, C. E. An electron- and light microscope study of sinus structure in perfused rabbit and dog spleens. *Amer. J. Anat., 120:*527 (1967).

WEISS, L. The structure of fine splenic arterial vessels in relation to hemoconcentration and red cell destruction. *Amer. J. Anat., 111:*131 (1962).

———. Appendix. The role of the spleen in the removal of normally aged red cells. *Amer. J. Anat., 111:*175 (1962).

PLATE 38

Skeletal Muscle and the Sarcoplasmic Reticulum

PLATE 38

Skeletal Muscle and the Sarcoplasmic Reticulum

THE cross striations that characterize skeletal and cardiac muscle reflect the patterned organization of contractile fibrils that fill the cytoplasm of each large, cylindrical multinucleated cell or fiber. Several of these fibrils (∗) located in the marginal zone of a fiber are shown in this micrograph. They in turn are clearly constructed of filaments, and the distribution of these is related to the alternating light and dark bands. Since in separate fibrils these bands are in precise register, the total effect results in the well-known striated appearance of the cell.

Each repeating sequence of striations constitutes what is referred to as a sarcomere, and the segment thus defined is considered to be the functional unit of contraction. From among the several bands in the striation pattern, the Z line is commonly selected as marking the limits of the sarcomere. This line is unusually dense, especially in contracted fibrils, and may be correctly regarded as a kind of septum that is continuous transversely across the fibril. Other bands in the sarcomere are labeled. The isotropic band, I, is bisected by the Z. The anisotropic, A, is the more dense and is bisected by a narrow light band, the H. And frequently a line, called the M, appears along the middle of the H band.

Careful studies of the fine structure of myofibrils have revealed the presence of at least two kinds of filaments in the fibrils. Of these, the thicker and more prominent run along the length of the A band. In part they represent the protein myosin, which among other properties possesses ATP-ase activity. The second type of filamentous unit is thinner and less obvious than the first. It intermingles in a highly ordered pattern with the myosin filaments and in each sarcomere extends from the Z line to the edge of the H band. In contraction, these actin filaments slide between the myosin units with the consequent disappearance of the I and H bands. The myosin filaments have small lateral projections, which introduce a finer, transverse periodicity into the fibril and which are thought to function in the sliding motion of contraction and in binding the two filament systems together.

In addition to the fibrils, this micrograph shows a prominent vesicular component in the interfibrillar cytoplasm or, as it is called in muscle, the sarcoplasm. This is the endoplasmic reticulum of the muscle cell, referred to appropriately in muscle as the sarcoplasmic reticulum or SR. As in other cells it is made up of interconnected, anastomosing tubules and vesicles, but in this instance they are without attached ribosomes. It can thus be thought of as a smooth form of the reticulum (see Plates 2, 7, 18, and 19). There are other peculiar features about it, one being a structural pattern that repeats with respect to each sarcomere of the myofibril. Thus one can notice in the micrograph that the lacelike reticular structures (SR) are interrupted in their continuity at each Z line and seem to terminate in dilated sacs (SR′). The latter are closely apposed to an interposed vesicular element (TS), which is positioned exactly opposite the Z line. This third element of the triad (text figure 38a) is now known to be part of a transverse membrane system, called the T-system (TS), which is continuous with the sarcolemma, the limiting membrane of the muscle fiber.

The recognition of this T-system elucidated, if not solved, a basic problem of muscle contraction—that is, the surprising fact that myofibrils within the center of a fiber, perhaps 50 microns from the surface, contract simultaneously with fibrils at the surface and near to the electrical excitation which moves over the sarcolemma just in advance of contraction. Since diffusion rates within cytoplasm would be too slow to account for such a rapid propagation of excitation throughout the fiber, it was argued that a structural element must be involved. Therefore, against this background of physiological information and theory, the discovery of the T-system and more especially its continuity with the sarcolemma initiated a new series of investigations focused on the mechanisms of excitation-contraction coupling. Comparative morphological studies have revealed that in some muscles, particularly the more rapidly contracting ones, the T-system with associated SR vesicles is more elaborately and extensively developed and appears opposite the two halves of the I band, at the level at which A and I bands meet. Biochemical studies on isolated fragments of the SR (muscle microsomes) have shown them to possess a remarkable capacity to take up and store calcium ion

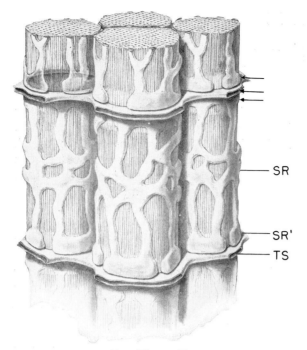

— SR

— SR'
— TS

Text Figure 38a

This three-dimensional drawing is designed to clarify the structural relationship between the myofibrils and two smooth membrane systems, the sarcoplasmic reticulum and the T-system, found in skeletal muscle fibers. The myofibrils are cylindrical shafts of closely packed filaments. At the top of the drawing, four fibrils are seen cut in cross section. As described in Plate 38, the fibrils are made up of repeating units, the sarcomeres. These are drum-shaped segments, all of equal size, piled end to end, and each one is in register with those adjacent to it. Curtains of anastomosing tubules, all parts of the sarcoplasmic reticulum (SR), occupy the sarcoplasm between the myofibrils and envelop each sarcomere. The reticulum is usually expanded in the region of the I band (SR'). At the levels of the Z lines, marking the limits of the sarcomeres, the expansions lie close to the membranes of the T-system (TS), forming the so-called triad (3 arrows). The T-system represents deep, narrow infoldings of the sarcolemma or plasma membrane of the muscle fiber. Its inner space is therefore continuous with the extracellular space. There is no evidence that it ever becomes confluent with cavities of the sarcoplasmic reticulum or any other intracellular space. The T-system may be pictured as a grid perforated by pores, through which pass the myofibrils. This structure is indicated at the upper left in the drawing, where the fibril is drawn as if it were transparent. As a whole, then, the T-system resembles a series of perforated lamellae or grids, partitioning the elongated muscle cell at regular sarcomeric intervals. It is obviously in close contact with the myofibrils, as well as with the vesicles of the sarcoplasmic reticulum, providing relationships that are essential for the rapid contraction and relaxation of the muscle cell.

in the presence of ATP. More recently *in situ* tests have pinpointed the large terminal vesicles of the SR as the storage site. Presumably the excitation (depolarization) that moves over the sarcolemma preceding muscle contraction is transported internally into the fiber along the membranes of the T-system. At the triad levels this disturbance is transmitted to the adjacent SR vesicles and triggers the release of calcium ion. After initiating contraction of the adjacent myofibrils, the calcium is quickly recaptured by the SR membranes and stored for the next excitation. The relationships of these two membranous systems, the SR and the T-system, to the myofibrils is illustrated further in the three-dimensional diagram in text figure 38a.

Tadpole segmental muscles are unusual in possessing very few mitochondria (sarcosomes), of which none appears in this particular field. This peculiarity reflects the fact that the muscle of origin is used by the animal only for short bursts of activity between relatively long periods of rest.

From the tail muscle of a leopard frog tadpole
Magnification × 29,000

150

COSTANTIN, LeR. L., FRANZINI-ARMSTRONG, C., and PODOLSKY, J. Localization of calcium-accumulating structures in striated muscle fibers. *Science, 147:*158 (1965).

EBASHI, S., and LIPMANN, F. Adenosine triphosphate-linked concentration of calcium ions in a particulate fraction of rabbit muscle. *J. Cell Biol., 14:*389 (1962).

FAWCETT, D. W., and REVEL, J. P. The sarcoplasmic reticulum of a fast-acting fish muscle. *J. Biophysic. and Biochem. Cytol., 10:* Suppl., 89 (1961).

FREYGANG, W. H. Tubular ionic movements. Symposium on excitation-contraction coupling in striated muscle. *Fed. Proc., 24:*1135 (1965).

HASSELBACH, W. Relaxation and the sarcotubular calcium pump. *Fed. Proc., 23:*909 (1964).

HUXLEY, A. F., and TAYLOR, R. E. Local activation of striated muscle fibers. *J. Physiol., 144:*426 (1958).

HUXLEY, H. E. The double array of filaments in cross-striated muscle. *J. Biophysic. and Biochem. Cytol., 3:* 631 (1957).

PEACHEY, L. D. The sarcoplasmic reticulum and transverse tubules of the frog's sartorius. *J. Cell Biol., 25* (No. 3, part 2): 209 (1965).

PORTER, K. R., and PALADE, G. E. Studies on the endoplasmic reticulum. III. Its form and distribution in striated muscle cells. *J. Biophysic. and Biochem. Cytol. 3:*269 (1957).

SMITH, D. S. Reticular organizations within the striated muscle cell. An historical survey of light microscope studies. *J. Biophysic. and Biochem. Cytol., 10:* Suppl., 61 (1961).

ZADUNAISKY, J. A. The localization of sodium in the transverse tubules of skeletal muscle. *J. Cell Biol., 31:*C-11 (following p. 214) (1966).

151

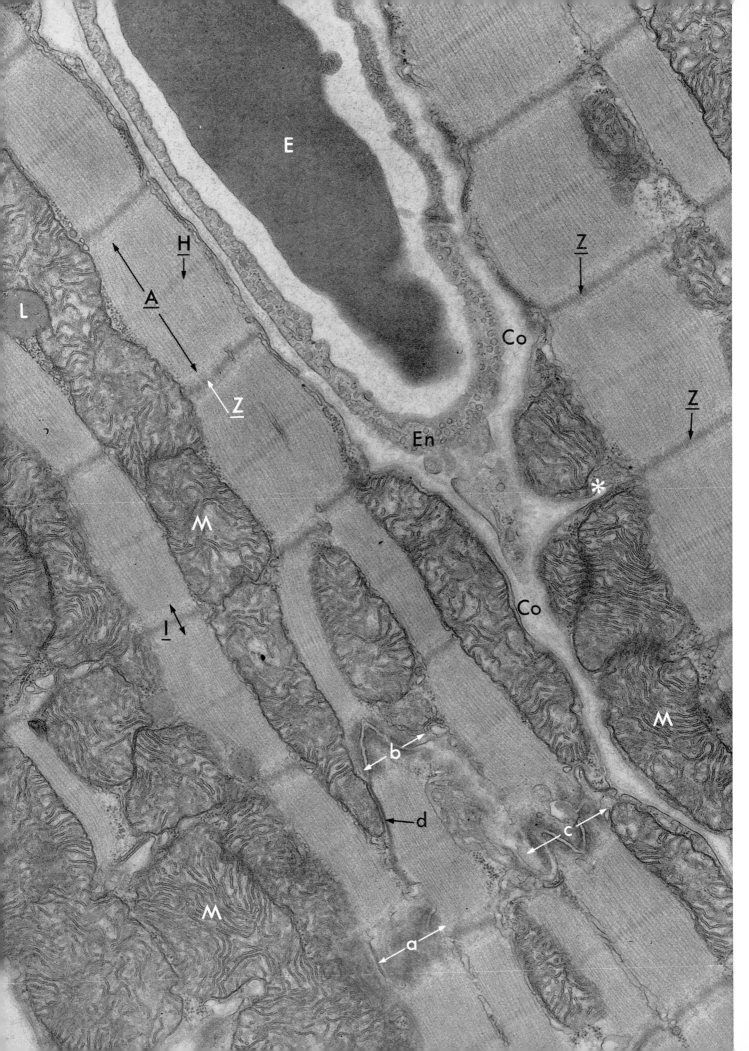

PLATE 39

Cardiac Muscle

CARDIAC muscle, like skeletal muscle, is striated, and the organization of the contractile fibrils and other components differs from that of skeletal muscle in detail only. In this micrograph portions of the cytoplasm of several cardiac muscle cells (fibers) may be examined. The cell at upper right is separated from the lateral surfaces of the column of cells at left by a thin layer of fine connective tissue fibrils (Co), within which is lodged a capillary of this well-vascularized tissue. The vesicular cytoplasm of the endothelial cells (En) and a profile of an erythrocyte (E) are evident.

As in skeletal muscle, myofibrils run parallel to the long axis of the cell, but unlike the fibrils in skeletal muscle, these may branch. The sarcomeres show the same pattern of banding as that of skeletal muscle. In this micrograph the Z lines (Z) delimiting the sarcomere are prominent and readily identified. However, the muscle is contracted so that the I band regions (I) have nearly disappeared, and the A band (A) occupies most of the sarcomere length. In the contracted state, a dark band normally appears at the position of the H band (H).

Cardiac muscle is noted for the size and the number of its mitochondria or sarcosomes (M), presumably present to satisfy the cell's unusual requirements for ATP. These are aligned in columns between the myofibrils. Often lipid droplets (L) lie alongside the sarcosomes.

For many years cardiac muscle was thought to be a syncytium. Now, however, the significance of the intercalated disk, long a puzzle to light microscopists, is understood. The disk is really an elaborate region of attachment that links the elongated cells end to end. Thus parallel columns of fibers are formed. In this micrograph two cells are joined by an intercalated disk (a, b, c). Though the disk always occurs at the level of the Z lines, it does not always occur at Z lines that are in register: i.e., the level of the disk may shift by the length of one sarcomere. Thus in this micrograph the central portion of a disk (b)

is at the level of a different Z line from those portions on either side (a, c). It follows that the boundaries of adjacent cells are not all in one plane but essentially interdigitate with one another. Along this specialized junction the plasma membranes of the attached cells can be followed, and along their cytoplasmic surfaces a dense material is accumulated. From the standpoints of morphology and function these regions within the intercalated disk may be regarded as elaborate desmosomes (see Plate 9). On the other hand, the plasma membranes (d) lateral to the sarcomere come close to one another to form a junction with a gap of about 20 A between adjacent cell membranes. When fine colloidal particles are introduced experimentally into the tissue, they can penetrate this gap, thus providing a negative stain that reveals hexagonally packed structures (each 70–75 A wide) spanning the gap. Such junctions are believed to be the sites where an electrical impulse can be transmitted from one muscle fiber membrane to the next. Thus the excitatory impulse sweeping as a wave over the plasma membrane of one fiber does not require chemical mediators for transmission to neighboring fibers (cf. Plates 42 and 43). In the propagation of the excitatory impulse that precedes and in effect causes contraction, cardiac muscle does then behave as if it were a syncytium.

The sarcolemma of the lateral surfaces of the cardiac muscle fiber is invaginated at the level of the Z line (∗). By this device the plasma membrane is brought into close contact not only with smooth-walled elements of the sarcoplasmic (endoplasmic) reticulum but also, as in the case of skeletal muscle, with the fibrils more deeply situated in the fibers. The infoldings of the sarcolemma therefore constitute the T-system of cardiac muscle (cf. Plate 38). Cardiac and skeletal muscles are therefore provided with specialized intracellular membrane systems, which are undoubtedly involved in the contractile process.

From the heart of the bat
Magnification × 30,500

References

ESSNER, E., NOVIKOFF, A. B., and QUINTANA, N. Nucleoside phosphatase activities in rat cardiac muscle. *J. Cell Biol.,* 25 (No. 2, part 1):201 (1965).

FAWCETT, D. W., and SELBY, C. C. Observations on the fine structure of the turtle atrium. *J. Biophysic. and Biochem. Cytol., 4:*63 (1958).

NELSON, D. A., and BENSON, E. S. On the structural continuities of the transverse tubular system of rabbit and human myocardial cells. *J. Cell Biol., 16:*297 (1963).

REVEL, J. P., and KARNOVSKY, M. J. Hexagonal array of subunits in intercellular junctions. *J. Cell Biol., 33:* C-7 (following p. 450) (1967).

SIMPSON, F. O., and OERTELIS, S. J. The fine structure of of sheep myocardial cells; sarcolemmal invaginations and the transverse tubular system. *J. Cell Biol., 12:*91 (1962).

SJÖSTRAND, F. S., and ANDERSSON-CEDERGREN, E. Intercalated discs of heart muscle. *In* The Structure and Function of Muscle. G. H. Bourne, editor. New York, Academic Press, vol. I (1960) p. 421.

PLATE 40
Smooth Muscle

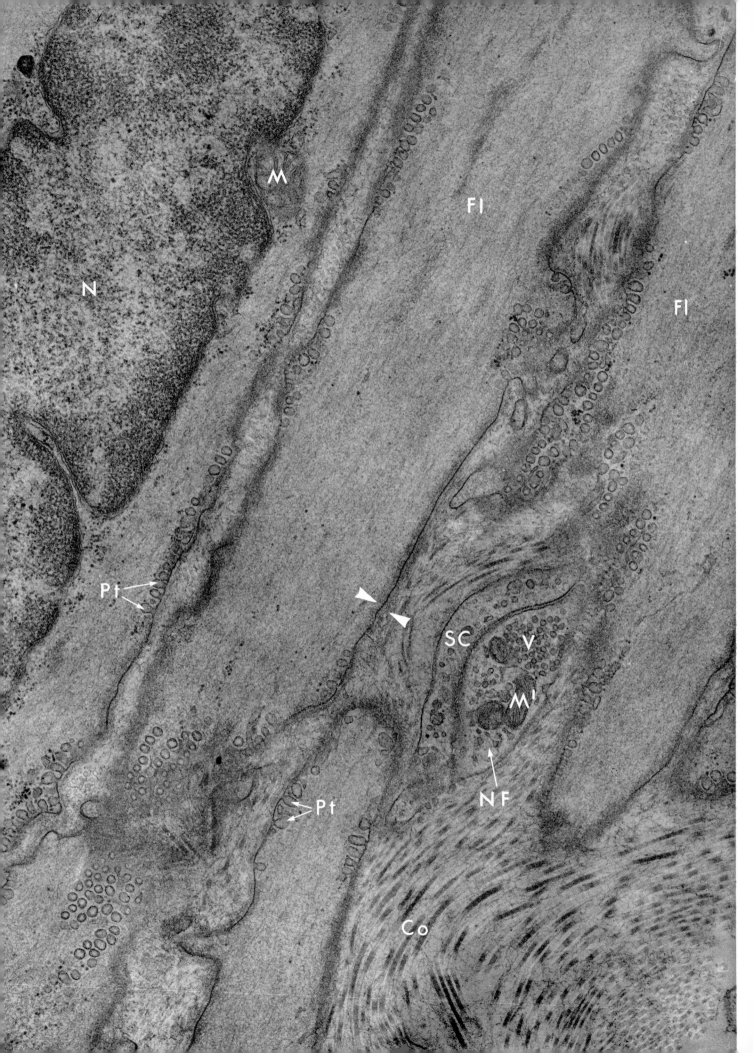

PLATE 40

Smooth Muscle

SMOOTH muscles, which contract involuntarily, are found in numerous places in the vertebrate body, such as in the walls of the intestinal tract, the blood vessels, and the uterus. They are characterized by several physiological features, of which their slow contraction time is outstanding. In some instances seconds, or even minutes, are required to complete a single contraction.

The tissue itself is made up of spindle-shaped cells containing a system of contractile proteins. The cells are intimately associated with the connective tissue fibers that bind them together. In these respects smooth muscle is similar to striated muscle, but unlike the latter the contractile elements are not organized into any obvious pattern for which microscopists have been able to provide a satisfactory functional interpretation (cf. Plates 38 and 39). Very thin filaments (Fl) can be seen to run parallel to the long axis of the cell (fiber) and to constitute the bulk of the cytoplasm. Thick filaments, common in striated fibers and identifiable with the protein myosin, are not obvious and have been observed only rarely in smooth muscle cells. Mitochondria (M) usually cluster near the irregular border of the nucleus (N). The endoplasmic reticulum is represented only by a few smooth-surfaced vesicles lying in the perinuclear region and in sparsely distributed channels among the fibrous elements.

Aside from the abundance of contractile material, specialized structural features associated with the plasma membrane distinguish smooth muscle cells. Representative of these are certain flasklike invaginations (pits) of the membrane (Pt) lying in the peripheral cytoplasm. The form of these suggests a structural device by which substances may be incorporated into the cells by a process akin to pinocytosis. Until now, however, evidence of uptake by these vesicles is lacking, and there is certainly no reason to believe that they transport selected molecules across the muscle fibers as they may across cells of the vascular endothelium, where they occur in similar form and number (cf. Plate 10).

Also associated with the plasma membrane are fine feltworks of moderately dense material lying on opposite sides of the line representing the membrane (arrows). Of these, the extracellular material is closely interwoven with the matrix and fibrils of the surrounding connective tissue, and it seems probable that the feltwork is homologous with the basement membranes (basal laminae) of other tissues (see Plates 10, 24, and 28). As such it serves to bind together the muscle cells and connective tissue fibers such as those seen at lower right (Co).

Studies of smooth muscle have revealed that, as in the case of striated muscles, actin and myosin are both present as the contractile proteins. Surprisingly they are similar in most respects to their counterparts in striated muscle, even though their disposition within the cell is strikingly different. The thin filaments, already mentioned, correspond to actin and may be isolated readily in filamentous form. The thick filaments, which are seemingly rare, probably represent myosin, but thus far this protein has been isolated as filaments only under rather special experimental conditions. It appears that most of the myosin in smooth muscle cells exists in a disaggregated form. Since the diameter of the thin filaments does not change measurably during contraction, models have been proposed in which myosin dimers act as lateral bridges that join arrays of actin filaments sliding past each other during contraction.

Comparison of relaxed and contracted smooth muscle indicates some of the morphological events accompanying shortening. Thin filaments become straighter and more clearly organized into bundles. At the same time areas of the plasma membrane lined with a dense layer of material (left arrow) fold inward as if the thin filaments were attached to and exerting a force on them. As though to emphasize this, intervening areas of the plasma membrane, where pits (Pt) are abundant, bulge outward. The strandlike cytoplasmic densities, called dense bodies (above label Fl), become longer. Like the cortical dense material, they also represent regions where actin filaments insert or are anchored. Thus these intracellular densities and those associated with the plasma membrane correspond to the Z lines of the striated muscle fibril. As contraction occurs, the nuclear envelope also becomes folded, and the mitochondria, ribosomes, etc., are aggregated at the nuclear poles.

Recently there have been observed special regions of attachment in which plasma membranes of adjacent smooth muscle fibers are closely associated, and no connective tissue fibers intervene between them. In some instances a fusion of the outer leaflets of the unit membranes is achieved and a tight junction (text figure 7a) is formed. In others the contact is less intimate and a space of ~100 A persists. It has been proposed that such regions of contact, particularly the tight junctions, may function in the transmission of excitation (the stimulation to contract) from one fiber to another.

A cross section of a small autonomic nerve process (NF) lies near the muscle fiber on the right-hand side of the picture. Mitochondria (M′) and vesicles (V), both of which are found near the regions of the synapse between nerve and muscle (or nerve), indicate that this is a terminal portion of a nerve fiber. However, an actual synapse, represented by the close approximation of two plasma membranes (see Plate 43), is not included in the section. The cytoplasm (SC) covering one side of the nerve fiber belongs to a Schwann cell. The structure of nervous tissue is discussed in details in Plates 42 through 45.

From the esophagus of the bat
Magnification × 38,500

References

CAESAR, R., EDWARDS, G. A., and RUSKA, H. Architecture and nerve supply of mammalian smooth muscle tissue. *J. Biophysic. and Biochem. Cytol., 3:*867 (1957).

DEWEY, M. M., and BARR, L. Intercellular connection between smooth muscle cells: the nexus. *Science, 137:* 670 (1962).

ELLIOTT, G. F. X-ray diffraction studies on striated and smooth muscles. *Proc. Roy. Soc., Series B, 160:*467 (1964).

KELLY, R. E., and RICE, R. V. Localization of myosin filaments in smooth muscle. *J. Cell Biol., 37:*105 (1968).

LANE, B. P. Alterations in the cytologic detail of intestinal smooth muscle cells in various stages of contraction. *J. Cell Biol., 27:*199 (1965).

———, and RHODIN, J. A. G. Cellular interrelationships and electrical activity in two types of smooth muscle. *J. Ultrastruct. Res., 10:*470 (1964).

OOSAKI, T., and ISHII, S. Junctional structure of smooth muscle cells. The ultrastructure of the regions of junction between smooth muscle cells in rat small intestine. *J. Ultrastruct. Res., 10:*567 (1964).

PANNER, B. J., and HONIG, C. R. Filament ultrastructure and organization in vertebrate smooth muscle. Contraction hypothesis based on localization of actin and myosin. *J. Cell Biol., 35:*303 (1967).

SHOENBERG, C. F., RÜEGG, J. C., NEEDHAM, D. M., SCHIRMER, R. H., and NEMETCHEK-GANSLER, H. A biochemical and electron microscope study of the contractile proteins in vertebrate smooth muscle. *Biochem. Z., 345:*255 (1966).

PLATE 41

The Arteriole

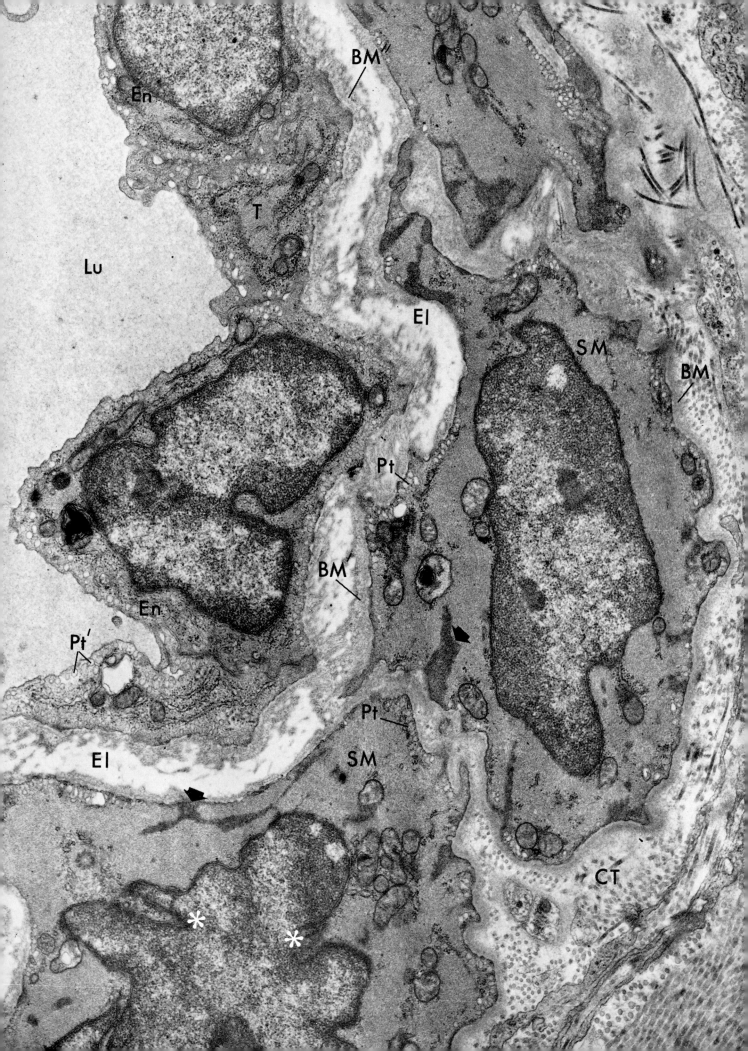

PLATE 41

The Arteriole

THE terminal arterioles, among the smallest branches of the arterial tree, are part of the strong-walled muscular system of vessels that conduct and distribute the blood to the capillary beds. They receive blood from the larger arteries that carry it from the heart. From them in turn the blood passes through the precapillary sphincters, then into small vessels called metarterioles, and finally into the capillaries. In contrast with capillaries, the importance of the arterioles and the sphincters lies not in their ability to bring about exchanges of metabolites between the capillary lumen and the surrounding tissues, but rather in their effectiveness in regulating blood pressure. The caliber of the arterioles changes in response to nervous stimulation and to changes in the composition of the blood. They thus serve as a kind of dam and floodgate, helping to regulate the flow of blood into the capillaries. Since capillary beds, such as those in the abdominal viscera, may accommodate the entire normal volume of blood, general dilation of arterioles that lead to these capillaries would result (as it does in certain cases of shock following sudden trauma) in a precipitous drop in blood pressure. Under conditions that usually prevail, the narrowing of the arterioles makes an important contribution to the maintenance of normal blood pressure and the allocation of blood to the various capillary beds.

The wall of a terminal arteriole, which may be examined in this micrograph, is made up of an endothelium (En) lining the lumen (Lu) of the vessel, a layer of elastic connective tissue (El), a circumferentially arranged layer of smooth muscle (SM), and a peripheral layer of collagenous connective tissue (CT).

It is, of course, the contraction and relaxation of the smooth muscle that controls directly the size of the arteriole lumen. The terminal arteriole has been defined as a vessel having a diameter of less than 50 μ and having a complete muscular layer one cell thick. The muscle cell layer forms the sphincter at the bases of smaller (less than 15 μ in diameter) vessels branching from the arterioles and then gradually disappears as the vessels (metarterioles) lead into arterial capillaries.

The muscle fibers seen here in cross section are in a contracted state, as evidenced by the irregular folds of the nuclear envelope (∗) and the outward bulging of the plasma membrane in regions containing many pits (Pt). The latter regions alternate with infoldings where dense bodies (arrows) are contiguous with the inner surface of the plasma membrane (cf. Plate 40). The basal lamina (BM) surrounding the muscle fibers is more compact on the sides of the cells facing the collagenous connective tissue layer (CT) or adventitia. Careful examination of the small arterioles has demonstrated that there are abundant nerve endings associated with muscle cells. Both vasoconstrictor and vasodilator nerve fibers are found, but the former are believed to be of prime importance. Furthermore, tight junctions between smooth muscle cells also occur regularly. These junctions probably facilitate the spread of the excitatory impulse for contraction from muscle cell to muscle cell.

Elastic fibers (El), which are unstained in this preparation, form a thin connective tissue layer that is enmeshed with basement membrane material, both with that surrounding the smooth muscle (BM′) and that underlying the endothelium (BM″). Elastic fibers are stretched as the vessel is distended and due to their elasticity add to the force exerted by contracting muscle fibers in narrowing the vessel lumen. In the large arteries, elastic connective tissue is extensively developed. There its property of resisting deformation is important in helping to maintain tension of the arterial wall.

The endothelium (En) lining the terminal arteriole is a thick layer when compared to many capillary linings (see Plates 10 and 24). The cells making it up are probably capable of expanding and contracting passively as the diameter of the lumen varies. Bundles of tonofilaments (T) may strengthen this layer. Cells of the endothelium are joined closely together, and fenestrae are lacking. As in other endothelial cells, pits (Pt′) and vesicles derived from them are prominent structural features.

In the terminal arterioles and precapillary sphincters there exist special areas of contact between endothelial cells and muscle fibers, such as those in text figure 41a (X). Tongues of endothelial cell cytoplasm extend through the underlying basement membrane to form myoendo-

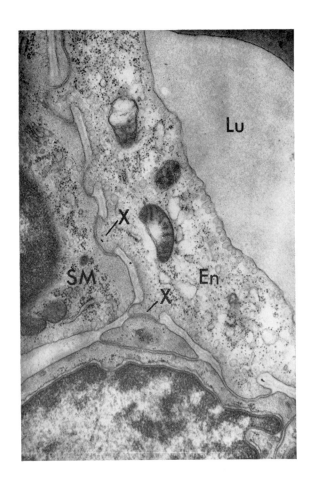

Text Figure 41a

Endothelial cells of terminal arterioles and precapillary sphincters, such as that shown here (En), frequently have footlike processes (X), and each makes a special contact with smooth muscle fibers (SM) of the vessel wall. The processes extend through the basement membrane material separating the two types of tissue. At the region of contact with the smooth muscle cell an intercellular gap of only 45 A remains. Such myoendothelial junctions may facilitate transmission of humoral agents from the blood in the vessel lumen (Lu) to muscle fibers, thus helping to regulate the dilation and constriction of the smallest arterial vessels. Micrograph courtesy of Dr. J. A. G. Rhodin. It is reprinted from Figure 24, *J. Ultrastruct. Res., 18:*181 (1967).

From the thigh muscles of the rabbit (*Oryctolagus cuniculus*)
Magnification × 25,500

thelial junctions with smooth muscle fibers. The two cells are separated by a 45 A gap but not by intervening basement membrane material.

Observations on small arterial vessels deprived of nervous connections have indicated that in some cases, such as in skeletal muscle, a strong muscular tone remains. These results have been interpreted as an indication that substances present locally can control the vasomotor responses. The presence of myoendothelial junctions may facilitate transmission of humoral substances from the blood to muscle fibers. Possibly for substances diffusing across the endothelium the junctions serve as pathways direct to the muscle. Perhaps more intriguing is the speculation that certain of the endothelial cells may act as receptors that respond to local concentrations of agents in the blood by depolarization of the plasma membrane. This excitation would then be transmitted to the muscle membrane at the junctional contacts.

From the epididymis of the hamster (*Cricetus cricetus*)
Magnification × 21,500

References

FAWCETT, D. W. The fine structure of capillaries, arterioles and small arteries. *In* The Microcirculation. S. R. M. Reynolds and B. W. Zweifach, editors. Urbana, Ill., University of Illinois Press (1959) p. 1.

GREENLEE, T. K., JR., ROSS, R., and HARTMAN, J. L. The fine structure of elastic fibers. *J. Cell Biol., 30:*59 (1966).

KARRER, H. E. Electron microscope study of developing chick embryo aorta. *J. Ultrastruct. Res., 4:*420 (1960).

RHODIN, J. A. G. The ultrastructure of mammalian arterioles and precapillary sphincters. *J. Ultrastruct. Res., 18:*181 (1967).

STEHBENS, W. E., and SILVER, M. D. Unusual development of basement membrane about small blood vessels. *J. Cell Biol., 26:*669 (1965).

162

PLATE 42
The Myoneural Junction

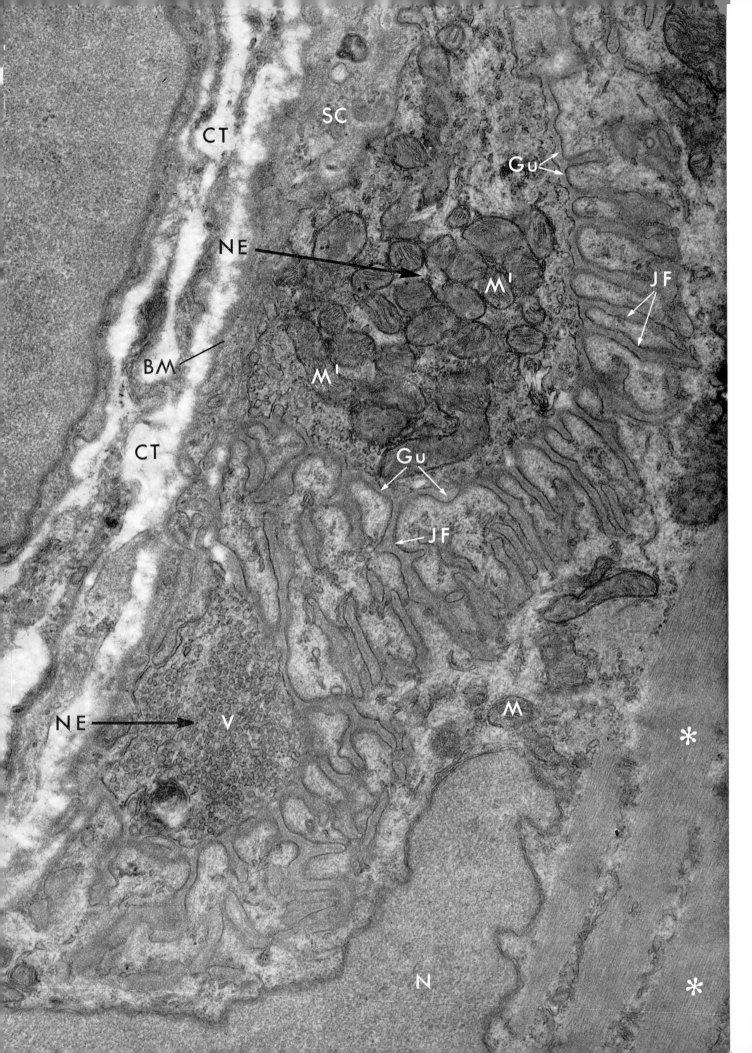

PLATE 42

The Myoneural Junction

THE stimulus to contract is brought to the fibers of skeletal muscle by axon processes of motor neurons, and the region of contact between the two cell types is especially differentiated to achieve the transmission. In the accompanying micrograph several myofibrils (*) identify the striated muscle fiber (cell). Where the axon terminal reaches the muscle, it inhabits a depression called a trough or gutter (Gu), which indents the surface of the fiber. Deep infoldings of the sarcolemma, called junctional folds (JF), extend from the bottoms of the troughs into the underlying cytoplasm, or sole plasm, of the fiber. Mitochondria (M) and the nucleus (N) of the muscle cell occur typically in this region of the fiber. The subneural apparatus, i.e., the gutters and junctional folds, are filled with a moderately dense, amorphous material that is similar to and continuous with that covering other regions of the muscle surface; it is essentially a basement membrane. The nerve cell endings (NE), on the other hand, lie naked in the trough; no cellular sheath is interposed between them and the muscle fiber. Rather, the two cells are separated from each other only by the layer of amorphous material described above. The Schwann cell sheath that encloses the axon as it approaches the myoneural junction pulls away from the axon terminal and remains only as a lidlike cover over the junction area. A portion of a Schwann cell (SC) can be seen in this illustration. It is surrounded by a basement membrane (BM) and connective tissue fibers (CT) of the endomysium. These structural relationships are diagrammed in text figure 42a.

At their tips, axons are filled with many small synaptic vesicles (V) and abundant mitochondria (M'). Because these vesicles are constantly present near the region of contact between nerve and muscle, as well as near synaptic junctions in the nervous system (see Plate 43), they have aroused considerable interest. Out of this has grown the theory that such vesicles, which measure 30 to 40 mμ in diameter, contain the humoral transmitter, acetylcholine. This localization has been established by chemical analysis of isolated synaptic vesicles. Cholinacetylase, an enzyme necessary for the formation of acetylcholine, is probably closely associated with the vesicles as well. Presumably the release of the transmitter substance through the presynaptic membrane and into the intercellular subneural space would bring about permeability changes and subsequently changes in the electrical potential across the postsynaptic membrane of the muscle. The resulting excitation and its propagation along the muscle fiber leads finally to the contraction of the myofibrils.

Once acetylcholine has served its function, it is rapidly destroyed by the enzyme cholinesterase. Histochemical studies of isolated synaptic membranes and use of autoradiographic techniques adapted for electron microscopy indicate that the enzyme is localized in the junctional folds and is probably an integral part of the postsynaptic membrane. The junctional folds provide a sixfold increase in the surface of the muscle fiber in the junctional region. This specialization would therefore seem to ensure high concentration of enzyme and prompt breakdown of acetylcholine, thus preventing continuous action of the neurohumor. Due to the extreme rapidity of this reaction the muscle fiber is almost immediately ready to be stimulated once more.

From rat diaphragm
Magnification × 32,000

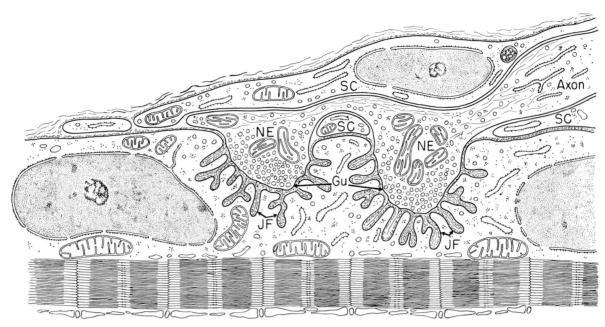

Text Figure 42a

This line drawing shows diagrammatically the relationship of the muscle fiber, nerve ending, and Schwann cell within the myoneural junction. It is based on a diagram by Couteaux, 1960.

A small part of a muscle fiber is shown in the lower half of the figure, identified by a myofibril. Nuclei lie right and left of the troughs or gutters (Gu), which indent the surface of the muscle cell. In the region of the troughs, the sarcolemma or plasma membrane is thrown into folds. These are called junctional folds (JF), and the material lining them is continuous with that covering the entire sarcolemma. This coating resembles a basement membrane and separates the muscle fiber from the nerve endings (NE) that reside in the gutters. As the axon reaches the region of the myoneural junction, its myelin sheath terminates, so that the neurolemma has no extraneous coverings except that represented by a Schwann cell (SC), which forms a lid enclosing the region of contact between the muscle and nerve cell. The axoplasm of the nerve endings is dominated by large numbers of synaptic vesicles, which crowd toward the zone of contact between the plasma membrane of the ending and the sarcolemma limiting the gutters.

References

COUTEAUX, R. Motor end-plate structure. *In* The Structure and Function of Muscle. G. H. Bourne, editor. New York, Academic Press, vol. I (1960) p. 337.

DE ROBERTIS, E. Ultrastructure and cytochemistry of the synaptic region. *Science, 156*:907 (1967).

——, RODRIGUES DE LORES ARNAIZ, G., SALGANICOFF, L., PELLEGRINO DE IRALDI, A., and ZIEHER, L. M. Isolation of synaptic vesicles and structural organization of the acetylcholine system within brain nerve endings. *J. Neurochem., 10*:225 (1963).

SALPETER, M. M. Electron microscope radioautography as a quantitative tool in enzyme cytochemistry. The distribution of acetylcholinesterase at motor end plates of a vertebrate twitch muscle. *J. Cell Biol., 32*:379 (1967).

166

PLATE 43

The Motor Neuron of the Spinal Cord

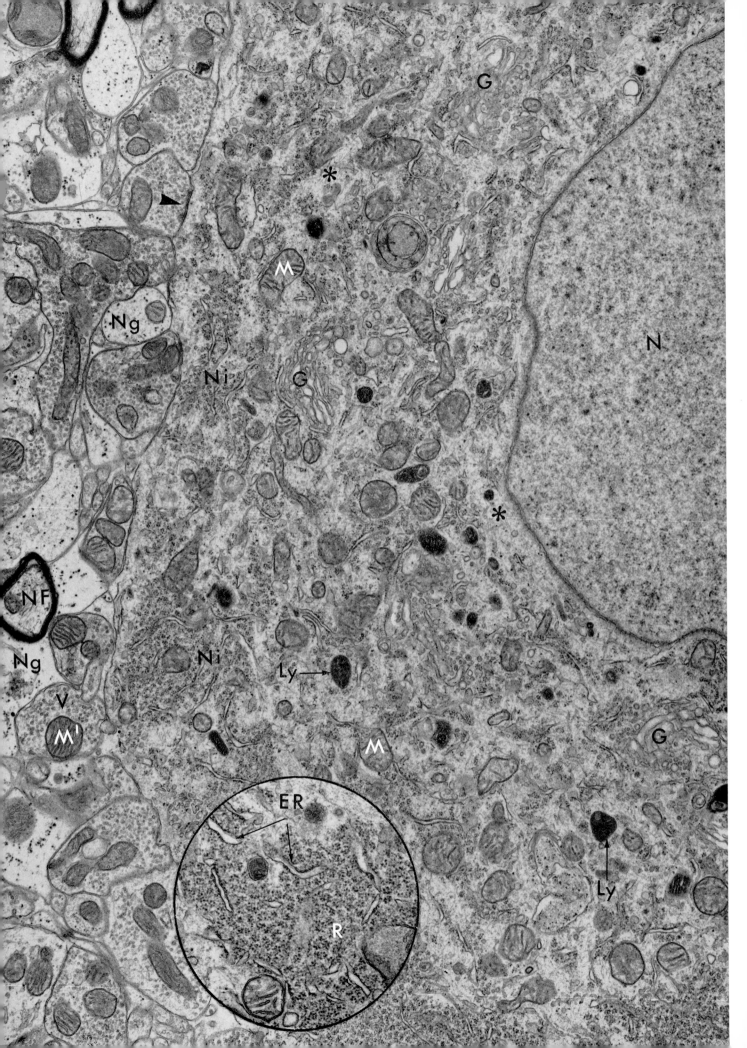

PLATE 43

The Motor Neuron of the Spinal Cord

THE motor neurons of the spinal cord, like neurons in general, are large cells. Only a small part of their total size is represented by the nucleus and perikaryon (the cytoplasm of the cell body), the greater part being in their processes, the axons and dendrites. Despite this unusual fact, the perikaryon is essential to the continuing function of the entire cell. It is the site of synthesis of the axon cytoplasm and that of the dendrites as well, and regeneration of nerves depends on the intact functioning of this central structure.

This micrograph depicts about half of a cross section through the perikaryon of a motor neuron and half its large nucleus (N). The perikaryon is rich in organelles, which in their morphology show variations on the themes displayed in other cells. The mitochondria (M) are small, fairly numerous, and more or less evenly distributed. Lysosomes (Ly) are commonly present. The Golgi region (G), which in its entirety is a complicated reticular structure in these cells, appears in section as scattered profiles of stacked cisternae and vesicles. Masses of ribosomes interlaced with profiles of ER cisternae represent the basophilic Nissl bodies (Ni), which are typical of neuronal cytoplasm. As shown in the inset, the bulk of the ribosomes (R) are not attached to ER membrane surfaces (ER), and presumably this distribution indicates that they are most active in the synthesis of proteins for retention by the neuron or its processes. Other intervening regions of the cytoplasm appear less dense than the Nissl material and can be seen in favorable instances to contain fine filaments, neurofilaments (*), which are especially common in axoplasm (see also Plates 44 and 45).

While the functional significance of the various components of the neuron cytoplasm (the perikaryon) can be surmised from generalizations based on our knowledge of cell fine structure, the specific and possibly special roles they perform in nerve cells are not as yet completely known. Only fragmentary but interesting observations are available. For example, the rough-surfaced ER, which is part of Nissl bodies, has been shown to be rich in cholinesterase. Presumably this enzyme, synthesized and sequestered in the ER, is thence transported to sites of ac-

tivity near the cell surface (cf. Plate 42). The lysosomes, also prominent in neurons, have been demonstrated to be rich in acid phosphatase. But less is known about the special roles of the masses of ribosomes also in the Nissl bodies, the neurofilaments in the cytoplasmic ground substance, and the Golgi, a vast and complex component of these cells. Evidence from autoradiographic studies suggests that in the neuron the Golgi is not involved in the packaging of a product for secretion, but its importance to the neuron has not been discovered.

We have noted before that in some instances functional information about cell organelles can be gleaned from exposing the cell to some well-defined physiological stress. When, for example, a motor neuron is deprived of its axon, it undertakes at once to regenerate a new one. As part of this phenomenon the Nissl bodies seem to lose their intense staining properties and are said to undergo chromatolysis (cf. text figure 4a). At the fine structural level the arrays of ER cisternae are seen to separate and to become fenestrated. The system of ribosomes and cisternae representing the Nissl body opens up and is essentially diluted by other cytoplasmic components with a consequent loss in staining intensity. It is apparent that the protein synthesizing machinery of the cell (ER and ribosomes) is dramatically affected by a situation that calls for a greater than normal production of new axoplasm in nerve regeneration. One can properly infer, therefore, that the Nissl is ordinarily involved in the slow but constant replacement of neuron cytoplasm.

In the spinal cord tissue just outside the neuron body, many nerve fibers can be seen in cross section. Of these some are myelinated (NF), that is, covered by a sheath, but others are not. The derivation and structure of myelin is discussed in relation to Plate 44. The structures most closely applied to the neuron surface represent nerve terminals. These are characterized by numerous synaptic vesicles (V) and a few mitochondria (M'). In the area of functional contact between neuronal elements, that is, in the synaptic region (arrowhead), the plasma membranes of the fiber and the neuron are intact and separated from each other by a space of about 80 A. Each appears denser, however, than in nonsynaptic areas. Because impulse conduction is uni-directional (in this case from fiber to cell body), the synapse plays a crucial role in integrating activities of the nervous system.

This synapse is one in which transmission is chemically mediated; that is, a substance liberated from the nerve ending of one cell brings about excitation in the plasma membrane of the next. In many cases acetylcholine fulfills this function just as it does in the myoneural junction (see Plate 42). In other instances norepinephrine plays a similar role, although in these instances some structural differences in the synapse are found. Transmission of nerve impulses without chemical mediation—electrical transmission—has also been detected. In these instances specialized low-resistance connections exist, coupling the pre- and postsynaptic neurons and resulting in ex-tremely rapid transmission. In all cases in which electrical transmission has been discovered a par-ticular structural type of intercellular junction has also been present. This resembles a "tight" junc-tion in which the adjacent plasma membranes are fused (cf. text figure 7a).

In the central nervous system the nerve cells and their processes are supported and perhaps nourished by neuroglial cells. The small sections of membrane-limited cytoplasm (Ng) containing an occasional mitochondrion, sparsely scattered filamentous material, small vesicles of the endo-plasmic reticulum, and darkly staining glycogen particles probably belong to these neuroglial ele-ments.

From the spinal cord of the bat
Magnification × 16,000

References

BENNETT, M. V. L., ALJURE, E., NAKAJIMA, Y., and PAPPAS, G. D. Electrotonic junctions between teleost spinal neurons: electrophysiology and ultrastructure. *Science, 141:*262 (1963).

BODIAN, D., and MELLORS, R. C. The regenerative cycle of motoneurons with special reference to phosphatase activity. *J. Exp. Med., 81:*469 (1945).

BUNGE, M. B., BUNGE, R. P., PETERSON, E. R., and MUR-RAY, M. R. A light and electron microscope study of long-term organized cultures of rat dorsal root ganglia. *J. Cell Biol., 32:*439 (1967).

DEITCH, A. D., and MOSES, M. J. The Nissl substance of living and fixed spinal ganglion cells. II. An ultraviolet absorption study. *J. Biophysic. and Biochem. Cytol., 3:*449 (1957).

ECCLES, J. The synapse. *Sci. Amer., 212:*56 (January, 1965).

FURSHPAN, E. J. "Electrical transmission" at an excitatory synapse in a vertebrate brain. *Science, 144:*878 (1964).

HOLTZMAN, E., NOVIKOFF, A. B., and VILLAVERDE, H. Lysosomes and GERL in normal and chromatolytic neurons of the rat ganglion nodosum. *J. Cell Biol., 33:* 419 (1967).

PALAY, S. L. The morphology of synapses in the central nervous system. *Exp. Cell Research, Suppl. 5:*275 (1958).

———, and PALADE, G. E. The fine structure of neurons. *J. Biophysic. and Biochem. Cytol., 1:*69 (1955).

PANNESE, E. Investigations on the ultrastructural changes of the spinal ganglion neurons in the course of axon regeneration and cell hypertrophy. I. Changes during axon regeneration. *Z. Zellforsch., 60:*711 (1963).

ROBERTSON, J. D., BODENHEIMER, T. S., and STAGE, D. E. The ultrastructure of Mauthner cell synapses and nodes in goldfish brains. *J. Cell Biol., 19:*159 (1963).

PLATE 44
Peripheral Nerve Fibers

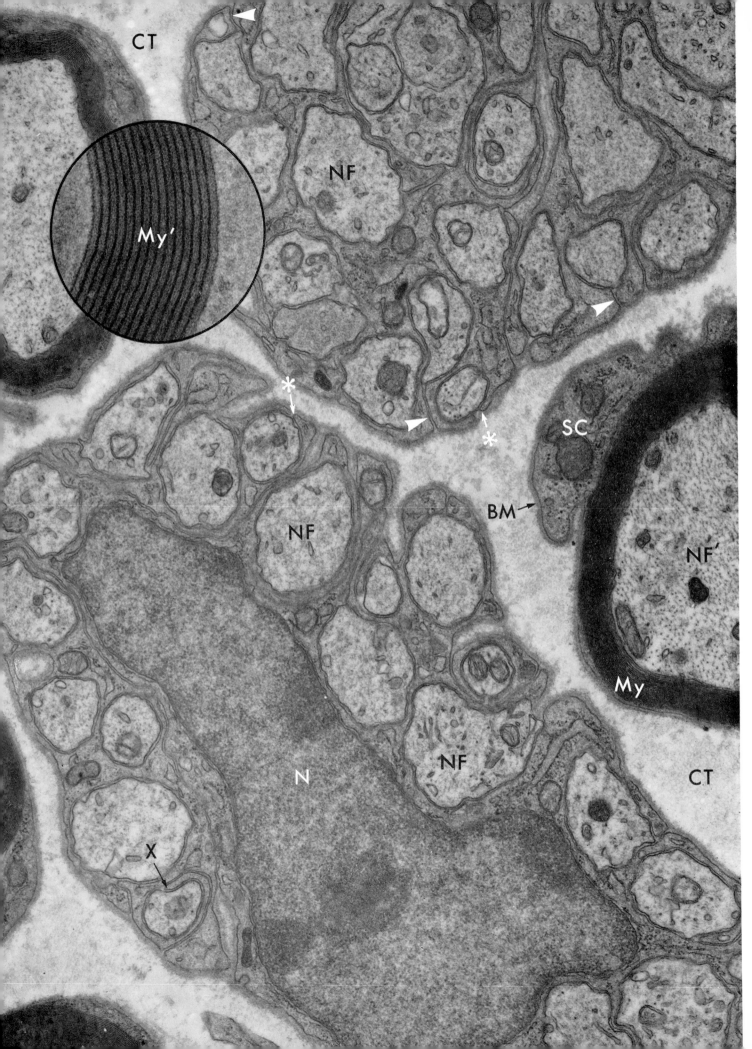

PLATE 44

Peripheral Nerve Fibers

THE long processes (fibers) of neurons are bundled together to form the "nerves" of gross anatomy. In cross sections of such nerves, as shown in this micrograph, the relationships of the fibers to special sheaths, coverings, and supporting connective tissue can be examined. Thus it has been learned that small, slow-conducting nerve fibers are not "naked" as was formerly believed but rather are enclosed by the cytoplasm of Schwann cells. Cross sections of many nerve fibers (NF) may be disposed around the nucleus (N) of a single Schwann cell, each enveloped by cytoplasmic extensions of the sheath cell. In favorable areas, the plasma membrane of the Schwann cell can be traced without discontinuity as it folds in from the surface and surrounds the fiber (*). Where the fiber is deeply embedded in the Schwann cell, a narrow channel is defined by the apposition of lips of Schwann cell cytoplasm (arrows). The channel and membranes facing it constitute the mesaxon.

Larger nerve fibers with faster conduction rates (NF') are covered by a myelin sheath (My). The formation of the sheath and its relationship to the nerve fiber has in recent years been greatly clarified by fine structural studies. Briefly, it has been found that the lamellae of the sheath (see inset, My') are derived from successive layers of Schwann cell plasma membrane. In this micrograph, the image at X could represent an early phase in the development of this sheath. As myelination proceeds, a lip of cytoplasm, such as that at the point of the arrow, extends itself around the axon by synthesizing membrane as it goes. Behind this lip, the cytoplasm is squeezed out to the point where the two membranes of the Schwann cell behind the lip come together and fuse at their inner (cytoplasmic) surfaces (see text figure 44a). This fusion forms the strong or major dense line of the sheath image (inset). The space between the lines represents the face-to-face contact of two plasma membranes, in which contact the outer leaflet of the unit membrane loses its clear identity (see text figure 44a). By this progressive membrane growth at the margins of the cytoplasmic lips, the mesaxon is greatly extended, and the resultant sheath becomes a multilayered structure. Thus it is evident that the large nerve fibers, like the smaller ones, are enclosed by a living cellular sheath. Portions of the enveloping Schwann cell (SC) may be identified at the periphery of the sheath. Each Schwann cell is surrounded by an amorphous basement membrane (BM) that separates it from the connective tissue of the endoneurium (CT).

The evenly spaced, layered structure of myelin described above can be related to the known chemical composition and the arrangement of the macromolecules represented. As already pointed out, it has been learned from studies on the development of myelin that each major period, i.e., from center to center of each dense line ($\sim$120 A) represents two unit membranes in face-to-face compression. The sheath is therefore pure membrane, which upon analysis is found to contain phospholipids, proteins, polysaccharides, salts and water. X-ray diffraction studies, combined with electron microscopy, have revealed that the low density regions represent the long hydrocarbon tails of the lipid molecules, regularly arranged and oriented perpendicular to the plane of the membrane. The denser bands, on the other hand, represent the polar groups of the lipid in combination with proteins. Why these combine on the back face of the unit membrane to give the major dense band in the myelin as opposed to the thinner and lighter line at the other face has not been explained.

From the skin of the mouse
Magnification $\times$ 27,500
Inset $\times$ 115,000

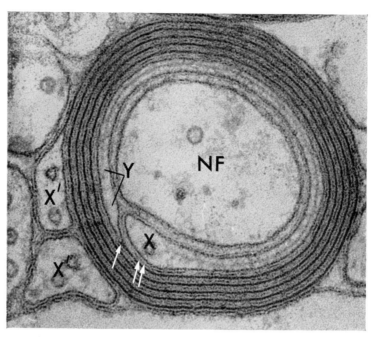

Text Figure 44a

This excellent micrograph shows clearly the structure of the myelin sheath and illustrates how the layers are formed within it as the neuroglial cell, the counterpart of the Schwann cell in the central nervous system, envelops the axon. The growing lip of cell cytoplasm (X) is advancing around the axon process (NF) and insinuating itself into the space between the plasma membrane of the axon and the membrane that limits the thin layer of cytoplasm (Y) left behind by the growing lip during its previous turn. This cytoplasmic layer disappears as the inner leaflets of its plasma membrane fuse to form the major dense line of the myelin sheath. This process is occurring at the point indicated by the single arrow. The outer leaflet of the plasma membrane surrounding the lip fuses with its own outer leaflet laid down on the previous turn. The two outer leaflets thus give rise to the less dense intermediate line of the sheath (double arrow). The cell body from which the investing cytoplasmic sheet originated cannot be seen in this micrograph, but cytoplasm within the lateral margins of the sheet do appear (X'). This micrograph was generously provided by A. Hirano and H. M. Dembritzer. It originally appeared in *J. Cell Biol., 34*:555 (1967), where a more complete explanation of myelin sheath formation is provided.

From the brain of the rat
Magnification × 166,000

References

BUNGE, M. B., BUNGE, R. P., and RIS, H. Ultrastructural study of remyelination in an experimental lesion in adult cat spinal cord. *J. Biophysic. and Biochem. Cytol., 10*:67 (1961).

ELFVIN, L.-G. Electron microscopic investigation of the plasma membrane and myelin sheath of autonomic nerve fibers in the cat. *J. Ultrastruct. Res., 5*:388 (1961).

FERNÁNDEZ-MORÁN, H., and FINEAN, J. B. Electron microscope and low-angle X-ray diffraction studies of the nerve myelin sheath. *J. Biophysic. and Biochem. Cytol., 3*:725 (1957).

GASSER, H. S. Properties of dorsal root unmedullated fibers on the two sides of the ganglion. *J. Gen. Physiol., 38*:709 (1955).

GEREN, B. B. The formation from the Schwann cell surface of myelin in the peripheral nerves of chick embryos. *Exp. Cell Res., 7*:558 (1954).

HIRANO, A., and DEMBITZER, H. M. A structural analysis of the myelin sheath in the central nervous system. *J. Cell Biol., 34*:555 (1967).

MATURANA, H. R. The fine anatomy of the optic nerve of Anurans—an electron microscope study. *J. Biophysic. and Biochem. Cytol., 7*:107 (1960).

O'BRIEN, J. S. Stability of the myelin membrane. *Science, 147*:1099 (1965).

PETERS, A. The formation and structure of myelin sheaths in the central nervous system. *J. Biophysic. and Biochem. Cytol., 8*:431 (1960).

———, and VAUGHN, J. E. Microtubules and filaments in the axons and astrocytes of early postnatal rat optic nerves. *J. Cell Biol., 32*:113 (1967).

PLATE 45

The Node of Ranvier

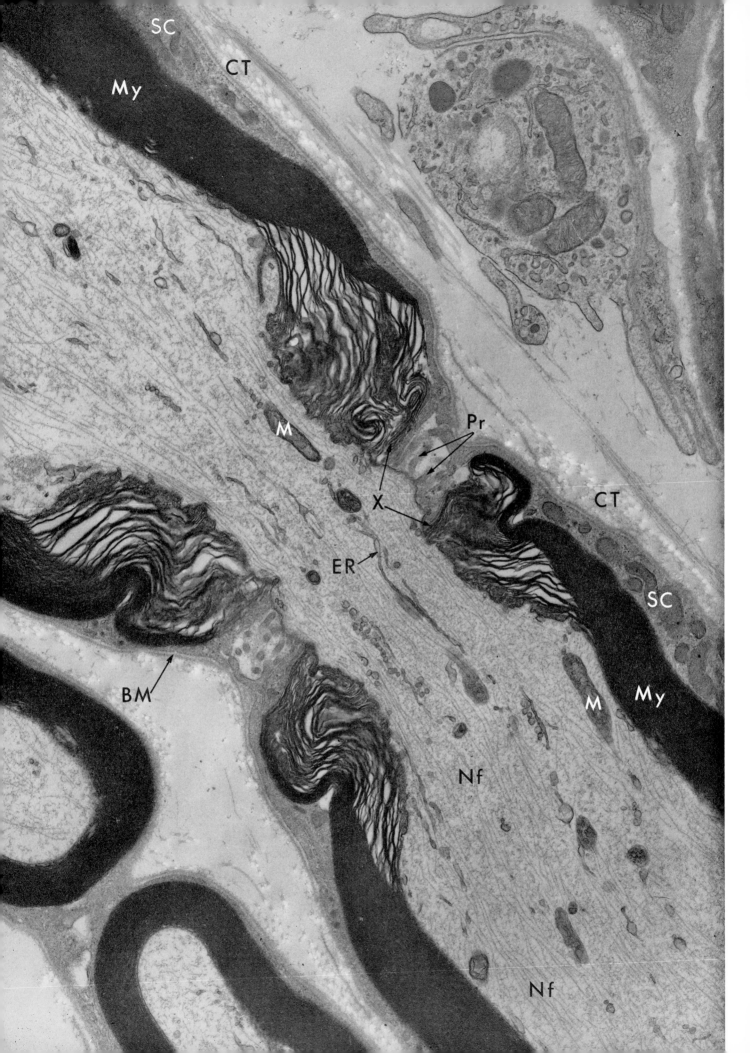

PLATE 45

The Node of Ranvier

THE myelin sheath of peripheral nerve processes (fibers) is periodically interrupted, and the gaps in this sheath are referred to as the nodes of Ranvier. Subsequent to understanding the nature of the myelin sheath (see Plate 44) we have come to learn more about this nodal structure. It has been found, for example, that a single Schwann cell is associated with each segment of the nerve fiber. The sheath of myelin, resulting from successive layering of Schwann cell plasma membranes, forms a compact tube (My) over most of the internodal areas. Near the node, some Schwann cell cytoplasm remains in the extended margins of the sheath layers and occupies a series of liplike folds (X), which envelop the fiber. In the region of the node itself, however, only fingerlike processes (Pr) of neighboring Schwann cells (SC) interdigitate and cover the nodal area. A basement membrane (BM) and connective tissue fibers (CT) of the endoneurium complete the wrappings of the fiber.

What is the significance of the nodes? An answer has been provided, based on the observation that the speed of conduction of myelinated fibers exceeds that of non-myelinated ones. According to a theory now widely favored, depolarization of myelinated nerve fibers occurs only in the region of the node, where the lipoprotein sheath of myelin, acting as an insulator, is absent. Thus the current can flow only in the nodal areas, and the impulse "jumps" from node to node. This phenomenon is called saltatory conduction. Good correlation has therefore been obtained between the fine structure of the node, observed by electron microscopy, and a large accumulation of physiological data.

While the primary events of impulse conduction are associated with the axonal plasma membrane, the membrane can function over a long period only when it is the limiting layer for a living core of axoplasm. The latter, it may be noted, is rich in neurofilaments (Nf) and contains slender elements of the ER and small numbers of thin mitochondria (M). Of special interest are the neurotubules, really microtubules (see text figure 45a), because these structures are probably involved in flow of protoplasm along the axonal fiber. The movement of protoplasm distally from the cell body has been documented by a number of work-

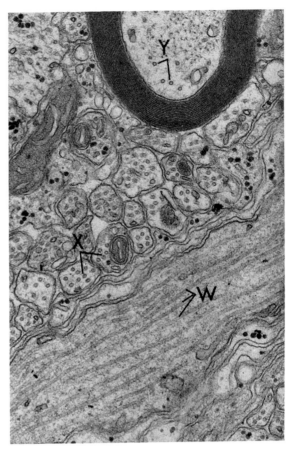

Text Figure 45a

This thin section of frog cerebellum demonstrates the presence of microtubules or, as they are called in this tissue, neurotubules, in the axoplasm of neurons. Profiles of tubules cut in cross section are found both in the small, nonmyelinated (X) nerve processes (dendrites) and in larger myelinated ones (Y) (axons). Longitudinally sectioned neurotubules (W) are present in the dendrite running diagonally across the lower part of the field.

From the cerebellum of the frog
Magnification × 36,000

ers. Although estimates of flow rate have varied, in general they resolve themselves into two: one about 1.2 mm per day and another of the order of 100 to 200 mm per day. Presumably the former represents a growth rate and the latter the protoplasmic streaming that might carry formed structures down the axon. Neither of these could easily provide for the local metabolic needs of the axon at all levels along its length, and so it remains reasonable to look for other sources. Recent autoradiographic studies, tracing the incorporation of labeled amino acid into neurons, indicate that molecules may pass through the myelin sheath and enter the nerve cell process at points far removed from the nerve cell body. While the role of the sheath as a kind of insulator in the internodal regions has been noted (see above), attention is directed to the possibility that the sheath provides at the local level specific nutrients to the axon.

From the sciatic nerve of the mouse
Magnification $\times$ 22,500

References

ELFVIN, L.-G. The ultrastructure of the nodes of Ranvier in cat sympathetic nerve fibers. *J. Ultrastruct. Res., 5:* 374 (1961).

ROBERTSON, J. D. Preliminary observations on the ultrastructure of nodes of Ranvier. *Z. Zellforsch., 50:*553 (1959).

SINGER, M., and SALPETER, M. M. The transport of ^{3}H-l-histidine through the Schwann and myelin sheath into the axon, including a re-evaluation of myelin function. *J. Morph., 120:*281 (1966).

UZMAN, B. G., and NOGUEIRA-GRAF, G. Electron microscope studies of the formation of nodes of Ranvier in mouse sciatic nerves. *J. Biophysic. and Biochem. Cytol., 3:*589 (1957).

WEISS, P., and HISCOE, H. B. Experiments on the mechanism of nerve growth. *J. Exp. Zool., 107:*315 (1948).

PLATE 46

The Rod Outer Segment

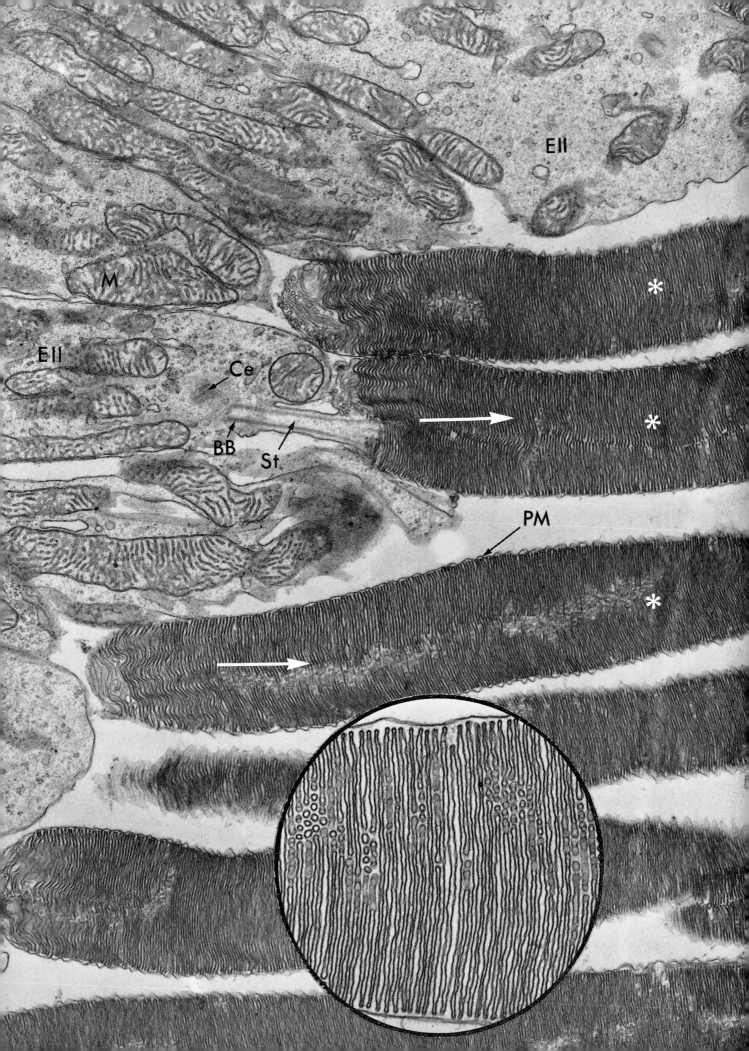

PLATE 46

The Rod Outer Segment

The retina is a photosensitive epithelium which, when excited by light, is able to transmit to the brain impulses that are interpreted as visual images. The epithelium consists of two types of bipolar neurons, which are named for the shapes of their sensory tips or outer segments, that is, the rods and cones. Rods are sensitive to dimmer illumination, but unlike the cones, which require more light for excitation, they cannot perceive color. The neuron cell bodies, from which the outer segments project, harbor the cell nucleus together with cytoplasmic organelles such as ribosomes and mitochondria. An axon extends from the pole of each cell opposite the sensory ending.

In this micrograph only parts of six rod outer segments (∗) and portions of neuronal cytoplasm, the so-called ellipsoids (Ell), are seen. These accommodate a large population of mitochondria (M). Other parts of the rod cell extend out of the picture to the left. Cones, on the other hand, are absent from the retina of the nocturnal kangaroo rat, the source of this specimen. However, we can observe a number of interesting structural features of the rods and attempt to evaluate their functional significance.

Rod outer segments are slender, cylindrical structures about 1.2 microns in diameter and 15 to 20 microns long. Their limiting membrane (PM) is continuous with that of the rest of the rod cell by way of a slender connecting stalk (St). The latter has the structure of a cilium (see Plate 8) and extends from a basal body (BB). Nearby one can identify part of the centriole (Ce) that is constantly associated with the basal body. The remarkable feature of these rod outer segments, which was early revealed by electron microscopy, is the laminated structure of their contents. They are essentially stacks of thin, membranous sacs (see inset). These are shaped like coins or disks with, however, some central perforations. In some species the margins of the lamellae are indented to form fissures, and thus in cross sections of the rod the disks have a scalloped profile.

Since the visual pigments are known to reside in the outer segments, the layered membranes provide strata in or on which pigments are oriented with respect to impinging light rays. These, by virtue of the structure of the eye, follow a path along the long axes of the outer segments (in the direction of the white arrows). Meticulous study of the light absorbing properties of small pieces of the retina and also of individual cells therein has indicated that the rod-shaped pigment molecules are located transversely with respect to the long axis of the segment and are therefore in a position to absorb maximally.

When the membranes of the disks are examined in face view at high magnifications with the electron microscope, small circular particles (30 mμ in diameter) may be found evenly distributed over them. These particles have also been described as disks with about the same thickness as the membrane (50 A). Although the micrographs cannot reveal their composition, it is reasonable to postulate that the visual pigments are concentrated in them. In support of this, calculations have shown that the amount of visual pigment in a rod could be included within these particles.

The visual pigments are made up of an aldehyde of vitamin A (a retinal) joined to a specific protein. The light in striking the pigment isomerizes the aldehyde, and this leads in turn to the separation of the retinal from the protein and to the exposure of presumably reactive groups on the protein. In some as yet unknown way these initial reactions lead to electrical excitation of the neuron and thereby give rise to impulses transmitted to the brain. It is thought that the excitation is elicited in the plasma membrane enclosing the disks of the rod and from that area moves as a wave of depolarization over the cell body and axon. These phenomena are analogous to those encountered in excitation of neurons in general (see Plate 43).

The origin of membranes in the outer segment of the rods (and cones) and indeed of the segments themselves has intrigued cytologists. Here as in other sensory epithelia (see Plate 47) the receptor ending seems to be a modified cilium. The disks, however, do not arise from ciliary microtubules but rather as infoldings of the plasma membrane at the bases of the outer segments. This is true of both cones and rods, although it is only in the latter that the membranes lose their continuity with the plasma membrane so that they encompass a closed space. This spectacular production of membrane depends in some way upon the presence of the cilium, or at least

181

the basal body, and also upon the presence of vitamin A. Vitamin A deficiency causes progressive degeneration of the outer segments, but recovery is possible when vitamin A is supplied and when the basal body has not been destroyed. Recently it has been found that normally the disks are being continuously renewed even in the mature animal, with new ones presumably being added at the base of the outer segment.

The retina of the kangaroo rat (*Dipodomys ordi*)
Magnification × 30,000
Inset × 59,000

References

BROWN, P. K., GIBBONS, I. R., and WALD, G. The visual cells and visual pigment of the mudpuppy, *Necturus*. *J. Cell Biol., 19:*79 (1963).

DeROBERTIS, E. Electron microscope observations on the submicroscopic organization of the retinal rods. *J. Biophysic. and Biochem. Cytol., 2:*319 (1956).

DOWLING, J. E. Night blindness. *Sci. Amer., 215:*78 (October, 1966).

HUBBARD, R., and KROPF, A. Molecular isomers in vision. *Sci. Amer., 216:*64 (June, 1967).

NILSSON, S. E. G. Receptor cell outer segment development and ultrastructure of disk membranes in the retina of the tadpole (*Rana pipiens*). *J. Ultrastruct. Res., 11:*581 (1964).

SJÖSTRAND, F. S. Electron microscopy of the retina. *In* The Structure of the Eye. G. K. Smelser, editor. New York, Academic Press (1961) p. 1.

WALD, G. General discussion of retinal structure in relation to the visual process. *In* The Structure of the Eye. G. K. Smelser, editor. New York, Academic Press (1961) p. 101.

YOUNG, R. W. The renewal of photoreceptor cell outer segments. *J. Cell Biol., 33:*61 (1967).

AMOORE, J. E., JOHNSTON, J. W., JR., and RUBIN, M. The stereochemical theory of odor. *Sci. Amer., 210:*42 (February, 1964).

DE LORENZO, A. J. D. Studies on the ultrastructure and histophysiology of cell membranes, nerve fibers and synaptic junctions in chemoreceptors. *In* Olfaction and Taste. Wenner-Gren Center International Symposium Series. Y. Zotterman, editor. New York, The Macmillan Company, vol. I (1963) p. 5.

GASSER, H. S. Olfactory nerve fibers. *J. Gen. Physiol., 39:*473 (1955).

GESTELAND, R. C., LETTVIN, J. Y., PITTS, W. H., and ROJAS, A. Odor specificities of the frog's olfactory receptors. *In* Olfaction and Taste. Wenner-Gren Center International Symposium Series. Y. Zotterman, editor. New York, The Macmillan Company, vol. I (1963) p. 19.

LE GROS CLARK, W. Inquiries into the anatomical basis of olfactory discrimination. *Proc. Roy. Soc. London, Ser. B., 146:*299 (1957).

OKANO, M., WEBER, A. F., and FROMMES, S. P. Electron microscopic studies of the distal border of the canine olfactory epithelium. *J. Ultrastruct. Res., 17:*487 (1967).

OTTOSON, D. Generation and transmission of signals in the olfactory system. *In* Olfaction and Taste. Wenner-Gren Center International Symposium Series. Y. Zotterman, editor. New York, The Macmillan Company, vol. I (1963) p. 35.

REESE, T. S. Olfactory cilia in the frog. *J. Cell Biol., 25* (No. 2, part 2): 209 (1965).

Notes on Technique

CERTAIN features in the construction and operation of the electron microscope oblige the microscopist to use special techniques in the preparation of his specimens. Foremost among these is the high vacuum required in the column of the microscope during operation. Obviously, the cell or other specimen exposed to this vacuum cannot be kept alive or even hydrated under ordinary conditions of observation. It must instead be preserved or "fixed" in a form that as closely as possible resembles the morphology of the living state. Though a number of chemical reagents can be used for this fixation, none has greater over-all value than osmium tetroxide (OsO_4). In addition to preserving quite faithfully the form of the living material, it reacts differentially with cell components. The resulting uneven deposition of osmium atoms exaggerates density differences in the specimen and gives it the appearance of being stained. This effect is important in giving the image enough contrast to permit the observer to distinguish one structural component from another in areas where natural density differences would be insufficient. In spite of these demonstrable values of OsO_4, the search for better reagents continues. Investigators are currently finding formaldehyde and glutaraldehyde, followed by osmium tetroxide, more reliable for the preservation of the complete complement of materials making up the cell's fine structure.

Another problem of specimen preparation develops from the fact that the electron beam will penetrate only a very thin layer of organic material. To meet this limitation, the microscopist must prepare extraordinary thin sections, not thicker than 0.05 to 0.1 microns. Therefore, in its preparation for microtomy the specimen is first dehydrated with alcohol and subsequently infiltrated with a resin or plastic in monomeric form. This, in turn, in polymerized by heat and catalysts, and the tissue, now embedded, is hard enough to section with a glass or diamond knife on microtomes designed especially for the task. The resulting thin sections may be given an additional staining with a salt of some heavy metal, such as lead or uranium, and the resulting specimen is ready for microscopy.

The micrographs originating in the Laboratory for Cell Biology at Harvard University were taken with a Philips 200 electron microscope (EM). This instrument is similar to others currently available in yielding resolutions at least 100 times greater than those given by the light microscope. Such resolutions make it feasible to take pictures with the EM at magnifications of 40 or 50 thousand times and to separate or resolve points of density as close together as 10 Angstrom units (10 A). For many purposes, however, especially for forming first impressions of the fine structure in a cell or tissue, lower magnifications are preferable. Thus, many of the originals of these pictures were taken at magnifications of only 3 to 5 thousand and thereafter were enlarged photographically.

With a knowledge of the magnification, one can, of course, measure the dimensions of objects in the pictures. This is commonly done in terms of small units of length: microns (μ), millimicrons ($m\mu$), and Angstrom units (A). In this connection the student will recall that

$$1\ \mu\ = 1/1000 \text{ of a millimeter (mm)}$$
$$1\ m\mu = 1/1000 \text{ of a micron } (\mu)$$
$$1\ A\ = 1/10 \text{ of a millimicron } (m\mu)$$

It follows that in a micrograph having a magnification of $1000\times$, a μ length is represented by 1 mm on the picture, or that at $30,000\times$, 1 μ is represented by 30 mm. Fractions of these distances, as measured with a millimeter scale or a pair of calipers, can be readily translated into $m\mu$'s or A's, and the dimensions of the object thereby determined.

Index

Numerals in *italics* refer to illustrations.